THE CHILD SEX SCANDAL
AND MODERN IRISH LITERATURE

IRISH CULTURE, MEMORY, PLACE
Oona Frawley, Ray Cashman, and Guy Beiner, editors

THE CHILD SEX SCANDAL
AND MODERN IRISH LITERATURE

Writing the Unspeakable

Joseph Valente and Margot Gayle Backus
Foreword by Fintan O'Toole

Indiana University Press

This book is a publication of

Indiana University Press
Office of Scholarly Publishing
Herman B Wells Library 350
1320 East 10th Street
Bloomington, Indiana 47405 USA

iupress.org

Manufactured in the United States of America

First printing 2020

Cataloging information is available from the Library of Congress.

ISBN 978-0-253-05317-6 (hdbk.)
ISBN 978-0-253-05318-3 (pbk.)
ISBN 978-0-253-05319-0 (web PDF)

To our respective children,
Jerilyn Backus Tennison and Matthew Elijah Valente

CONTENTS

List of Illustrations ix
Foreword xi
Preface xv
Acknowledgments xxiii

Introduction: The Enigmatic History of Imperiled Innocence 1

1. "An Iridescence Difficult to Account For": Sexual Initiation in
Joyce's Fiction of Development 41

2. Between (Open) Secret and Enigma: Kate O'Brien,
The Land of Spices, and the Stylistic Invention of Lesbian (In)visibility ... 73

3. Country Girl: Groomed, Seduced, and Abandoned 99

4. "From the Pits and Ditches Where People Have Fallen":
Sex Scandal and the Reinvention of the Irish Public Sphere
in Keith Ridgway's *The Long Falling* 131

5. Retrofitting Ireland's Architecture of Containment in
Tana French's *In the Woods* 163

6. "Roaring Inside Me": The Enigma of Sexual Violence in *The Gathering* ... 196

Epilogue: What about Brendan? 232

Notes on the Illustrations 243
References 253
Index 265

ILLUSTRATIONS

For full bibliographic details for each illustration, see Notes on the Illustrations.

Cover: Strange silence falls on scene of shame

Figure 0.1. The "spider web" of Tuam could touch anywhere

Figure i.1. *Homeless*

Figure i.2. A dream of green fields

Figure i.3. Women of Britain say—"Go!"

Figure i.4. Orpen's war exam

Figure i.5. True to tradition

Figure i.6. Food kitchen in Liberty Hall

Figure i.7. *The Faith* saves "Irish Child" from "Socialism"

Figure i.8. Saving Dublin children

Figure i.9. Staging of Larry Kirwan's *Rebel in the Soul*

Figure i.10. State of shame

Figure i.11. "The introduction of internment . . . for fourteen-year-old girls."

Figure i.12. Credo that protected a monster

Figure i.13. Shadow of a trauma

Figure i.14. "Pretty twisted stuff. It's almost Kafkaesque."

Figure 3.1. Ann Lovett: Death at the grotto

Figure 5.1. The Battle of Soldiers Hill

Figure 5.2. Names of 796 Tuam babies written on white sheets

Figure 7.1. The crumbling St Ita's Hospital, Portrane, Co. Dublin

Figure 7.2. The hospital was divided

FOREWORD

INSTITUTIONALIZED CHILD ABUSE IS A global reality, unconfined by national, cultural, or religious boundaries. Ireland is not unique in creating, sustaining, justifying, and eventually exposing a large-scale system of coercive confinement in which women and children were rendered vulnerable to every form of physical and psychological violence and exploitation. It is probably true, nonetheless, that there are few if any countries where this system was so central to the very nature of the state. The tight intertwining of the Catholic Church with both the institutions of government after Irish independence in 1922 and the moral and ideological underpinnings of independence itself meant that the control of sexuality, reproduction, and childhood could never be marginal to the definition of Irishness, of respectability, of citizenship, and of belonging.

This in turn meant that the exposure from the early 1990s onward of the whole archipelago of institutional abuse—industrial schools, Magdalene laundries, mother-and-baby homes, and (still underexposed) mental hospitals—had a very particular drama. It both coincided with and hastened an epochal shift, the fall of Catholic Ireland. Because so much abuse had taken place within institutions run by Catholic religious orders, the revelations of horrific crimes (and the doomed attempts to deny them) shattered the moral authority of the church and rocked the state that had been so closely allied to it. The question of the state's collusion in the church's crimes against children and women could never be a mere reckoning with the past—it also must be a force for reshaping the future.

And yet, not quite. In 2019, the *Irish Times* ran a yearlong campaign called No Child 2020 to mark the centenary of the Democratic Programme adopted in January 1919 by the First Dáil, the parliament formed by the majority of those who had won seats in the previous month's Westminster elections but chose, in line with the policy of Sinn Féin, to secede and form their own national assembly in Dublin. In particular, the campaign drew attention to the contrast between the extraordinarily progressive nature of the Democratic Programme—its imagining of children as citizens of the republic and promise to prioritize their needs—and the abject failure to keep those promises.

The program had claimed that "it shall be the first duty of the Government of the Republic to make provision for the physical, mental and spiritual well-being of the children, to secure that no child shall suffer hunger or cold from lack of food, clothing, or shelter, but that all shall be provided with the means and facilities requisite for their proper education and training as Citizens of a Free and Gaelic Ireland." A century on, it was obvious not only that the state that emerged from the revolutionary period made a mockery of these pledges but also that, even in 2019, long after the exposure of this hypocrisy, it was still doing so.

It was not that the revelations had made no difference but that they had been somehow compartmentalized. They existed in a domain of horror and scandal and deeply felt shame. They did not transform life outside that domain. There were still scandals that were not scandals—a doubling of child poverty because children were the primary victims of the austerity policies that followed the great banking collapse of 2008, a huge rise in the number of homeless children being raised in objectively abusive accommodation, a crisis in mental health services for children and young people, a system of "direct provision" for asylum seekers that was acknowledged as grossly unsuitable for the children living in it. The great scandals had in fact done little to change the way vulnerable children were being treated.

This is the paradox: the exposure of child abuse was at once profoundly political and largely depoliticized. It was fully understood in and of itself as a story about power and belonging, about inclusion and exclusion, about gender and class, about nationhood and religion. But it did not (perhaps one should add, so far) fundamentally alter the way those forces operate in Ireland. It was certainly the case that the undermining of the political authority of the church had real indirect political consequences (most obviously in referendums to allow same-sex marriage and legalized abortion). Yet Ireland in 2019 was no closer to being a republic whose "first duty" was to the welfare of children than it had been in 1919, 1949, or 1999. The story of the great scandal was somehow both absorbed and deflected.

This raises the great questions that this brilliant book grapples with. What are the psychological mechanisms of abuse? How is it conceptualized and imagined? How can it be at once seen and unseen? I have suggested in writing about it that child abuse has been Ireland's variation on Donald Rumsfeld's epistemological musings. It is not the known unknown. It is our unknown known, always apprehended but never comprehended. Joseph Valente and Margot Gayle Backus use as one of their main analytic tools a more sophisticated version of this idea, Jean Laplanche's concept of the "enigmatic signifier": "sexually uninitiated juvenile narrators who can see things they have not yet learned *not* to see."

When they write that "in twentieth-century Ireland, the vulnerability and trauma of children operated as a collective enigmatic signifier imbued with unspeakable appeal and saturated with shame, both personal and collective," the words apply just as much to the twenty-first century. The documents of the scandal—the official reports, documentaries, films, journalism, and political speeches—themselves became a kind of enigmatic signifier, powerfully attractive, even seductive, but resistant to being configured as a political program.

And when Valente and Backus take us into the extraordinary ways in which so many Irish fiction writers have used the point of view of "uninitiated innocents who encounter taboo material," it is hard not to think that this also became a pose through which Irish society managed to present itself in relation to the scandals. A society that was in fact deeply collusive with the mechanisms of exclusion and cruelty at the heart of the abusive institutions managed to think itself into the attitude of an innocent child shocked by its encounter with this taboo material.

Through their psychoanalytic readings of selected twentieth- and twenty-first-century short stories and novels, Valente and Backus give original, subtle, and acute accounts of the ways in which Irish writers interacted with, subverted, and transformed existing British narratives of imperiled innocence. Those narratives, privileging children's supposed moral and religious well-being over their actual physical and psychological safety, are at the heart of the grotesque irony: using a narrative of vulnerability to turn children and women into prey, purporting to protect children and women from danger while exposing them to it, and rendering them defenseless by removing them from social and legal supports in the name of defending them from spiritual threat.

What these readings convincingly point to is "the endemic operation of sexual or sexualized abuse" in Irish society. This of course is the other paradox: fiction is much more "factual" in this sense than the vast bulk of contemporary journalistic and political discourse. It picks up on the intimacies that are so carefully occluded in official discourse. But it also maps the complex relationships between what can be said and what can be written. In life, much of what children know is communicated between them only in quiet speech—the unspeakable is really the unwritable. In art, it is writing that occupies the place of this speech, that broaches, more or less explicitly, what is not being said, either by the young characters themselves or by the world around them.

Writing the Unspeakable aims "to find out how and why the strong reactions stirred up by scandalous accounts of betrayed youthful innocents so often reaffirm rather than challenge a society's complacent belief in its collective commitment to children and their welfare." This is, to a large extent, the process that took place in Ireland in response to the great scandals of child abuse. Valente and Backus therefore achieve much more than a highly provocative and illuminating act of literary criticism. They open up a field of great importance, not just to Ireland but to every society that is seeking to grapple with the implications of systematic and endemic cruelty. The point, as they implicitly suggest in this bold and sure-footed expedition into dark psychological terrain, is not merely to interpret the cruelty, exploitation, and trauma. It is to change the society that colludes in them.

Fintan O'Toole

PREFACE

THE MEDIA FUROR THAT SURROUNDED the 2014 disclosure of the names of the 796 orphans disposed of and forgotten by Ireland's Bon Secours Mother and Baby Home in Tuam, Galway, is just one of the latest in a series of international scandals over the abuse and exploitation of children that dates back to the late nineteenth century. These scandals have involved child labor, homelessness, and malnutrition; children sold as brides or as sex slaves; physical and emotional abuse in schools, prisons, detention facilities, and refugee camps; sexual abuse by priests, family members, and neighbors; and child victims of war and gun violence.

At a minimum, the inexorability with which one "imperiled child" scandal is followed by yet another raises the question of why, if modern societies are as concerned about children's well-being as they profess, so many of the world's children remain, in the words of Anne Enright's protagonist in *The Gathering*, "manifestly *of little account*" (2007, 236; emphasis in original). In a mass-mediated world in which public opinion on many issues is routinely and powerfully influenced by representations of children at risk, why are the lives of so many children as precarious as ever? Furthermore, if children's status has not been improved by more than a century of scandals calling attention to children at risk, how *have* these scandals affected children, and why?

The Child Sex Scandal and Modern Irish Literature: Writing the Unspeakable suggests answers to these timely and urgent questions by applying the filter of psychoanalytic theory to modern and contemporary literary representations of scandals of child imperilment in Ireland. Moving beyond the indisputable conclusion that such scandals are at times deployed cynically to manipulate public opinion, our inquiry asks what it is in the human psyche that makes us not only susceptible to such cynical manipulations but also liable to misdirect our outrage even when legitimately outrageous abuses of children are brought to light.

In *Writing the Unspeakable*, we examine influential literary depictions of childhood sexual initiation, consciously organized in relation to influential Irish sex scandals, to find out how and why the strong reactions stirred up by scandalous accounts of betrayed youthful innocents so often reaffirm rather than challenge a society's complacent belief in its collective commitment to children and their welfare. Revisiting key turning points in what Tom Inglis (1998) describes as the rise and fall of the Irish Catholic Church's "moral monopoly," we apply our training in theories of representation to produce a more nuanced and holistic reading of metonymic media depictions of endangered juveniles. By broadening our reading of these scandals to include their literary afterlives, we aim to produce a representationally, politically, and psychoanalytically sophisticated account of how a series of sensational media representations of child endangerment precipitated a series of moral adjustments in Ireland that successfully directed the public's aroused sense of militant protectiveness toward state, institutional, or movement-defined objects.

As Moira J. Maguire and other historians make clear, the new moral frameworks that Irish media consumers periodically embraced in response to media outcries aligning children's imperative needs with those of the state, the Catholic Church and its prelates, business owners, or various political movements were seldom at odds with their own self-interest. It is beyond dispute that the Catholic Church and its various institutions and officials—Magdalene laundries, orphanages and industrial schools, mother-and-baby homes, and pedophilic clerics—were especially notorious for perpetrating violence against children and especially venal in concealing it. But it is no less true that the atrocities did not begin, and the cover-ups did not terminate, in convents, homes, or sacristies. As Maguire observes, "People at all levels of Irish society often acted out of little more than self-interest and self-preservation, especially when it came to the treatment of poor, illegitimate, and abused children" (2009). Yet clearly the Irish people did not consciously think of their treatment of poor, illegitimate, and abused children as based on self-interest or self-preservation. Rather, sensational media accounts of horrific threats posed either to or by such children lent a very persuasive veneer of altruism to an array of now infamous institutions and measures and to all but the most anomalous acts of self-interest and self-preservation.

The powerful sentiments aroused by accounts of children in danger are firmly rooted in protective instincts that are sincere, worthy, and to some extent biologically hardwired. By its nature, however, the scandal of imperiled innocence constitutes any abuse it discloses as axiomatically other, as distinct in its very unthinkability from the time or place of the scandal's enlightened public. Accordingly, even media accounts of child abuse uncovered by irreproachably motivated researchers, activists, or officials inspire little public will to identify and insure against analogous contemporary abuses. For instance, in 2014 local historian Catherine Corless released to the media the names and ages of the orphans of the Tuam Mother and Baby Home dumped on waste ground in County Galway from the 1940s through the 1960s. The Irish public was suitably horrified, yet the resulting scandal failed to translate into public indignation concerning the comparable conditions of Irish-born children of immigrants institutionalized in contemporary Ireland under the notoriously harsh "direct provision" system. So long as the Irish media relies on the conventions of the imperiled child scandal when covering harm done to children, such news stories will continue to emphasize these events' distance from the Irish public's current stipulated state of good sense and goodwill, and Ireland, like many modern societies around the globe, will remain as deeply in thrall to the child scandal's moralizing rationalizations as ever.[1]

Scholars of newspaper and media studies, social historians, and queer theorists before us have scrutinized media coverage, legal records, case studies, interviews, advertising, and journal entries to investigate how allegations of harm to children can empower the already powerful, often at children's expense. While we build on these earlier insights, our literary source materials uniquely capture the earnestness and the unconscious self-concern that are inevitably conjoined in scandals of abused youth. As a nation whose values and institutions have been shaped by child-related scandals dating back to the origins of the modern media scandal, Ireland has produced a wealth of fictional narratives on the subject, which provide the rich primary-source materials for our investigation.

Figure 0.1. "The 'spider web' of Tuam could touch anywhere." A memorial commemorating the discarded lives and bodies of 796 infants and children from the Tuam Mother and Baby Home. *The Irish Examiner,* July 27, 2018. © Eamon Ward.

This study originated in a series of essays we coauthored on child sexual initiation in the works of James Joyce and Kate O'Brien. Our collaborative work evolved into the present book as we became increasingly aware of how many of modern Ireland's most highly regarded and influential literary narratives depict sex scandals as seen through the eyes of children. In the course of our work, we discovered a widespread, long-established subgenre that we term the *literature of scandal*, which appears to have significantly influenced not only modern Irish literature but also the larger Irish public sphere. The literature of scandal has exerted this influence, we argue, by making the culturally taboo visible, placing the reader in the position of an uninitiated child experiencing something both horrible and compelling that she cannot comprehend but that the reader can. By slowing down and demystifying the usual slam-bang immediacy of scandals of violated innocence, the literature of scandal has been a consequential participant in a broader public discourse in Ireland concerning outrages against children.

In our introduction, we map the generative context of the Irish literature of scandal by describing how the British trope of child imperilment took on a new and socially decisive form in early twentieth-century Ireland. In the first two of the introduction's six sections, we describe the sentimentalization of poor women and children in eighteenth- and nineteenth-century Britain and the role of the scandal of imperiled innocence in the emergence of the New Journalism in Britain. In our third and fourth sections, we analyze the ensuing contribution of the New Journalist child sex scandal to Irish media coverage of the 1913 "Campaign to Save the Kiddies." Here we also show how the Irish child imperilment scandal reinforced the broad sexualized shaming of irreligion and dissent that provided the nascent Irish state with a powerful means to quell the class and regional conflicts that often spell disaster for newly decolonized nations. The introduction concludes by outlining the psychoanalytic implications of each of these developments. Here we explain how our psychoanalytic framework serves to articulate the historical contexts for modern Ireland's distinctive literary portrayals of child sexual abuse with the experience of reading and responding to this pervasive yet pervasively denied form of harm. We set forth, in broad strokes, how a rigorously psychoanalytic critical lens makes evident the specific and indispensable contribution Irish literature has made to Irish society's now-ongoing reckoning with this long-hidden corruption.

In chapter 1, "'An Iridescence Difficult to Account For': Sexual Initiation in Joyce's Fiction of Development," we present the central theoretical framework of the study: Jean Laplanche's concept of the enigmatic signifier and its reference to ambiguous or coded sexual messages that elicit a traumatic enjoyment in children, permanently shaping their psychic subjectivity. We borrow this construct to argue that in twentieth-century Ireland, the vulnerability and trauma of children operated as a collective enigmatic signifier imbued with unspeakable appeal and saturated with shame, both personal and collective. Our research reveals that the enigmatic signifiers that mediate the seduction of specific boys in Joyce's *Dubliners* (1914) and *A Portrait of the Artist as a Young Man* (1916) also mediate the seduction of the reader by these narratives.

Our second chapter, "Between (Open) Secret and Enigma: Kate O'Brien, *The Land of Spices*, and the Stylistic Invention of Lesbian (In)visibility," examines the literary strategy by which O'Brien's novel undoes and reties the entangled, obscure knot conjoining sexual desire, trauma, and the shaming and silencing effects of scandal. As a sexually nonconforming Catholic intellectual, O'Brien depicts and narratively enacts the ad hoc flexibility and moral responsiveness that were contingently accessible in the world in which she came of age. That world's oral networks of girls and women, we argue, provided her with a publicly accessible purchase on the enigmatic signifier, through which she could convey an alternative account of erotic desire and interpersonal ethics.

Our third chapter addresses the scandal reflected on and given in turn by Edna O'Brien's first novel, *The Country Girls*. We are particularly concerned to examine how Caithleen Brady's juvenile development is keyed to the symbiotic relationship between overt physical and coded sexual abuse, and then again between both forms of child abuse and the predatory eroticization of young girls like her in the rural community of her adolescence. Her compulsion to repeat as well as repair the unconscious sexual elements of her family trauma, which are retroactively ignited by her father's proprietary violence, leaves her prey to a series of likewise abusive yet socially approved paternal surrogates. O'Brien illustrates how this process of normalized predatory acculturation deflects and obscures the more dissident or queer aspects of Caithleen's sexual disposition, long overlooked in the readings of this *bildungsroman*. Among its other aims, chapter 3 looks to refute the impression of O'Brien's early work as aggressively heterocentric.

In chapter 4, "'From the Pits and Ditches Where People Have Fallen': Sex Scandal and the Reinvention of the Irish Public Sphere in Keith Ridgway's *The Long Falling*," we examine how a prominent child imperilment scandal, the so-called X case, forced significant changes in certain aspects of the Irish public sphere while encountering insuperable resistance in others. The period's more accessible but still radically restricted public sphere is emblematized in the novel in the person of Sean, a gay Irishman and established Dublin-based journalist whose power to designate what is news and what is not is pivotal to the narrative. In his novel, we argue, Ridgway transforms the X of the X case into a national enigmatic signifier, which he calls "a new symbol . . . the enigmatic figure, the cross fallen sideways" (175).

In chapter 5, "Retrofitting Ireland's Architecture of Containment in Tana French's *In the Woods*," we analyze how French pushes the implications of the enigmatic signifier to a logical extreme in order to examine the violent psychopathology of everyday Irish life. As we demonstrate, the realist surface of *In the Woods* (2007) is distorted by frightening glimpses of a supernatural, predatory, archaic Other, which corresponds to a fantastic and appalling childhood trauma that resists explanation. At the same time, French meticulously analogizes these elements of gothic detective fiction to the operation of the masculinist, neoliberal forces of postindependence Catholic nationalism. In French's hands, a social critique of child sexual abuse thus dovetails with a representation of child sexual abuse as social critique.

In chapter 6, "'Roaring Inside Me': The Enigma of Sexual Violence in *The Gathering*," we analyze Enright's lauded contribution to the tradition of uncomprehending child narrators in the Irish literature of scandal. As we show, *The Gathering* (2007) mimetically reproduces the elisions, gaps, and doubts that are the legacy of severe childhood trauma in a way that also thwarts the reader's attempts to definitively identify an individual perpetrator. Enright's narrator, Veronica, speaks simultaneously as an individual and as a personification of the Irish public sphere, observing that "over the next twenty years, the world around us changed and I remembered [a scene of abuse]. But I never would have made that shift on my own—if I hadn't been listening to the radio, and reading the paper, and hearing about what went on in schools and churches and in people's homes" (172–73).

Our focus on the literature of scandal allows us to transcend narrow disciplinary boundaries by examining ways in which literature both complexly incorporates and effectively interacts with other discourses. Through our psychoanalytic readings of selected twentieth- and twenty-first-century short stories and novels, we are able to give an original and nuanced account of how early to mid-twentieth-century Irish scandals of imperiled innocence emphasized children's purported moral and religious well-being to the exclusion of their physical and emotional security, thereby profoundly and destructively influencing the social infrastructure and moral priorities of the modern Irish state. And through our close examination of the influence of these texts within the larger Irish culture, we describe the contribution that many of Ireland's authors, far more of them than we are able to include, have made to democratizing the Irish nation along generational lines.

We hope our findings will prove valuable and generative for those current and future scholars in a range of disciplines who will continue to explore the relationship between intensely felt and widely accepted moral frameworks and the capacity (or incapacity) of modern mass-mediated societies to generate solutions to the real problems that afflict real children.

NOTE

1. In the summer of 2014, local and international media consumers reacted with horror to the exhumation of 796 skeletons of babies and children buried years ago without ceremony by the nuns of the Tuam Mother and Baby Home. Conversely and contemporaneously, there was minimal media coverage in that same summer of immigrant children who had been held in Irish refugee camps for over three years.

ACKNOWLEDGMENTS

WE WOULD LIKE TO THANK the friends and colleagues who read parts of this manuscript and from whose comments we benefited, including Hosam Aboul-Ela, Jeanne Barker-Nunn, Lauren Berlant, Sreya Chatterjee, Betsy Dougherty, Jed Esty, Claire Bracken, David Mazella, Anne Mulhall, Eibhear Walshe, Karen Fang, Sean Kennedy, Sarah McKibben, and Gretchen Van Deusen. We would also like to express our appreciation of those friends and colleagues who have lent intellectual support to this project, including Marjorie Howes, Kathryn Conrad, Nessa Cronin, Oninye Ihezukwu, Lucy McDiarmid, Tina O'Toole, Paige Reynolds, Michael Snediker, Ed Madden, Cormac O'Brien, Eve Watson, Renee Fox, and Abby Bender. Vicki Mahaffey deserves special mention as she midwifed this project when she assigned the two of us a collaborative essay on James Joyce's "An Encounter" for her edited collection, *Collaborative Dubliners*.

We are greatly indebted to a large number of individuals who helped us obtain permissions and high-resolution images for our cover art and illustrations. Owing to their enthusiasm, generosity, ingenuity, and solidarity, many of the following individuals merit recognition as active contributors to this project. In particular, the help, guidance, and generosity of some of the professionals and activists who actively brought about the cultural sea changes this study engages greatly enriched its production and, we trust, the quality of the work itself. Those who helped us include Aedin Clements, interim head, Rare Books and Special Collections, University of Notre Dame Hesburgh Library; Steve Coleman, lecturer in anthropology, National

University of Ireland, Maynooth; Ida Milne, lecturer in European history at Carlow College, St. Patrick's; Lisa Fane, general manager, Irish Repertory Theater; Glenn Dunn and Justin Furlong, National Library of Ireland; Beatrix Faerber, University College Cork, CELT Project manager; James Grange Osborne, archives assistant, *Irish Independent* and *Sunday Independent*; Declan Howard, production manager, Avondhu Press; Brendan Maher, assistant images and licensing officer, National Gallery of Ireland; Ronan Duffy; Christine Bohan and Aoife Moore; Mark Yzaguirre; Andrew Martin, Irish Newspaper Archives; Carol Rosegg; Dave O'Connell, group editor, *Connacht Tribune*; Donal O'Keefe; Emma Busowski Cox and Tansy Curtin, curatorial manager, Bendigo Art Gallery; Natalie Jones, Mirrorpix; Flora Smith, managing partner, Topfoto.co.uk; Andrew Corless, chief editor, Media Drum World; Linda Briscoe-Meyers and Cristina Meisner, University of Texas Harry Ransom Humanities Research Center; Lynda O'Keefe, Editor's Office, *The Irish Times*; Johnathon Vines, image and brand licensing manager, and Chris Rawlings, licensing assistant, British Library; Jim Coughlan, *Irish Examiner*; Emily Vinson and the University of Houston Libraries Copyright Team; and straight-up agents of cultural change Piotr Ambroziac, Erin Darcy, Larry Kirwan, David Rooney, Wendy Shea, Martyn Turner, Dinny Wheeler, and Padraig Yeates.

Our editor, Jennika Baines, has believed in and enthusiastically supported this project virtually from the point at which we first figured out that the conference papers and articles we had been coauthoring since 2004 were part of a larger whole. Her guidance has been wise, deft, and spot on. We are particularly grateful to our two external readers for Indiana University Press, whose feedback was detailed, insightful, and extremely helpful.

Gretchen Van Deusen's contributions to this volume have been long-standing and thoroughgoing. For this coauthored work, her extensive support in the areas of chapter transcription, grant writing and management, and travel logistics and her oversight of rounds of chapter revision, manuscript preparation, and permissions have been indispensable. We are also indebted to Kezia Whiting for her invaluable editorial assistance and insight. Finally, we are indebted to Gretchen Van Deusen and Kezia Whiting for proofreading and, with Jerilyn Backus Tennison, for help with copy editing.

Both authors have benefited from extensive institutional support. Joseph Valente benefited from a Critical Research Initiative Grant from the University of Illinois in 2004 and subsequently from a Humanities

Research Award from the University of Illinois in 2006, both of which supported work on the early stages of this project. From his present institution, the University at Buffalo, he received a Research Leave for the spring of 2012 and a second Research Leave for the academic year 2016–17, both of which facilitated important stages in the writing of the manuscript. Finally, he was awarded a Humanities Institute Fellowship for the academic year 2018–19, during which period the manuscript was completed. In addition, an annual research grant during his time at Buffalo helped defray the costs of research materials, travel, and conference expenses dedicated to the present volume. Margot Backus received a year of supported leave in residence as 2007–08 Irish American Cultural Institute Fellow at the National University of Ireland–Galway's Martha Fox Centre for Irish Studies made possible, in part, through a University of Houston research leave. Subsequent work on early chapter drafts was supported by a two-year Houstoun Research Professorship, funded by the Houstoun Endowment through the University of Houston's Department of English, University of Houston grants-in-aid, UH Provost's travel grants, and two generous University of Houston's Women's, Gender and Sexuality Studies Summer stipends.

Margot Backus's work was also facilitated by a teaching-research semester as 2015 Fulbright Scholar of Anglophone Irish Writing at the Seamus Heaney Centre at the School of English at Queen's University Belfast, which was also partly funded by the University of Houston; a month in residence at the University at Buffalo as 2015 James Joyce Research Fellow; and, also in the fall of 2015, a half-year of supported research leave from the University of Houston. Chapter revision, manuscript preparation and permissions, and photo duplication were funded through three small research grants from the University of Houston English Department's Houstoun Endowment and a small University of Houston project completion grant. The University at Buffalo library has lent its support to an open-access platform of our book through the TOME project. Thanks to both institutions for their generosity and encouragement.

We have ordered our names in terms of seniority rather than alphabetically, an alternate convention to which we are calling attention because we are strong supporters of collaborative work in the humanities, and we understand that explanations of the significance of name order will be badly needed by scholars whose work is likely to be reviewed by promotion and tenure committees whose members may be accustomed to name order as reflecting the relative significance of each author's contribution to a given publication. In our case, and presumably in most collaborative work in the humanities, authors' contributions are, owing to the inherently iterative and dialogical nature of humanities scholarship, equal. It is to be expected that each author is fully responsible for every aspect of the project and that, indeed, each of us did as much work, in coauthoring this book, as we have done in the past in authoring our single-authored books. The benefit of collaboration in the humanities has nothing to do with labor reduction. Having each other as built-in interlocutors, first readers, sources of additional citations and knowledge bases, copy editors, and proofreaders has not reduced the per-scholar work that went into the production of this study, but it has significantly enhanced the quality and complexity of our analysis; the richness of the theoretical, historical, and critical context in which we can couch this analysis; and the clarity and style with which we have been able to convey it.

THE CHILD SEX SCANDAL
AND MODERN IRISH LITERATURE

INTRODUCTION

The Enigmatic History of Imperiled Innocence

IN A 2010 INTERVIEW, EMMA Donoghue lucidly explicated the literary trope around which *Writing the Unspeakable* coheres: childhood encounters with an unbearable signifier. According to Donoghue, her novel *Room*'s extraordinary child's-eye-view from inside a world-scale sex scandal builds on "painful moments" in earlier child-narrated novels such as Roddy Doyle's *Paddy Clarke Ha Ha Ha*: "When the reader deduces something going on between the adults that the child doesn't understand, though the child is aware that *something is missing*. . . . Sex is fundamentally a mystery to children, and many adult decisions are motivated by questions of sex. Child narrators who are confused about adult sexuality are particularly useful" (Derbyshire 2010; emphasis added). In other words, Donoghue built *Room* on a preexisting literary edifice organized around sexually uninitiated juvenile narrators who can see things they have not yet learned *not* to see. As Donoghue makes clear, such narrators are "particularly useful" for defamiliarizing the "painful moments" their point of view affords, which can fairly be described as otherwise inaccessible glimpses of the sexually scandalous.

Donoghue's observation highlights the literary device at the heart of our study of children in Irish literary representations of sex scandal. In our earliest collaborative work on representations of child sexual initiation in James Joyce and Kate O'Brien, we began theorizing moments similar to those Donoghue describes.[1] We have since discovered that throughout the twentieth century an astonishing number of Irish authors, including Donoghue, have been finding child protagonists "particularly useful" in this way.

Indeed, modern and contemporary Irish literature teems with uninitiated innocents who encounter taboo material otherwise representable only in the oral register of the open secret, in the quasi-journalistic genre of "sensational childhood" (Dougherty 2007, 52), and most pervasively, in the culturally influential phenomenon of the child sex scandal.

As we show in this book, the fictional narratives we collectively term *literature of child sex scandal* emerged in modern Ireland in direct conversation with British and Irish media scandals involving sexual (i.e., moral) threats to youthful innocence.[2] This influential literary subgenre is distinguished by uncomprehending child narrators whose point of view narratively reframes events that adults are socialized not to see, constituting them as enigmas—as "something missing"—that both child and reader need to interpret in order to make sense of the narrative as a whole. Since the early twentieth century, Irish authors have been employing and developing the generative (and generational) gap produced through depictions of an enigmatic encounter with something a child can apprehend but cannot understand or name, thereby systematically forcing into view appalling realities that the Irish public was culturally bound not to see.

Thus, in *Writing the Unspeakable*, we describe and account for the process whereby a loose coalition of modern and contemporary Irish authors collectively developed and built on the above-described literary effect, which, drawing on French psychoanalyst Jean Laplanche, we term the *enigmatic encounter*. These authors played a significant role in Ireland's social development by forcing into public view a whole stratum of disavowed child abuse and exploitation that was otherwise both obscured and enabled by the cordon sanitaire the modern sex scandal produces. In this critical study of several especially seminal works in this subgenre's development, we offer an account of how Ireland's literature of child sex scandal helped make possible more open, rational, and democratic public conversations concerning the position of children—and ultimately, other marginalized groups—in Irish society.[3] This literature's influential role is theoretically and ethically worthy of such systematic consideration, as it has documentably helped make publicly discernible the needs and well-being of groups whose experiences had been historically set off limits through the silencing, stigmatizing power of the modern, media-driven moral panic that is sex scandal.[4] In *Writing the Unspeakable*, we offer close critical readings of a series of significant modern Irish coming-of-age novels and short stories, taking advantage of literature's capacity to simultaneously display the individual and the collective, the psychoanalytic and the social, so as to produce a more nuanced account of the complex interrelations between children's subjective, lived experience (and its afterlife in the adult psyche) and children's objective political standing. Our methodology, applied to descriptions of influential child imperilment scandals found in newspapers, historical studies, and literature, reveals a public sphere ardently committed to Irish children's souls yet piously oblivious to their physical welfare, and comprising individuals who simultaneously knew and did not know that abuse and neglect were inescapable realities for many Irish children.

To unpack this phenomenon of knowing and not knowing, we draw on psychoanalytical theorist Laplanche's concept of the *enigmatic signifier*: a constitutive psychic blind spot incurred in a child's traumatic encounter with adult sexuality. This encounter, which can be neither integrated nor dismissed owing to its simultaneous inscrutability and affective intensity, is experienced by the child as both unbearably shameful and ecstatically pleasurable. Our historically contextualized and psychoanalytically informed readings of literary scandal narratives by six notable modern Irish authors trace their continually reinvented deployments of the enigmatic signifier as a literary device and instrument of social intervention. By placing these texts within a larger counterdiscourse that has forced the taboo topic of child sexual abuse into visibility, we have identified a rich and previously neglected historical archive of psychically and socially disavowed elements of Irish children's lives and the social world that shaped them.

"Who Make Up a Heaven of Our Misery"

The theme of imperiled innocence that would become central to the politics of twentieth-century Irish nationhood can already be found in such classical plotlines as the sacrifice of Iphigenia, Medea's murder of her children, Cain's murder of Abel, Solomon's choice, Abraham's intended sacrifice of Isaac, and Christianity's central, brutal sacrifice. In the British Isles, however, imperiled innocence reached its cultural apogee in the eighteenth-century gothic and its offspring, melodrama, genres so pervasive that by the turn of the nineteenth century imperilment was implicit in any attractive youth looking sad, scared, or disheveled.

Figure i.1. *Homeless* (1890). Painting by Thomas Kennington. © Bendigo Art Gallery.

In Britain, the sentimentalization of endangered innocence was coterminous with and paralleled women's and children's broad exclusion from factory work by factory owners whose newfound moral discernment appealed to adult male workers by giving their horrible jobs new prestige and their horrible wages new comparative value.[5] Arguably extending the eighteenth-century domestication of the child/maternal body-dyad that Ruth Perry describes (1992, 208), newfound national solicitude for poor women and children inspired public rituals dramatizing British society's protective stance toward its most vulnerable constituents, such as the ones William Blake immortalized in his "Holy Thursday" poems.

In a manner that prefigures the role of innocent children in the consolidation of the twentieth-century Irish nation-state, early imperial Britain created public displays of magnanimity toward rescued or reformed indigents as moral rituals of political consolidation.[6] In both of the "Holy Thursday" poems, Blake emphasizes the political nature of such public displays of benevolence. In the *Songs of Innocence* version, the "aged men wise guardians of the poor" sit "beneath" the orphans on display (Blake 1982, 13), an image that might suggest the humility of these kindly men but that also evokes an audience watching a play, with the orphans as an allegorical *tableau vivant*, positioned to convey through their very abjection the magnanimity of the Anglo-Protestant state. In the *Songs of Experience* version, Blake more pointedly delineates the vast ritual of beneficent power that public displays of "rescued" children produce. Blake's orphans are fed with a "cold and usurous hand" (19–20), a word choice that points to the profit motive, suggesting that the Anglican Church and the British state are invisibly extracting something from the destitute children they spectacularly nurture. As Blake describes it, through an elaborate display of symbolic munificence in a society whose abundant resources they themselves control, the English ruling class makes its goodness, and hence its legitimacy, socially manifest. In the words of "The Chimney Sweeper," through such actions, powerful adults mount displays of purely apparitional compassion to make "a heaven of [poor children's] misery" (22–23).

Blake's depictions of poor children as a source of hegemonic legitimation in the consolidating British empire closely anticipate the position in which twentieth-century Irish poor children would find themselves in the consolidating Irish state. During both periods of political transition, while public demonstrations of charity toward vulnerable innocents were reconstituting poor children as moral and symbolic capital, organizations devoted to this rescue work were rapidly reconstituting their beneficiaries as sources of literal profit. Frances Finnegan, in her history of the Magdalene asylums, describes the brawls over prospective penitents that were starting to break out between competing British rescue organizations around the time Blake was composing the "Holy Thursday" poems (2004, 11–12). Portentously, although England's Magdalene asylums were originally established to provide destitute girls and women with skills to improve their earning power, by Blake's time they were shamelessly exploiting the gratis labor of their charges. By the early to mid-nineteenth century, religiously-minded entrepreneurs along the lines of Charlotte Bronte's Mr. Brocklehurst were employing an array of strategies for transforming morally endangered or suspect youth from a deficit into an asset.[7] Most tellingly, as the symbolic potency of imperiled innocence grew throughout the nineteenth century, particularly once it had become a staple of the New Journalist sex scandal, the representability and even perceptibility of the needs of actual poor children concomitantly declined.[8]

In Britain, over the course of the nineteenth century, representations of endangered innocence already central to the gothic and realist novels engendered two additional print capitalist genres: first, the melodrama, with its further sentimentalization of imperiled women and children, and subsequently, the late nineteenth century's New Journalist sex scandal.[9] In 1885, W. T. Stead famously originated the modern political sex scandal through a series of articles collectively entitled "The Maiden Tribute of Modern Babylon." In his writing itself, and in his articles' splashy placement in the daily newspaper he edited, the *Pall Mall Gazette*, Stead sensationally publicized his own purchase, abduction, and involuntary detention of Eliza Armstrong, or "Lily," a thirteen-year-old gynecologically certified virgin. Stead published the "Maiden Tribute" series laudably aiming to confront the British public with the harsh realities of child prostitution in order to pressure Parliament to raise the age of consent for girls. In this regard, he succeeded, launching a moral panic of unprecedented proportions, in particular among members of the House of Lords who were heretofore complacent about the youthful streetwalkers visibly populating British urban thoroughfares.[10] From the standpoint of genre, Stead achieved his social effects by importing into hard journalism the sort of imperiled innocent already familiar to British readers from novels and the stage.

In "The Maiden Tribute of Modern Babylon," Stead thus originated a new and powerful journalistic subgenre: the scandal of imperiled innocence. And a nascent conservative Irish Catholic state would establish its moral and institutional supremacy in the early decades of the twentieth century through an adapted version of this very "imperiled child" scandal script. As we shall see, conservative Catholic nationalism deployed powerful, conventional media depictions of children in peril in a manner that both relied on and intensified the consolidation of interlocking church/business/media

A DREAM OF GREEN FIELDS.

Mr. Punch. "NOW, MISTRESS CHARITY, CAN'T WE MANAGE TO MAKE THE DREAM COME TRUE—JUST FOR A FORTNIGHT?"

[The Children's Country Holidays Fund is in great need of assistance. The Hon. Treasurer is the Earl of Arran, 18, Buckingham St., W.C.]

Figure i.2. "A dream of green fields." *Punch, or the London Charivari,* August 10, 1904. © Punch Cartoon Library/Topfoto.

directorates that would form the basis of what Jim Smith (2007) has termed "Ireland's architecture of containment." The Steadian child sex scandal in its first several decades exerted a considerably more consistent and extreme influence in Ireland than it had in either Britain or the United States. Beginning in the later twentieth century, however, the Irish scandal of imperiled innocence shifted radically. Over the long turn of the twenty-first century, Irish feminists, socialists, republicans, and LGBTQ activists began—and are continuing—to make canny use of endangered innocence to discredit the very Irish institutions that had most certainly been making for themselves a heaven of poor children's misery.

The underlying principle shared between the Anglo-American scandal of imperiled innocence Stead originated and its subsequent Irish offspring is a reliance on the perpetual vulnerability of poor children (and other vulnerable innocents) to exploitation as a renewable resource that can be readily sensationalized (and also neutralized) at will, and in the name of virtually any political cause that a society's powerful might deem expedient.

Sentimentalized for its precarious innocence, the figure of the child keyed the project of *soul-making*, on which basis Irish Catholic nationalism, like Anglo-Protestant imperialism, staked its claim to a manipulative, overbearing moral authority over gender norms, sexual expression and the wideranging social policies they underwrite.

The Imperiled Child in Turn-of-the-Century Ireland

As James Joyce's earliest fiction delicately but repeatedly indicates, late Victorian Ireland's educated reading publics were well aware of scandalous disclosures in the British press. Joyce's child protagonists come of age—as Joyce did—well aware of the "nauseous tides of seductive debauchery" to be found in British newspapers.[11] In *A Portrait of the Artist as a Young Man*, Stephen Dedalus's companion in the Clongowes infirmary, Athy, speaks knowingly but vaguely of newspaper scandals, and the young Stephen responds to these oblique allusions with a dream that makes clear how much he has already absorbed by osmosis about the Parnell scandal (Joyce 1992b, 25–27).[12] Joyce's eponymous Eveline, as both Katherine Mullin and Anne Fogarty have argued, fears "leaving home" not owing to generally misplaced loyalty but in response to the Irish nationalist press's various reactions to perceived British (mediated) depravity (Mullin 2003, 56–82; Attridge and

Figure i.3. "Women of Britain say—'Go!'." A propaganda poster appealing to Britain's women (in their role as children's primary protectors) to ensure that their men enlist. © The British Library Board (World War One propaganda collection).

Figure i.4. "Orpen's war exam." William Orpen (1878–1931). Graves Collection of William Orpen Letters, Prints and Drawings, National Gallery of Ireland. NGI.7830.302. Photo © National Gallery of Ireland.

Fogarty 2012, 97–106). Yet, although the British, Steadian scandal of imperiled innocence was powerfully affecting Ireland from its inception, the scandal script itself came late to the Irish press.[13]

Until the time of the Dublin Lockout, which began in September 1913, the vulnerability and suffering of destitute children like "The Maiden Tribute's" so-called Lily went unmentioned in the Irish media, owing, as Diarmaid Ferriter observes, to the extreme sensitivity of the Irish to any insinuation that "the maternal isle" was "maltreating" her children (2005, 48). Most saliently, at the turn of the twentieth century the Irish nationalist press was still reeling due to its own involuntary part in the ongoing effects of the Great Famine and, little more than a generation later, in the politically and socially cataclysmic fall of Charles Stewart Parnell.[14]

In the late nineteenth century, the Irish press was operating in a strangely liminal society where, within living memory, over a million men, women, and children had "d[ied] in conditions that would have seemed primitive to a medieval peasant," while, owing to rapid technological advances, appalling "reports of those deaths could be whisked to Dublin and London . . . in a matter of days" (Morash 2010, 80).[15] Already ambiguously situated in a traumatized and guilt-ridden post-Famine society, "the mainstream nationalist press next found itself calamitously entangled in a network of telegraph wires, an informational field in which a [forged] letter published in a London newspaper alleging an Irish politician's involvement with an American newspaper would become an event that resonated throughout a new trans-Atlantic field" (96).

Culminating in 1890, several media-related Irish shame vectors converged, catalyzed by the series of London newspaper exposés that targeted and finally toppled Parnell, arguably the one Irish nationalist leader ever to have passed the manliness litmus test (Valente 2011, 27–62). Parnell's unmanning fall and his craven betrayal by his political allies and followers at the instigation of the Irish Catholic Church left behind a post-Parnellite public sphere haunted by sins and failures too shameful to acknowledge and too terrible to forget. This ambient post-Famine, post-Parnellite shame and guilt, in turn, gave rise to the hypersensitivity Ferriter (2005) describes.

Irish newspapers were doing their best to cope in a society that had been slammed with two society-wide affective shock waves. And they increasingly responded—as they tellingly urged Irish housewives to do—by fighting tirelessly against dirt and disorder in newly defined and intensely promoted Irish Catholic spaces of cleanly respectability (Attridge

and Fogarty 2012, 102–6).[16] The diligent housekeeping and home beautifica-
tion both promoted and figuratively undertaken by the mainstream nationalist press entailed keeping "well away" from all distressed Irish children,
along with anything else that might signify Irish abjection (see Walshe 2011,
12–16). At the same time, clean, well-educated, and well-scrubbed middle-
class Catholic children were increasingly set forth as a significant, even valo-
rized newspaper category.[17]

At-Risk Children as Human Shields in the 1913 Dublin Lockout

Starting on September 4, 1913, a coordinated initiative by roughly four hundred Dublin employers pointedly threatened the families of organizing
workers with starvation by collectively locking out all workers who refused
to sign a pledge forswearing membership in Jim Larkin's powerful syndical-
ist union, the ITGWU.

In the ensuing Lockout, food became profoundly politicized, with
"Catholic and Protestant food kitchens [competing] to win souls by feeding the starving" (Yeates 2001, 34). By mid-October, moved by her own
observations of starving children foraging through garbage piles, British
socialist and union sympathizer Dora Montefiore was organizing what she
termed a campaign to "Save the Kiddies." Using her valuable connections,
she arranged for the first of what were meant to be several designated ships
that would transport the children of locked-out workers to temporary foster
homes with sympathetic British families.

In the third week of October 1913, Dublin's Archbishop Walsh took the
church's long-established unwillingness to relinquish prerogatives regard-
ing children to new extremes when he blasted the Save the Kiddies scheme
from the pages of both Irish nationalist daily newspapers.[18] The formula
Walsh employed—one the nationalist press was to make its own—was that
Irish children were better off dead than exposed to any worldview outside
of that authorized by the Catholic Church (McDiarmid 2004, 141). Walsh's
statement opened the floodgates: political cartoons and newspaper commentary commenced stridently to accuse those workers who refused to
sign Martin Murphy's pledge of starving their own children and to laud the
Irish Catholic Church as the children's heroic savior. Walsh's updated scandal of imperiled innocence, which equated the succor of starving children

Figure i.5. "True to tradition." *Daily Herald* cover, October 7, 1913: "The police have bludgeoned women and children in Dublin." © Mirrorpix/British Newspaper Archive.

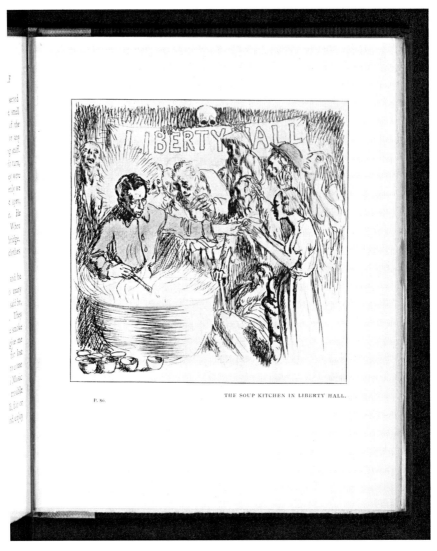

THE SOUP KITCHEN IN LIBERTY HALL.

P. 86.

Figure i.6. "Food kitchen in Liberty Hall." Illustration from 1913 by William Orpen, depicting efforts by trade unionists and sympathizers to feed families during the 1913 Dublin Lockout.

with perversion, directed torrents of public outrage, akin to those Stead had incited through the "Maiden Tribute" scandal, toward the children's would-be rescuers.[19]

In the bare-knuckled ideological brawl that ensued, children's exquisitely vulnerable souls came to epitomize everything that Dublin business owners and the Irish Catholic Church believed socialist syndicalism endangered. As Padraig Yeates reports, the "less than generous response of the city's middle classes to the hardship of workers was partly due to Larkin's promotion of the 'Dublin kiddies' scheme" (2001, 34).[20] Effectively speaking for the Irish Catholic Church, Walsh radically modified what had been a moderately sympathetic stance toward locked-out workers in response to the ostensible religious dangers implicit in Montefiore's plan. Walsh's representations of innocent Irish children threatened with unspeakable perversion and the ultimate child abuse—perpetual damnation—powerfully conveyed to the Irish mainstream the intolerable threat to Irish innocence posed by "godless" labor, socialist, and feminist initiatives.

On October 22, 1913, hundreds of parents and activists attempting to see workers' children onto the first transport ship bound for Liverpool were set upon by priests, police, and organized lay Catholics determined to unsave, or countersave, those same children. Montefiore and even some parents were formally charged with kidnapping. Only a few children made it onto the ship, and "the supply of children rapidly dried up when the Murphyite press began publishing the names and addresses of parents" (Yeates 2000, 34). The nationalist press ascribed all this mayhem to the workers, who were accused not only of widespread child abduction but also of unprovoked assaults on members of the police and the clergy. Thus, over the course of the Dublin Strike and Lockout, from September 1913 through the strike's final collapse in February 1914, the church's position in mainstream Irish nationalism as the rightful arbiter of Irish children's well-being was firmly established.[21] As we shall see, the new emphasis in Irish public discourse on children's well-being as exclusively defined by the religious affiliation of their guardians was to influence profoundly both the institutional and moral infrastructure of the modern Irish state.

What might reasonably be termed the 1913 clerical "Campaign to *Starve the Kiddies*" would be only the first in a series of national controversies demonizing anyone who sought to improve the welfare of children, women, or both, or conversely demonizing both women and children who showed

Figure i.7. *The Faith* saves "Irish Child" from "Socialism," celebrating the defeat of Dora Montefiore's "Save the Dublin Kiddies" campaign. This illustration appeared in the *Sunday Independent* on October 26, 1913. Photo credit: TheJournal .ie (with permission of the National Library of Ireland).

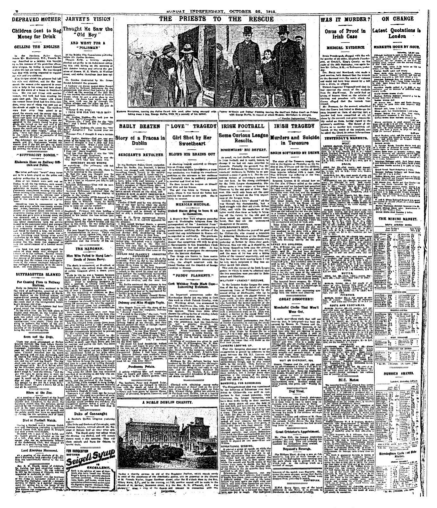

Figure i.8. "Saving Dublin children." Dora Montefiore's arrest (left) and two priests who have taken custody of the boy Montefiore had been escorting. *Sunday Independent,* October 26, 1913. © INM (Independent News and Media).

symptoms of resisting the church's beneficent attention. Such controversies would resurface across the decades, from the 1913 Lockout to the 1931 Carrigan Report to the defeat by impassioned lay Catholics of the Mother and Child Scheme in the early 1950s. A pattern of public exposés decrying ostensible threats either to children or to the Irish Catholic Church (and hence to the nation's spiritual purity) incontrovertibly established the church's sovereignty over Irish Catholic youth.[22] In the process, a newly unified church-media-government complex came into being.

THE CHILDREN OF THE NATION

The year 1913 thus saw the effective fulfillment of the Irish Catholic clergy's long-standing efforts to establish itself as speaking for the Irish people as a whole and to eliminate or discredit all competing ideologies in Ireland. Out of the chaos of the strike and its subsequent collapse emerged a vastly empowered Irish Catholic Church that increasingly presented itself as the future Irish state in utero.[23]

Immediately after the post-Treaty Irish Civil War (June 1922–May 1923), what we term a new *moral episteme* was further shaped in surprising ways by the nascent state's and nationalist media's emphasis on a caste of culpable children whose corruption posed a threat to Irish society's inherent purity. Poor juveniles, whom Walsh had originally sensationalized as probable victims of ideological (and subliminally, other forms of) perversion, were transformed into scandal perpetrators who themselves posed a threat to Ireland's high moral standing, now symbolically vested in adults—especially in Irish men. Through a series of shocking reports, documentaries, and scholarly studies, an ever-clearer picture of this period is now emerging, detailing the abuse and the commodification of babies and juveniles of both sexes in early to midcentury Irish orphanages and industrial schools, and of course, at the hands of those clergy and lay people who used the rituals of the church to groom their victims. While Ireland's dominant scandal culture up to the time of the 1992 Bishop Casey scandal focused obsessively on girls and women as sex scandal perpetrators, and gradually as scandal victims, the archival record shows clearly that in Ireland's architecture of containment, both boys and girls suffered terribly.[24]

The church's enhanced claim to be the only legitimate arbiter of Irish national interests palpably foreclosed the space in which representations of the material needs or interests of children could be articulated in the new Irish state. Even in Sean O'Casey's *The Plough and the Stars*—his aggressive critique of the nationalism animating the Easter Rising—the central emblem of the plight of poor children, Mollser (the play's doomed slum child), is devoid of particularity, serving far more as an allegory in death than as a living representative of the everyday experiences of slum children.

However, as we will show, this pervasive allegorization of the child was significantly contested by Irish modernists like James Joyce and Kate O'Brien and, starting around midcentury, in the hyperrealism of Edna O'Brien and John McGahern.[25] This pattern of literary contestation was then taken up by far more writers and creatives than we can possibly credit: hundreds have engaged in a collective transtemporal project of restoring to the poor or otherwise abjected child—and thereby indirectly to all the constituencies that Ireland's war on children had rendered voiceless—the embodied subjectivity that the scandal of imperiled innocence took from them.[26]

Throughout the decades of the Irish Catholic Church's closest alignment with Irish nationalism, the Irish media, and the Irish state, children were conceived of as empty vessels whose virtually coterminous spiritual and sexual purity was absolutely secured by the church's social and moral oversight. Those children, young women, and the disabled, who could not be construed as healthy, well-cared-for embodiments of Catholic purity, were effectively criminalized and shunted into Catholic institutions that served as pressure-release valves within Ireland's architecture of containment. Over time, these institutions swelled with sexually suspect girls, insubordinate children of impoverished families, and babies whose visible presence in their birth communities would have threatened the symbolic purity so crucial to the national imaginary. While the teeming ranks of Ireland's discarded minors fortified the church's finances and social clout, these arrangements also served to reduce some of the vast social and economic stress imposed on the ordinary Catholic citizen-subject in what Tom Inglis terms "the Irish Catholic habitus" (2008, 250).

By the early 1950s, the charge of child imperilment could be potently deployed even against a Catholic political leader who was unambiguously championing children's welfare. Noël Browne, Ireland's second minister for health (1948–51), became a high-profile casualty of his own determined efforts to combat Ireland's soaring child and infant mortality. The church objected to Browne's Mother and Child Scheme lest it open the door to Irish Catholics having access to medical (especially gynecological) care from sources outside the church's purview. A Trinity-trained MD who went into politics specifically to fight the ravages of tuberculosis, Browne was forced from office through the back-door machinations of the church leadership, which had in public continually asserted its neutrality toward Browne's initiative. Browne accepted his inevitable defeat, but he did not go quietly.

Figure i.9. Staging of Larry Kirwan's *Rebel in the Soul*, Irish Repertory Theatre. (Patrick Fitzgerald as Dr. Noël Browne, and John Keating as Archbishop John Charles McQuaid.) © Carol Rosegg.

In his resignation statement, he told the Dáil that "the [Catholic Church] hierarchy has informed the government that they must regard the mother and child scheme proposed by me as opposed to Catholic social teaching," and that he had been informed by the archbishop of Dublin, John Charles McQuaid, "that Catholic social teaching and Catholic moral teaching were one and the same thing." Thus, Browne explained, as a good Catholic, he had no option but to resign because the church had now made its position unambiguously clear: the Mother and Child Scheme was immoral.[27]

As this last example, and indeed the above cultural history as a whole makes clear, the very idea of imperiled childhood innocence allowed for considerable moral, political, and definitional leverage that extended far beyond the material welfare of actual children, and indeed often had little or nothing to do with children at all. In keeping with this politically cynical instrumentalization of victimage, the most effectively spectacular "innocent children" have typically been those who become the object of (our) collective solicitude when their vulnerability is abruptly, sensationally revealed as ascribable to some unthinkable external threat, whether foreign, supernatural, or unspeakably depraved. From the diabolical white slave trade made public by Stead's "Maiden Tribute" series, to the Irish Catholic media campaign linking trade union activity to child abduction, child endangerment has regularly been attributed to some individual or group other, whose exile from the approved social order would reinforce the prevailing power structure.

Since the 1990s, the Irish mainstream has increasingly come to see the mid-century nationalist church/state axis as likewise inexplicably alien. Nonetheless, as Moira Maguire (2009) has shown in *Precarious Childhood*, significant evidence exists to document a surprisingly high degree of complacency on the part of the Irish people with respect to the church's openly extreme treatment of specific women, children, and babies in perceived violation of Ireland's moral episteme.[28] Ultimately and importantly, the absolute nature of ecclesiastical authority allowed the Irish Catholic Church and its followers to define the nation's moral episteme to suit themselves. In a representational environment defined by censorship, direct ecclesiastical control over education and other social services, and indirect control over the media and political and legal processes, the Irish Catholic Church and its functionaries eventually accumulated more than enough rope to hang themselves in the eyes of an appalled, if unconsciously complicit, Irish public. Crucially, Ireland's growing rejection of the church's strictures in response to the very scandal conventions that had previously reinforced them has ameliorated, but by no means resolved, the threats to children's well-being posed by the child sex scandal. Such an awakening could not have occurred without the mediating role played by a broad front of Irish authors and public intellectuals whose novels, short stories, and literary criticism were too greatly admired by readers and scholars beyond Ireland to be feasibly suppressed within Ireland.

Conversely, the Irish child sex scandals of the late twentieth century proved to be so explosive precisely because they revealed the main threat to Ireland's youth to be decisively *internal*—internal to Ireland, internal to respectable Catholic society, and, most unsettling of all, internal to the very agencies ostensibly most concerned to protect childhood innocence. Under these circumstances, the moral and political leverage that scandal had afforded the dominant institutions of Irish society could be, and were, turned against them.

Contemporary Irish sex scandal has taken its seismic force from its tendency to upset rather than stabilize the ideological applecart. Beginning in the mid-1980s, the hegemonic position of the Irish Catholic Church began

Figure i.10. "State of shame." Three boys sewing at an industrial school. *Irish Independent*, May 21, 2009. Horrified response to the Ryan Report (released May 20, 2009). © INM (Independent News and Media).

to visibly give way when the indifference of both church officials and the broader Irish public to the welfare of minors was made palpable through a series of child sex scandals in which the terms *victim* and *victimization* began to be defined in new ways. In 1984, fifteen-year-old Ann Lovett died in childbirth, along with her newborn infant, at the grotto of the Virgin Mary in Granard. She had carried a pregnancy to term without anyone in her piously Catholic community intervening to help her or, indeed, her baby once it was born. In the same year, the discovery of a dead infant in County Kerry led to the prosecution of a woman deemed to be the mother/murderer that continued even after she proved her own baby had been still-born. The determined prosecuting tribunal, evidently fixated on the bereft mother's guilt as a woman who had had extramarital sex, theorized that she might have had two different babies from different fathers within a short period (Conrad 2004, 86). The new legibility of such cases in the mid-1980s was most proximately indebted to the courageous work of Irish feminists, who since the 1960s had been organizing tirelessly to connect the teachings of the Catholic Church to the fates of such women and babies. However, both the arguments that Irish feminists made and the capacity of some portion of the Irish populace to make even limited sense of these arguments strongly relied on an alternate moral vocabulary and an alternate ethical lens that were being largely supplied by Irish authors.

By the early 1990s, the high price that some Irish women and children had been paying to subsidize the nation's surface appearance of Catholic piety was becoming apparent, still largely through scandals involving wronged girls and women. In February 1992, the so-called X case began to make headlines after fourteen-year-old Girl X traveled with her parents to London to terminate a pregnancy resulting from her rape by a family friend who had been sexually abusing her for years. Before the abortion could take place, she was ordered to return to Ireland in strict obedience to the Eighth Amendment of the Irish Constitution (Conrad 2004, 102).

In May 1992, *Irish Times* headlines rightly treated Father Eamonn Casey's sudden resignation as Bishop of Galway as a de facto admission that he had had an affair and fathered a child with Annie Murphy, an American. Only in 1993, when Murphy published *Forbidden Fruit: The True Story of My Love Affair with Ireland's Most Powerful Bishop*, did the Irish reading public learn that Casey had sought to involuntarily confine Murphy in an Irish convent and force her to give up his child for adoption. For the powerful and sexually

Figure i.11. "The introduction of internment . . . for fourteen-year-old girls." Martyn Turner's celebrated rejoinder to the "Girl X" case. © Martyn Turner.

conservative Casey, who was fully prepared to treat Murphy like any other erring Magdalene, this solution was clearly standard operating procedure. Also in 1993, a mass grave in which 133 Magdalenes who had been incarcerated for life by Dublin's Sisters of Charity was unexpectedly unearthed, bringing to widespread attention the previously unacknowledged scale and intensity with which sexually erring or suspect women had been extrajudicially incarcerated and exploited in Ireland's Magdalene laundries.

Illicit heterosexual conduct had been the dominant theme of Irish scandal culture since the early days of the Irish republic, but these particular stories exploded on contact with that scandal culture, forcing a virtual reversal in the moral force field that bourgeois nationalism had long enforced. A long-established tradition of media silence concerning the abuse of children and cases of ecclesiastical hypocrisy gradually gave way as a virtual avalanche of long-suppressed clerical abuse surged into public view. By 1994, the public attitude toward the Irish Catholic Church and its long-accepted prerogatives was detectably shifting. In this year, the Irish press began to report on the Irish state's ongoing failure to extradite Northern Irish Tridentine priest Fr. Brendan Smyth back to Northern Ireland, where he was to face charges relating to his molestation of seventeen boys and girls (a small fraction of the enormous number of children Smyth molested over the course of four decades).

Understandably, Taoiseach Albert Reynolds's coalition Fianna Fáil–Labour Party government hewed to the established terms of the post-Treaty church-state alliance, dragging its heels, backing the voraciously pedophilic priest, and counting on the Irish Church hierarchy's power to protect them in return. And for the first time it was the Reynolds government, Smyth, and the church-state system they represented, rather than a panoply of socialists, feminists, and labor unionists, whom the Irish media and Irish audiences would see as endangering innocent children. In the end, the coalition government collapsed, and Smyth died in prison.

Psychoanalyzing the Enigma of Sexualized Innocence

While any turnabout whereby the shepherd becomes the wolf is ironic, even counterintuitive, it is also, from a psychoanalytic point of view, anything but inexplicable. Insofar as sexuality, constituted as the foremost threat to Catholic youth, remains at the same time a radically if problematically constitutive element of subjectivity, it cannot be finally squelched or purged. Any attempt to do so, whether by sacramental dispensation, state censorship, vows of celibacy, reproductive imperatives, institutional sanctions, ascetic regimens, or shaming rituals, can only fuel, shape, and ultimately solidify further displaced modalities of sexual expression. This might, indeed, be termed the first law of psychoanalysis. Further, because desire itself is mobilized by the signifier, the symbolic nexus between subjects and

Figure i.12. "Credo that protected a monster." Wendy Shea's depiction of Brendan Smyth as a bloated, amoeboid figure preparing to incorporate his next victim. *Sunday Independent*, October 16, 1994. © Wendy Shea.

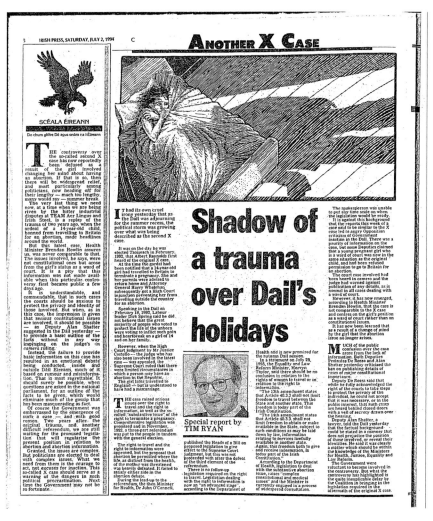

Figure i.13. "Shadow of a trauma." This illustration of a child cowering under a looming shadow illustrates the imagined reaction of the Irish Dail to a second X case. *Irish Press*, July 2, 1994. © David Rooney.

the social order to which they belong, the displacement of sexuality attendant to its suppression affects not only the parties under restriction—in this case, the imperiled innocents—but also the restricting parties and agencies. Hence, we might express the following as an indispensable corollary to the first law of psychoanalysis: the policing of eroticism inevitably becomes an erotic and an eroticizing activity all its own, whether voyeuristic, sadistic, or narcissistically self-aggrandizing. Having assumed (in every sense) a nearly absolute, sometimes divinely appointed authority, including a pretense to mastery over the vagaries of sexuality itself, certain officials and associates of Irish Catholic institutions wound up eroticizing the sanctified powers and the entitled sanctity with which they had been invested. That is to say, even as the authority to protect innocence was consciously "taken" (in the sense of both "construed" and "appropriated"), sexual license and gratification were likewise unconsciously taken (again in both senses) as that sanctified authority's prerogative.

We can see this reflexive turn of erotic energy in the disavowed jouissance, the enjoyment in disgust, at work in those agents', often clerics', judgments concerning the perceived sexual delinquency of those under their charge and in the brutal disciplining of those marked as sexually corrupted—whether by internment, chastisement, forced labor, stigmatization, mutilation, some combination thereof, or by the implicit encouragement of the wider populace to engage in cognate acts of moralizing abuse, from ostracism to confinement. We also see this sort of reflexive turn in individual mentors' (clerical and otherwise) grooming for sexual seduction and abuse of those minors and spiritual dependents under their tutelage. Finally, we see just this sort of reflexive turn illustrated in Sebastian Barry's tour de force, *The Secret Scripture*, where "savage" nuns beat the sexual errancy out of the poorer girls "with every ounce of energy in their bodies," a practice that just exudes the exorbitant release of libidinal energy (2008, 90).[29]

As this example intimates, the officers of the Catholic Church are especially liable to the reflexive turn we have theorized. In representing the always equivocal signifiers of divine law and purpose, in channeling the always projected will of God, the Catholic clergy occupy an equivocal position of their own, wherein the ineluctably phantasmatic aspect of religious faith could slip unnoticed into the religious, faith-based legitimation of personal fantasy. Predicated on an identification with the received canons of sanctity, the clerical exceptionalism endemic to the church-state complex of Ireland could easily induce a sense of exception, or exemption, from the binding force of those same canons.[30] Put another way, the different strains of the church fathers' (and brothers' and sisters') desire could and sometimes did inform and/or distort, infuse and/or contaminate, supplement and/or supplant the particular expressions of the sovereign demand they supposedly relayed as deputies of the Godhead. In conceiving themselves

Figure i.14. "Pretty twisted stuff. It's almost Kafkaesque." Speech by Fine Gael TD John Deasy on the Grace foster abuse scandal, published in the *Irish Examiner*, March 9, 2017. © *Irish Examiner*/Getty Images stock photo.

as representatives and instruments of divine will, members of the clergy in particular run the risk of enlisting the deity, unconsciously or not, as the guarantor of their own occluded desires. By extension—and here is where the real danger lies—they risk positioning their young pastoral wards as instrumental objects of their own disavowed wishes, under color of rendering them instruments of God's will as well. What is more, the surpassing authority they enjoy for the faithful can (and often does) create a similar confusion on the part of their spiritual followers.[31]

Although the grounds for mystifying the impetus and misrecognizing the implications of child sexual abuse are especially prevalent within the morally authoritative walls of the Irish Catholic Church, it would be inaccurate and unfair to suggest that such infractions are the sole province of church institutions. To the contrary, as Maguire argues, the connivance at, complicity with, and even commission of child sexploitation radiated through every quarter of Irish society. But owing to the preeminence of the church as moral arbiter and political power broker, the entire scandal can be laid, as well-known abuse survivor and advocate Colm O'Gorman contends, at the doorstep of that conjoined national edifice, the virtual, postindependence Catholic theocracy (Maher and Littleton 2010, 8). The site of intensive and extensive ethno-identification under de Valera, this virtual theocracy was consolidated in law (the Constitution of 1937), in actual governance (the partnership of the church and state apparatus), and in the ideology of the everyday (instilled in practices of childhood education, adolescent supervision, and adult surveillance; Inglis 1998, 10–13).

Given the finely calibrated hierarchy of church organization, its circumambient role in normative regulation and the social welfare apparatus of an impoverished nation, and the extremely localized (not to say personalized) exercise of power in the ranks of both the clergy and the laity, Irish theocracy functioned as a network of Foucaultian micropower, its top-down impetus at once diffused and enhanced via a dense mesh of disciplinary, tutelary, and pedagogical relationships. Like any such microcircuit, on Michel Foucault's (1980) account, this one operates not on a strictly repressive basis (all appearances to the contrary) but through an alternating and symbiotic current of constraint and provocation, the inhibition and implantation of desire. This current manifests itself, of course, in the structural oscillation between scandals of oppression (the Lovett and Kerry baby cases) and scandals of predation (the Brendan Smyth case and the Ferns Diocese scandal) and in the combination of oppression and predation in single episodes such as the X case. Most tellingly, it manifests in the way erotic energies feed on the practices and rituals of correction throughout the entire system. For in the attempt to confine and canalize the unruly longings of its charges and dependents, the regulatory machinery of the Irish church wound up saturating certain sites of disciplinary constraint and purgation—orphanages, industrial schools, convents, rectories, laundries, and "homes" both public and private—with the very libidinal stirrings it sought to tame.[32] The recursive arc of this libidinal economy comprehended more than the illicit romances of popular bishops or the serial abuses of rogue priests. Rather, it extends along a continuum that comprises not only these overt sexual acts, but an entire repertoire of avidly punitive cruelty whose erotic undercurrents cannot be ignored. Indeed, these are cruelties often associated with the most infamous sexual predators: the corporal punishment administered to children of industrial schools and the inmates of Magdalene laundries; the long-term forced imprisonment of these same populations, with mandatory labor superadded; forced childbirth, even following rape; the extravagant shaming and ostracism of "wayward" girls; the sexual exploitation of minors of both sexes; the forced appropriation, commodification, and mistreatment of the offspring of unsanctioned couplings—an entire jouissance of coercion enacted under the sign of moral correction.

Beyond shocking the conscience, such violations, being the outgrowth of unconscious dynamics, all but defy rational explanation. It is accordingly difficult to get past one's initial moral outrage and condemnation to perform a more in-depth and dispassionate analysis, especially if one takes at all seriously the claims to godliness lodged by many of the individual perpetrators, by the church institutions, and by the Irish nation itself, "where the faith and piety of our people are unquestioned" (Long 1950, 12). Here, literature has a crucial function to perform in confronting, interrogating, and dissecting the psychosocial complexities of Ireland's child sex scandal culture. Literature, we contend, has the capacity to form an unconscious reserve of history, what Bruce Fink calls the "censored chapters" of an approved narrative—in this case, a collective or ethnonational script (1995, 6). The novels we will be unpacking discharge this office by deploying what Walter Benjamin calls the "art of using allegory inconspicuously"—that is, as a cloaking device flush with the production of legible semiotic possibility, admitting and balking simultaneously the identification of its object (1998, 191). The strategic engagement with this "irreducible component of any text," as Paul de Man has it, enables these novels to serve as repositories of difficult, traumatic, and scandalous historical truths disclosed under the guard of Freudian disavowal—that is, to answer the knowing/not-knowing of the open secret with the saying/not-saying of muted revelation (1979, 77). In allegories of this sociopolitical stripe, represented scenarios—say, of child sexual predation—may, but need not, be taken to bear a specific historical reference and may, but need not, be understood as exemplifying a chronic social or institutional pathology; explicit witness to historical outrages against children may be borne, but in a fictive and therefore explicitly nontestimonial framework; and scandalous stories with a factual basis but without a factual warrant are retailed. In this fashion, literature records truths otherwise inaccessible to communal consciousness by way of figural practices that to some degree veil or leaven them. These novels traffic, we would say, in the enigmatic signifiers of the Real, signifiers that particularly suit them to the task of exploring the "hidden Ireland" of child sexual abuse.

Insofar as literary narratives form an unconscious reserve for real-time historical scripts, they remain, of course, a part of those very scripts—interleaved, ambiguously redacted passages in the margins of that history. Occupying such a position denies literature the possibility of distanced reflection on any factual referent of its allegory and precludes it from serving as an analyst of the collective symptoms it surveys. But it does not altogether deny literature—and herein lies a conundrum in need of theoretical elaboration—the capacity for critical and even therapeutic reflection. Without the power to perform a collective (psycho-)analysis of the national and sectarian pathologies it addresses, modern Irish fiction nevertheless has been able to open and hold open the possibility of such a collective analysis.

To illustrate by way of an earlier example, Barry's *The Secret Scripture* contains a neat allegory of this power dynamic, along with the sort of displacements that serve to disguise it. Upon the death of her disgraced father, the protagonist, a then-sixteen-year-old Roseanne, is visited by the parish priest, Father Gaunt, who proposes to see her provided for by way of an arranged marriage to Joe Brady, a corpulent fifty-year-old man who took her father's job. When Roseanne replies, "You'd have me marry an old man?" (2008, 94), the priest explains that Roseanne has received a gift from God, her sexual appeal (though he hems and haws about the term and settles on "beauty"), which allows him to make this advantageous, if precipitous, match. When Roseanne still resists, Gaunt deems that same quality, now unnamed, as a danger, a "temptation" to the "boys of Sligo." Thus, Roseanne's endowments are a supreme good, a "gift from God," so long as Gaunt enjoys the power to dispose of them (the original French meaning of the term *jouissance* is "rights over property"), but they deteriorate into evil should he fail to command that power. In other words, Father Gaunt seeks to possess Roseanne's body sexually by a form of remote control that would maintain the appearance of perfect, celibate self-denial. Not surprisingly, Father Gaunt's efforts to despoil Roseanne's reputation later in the novel seem undermotivated except as the revenge of the jilted. That the more directly spurned lover, Joe Brady, subsequently endeavors to take possession of Roseanne's body sexually by raping her—and then explicitly justifies the attempt as vengeance for her refusal of his advances—positions the two men as doppelgänger figures, each wanting to control Roseanne in his own way: one through the violence of (theocratic) law and one with a violence surpassing law altogether; one a priested pimp, one a rapist john; one the image of muscular Christianity (trim, athletic, and self-restrained, "Gaunt" his allegorical name), one a figure of diabolical excess (by way of his corpulent body and "swollen penis"; 105). But most importantly, the one serves the other as his agent, with profoundly allegorical implications: the authoritative figure of sexual repression, in concentrating libidinal energy around his authority to institute such repression, advances the cause within himself and his circle of sexual violence against the disempowered.

Although dramatically enhanced in literary texts by reason of their public availability, this capacity for immanent traumatic reflection is not specific to literature, nor was it first identified in aesthetic or cultural discourse. It is, rather, a paradox native to psychoanalysis—one of the great paradoxes of psychoanalysis—that traumatic manifestations and symptomatic formations constitute, in and of themselves, modes of reflection on their prompts and determinants. The object of psychotherapy is already (if not always) an agent of psychotherapy. Building on Sigmund Freud's notion of infantile sexual theory, Laplanche (1999) observes that analytical theory at its most general level (notably the theory of the drive) should show us how, in what conditions, with what results, with what failures, and with what costs the subject theorizes or metabolizes the enigmas that are posed to it from the outset by interhuman communication. Analytic theory is in this respect a metatheory in relation to the fundamental theorization that all human beings carry out, not primarily in order to appropriate nature but to bind anxiety in relation to the trauma that is the enigma (Laplanche 1999, 135).

For Laplanche, to be a subject at all is to be the subject of an always traumatic because enigmatic sexuality, and his point in the observation noted above is that there always resides a distinct if fugitive mental phase between the traumatic experience and its symptomatic reflexes on one side, and the psychoanalytic interpretation and traversal of the revealed fantasy on the other. This phenomenological interval Laplanche likens to a "fundamental theorization," an interlude wherein reflection inheres in the very traumatic, enigmatic experience to be reflected on. While such reflection stops short of theoretical analysis proper (what Laplanche christens "metatheory"), which entails the elaboration of a coherent, generalizable paradigm, it does "metabolize the enigma" of the experience by rehearsing it on other terms, representing it anew, and, in thus binding the trauma, it prepares the enigma for interpretive clarification and resolution. These novels, with their generic capacity for inconspicuous allegory, perform this function on the ethnonational stage, treating the traumatic realities of material dispossession, racial abjection, and cultural deracination in exemplary portrayals that bind the resulting affective distress for critical analysis. If anything, certain touchstones of modern Irish literature (including *Dubliners*, *A Portrait of the Artist as a Young Man*, *The Land of Spices*, *The Country Girls Trilogy*, *The Long Falling*, *In the Woods*, and *The Gathering*) offer a still more precise literary version of the "fundamental theorization" delineated by Laplanche. They both specify the universally traumatic nature of sexuality in a series of historically based sexual abuses and allegorize historically based sexual abuses in narratives implicating the universally traumatic nature of sexuality. The enabling mechanism of such "fundamental theorization" is the vehicle of traumatic sexualization itself, which Laplanche terms the "enigmatic signifier" (1997, 653–65).

According to Laplanche, parental or authority figures impart the energies of their own repressed desires and compromise formations to children in ambiguous psychic messages that take the form of enigmatic signifiers. This introduction of (adult) sexuality into the child's life horizon elicits a traumatic jouissance that furnishes the necessary condition of his or her accession to subjectivity. The vehicle of this traumatic enjoyment is precisely the signifier's enigmatic quality, which conveys a sensory or affective power exceeding its capacity for determinant meaning or function.

Jouissance occupies the material lining of the signifier (the acoustics of the word, timbre of the voice, sheen of the image) as an occult zone of undecidability, wherein the vicissitudes of unconscious parental desire touch and translate into the turbulent libidinal awakening of the child.[33]

At the same time, the eroticized occult penumbra of the signifier exists only insofar as it is propped on or attached to the potential for meaning or functionality—the everyday purpose of signification—and the articulation of jouissance in the enigmatic penumbra of the sign allows those specific contents and objects to take on sexual appeal, resonance, and power. The obverse holds as well: the contingent but requisite attachment of traumatic jouissance to vehicles of determinate meaning and valence entails that every experience thereof comes with the potential to be, in G. W. F. Hegel's phrase, "reflected into itself," to be or to become a locus of conscious attention and consideration (1977, 13). While the jouissance borne by the enigmatic signifier can lead, like any trauma, to psychic overload, shutdown, and repression, this very insertion in a signifying chain turns that traumatic enjoyment into a potential object of immanent reflection for the subject. With its post-Jamesian renderings of psychic interiority, modern Irish literature was poised to capitalize on this opportunity. The uncertainties and mystifications that sexualize juvenile experience in the texts we have cited simultaneously constitute occasions and catalysts for the juvenile protagonists to speculate on and wrestle with that experience. Representational strategies in such novels as *Down by the River* (E. O'Brien 1997) or *A Portrait of the Artist as a Young Man* (Joyce 1992b) are designed to highlight the dwelling in the enigmatic signifier and the hermeneutical binding of the anxiety aroused thereby.

In what follows, we provide a detailed examination of how featured twentieth- and twenty-first-century Irish novelists mobilized enigmatic signifiers to explore the mysteries of sexual initiation, seduction, and abuse. Not coincidentally, the figures we have been looking at are also exponents of the most sophisticated techniques for recording these feints and illuminations of consciousness: the use of unreliable and undecided narration, interior monologue, and, above all, subtle modes of free indirect discourse; all serve to position those traumatic enigmatic signifiers as textual kernels of immanent reflection.

To take matters a step further, unlike a journalistic account, which presumes an existential ground outside of its effect on the reader, literary fiction depends for its very being on the relationship between the depicted scenario and the transferential identification of the reader with its several elements (identification with identification). Tapping into this relationship, the texts studied here consistently syncopate the unfolding of the action so as to replicate for the reader an abstracted version of the experience of the enigmatic signifier as both affective or erotic trauma and hermeneutical lure. They thereby place the reader alongside the protagonist, as it were, nudging us to supply the "metatheory" that will confirm, correct, or elucidate the "fundamental theorization" in the text. Following this method, allegories or exemplary fictions of sexual exploitation utilize their structural condition of disavowal to immerse the reader on an individual, personal basis within a larger social and institutional pathology that itself unfolds on a person-by-person basis, at the very point where individual subjectivity is formed.

In the wake of the Irish Catholic theocracy's abrupt shift from the position of rescuer to that of persecutor in Ireland's national scandal framework, a key problem remained for supporters of alternate systems of public ethics and care. The long history of representations of children as imperiled innocents was what had made them such low-hanging fruit in the first place and such an easily misrepresented and easily spoken-for constituency on which to forge a power base, not to mention easy figures around which to weave elaborate fantasies. It is with such motivating and self-fulfilling fantasies—sexual, moral, and political, and on all sides of the issue—that our object texts and our readings concern themselves.

NOTES

1. See Valente and Backus (2009); Backus and Valente (2012, 48–68); Backus and Valente (2013, 55–73).

2. These fictional narratives reflect the efforts of several Irish authors over a period of decades to challenge the morally coercive powers of the media scandals, moral outrages, and government reports we term *the child sex scandal*. The child sex scandal co-implicates three categories—sex, children, and a threat or moral violation. These may include subliminally eroticized representations of physical and emotional cruelty or neglect of children, whether as justifiable punishment, protection, or horrifying abuse. They may also thematize the sexualized punishment of errant girls and women, especially through the forcible transfer of their infants or children to adoptive and foster families or orphanages. The child sex scandal can range from cases of infanticide to overt child sexual abuse. The literature we discussed here touches on all these variants and more; what they have in common is the capacity to confront the scandal consumers/observers with their own far-from-disinterested placement in the operations of the child scandal, and thus push individual readers and Irish society to think from outside

the moral episteme the child sex scandal serves to maintain when considering the needs and vulnerabilities of all Ireland's children.

3. As Jago Morrison and Susan Watkins note in the introduction to their *Scandalous Fictions: The Twentieth-Century Novel in the Public Sphere*, "one of the fascinating and provocative features of the novel in the course of its development has been its capacity to test the boundaries between the ostensibly separate spheres of public and private life" (2006, 3). The introduction and the volume's collected essays cover many of the diverse ways in which the novel, "an unruly or irresponsible form, . . . is also a mobile and plastic form" by closely attending to an array of stances the novel might allow a writer to take up with respect to "extremely determinate responsibilities before socio-political or ideological bodies" (12). In *Writing the Unspeakable*, we do not mean to imply that the pattern we trace is the only significant way that the novels we foreground might represent important sites—either disrupting or negotiating "cultural mores, social identity, and collective memory" (3). We would argue, rather, that over time the particular pattern we trace has had a recognizable impact on the Irish public sphere by influencing what is deemed scandalous and by determining how the outrage that child sex scandal continues to generate is collectively understood.

4. In other words, we are starting from the widely accepted presumption that (at least in Ireland's version of "the strange, lurid, and disgusting images [merging] media and popular reactions" (Herdt 2009, 1–2) characteristic of late-capitalist sex scandals) Gilbert Herdt's observation that moral panics, at their worst, completely occlude the humanity of their designated "folk devils" pertains equally to this scandal genre's innocent "folk victims" (2009, 1–2). As Herdt describes the effect of a full-blown moral panic on its designated folk devils, "in the worst cases, the rights of these persons are qualified or revoked, undermining citizenship and threatening democracy" (2). By "citizenship," Herdt explains, he means "the full rights, entitlements, and opportunity structures that support household security and wellbeing" (2). The modern moral panic we term, alternatively, the *child sex scandal* or *the scandal of imperiled innocence*, strips its designated victims of social standing and social legibility just as it does its folk devils—and, indeed, it sets up its folk victims for ready conversion into folk devils, and, sometimes, vice versa.

5. Child labor laws began in 1788 and came to maturity with the Factory Act of 1833. See Armstrong and Tennenhouse (1989, 229–78).

6. For further discussion of Victorian representations of the child, see Potter (2003), Makdisi (2014, 66), and especially Colley (1992, 226–27). Starting in the eighteenth century, the drama of the economically vulnerable and thus morally suspect woman's restoration to innocence is increasingly popularized or specularized by the Magdalene societies as a kind of living enactment of social melodrama.

7. "Up until the turn of the twentieth century, religious Magdalene laundries, no matter where they resided (France, Ireland, England, etc.) were, more often than not, labor abusive institutions organized under the rhetoric of spiritual reform, but run under the realities of material profit" (McCarthy 2010, 181).

8. For works that explore in detail the dynamics that can push adult actions taken on behalf of children in directions that in fact harm children, see Levine (2002), Lancaster (2011, 8–9), and Herdt (2009, 12–13). Even dedicated child rescuers are prone to unconsciously select from and frame available data in a manner that will most sensationally promote their own (or their constituency's) interests. "Noble cause corruption" is a useful term for describing the ways in which even well-balanced and well-intentioned adults can wind up colluding with baseless accusations of child victimization—even to the extent of distorting or fabricating testimony and to the detriment of the very children they seek to protect. See Grometstein (2010).

9. For melodrama and the nineteenth-century public sphere, see Soderlund (2013, 24–36), Walkowitz (1992, 85–102), Cvetkovich (1992, 97–127), and Hinton (1999, 7–12).

10. For examples of the abundant scholarship on W. T. Stead, the New Journalism, and the "Maiden Tribute" scandal, see Walkowitz (1992, 81–134), Mullin (2003, 56–82), and Soderlund (2013, 24–66). See also Steele's essay in Steele and de Nie (2014), Brake (2005), Backus (2013, 61–73), Eckley (2007), Ferriter (2009, 38–39), and Malone (1999).

11. This wonderfully telling phrase is taken from the title of Stephanie Rains's 2015 overview of the symbiotic relationship in turn-of-the-century Ireland among the Irish purity movement, the scandal-fixated British newspapers, and an Irish print industry pleased to piously promote its own wholesome output as a virtuous Irish alternative to British depravity.

12. See Attridge and Fogarty (2012) for a discussion of the ways in which Joyce responds to the scandal-reactive "household hints" columns in the *Irish Homestead*, which urge Irish women to take up their role in ridding Ireland of a residual and clearly British, media-imposed shame connected with dirt, animals in the home, untidiness, and so on. Fogarty and Attridge share Mullin's (2003) observation that "Eveline" rebuts the *Irish Homestead*'s treatment of British scandal representations as a reliable index of two different kinds of risk—one associated with leaving Ireland altogether (Mullin) and one associated with women "leaving home" in a more philosophical sense.

13. Throughout the nineteenth century and into the twentieth, Irish nationalist newspapers were content to interpret British journalists' accounts of endangered innocents in London and Manchester as evidence of Britain's moral depravity rather than its moral vigilance. See Rains (2015).

14. Seamus Deane (1995) found repeated references to shame in connection with the Irish language and culture among post-Famine rural dwellers' accounts of the Famine. Further, in *The Myth of Manliness*, Joseph Valente compellingly describes how the British quality of manliness, once enthroned as the sole and indispensable hallmark of male acceptability, slipped like quicksilver through the grasp of Irish men who sought to speak on Ireland's behalf (2011, 1–25).

15. During and following the 1846–51 Great Famine, Irish people whose lives had remained undisrupted by the storm of agony and death that raged across much of Ireland would have experienced survivor guilt unprecedented in degree and kind, owing to Ireland's rapidly developing media networks. Christopher Morash vividly conveys neighborly voyeurism through an 1847 newspaper passage describing the virtual hellscape an imagined reader on a train from Dublin to Cork might see, surrounded by "another world," in which "mothers [are] carrying about dead infants in their arms until they were putrid," perhaps in hopes that this horrible sight might "wring charity from the callous townspeople" (2010, 79).

16. For an overarching theory of literal cleanliness as expressive of moral purity, see Douglas (1966).

17. The Irish nationalist media reacted to British scandal journalism by gloatingly identifying England with the immoral excesses its newspapers exposed. It meanwhile posited Ireland as vice-ridden England's polar opposite, a society where innocents, principally virginal young women, were axiomatically safe—providing they stayed put (Mullin 2003, 73–75). As Ríona Nic Congáil (2009) has shown in her essay on the Fireside Club, the Irish nationalist media did begin to acknowledge some children during this period, but it did so by showcasing the well-being and achievements of Catholic Ireland's most prosperous children, who were depicted as representative of Ireland's children as a whole. See also Bobotis (2006).

18. The two mainstream Irish nationalist dailies were the *Freeman's Journal* and William Martin Murphy's *Irish Independent*.

19. Walsh's inflammatory denunciation used terms familiar from the vocabulary of the New Journalist sex scandal, including *innocence*, *exposure*, and *vulnerability*, as well as

perversion, to convert a plan to preserve children's lives into a sinister and vaguely sexualized abduction scenario. By framing Montefiore's plan as a scandal of imperiled innocence, Walsh and other influential Catholic leaders had found the means to speak out decisively in favor of the high rates of child mortality that the Lockout was on course to precipitate.

20. In a modifying clause that clarifies why he finds Jim Larkin to have been ill advised in supporting this plan, Yeates notes that its originator, Dora Montefiore, was "a member of a prominent liberal Jewish family" (2001, 34).

21. By recasting as innocents Irish children who had previously been treated as a kind of urban wildlife, the Irish Catholic Church used this episode to assert absolute moral sovereignty over Irish Catholic children. The church's account of what constituted child imperilment allowed employers to prevent internationalist networks from effectively supporting the striking workers, thus leveling a very serious blow against syndicalism across Europe. The church thus secured its dominant position and ensured the mutually reinforcing relationship of the Catholic Church and employers in the new Irish state.

22. As Fintan O'Toole argues, in "the years between 1922 and 1958 . . . the public rhetoric of the state was filled with this notion of an *ideal innocence*," and the presumption that "the Irish people, like innocent children liable to corruption from every side, were in need of protection" (2009).

23. This institution's social powers were exercised through a huge network of social service institutions comprising orphanages, hospitals, asylums, primary schools, and secondary schools, as well as the parish churches and convents that performed many state functions, such as feeding and caring for the local poor. See McDiarmid (2005, 127).

24. Jim Smith, in particular, has produced a detailed overview of the fledgling state's seizure of institutional control in the form of industrial and reformatory schools and Magdalene laundries, as well as a more general, society-wide intimidation of women and, as we would emphasize, of children. Smith sums up this Irish containment culture as concealing sexual crime while simultaneously sexualizing the women and children unfortunate enough to fall victim to society's moral proscriptions (2007, 4).

25. For decades, however, owing to the Irish state's notoriously hair-trigger system of censorship, the most effective such writers were not allowed a hearing in the Irish Symbolic Order. A historically consistent pattern emerges of the most pointed literary scandals either being censored outright or, as was the case with all of Joyce's writings, simply not being admitted.

26. As Jane Elizabeth Dougherty (2007) has pointed out, Irish girlhood has been effaced in modern Irish literature, far more so than Irish boyhood. As Dougherty noted in a private interview, from the 1920s through the 1990s the effacement of Irish girlhood was an effect caused in part by the double bind of a girl's position at the intersection of two allegorically overloaded subject positions, those of child and of woman.

27. See "A First-Person Account of Mother and Child Row," *Connacht Tribune*, November 21, 1986, 10.

28. For a discussion of Irish society's acceptance of these strictures, see also Maguire and Ó Cinnéide (2005).

29. See also the scene of a nun's wild release of rage into extreme and indiscriminate violence in response to Caithleen and Baba's note in the cloakroom in Edna O'Brien's *The Country Girls* (1960, 105–6).

30. Beginning with Freud's *Totem and Taboo* and continuing in the ethics of Jacques Lacan and Slavoj Žižek, one lesson of psychoanalysis has been the close psychic kinship between the father of the law and the father beyond the law, the *père du jouir*. See Freud (1950, 140–46).

31. As Inglis writes in *Moral Monopoly*, "The habitus, embodied in the home, school and church, produces specific Catholic ways of being religious and ethical. Through these

practices, people can attain religious capital by being a spiritually and ethically good person. . . . Being a good Catholic legitimates whatever economic, political, social and cultural capital already accumulated" (1998, 11).

32. As if to exemplify this dynamic, the Piarist order of seventeenth-century Rome made the preaching of sexual repression central to its teachings and stooped in short order to acts of child sexual abuse so conspicuous that after years of cover-up by the church hierarchy, the pope felt compelled to disband the order (Rigert 2008, 88–89).

33. See Valente and Backus (2009, 527–28).

THE CHILD SEX SCANDAL AND MODERN IRISH LITERATURE

1

"AN IRIDESCENCE DIFFICULT TO ACCOUNT FOR"

Sexual Initiation in Joyce's Fiction of Development

As Theodore Spencer observes in his introduction to the extant pages of Joyce's early, abandoned *Stephen Hero*, "much of the talk sounds as if it had been taken down immediately after it had been spoken" (1963, 9). This impression, that Joyce's early fiction represented photo-realist accounts (or Akashic records) of the Dublin circles in which he moved, is consistent with Joyce's known approach of accurately reproducing dialogue and sensory impressions in his "epiphanies," some of which he incorporated into the *Stephen Hero* manuscript. Certainly, the preponderance of the dialogue in *Stephen Hero* was either transcribed verbatim, like the epiphanies, or crafted in painstaking obedience to the social conventions of the world Joyce depicts—a social world punctuated by emotionally intense, semantically cryptic exchanges organized in relation to unspecified, enigmatic scandal referents.[1]

In many of these dialogues, it is possible to observe the relationship between the disconnect of the sentimental representation of children in public discourse from the actual treatment of children, and the circulation and socio-symbolic import of such cryptic scandal signifiers. The connections between child-love in theory and child-harm in practice, on one hand, and enigmatic scandal referents, on the other, is especially evident in two contiguous passages in *Stephen Hero* dealing with the harrowing death of Stephen's younger sister, Isabel. Isabel has returned from her convent school so steeped in Catholic doctrine that Stephen finds he must either patronize her, by speaking in the thoroughly reified, formulaic language of

Catholic piety, or threaten to corrupt her by speaking to her in any other way.[2] In Isabel's death scene, Joyce painfully juxtaposes children's idealized spiritual purity—the Catholic valorization of which prompts their mother to bid Isabel rejoice in her own imminent demise—with Stephen's reflections on all that Isabel's restrictive upbringing has stolen from even the short life she has had:

> Isabel seemed to Stephen to have grown very old: her face had become a woman's face. Her eyes turned constantly between the two figures nearest to her as if to say she had been wronged in being given life and, at Stephen's word, she gulped down whatever was offered her. When she could swallow no more her mother said to her, "You are going home, dear, now. You are going to heaven where we will all meet again. Don't you know? . . . Yes, dear . . . Heaven, with God" and the child fixed her great eyes on her mother's face while her bosom began to heave loudly beneath the bedclothes.
>
> Stephen felt very acutely the futility of his sister's life. He would have done many things for her and, though she was almost a stranger to him, he was sorry to see her lying dead. Life seemed to him a gift; the statement "I am alive" seemed to him to contain a satisfactory certainty and many other things, held up as indubitable, seemed to him uncertain. His sister had enjoyed little more than the fact of life, few or none of its privileges. The supposition of an allwise God calling a soul home whenever it seemed good to Him could not redeem in his eyes the futility of her life. The wasted body that lay before him had existed by sufferance; the spirit that dwelt therein had literally never dared to live and had not learned anything by an abstention which it had not willed for itself. (1963, 165)

In this agonizing passage, Stephen gazes into the prematurely aged face of his barely pubescent, dying sibling who has lived "by sufferance," debarred from the gratification of her every vital drive: to explore and experience, to question and learn, to communicate with others in a language that makes possible both intimacy and insight. Isabel has ultimately been denied the opportunity even to experience herself as alive. In the passage that follows, an exchange at Isabel's wake serves explicitly to indict the anti-sex, anti-body piety that Dublin's Archbishop Walsh already epitomized owing to his leadership role in Charles Stewart Parnell's destruction.[3] Stephen lays the responsibility for his dying sister's grim fate—the systematic eradication of every satisfaction from her short time on Earth—on Walsh's life-hating mode of Catholicism and the growing numbers of educated Irish nationalists who had, since the fall of Parnell, been embracing it in the name of social and career advancement.

Upon his arrival at Isabel's wake, Stephen and Isabel's uncle John is introduced in a single, breathless sentence as "a very shock-headed asthmatic man who had in his youth been rather indiscreet with his landlady's daughter and the family had been scarcely appeased by a tardy marriage" (166). Once Uncle John's three most distinctive characteristics are established, a friend of Simon Daedalus, "a clerk in the police courts," ventures what seems a practiced conversational gambit. He tells nearby mourners about a friend of his in Dublin Castle whose impressive and somewhat titillating charge it is to "examin[e] prohibited books." Getting wound up in response to his own icebreaker, possibly owing to the gravity of the occasion, the clerk bursts out, concerning materials that he himself cannot have seen, "such filth. . . .You'd wonder how any man would have the face to print it" (166). Uncle John, whose personal sex scandal, as the narrator's establishing shot makes clear, is both known to and studiously concealed by his community, follows the clerk's highly emotional bid—"such filth"—with his own enigmatic horror story about a youthful encounter with some kind of similarly reprehensible print material. He recalls that "when [he] was a boy," he had gone to "a bookshop near Patrick's Close . . . to buy a copy of *Colleen Bawn*" (166). On that occasion, he recalls, in a tone and with body language that clearly convey a sense of horror, "The man asked me in and he showed me a book" (166).

This utterly cryptic account of a scandalous outrage, in which a bookseller shows a book to a regular patron who had gone to the bookshop to buy a book, subsides in ellipses, and the clerk, alert to the inward shudder signaled by Uncle John's pregnant silence, relieves him of the insupportable burden of going on by murmuring, "I know, I know." Thus validated in the sense of horror this memory has inspired, Uncle John bursts out, "Such a book to put into the hands of a young lad! Such ideas to put in his head! Scandalous!" (166). Stephen's brother, Maurice, gives his uncle's declaration a moment to land before asking curiously, "Did you buy the book, Uncle John?" (perhaps mischievously treating the exchange as an actual, ordinary conversation). Uncle John's auditors seem ready to laugh, but Uncle John himself grows angrier still, barking, "They should be prosecuted for putting such books on sale. Children should be kept in their places" (166).

These strangely unmoored and oblique allusions to unspecified books can have triggered the two men's outrage only insofar as the books in question had also titillated their interest. In other words, the police clerk, by expressing his revulsion, makes clear that his friend has shared scandalous particulars with him—or, at minimum, that he has a fantasy about what those books might be like. For his part, Uncle John, a known fornicator, erupts with outrage and calls for a crackdown on publishing *and* on children in response to a question that threatens to reconnect his own suppressed and denied desires to the vague scandal signifiers that the two men have taken shared, self-congratulatory pleasure in condemning. In a final effusion of defensive sadism, Uncle John commits what might be described as the Freudian slip of all time, climatically calling to further restrict Ireland's children at a gathering that centers on the body of a child who is already "in [her] place" forever, lying among them, dead in a box.

The men's encoded interchange exemplifies a paranoid hyperawareness on the part of Irish nationalists of every stripe concerning the dangers of sex scandals that gained new purchase in Irish society in the wake of Parnell's scandalous fall and subsequent death. A psychic and social mandate to misrecognize was broadly constitutive of adult civic subjectivity in post-Parnellite nationalist circles. Saturated with guilt, shame, and bitter disappointment and menaced by both social and psychic dangers associated with sexual exposure, Irish nationalists found in the pervasive encoding function of the scandal signifier both the means and the mandate to express and thereby exploit painful shared realities—personal, social, and historical—in encrypted form. The scandal-saturated air that James Joyce grew up breathing—what Joyce termed "the odour of corruption" that he sought to capture in *Dubliners* (1965, 89–90)—stimulated him to develop various techniques to amplify and play on the devious deniability that characterized turn-of-the-century Dublin's scandal-coded vernacular. As is well known, Joyce's obsession with the artfully encoded sex scandal reached its fullest expression (or got entirely out of hand, depending on whom you ask) in *Finnegans Wake*. As Margot Norris puts it, this sprawling word puzzle, seventeen years in the making, "greatly augments the normal tendency of discourse to consciously or unconsciously conceal, then inadvertently reveal those matters that are most important to the speaker" (1998, 5–6).[4]

The practical necessity of this pervasive scandal management is dramatized in the Christmas dinner-table scene in *A Portrait of the Artist as a Young Man* (Joyce 1992b), when Dante, an aging female and poor relation, single-handedly demolishes paterfamilias Simon Dedalus and his friend, Mr. Casey, whose aura of heroic nationalism is enhanced by his time in a

British prison. Oblivious to the newly emerging capacity of the scandal signifier to redefine and enforce collective moral priorities, Dedalus and Casey ill-advisedly enter into a verbal fight they cannot win. Still reeling from Parnell's death, they denounce the Irish Catholic hierarchy for its part in his fall, which, as they believe, has destroyed the prospects for Irish independence. Importantly, their dinner-table jousting first careens out of control around the point when Dedalus specifically heaps scorn on Dublin archbishop William Walsh, or "Billy with the lip" (35). Dante, through her undeviating, fulminating emphasis on Parnell's sex scandal, hammers away at her opponents as traitors to the nation—renegade Catholics, black Protestants, and blasphemers—because their focus on Ireland's lost opportunity for independence evinces their sinful, failure to fixate on sex.

As they struggle to set aside the question of Parnell's legally and clerically unsanctioned union with Katharine O'Shea in favor of what they understandably view as the weightier question of Irish independence, Dante repeatedly casts Casey and Dedalus as unforgivably indifferent to the enormity of Parnell's sin and thus as secret enemies of the Catholic Church and Ireland itself. In his attempts to respond to Dante's badgering accusations, Casey is at last provoked into open blasphemy, renouncing the Catholic Church altogether. This speech act precipitates both men's collapse into inchoate shame, visibly and tangibly ousted from a national community over which Catholicism, in any and all matters touching on sex (which, through the enigmatic signifier, all matters can be made to do), now reigns supreme.

In this microcosmic reenactment of the Parnell scandal's reconfiguration of the Irish national imaginary, Joyce reveals how censorious references to the Chief's private life could readily be wielded, with destructive force, against anyone foolish enough to defend or downplay his adultery. Thus in modern Ireland did the enigmatic signifier give rise to an acute sense of threatened exposure that had to be constantly indemnified by means of impinging silences, evasions, and opacities, and in irrational or self-contradictory assertions.

JAMES JOYCE, SEXUAL INITIATION, AND THE ENIGMATIC SIGNIFIER

James Joyce and Nora Barnacle's first, illicit sexual experience is famously commemorated in the date on which *Ulysses* is set. That romantic gesture has combined with Molly Bloom's rapturous last words recalling *her* first sexual encounter—"yes I said yes I will Yes" (Joyce 1986, 18.1608–9)—to give rise to the "Joyce of sex" phenomenon, the popular, and sometimes scholarly, assumption that Joyce affirms the potential of human sexuality to be fully liberatory and gratifying (Beja and Jones 1982, 255–66). Concomitantly, the early puritanical efforts of Anthony Comstock and the Decency societies to have *Ulysses* banned in the United States as obscene pornography have served to discourage the examination of the darker, more skeptical side of Joyce's erotic vision. Yet the sexual panegyrics in *Ulysses*, which align the novel with contemporary sexological discourses espoused by Havelock Ellis or Charles Albert,[5] are in fact counterbalanced by constitutively traumatic specimens of sexual initiation, most notably Stephen Dedalus's account of the seduction of William Shakespeare by Anne Hathaway, which corresponds to Stephen's own first sexual encounter with an older prostitute in *A Portrait of the Artist*. If we expand our idea of sexual initiation from the classic first-intercourse variety to the many forms of introductory sexual knowing that pervade Joyce's narratives, beginning with the earliest stages of infantile awareness, we discover that the alternative scenarios we have cited and the conflicting values they attach to sexual experience (shameful/validating, transgressive/compliant, exalting/scarring) are the outcroppings of a deep-structural aporia in the Symbolic Order itself: the mutual determination and disturbance of sexual affect and the signifying function. A kind of literary phenomenology of this aporia, Joyce's writing registers the radical psychic ambivalence that it produces, an ambivalence imbricating the meaning of sexuality and the sexualization of language.

In pursuing this project, Joyce never forgot (or perhaps his deeply Catholic, quasi-Jansenist culture did not let him forget) the cauterizing as well as the exalting aspect of sexual enjoyment, and this unremitting double vision has given him an honored place in the annals of post-Freudian psychoanalysis— psychoanalysis *après la lettre*, if you will—which is likewise magnetized by the inherent ambivalence of the erotic.[6] Joyce's work has not, however, been brought to bear on certain of the long-standing debates in psychoanalysis concerning sexual identity formation, particularly its underexplicated relationship to collective identity formation. To begin this discussion, we propose to examine the status of sexual initiation in Joyce's narratives of development— specifically, "The Sisters" and *A Portrait of the Artist*—focusing on aesthetic and representational strategies that achieve their effects by tapping a residue of sexualized trauma embedded at the level of the word.

Understanding the ways in which Joyce employs ambiguously sexual formulations that position both his characters and readers as imperfectly initiated allows for a fuller appreciation of the workings of his literary style. It also affords greater insight into how the social world leaves its most salient imprint on the individual subject through contingent personal experience and how, conversely, such highly individuated experience lends intense affect to larger social movements and ideologies. In Joyce's case, the most consistently impinging of such ideologies is Irish Catholic nationalism. This simultaneously ethnic and sectarian ideology stands as his test case for the shaping power that collective priorities and concerns exert on a child's ambiguously sexual stirrings, causing them to set and calcify within an always emergent Symbolic Order. Read in this light, Joyce's work continues to elucidate and expand the vocabulary of psychoanalytic theory.

JOYCEANCE

Late in his career, Jacques Lacan devoted his annual seminar to Joyce, for the purpose of introducing a last course correction in his long "return to Freud" (Lacan 1997a).[7] According to Lacan's model of subject formation at that point, the infant, on entering into language, forfeits or finds refuge from a traumatically intense mode of enjoyment—or jouissance—seated in the bodily connection to the mother. The child does so in acceding to the Symbolic Order, the register of cultural discourse, which is anchored by the *nom du père* (name/no of the father; Lacan 1997b). The reconciliation of the oedipal/castration complex, in other words, involves repression in its primary form. The paternal name or phallic signifier that forbids direct access to the maternal body likewise mediates and in a sense mummifies the child's experience of his or her own body, insulating somatic tissue within the tissue of representation. The effect is to replace an overwhelming sexual pulsion, steeped in the Real, with an ineradicable lack or desire, enchained to the figural displacements of language, a process Lacan described as "the sliding of the signified under the signifier" (Lacan 1999, 153). On this account, sexual initiation coincides with the genesis of subjectivity and unfolds according to the same logic. The substance of being, jouissance, is alienated in the domain of meaning, the signifying grid, which functions as a sort of generative prophylactic giving rise to a life form by stanching its primordial vitality.

In Joyce's work, however, Lacan discerned a reversal of this logic. From the "supple periodic prose" of *A Portrait of the Artist* to the portmanteau words of *Finnegans Wake*, Joyce's method of writing works to access and exude jouissance instead of inhibiting it. His progressive exploitation of the paronomastic and acoustic properties of language and the flamboyant unde-cidability of meaning effected thereby struck Lacan as a materialization of enjoyment at the level of the signifier itself (Lacan 1998). Joyce's exuberant wordplay even inspired Lacan to articulate his revisionary insights on this question in similarly homophonic terms. The traumatic enjoyment of jouis-sance finds its literary correlative in *joyceance*, which reveals that "punning . . . constitutes the law of the signifier" (Lacan 1990, 10). This discovery allows in turn for the possibility of *jouis-sens*, enjoy-meant, for which the signifier serves as vehicle rather than brake, vessel rather than limit. In the same motion, the symptom, the signifier of a pathic relation to the forbidden jouissance, becomes a *sinthome*, a primordial synthesis of being and mean-ing, the formation wherein jouissance lodges in the signifier.[8]

Lacan's seminar "Joyce le sinthome" not only altered the direction of *l'école Freudienne* but also fostered a Lacanian approach within Joyce stud-ies. What is surprising, however, is that the revisions introduced into Laca-nian analysis under the name of Joyce were not extended to the dynamics of sexual initiation, which they clearly implicate. For their part, Lacanian Joyce scholars have yet to systematically explore how the accommodation of jouissance in Joyce's writing might signal a different, less strictly repres-sive function of language in the emergence of sexuality; how, accordingly, Joyce's experiment with the signifier correlates with an alternative version of sexual genesis; and, finally, whether such a genesis makes itself evident in the initiation scenarios that figure so importantly in every one of Joyce's texts. It is this cluster of questions that we address here. But to confront them is to come face-to-face with the oldest, most stubborn dispute in psy-choanalysis, one centered precisely on the problem of sexual initiation. Did Freud do the right thing, on therapeutic or heuristic grounds, in jettisoning his theory of primal seduction in favor of a theory of primal fantasy?

THE FIRST CUT IS THE DEEPEST

At the dawn of psychoanalysis, Freud held the syndrome of conversion hys-teria, with its traumatically symptomatic modes of enjoyment, to derive from childhood molestation, typically committed by a parental figure. Increasingly doubtful as to whether incestuous abuse could be so rampant as his patients indicated, he concluded that their reported sexual encounters must be the unconscious, complexly mediated effects of repressed infantile fantasies.[9] Correlatively, the origin of libidinal affect shifted in Freud's account from the incitement of external contact that became sexualized on reaching a traumatic level of intensity to the endogenous operation of the "drives," which impart a traumatic sexual charge to contingently selected perceptual cues. On this view, the unconscious of the child organizes further libidinal development by converting innocuous stimuli, such as those associated with parental nurture, into dangerous excitations that demand to be misrecognized, the raw material of the repressive-cum-substitutive operation of oedipal desire.

Lacan's earlier model of subject and sexual formation presupposes the revisionist theory of primal fantasy. Traumatic jouissance is construed as endemic to the preoedipal stage, where phantasmatic, "primary process" thought predominates, and as impinging on the fully realized subject of language only in the distorted form of the symptom. With the Joycean *sinthome*, by contrast, Lacan locates jouissance in the body of the signifier, a move that implicitly binds the possibility of enjoyment to the social-symbolic order in which oedipal subjectivity is consolidated. We are left to infer that, far from issuing from the infantile fantasy of somatic continuity with the mother, jouissance (as *jouis-sens*) arises in connection with some external, socially intrusive force or presence, which would help explain its traumatic character. As we shall see, Joyce's signature sexual initiation scenarios make just this case in narrative terms. Taken whole, then, as both poesis and diegesis, *joyceance* not only prompts an epistemological break within Lacanian theory but points to the need for a like break *from* that theory, specifically the need for a still more radical return to Freud, one that salvages by strenuously complicating his original theory of primal seduction.

In this regard, Joyce's materialization of enjoyment in the written word may be seized upon less as an anticipation of the Lacanian phallic signifier, the signifier of lack, than as an anticipation of the so-called enigmatic signifier, the signifier of traumatic sexuality, conceived by Lacan's foremost rival in the lists of French psychoanalysis, Jean Laplanche. In the process of affirming the oedipal and castration complexes as the twin engine of sexual development as well as gender/subject formation, Laplanche has critiqued

Freud and his legatees, Lacan included, for eliding or minimizing the impact of the parental unconscious on the vicissitudes of infantile eroticism—a factor that Joyce, from the "mad" Father Flynn at the start of *Dubliners* to the "mad feary father" at the end of *Finnegans Wake* (1968, 628), remembers with an almost obsessive persistence.

Laplanche takes this psychoanalytic blind spot to be the result of Freud's decision not just to replace primal seduction with primal fantasy but to oppose them in the first place (Laplanche 1997, 653–66). By separating fantasy from seduction as the prior psychic determinant, Freud tends to cordon off the unconscious as a sort of private reserve that is delimited by the social symbolic in a mainly negative (repressive) manner. Laplanche seeks to conceptualize the properly interdependent psychogenetic agency of internal and external stimuli, endogenous theories and social experience, by returning to the original hypothesis of seduction but on a basis that is more ecumenical for being more precise. His general theory of seduction introduces a distinction between the give and take of seduction and the brute imposition of sexual assault, and for this reason it need not exclude childhood fantasy from its calculations. At the inaugural stage of sexuality, Laplanche finds the seductive transaction to be no less dialogic for being traumatic.

Because parental figures harbor repressed libidinal stirrings, the care they give their children unconsciously transmits ambiguously charged signifiers that Laplanche calls "enigmatic" (1997, 661). An enigmatic signifier is coded material that enables without demanding, solicits without enforcing sexual constructions and responses at the unconscious level. For Laplanche, such enigmatic signifiers come freighted with a traumatic enjoyment that forms the substance of the child's developing subjectivity. That substance in turn inheres not in the meaning but in the materiality of the signifier, which possesses the primary power to engender and elicit psychic affect in general and jouissance in particular. The sensory properties of the signifier (the acoustics of the word, the timbre of the voice, the sheen of the image) and the already felt anticipation of meaning constitute what we, paraphrasing Frantz Fanon (1968), call an "occult zone of undecidability," wherein the virtualities of hidden parental desire are confounded with the libidinal possibilities that they awaken in the child. Because the signifier is inherently iterable, the jouissance with which it is vested in moments of sexual initiation remains available to be reactivated under special circumstances, as Lacan found in the work of Joyce. The profound impact of primary libidinal excitation is thus a contingently renewable resource that fuels sexuality in its various manifestations, including subsequent instances of sexual initiation—prepubescent, pubescent, and so on. On the one hand, because the sensory erotic penumbra of the signifier is constituted in anticipation of the meaning to be conveyed, the jouissance it comes to bear upon reactivation can never arise in the absence of specific, highly determinate objects or contents, even though it emerges only in exceeding those objects and contents. On the other hand, the same logic holds in reverse: it is the articulation of jouissance in the enigmatic penumbra of the signifier that eroticizes the objects or contents themselves. The concept of the enigmatic signifier thus permits us to understand:

A. the dynamics of Freudian *nachträglichkeit*, or "afterwardness" (Laplanche 2016, xi): how an infantile episode of sexualized trauma and enjoyment may be not only recalled in but constituted by a cognate later episode, wherein the meaningful potential anticipated in the initial enigmatic signifier becomes accessible to re-cognition; and
B. the dynamics of Freudian desire—how a wide array of objects, scenarios, and experiential categories come to be libidinally saturated and how their cultural importance might be constitutively tied to their eroticization. But more than that, in locating primary jouissance in terms of an already symbolizable, rather than a preoedipal, fantasy formation, the concept of the enigmatic signifier elucidates how various sorts of distinctively social attitudes and valuations, including those relative to ideologically charged predicates such as race, class, disability, and ethnicity, come to be integral to the sexual organization of the subject espousing them.

Such a dynamic, in which sexual initiation and ideological inculcation dovetail inextricably, has obvious importance for questions of nationalism across the board, but perhaps especially so in the case of a metropolitan holding like Ireland. There, entrenched identificatory ambivalence (between imperial and colonial, Anglo and Gaelic culture) gave birth to a wide array of ethno-national signifiers and *figura* that were enigmatic in their own right, not least in their gender/sexual valences—the undecidable markers of what Fanon did in fact call an "occult zone of instability" (1968, 215).

Becoming James Joyce: The Acoustics of Sex

The modern fictive portraiture of the child sex scandal in Ireland can be traced back to Joyce and has been so traced by many of his successors in the genre—Kate O'Brien, Edna O'Brien, Patrick McCabe, Keith Ridgway, Jamie O'Neill, Anne Enright, and others—for whom he has figured not as a daunting, inescapable shadow but as a welcome, empowering interlocutor on a difficult topic. The traumatic intrusion of adult sexuality into children's lives and psyches runs throughout Joyce's corpus: in "An Encounter," "The Boarding House," "Eveline," the pandying scene in *A Portrait of the Artist*, Milly's exile to Mullingar in *Ulysses*, and recurrently in *Finnegans Wake*. But the exemplary narrative for our purposes is Joyce's first effort along these lines, which is also his first published fiction: "The Sisters."

In a sense, the writer we know as James Joyce came into being with his discovery and deployment of the enigmatic signifier, the semiotic vehicle of a jouissance attendant on the scene of sexual initiation. Or to put it another way, Joyce's treatment of the mysteries of sexual initiation in the short story "The Sisters," which originally appeared in the *Irish Homestead*, constituted his own rite of passage into many of the signifying practices for which he is best known. For the story's inclusion in *Dubliners*, Joyce altered the first paragraph so as to frame both the story and the volume as a whole. Most strikingly, of course, he added the three famous leitmotifs—paralysis, simony, and gnomon—which are correctly read as interpretive keys to the collection. There is prima facie evidence, however, that Joyce intended these leitmotifs to be read for something other than their meaning: "Every night as I gazed up at the window I said softly to myself the word *paralysis*. It had always sounded strangely in my ears, like the word *gnomon* in the Euclid and the word *simony* in the Catechism. But now it sounded to me like the name of some maleficent and sinful being. It filled me with fear, and yet I longed to be nearer to it and to look upon its deadly work" (1992a, 1). It is the acoustic properties of the word *paralysis*, how it "sounded . . . in [his] ears," that affect the boy primarily, that ground its relation to the other key words, and that give it a certain precedence over them ("but now it sounded to me . . ."). The effect it has "in" his ears gives the word *paralysis* its strange power to fill the boy with fear and fascination, an ambivalent state akin if not equivalent to traumatic enjoyment. As the material lining of the signifier, its acoustics not only house its capacity to transmit jouissance, they do so because they form a tissue of undecidability, registering in their fusion of possible sense and pure sensation how the life of the signifier at once affixes to and exceeds its meaning or content. In this case, significantly, the shadowy zone consolidated in the word's sound stretches between opposed constructions of the term *paralysis*: ordinary paralysis caused by the three strokes Flynn suffered and general paralysis of the insane, or tertiary-stage syphilis, which might have caused those strokes. In the first take, paralysis would represent a properly "maleficent being," a medical scourge, while in the second it would signal the priest's own "sinful being," implicating him in sexual misconduct. Accordingly, the kind of initiation that Flynn has given his young protégé remains properly enigmatic, soliciting without enforcing a libidinal diagnosis—both from the reader (who may or may not credit Oscar Wilde's homoerotic "The Priest and the Acolyte" as a prototype of "The Sisters")[10] and from the boy himself, who suffers the priest's death in ambiguously sexual terms throughout the story. Joyce hereby intimates that the problem of sexual abuse can be found already lurking in the dynamics of sexual initiation as such.

The enigmatically sexual nature of the priest's relationship to the boy represents a point of discernible complicity or at least connivance on the part of his friends and family. An uneasy awareness of something awry emerges in their dinner conversation but remains frozen at the level of knowing non-assertion, marked by a series of ellipses: "No, I wouldn't say he was exactly . . . but there was something queer . . . there was something uncanny about him. I'll tell you my opinion" (Joyce 1992a, 1). As these snippets indicate, the ellipsis serves as the punctual symbol of that staple of cultural scandal, the open secret, a shadowy form of group consensus designed to exist under erasure. Nowhere is Joyce's work—an oeuvre preoccupied with such things—more prescient as to the dynamics of child sex scandal in twentieth-century Ireland, where revelations have often triggered retrospective acknowledgements of suspicions unpursued and apprehensions willfully uncorroborated.

This complicity of the boy's family in the potential scandal is not unrelated to the central role played by the priest, who commands in his office all of the respect he fails to command in his person. Indeed, Father Flynn's personal failure to meet the demands of his office serves as a metonym for the scandalous cloud that has gathered about his memory. His own sister and the boy's aunt actually believe that this failure *is* the scandal: "The duties of the priesthood was too much for him" (9). But the narrative structure of the tale and the bullying nature of Flynn's sexualized mentorship of the boy combine to suggest that he seeks to control and humble his charge in compensation for his "crossed" life and career. In this light, the lenient speculations of the women, like the accusatory but abortive pronouncements of "old Cotter," appear as a most effective strategy of Freudian disavowal, half steps toward the truth that prevent or protect them from ever actually arriving. Joyce's decision to render the sexual tenor of the boy's discipleship fuzzy and obscure from the start enjoins upon the reader a like sense of complicity. In this way, Joyce refuses to portray the scandal of child sexual abuse as purely external to any imagined community his work might reach.

UNSEEING THE UNBEARABLE

The enigmatic force of the boy's initiation in "The Sisters" begins with the impact of the signifier *paralysis* in the boy's ears, in order to affirm the originary status of such an occult signifier to the always indefinite process of seduction. Is the uncanny stimulation that the word gives to the boy's tympanum merely a symbolic residue of the often arcane and exotic knowledge the priest had poured into his ear during their daily sessions? Or does this stimulation figure forth the medieval notion of spoken communication as a variant on sexual penetration, with the ear serving as a displacement of the anus or vagina (a notion Joyce mobilized in the "Sirens" episode of *Ulysses* and again in the Persse O'Reilly section of *Finnegans Wake*)? To say that this electric signifier reverberates with both options but need not speak to either is precisely the point. The seductive force concentrated in the signifier and exfoliated in the narrative, their potential reservoir of jouissance, gathers experientially in the zone of uncertainty between the sexual and the nonsexual, around the enigma, if you like, about whether something—a word, a gesture, a relationship, a program of instruction—is properly sexual or not. That is to say, Joyce narrativizes what Laplanche would later theorize, an initiation/seduction that is all the more traumatically enjoyable and sexually charged for being indefinitely so. Since "The Sisters" is in turn the reader's initiation to the eroticized textuality of *Dubliners*, it is cunningly apt that Joyce restages undecidable traumatic enjoyment at the level of the narrative action, the claustrophobic sexual *power* of which arises entirely from the boundless uncertainty as to its sexual *tenor*.

The enigmatic penumbra of paralysis radiates to other key signifiers in the story as well. On the one hand, its enigmatic quality is shared by the leitmotif simony, with its homophonic play on the word *sodomy*, which for its part names a practice strictly germane and yet largely inaccessible to the narration of the story. That the sound of a taboo sexual signifier should thus lurk (hide/linger) in the acoustic precincts of other signifiers serves to mirror, at the level of poesis, the relationship of sexuality to signification more generally. On the other hand, the sense of the word *paralysis* materializes in the oral incontinence of the priest, which images forth a sensual excess or avidity consistent with the more perverse, if deliberately indefinite, assessments of his character and agenda ("I wouldn't like children of mine," says Cotter, "to have too much to say to a man like that"; 2).

These two enigmatic signifiers (paralysis and simony) come together, appropriately, in the boy's memory of his previous night's dream, a theater of unconscious desire and its conflicted representation: "I felt my soul receding into some pleasant and vicious region; and there again I found it waiting for me. It began to confess to me in a murmuring voice and I wondered why it smiled continually and why the lips were so moist with spittle. But then I remembered that it had died of paralysis and I felt that I too was smiling feebly as if to absolve the simoniac of his sin" (3). Attuned as they are to power dynamics, our preferred methods of reading would doubtless identify the boy's dream wish with the reversal of positions, wherein he assumes the divine authority of absolution and the priest assumes the boy's more accustomed role as penitent.[11] But to qualify the surplus enjoyment adhering to the boy's wish, it is first necessary to recognize how far his dream scenario replicates the structure of his daily interviews with Father Flynn. After all, in the confessional, the priest's latticed ear is carefully poised to "sound" with secret knowledge and with the effusions of the illicit, much as the boy's ears were in Flynn's "little dark room behind the shop" (4). And just as these conversations afforded the boy traumatic enjoyment so too does the prospect of hearing the priest's sins, as the phrase "some pleasant and vicious region" betokens. Where the dream differs from the everyday experience—and here we can detect the distinctive pressure of the dream wish—is in the promise the confessional scenario affords for a simultaneous consummation and dissolution of that traumatic enjoyment.

In confession, the secret knowledge the priest receives is a secret knowledge about the illicit, particularly, in this case, whether and to what degree the penitent has in the past introduced his young confessor to the traumatizing element of adult sexuality. That this promise of the dream goes unfulfilled, and that the boy's jouissance accordingly persists, can be inferred from several pieces of textual evidence: the use, at the point of absolution, of the term *simoniac*, which sustains the air of euphemistic eccentricity around the priest's "troubles" (with simony serving as a substitute or malaprop for sodomy in this homoerotic context); the mirroring of the priest's slobbering smile in the feeble smile of the boy, which suggests that the enigmatic message of the former has been received and internalized by the latter; and the boy's insistence on returning to the dream, still fascinated and still unsatisfied, only to find a strange room furnished with the resolutely ambiguous motifs of orientalized sensuality (6).

After this confession scene, the boy's occult, oppressive enjoyment progressively focuses on the sacramental and liturgical objects (vestments, chalice, confession box) and actions (prayer, last rites, communion) of the Roman Catholic Church. Like the transfer of sexualized acoustic energy from the word *paralysis* to the other strange leitmotifs, the narrative concatenation of fetish objects delineates how the jouissance concentrated in the enigmatic signifier in sexual initiation can, through mechanisms of symbolic association, disseminate its libidinal aftershocks across socially delimited fields of reference, identification, and praxis.

The founding conditions of this sort of transference are also the enabling conditions of that mysterious counteraction known as sublimation. Just as the exorbitancy of jouissance to whatever signifiers incite or animate it enables that libidinal affect to be readily displaced along a chain of associated symbolic forms and behaviors, so the same continuing exorbitancy lends those forms and behaviors an apparent yet effective margin of autonomy from whatever sexual energies infuse, enliven, and enhance them. The constitutive semidetachment of jouissance from its signifying source—to which it is wedged, not wedded—entails a like semidetachment of its signifying destinations from jouissance. If the riddle of sublimation, dating back to Freud, has been "how can the drive be desexualized yet satisfied without the pathological aid of repression," Laplanche's enigmatic signifier would seem to prise open a possible solution.[12] Precisely because it is as peripheral as it is profound, the relation of libidinal affect to signifying cause does not always and inexorably tend toward recognizably erotic manifestation, the absence of which, accordingly, does not always and inevitably signal some degree of constraint.

To be sure, a given symbolic practice must express in some form the associated jouissance that fuels it, but owing to its "external" character, the association itself, which is the emergence of sexual feeling, may go unremarked yet unrepressed, operating unobtrusively or in other terms without being inhibited or concealed. What we have called, then, the enigmatic signifier's "zone of undecidability" serves, and can only serve, as a space of transferential proliferation provided that it can alternatively function as a space of deferral and sublimation. As Slavoj Žižek argues, anything at all can be sexualized (Žižek 1994, 126), but, we must add, only on the condition that nothing at all can be categorically, exhaustively, or exclusively sexual. Institutionalized religious experience, particularly a variety as steeped in rite and symbol as Catholicism, clearly draws on both of these alternatives in their interdependency. In "The Sisters," for example, the boy's sexualization of the sacerdotal is part of his informal preparation for a celibate vocation. That Catholicism also represents the national religion of Irish Ireland extends the range of reflected jouissance and the corresponding opportunity for sublimation to include the dimension of ethno-national belonging, and in this respect points the way to the *bildung* of Stephen Dedalus in *A Portrait of the Artist.*

"Forbidding Such an Outlet"

The first two chapters of *A Portrait of the Artist,* leading up to Stephen's first sexual experience, are punctuated with visions of adult romantic or erotic bonding that are explicitly contoured relative to national norms. Introduced by Stephen's father, the moocow fable is at one level an adaptation of a nationalist myth, in which a white cow, allegorical of Ireland, abducts the child from home in order to school him in the arts of heroism (Gifford 1982, 131–33). At another level, the moocow is available to be read as a figure of the mother qua vehicle of nurture and pleasure. In the former case, Stephen is being interpellated to sublimate his domestic affections as a patriotic exponent of masculine virtue; in the latter, he is being inscribed within the likewise gendered plot of the oedipal romance, his desire catalyzed and canalized along approved heterosexual lines through the perilous pass of incestuous passion and taboo. Read in tandem, the national and oedipal romances validate mutually acceptable pathways of desire (the eroticism undergirding the patriotic love of "Mother" Ireland; the properly Irish Catholic embrace of reproductive heterosexuality) that remain parasitic on and haunted by the kind of proximate familial affections they help drive underground.

Stephen's first awareness of people beyond his own family aptly involves people beyond his national-sectarian family as well, the Anglo-Protestant Vances. His ill-fated pronouncement that he will grow up to marry their daughter, Eileen, sets off the moocow fable in reverse: his mother-figures administer a frenzied chastisement for his "betrayal" of the ethno-religious tribe, driving him under the table and threatening to *"Pull out his eyes"* (Joyce 1992b, 4). Not unlike the paternal entertainment, however, the maternal punishment harbors a contrary sexual affect. While the threat to Stephen's eyes plainly invokes oedipal castration, it also connects to Stephen's later recollection of Eileen having put "her hands over his eyes: long and white and thin and cold and soft" (36). In these juxtaposed images of trauma and pleasure, we can sense the open-endedness of the sexual signifier for Stephen, its enigmatic quality.

Stephen recalls Eileen again amid the Christmas dinner set-to over Parnell, where the question of a sexual alliance between individuals once again fuels a violent debate over nationalist sexual norms and, hence, allegiances. Set against the furor, Stephen's thoughts not only light on Eileen's hands, "long and white and thin and cold and soft," but merge them into a hitherto puzzling metaphor of the Blessed Virgin, *"Tower of Ivory"* (35). We are thus given to understand that libidinal desire for actual bodies, which can ignite national traumas, operates through signifiers whose lability allows for their sublimation into images of nationalist piety.

Shortly after his family relocates from suburban Blackrock to Dublin, Stephen reflects for the first time that "his father was in trouble" (66). The "slight change in his house," which he had once deemed "unchangeable," deliver many "slight shocks to his boyish conception of the world," and with them comes an "ambition which he felt astir at times in the darkness of his soul" (67). Important for the image pattern that we will follow is the close relationship between Stephen's "conception" of the world and the first "stirrings" in Stephen's soul, words that connote fertilization and the quickening of a forming embryo, in a pattern that, as Richard Ellmann (1982, 295–99) and others have pointed out, structures the overall narrative. Significantly, however, the beginnings of the gestation model here mark, without making entirely explicit, the prepubescent awakening of sexual appetite. The "stirring in a dark place" that tropes the earliest movements of a fetus and, metaphorically, Stephen's emerging artistic consciousness, also suggests the inadvertent but pleasurable stiffening of a penis under bedclothes.

As young Stephen begins a pattern of cruising—an apparent displacement of his sexual energies that ironically leads in time to actual sexual gratification—he fantasizes about a sexual encounter that will divest him of his body and purify him. He believes he will meet with an image that is insubstantial both because it is holy and because it is explicitly sexual and therefore, in a highly repressive society, indescribable. In language echoing the uterine "darkness of his soul" (67), Stephen envisions a sexual/spiritual coupling in some "secret place," where he and his partner "would be alone, surrounded by darkness and silence" (67). Rather than imagining this encounter in terms of physical or even emotional satisfaction, Stephen envisions it as a moment of self-transcendence. He "would be transfigured . . . would fade into something impalpable under her eyes" and through this sexual annihilation escape from both the limitations of his body and his emotions: "Weakness and timidity and inexperience would fall from him in that magic moment" (67).

The relationship between Stephen's worshipful and phallic attitudes toward the feminine has typically been taken as a version of the Madonna/whore dichotomy, which it undoubtedly resembles in certain respects.[13] But to overlook how far the absolute bipolarity that defines this complex has been undermined from the outset is to miss the subtlety of the psychodynamics Joyce uncovers. Stephen's fantasized Madonna figures are not set in opposition to lascivious whores; rather, sexual activity itself is fantasized as simultaneously an act of bodily conception and an exercise in spiritual transcendence. Thus, when "a strange unrest [creeps] into [Stephen's] blood," heralding the onset of uncontrollable sexual urges, he "rove[s] alone" in search not of the flesh that would satisfy them but of "the unsubstantial image which his soul so constantly beheld" (67).

As Stephen matures, he plumbs a similarly absolute yet traversable breach between "the real world" and "the unsubstantial image" that he wishes to meet in that world, enabling reveries that are simultaneously corporeal and incorporeal, carnal and pure. In his "Monte Cristo" fantasies, for example, his dignified renunciation of desire for the literary love object, Mercedes—encoded in the citation "Madam, I never eat muscatel grapes" (65)—holds her firmly within the universe of his bodily passion precisely by placing her beyond its limits. This type of sublimating discordia concors has its ultimate condition of possibility in the margin of undecidability, hence reversibility, intrinsic to the enigmatic signifier of intrusively adult sexuality. But Stephen borrows his specific strategy for conflating the sanctioned and the unsanctioned from a discourse of martyrology common to the Irish Catholic Church and advanced Irish nationalism. Both institutions infused their respective saints, secular and religious, with a potent eroticism insulated by their ambiguously rarefied status—that is, their voluntary, excess embodiment (as corpse) in the service of a spiritual ideal. This is also to say, both draw on their members' psychosexual development—their riveting encounter with underdetermined and therefore ambivalent sexual signifiers—to manipulate their enjoyment, mobilize their efforts, and ensure their fidelity.

In what amounts to Stephen's first adolescent "date," he turns his sense of alienation at the "Harold's Cross" party into a manner of attracting the interest of one of the girls in attendance. Taking the last tram home with her, Stephen experiences the sexually charged moment as a series of tantalizingly ambiguous signifiers—"her movements" up and down, in rhythm to the conversation; her eyes speaking from beneath a cowl; "her fine dress and sash and long black stockings" (72)—which entice but do not finally actuate him to fulfill their mutual desire for a kiss. Amid this near tryst, Stephen gives a passing but by no means insignificant thought to Eileen Vance (72–73). Her image puts in play a memory (unconscious in his case, conscious in ours) of his earliest infantile response to such riddling signifiers of sexuality, the direct expression of a romantic wish, and the painful humiliation it brought him from the most important women in his young life. Little wonder, then, that Stephen forgoes any direct expression of forbidden carnal longing in this case, but rather goes home to transform the fraught scene of seduction into the culturally mediated and approved form of a poem (followed by a long gaze at his own countenance in his mother's bedroom mirror). What is more, encouraged by the post-Romantic association of verse with the fashioning of ethereal ideals, Stephen contrives to represent the kiss bestowed as bearing the same aura of immateriality as the kiss eschewed: "There remained no trace of the tram itself nor of the trammen nor of the horses: nor did he and she appear vividly. The verses told only of the night and the balmy breeze and the maiden luster of the moon . . . and . . . the kiss, which had been withheld by one, was given by both" (74).

While poetry was conventionally taken to signal a commitment to the ideal over the real, writing also, as we have just seen, externalizes the ideal world and exposes its erotic motivations. Stephen's growing awareness of the dangers inherent in writing as sexual sublimation is made clear just before the Whitsuntide play. Stephen reflects that "the old restless moodiness," stirred anew by E. C.'s impending arrival, "had not," this time, "found an outlet in verse," owing to "the growth and knowledge of two years of boyhood . . . forbidding such an outlet" (81). The phrase *forbidding such an outlet* draws on the discourse of abstinence central to Catholic teachings concerning masturbation and points to the circle of authorities who enforce it. In this passage, poetry and orgasm are conjoined, and both are, as the older, wiser Stephen now knows, proscribed channels for his developing eroticism. It is unsurprising, then, that in the midst of Stephen's angry response to Heron's indelicacy on the subject of E. C.'s attractiveness, he recollects how a year earlier Heron had beaten him for defending the heretical Byron's preeminence as a poet (84–86). In this passage too, sex and writing are conjoined and associated with blame and physical punishment. Stephen was, we are told, spending "all the leisure which his school life left him . . . in the company of subversive writers whose gibes and violence of speech set up a ferment in his brain before they passed . . . into his crude writings" (82–83). Here, the "subversive" writing of poets such as Byron is figured as a form of violently inseminating material that, having in a crude, vegetative manner gestated in Stephen's brain, finds release in a form of literary ejaculation or birth.

Stephen himself has been singled out as heretical by the English master whose high assessment of his work had heretofore secured his predominance among his peers. He is then set upon by Heron, Boland, and Nash, who operate as the church's unofficial policemen. By praising the conventional "rhymester" Tennyson, they goad Stephen into another quasiheretical emission and maul him in response to his increasingly heated ejaculations, which are described in terms suggestive of incontinence and loss of bodily control. Stephen "turn[s] on [Boland] boldly," crying out "hotly," "I don't care what he was," and shouting, "what do you know about it?" (85–86). Wrenching himself away from the savage beating, he staggers off, "half blinded with tears, clenching his fists madly and sobbing" (86). Stephen's open subordination of doctrinal purity and sexual morality to the sensuous concerns of aesthetics and craft incur a brutal form of Catholic nationalist discipline; the crude ejaculations of his writing are violently reconstituted and reflected back to him in an obscene and shaming light. Through a sequence of verbal and then physical insults, the presumably articulate defense of Byron that Stephen could have made is rendered inchoate, reduced to a series of monosyllabic negations and ultimately to wordless sobs. Poetry becomes all the more sexualized as a form of expression, something closer to Julia Kristeva's "semiotike" (1980), for being muzzled in this fashion.

"Waking in Darkness and Secrecy and Loneliness"

The novel's images of an inner self under pressure, denied "outlet" and "hemmed in on all sides" while communing with "phantasmal comrades," are themselves suggestive of masturbation. And immediately following the above passage, a brief description of backstage goings-on is couched in distinctly onanistic terms: the made-up boys touch their faces "with their furtive fingertips" while a young Jesuit "rock[s] himself rhythmically . . . his hands thrust well forward into his side pockets" (89). Unsurprisingly, Stephen is "aware of some desecration of the priest's office or of the vestry itself" in these activities (89). Shortly thereafter, Stephen, made up himself and anticipating E. C.'s approving gaze, joins in the carnivalesque spirit of the occasion: "For one rare moment . . . clothed in the real apparel of boyhood" (90). But the masturbation imagery persists, legibly refigured in "the common mirth amid which the drop scene was hauled upwards by two able-bodied priests with violent jerks and all awry" (90), and it serves to extend throughout the scene the air of a sexuality all the more disturbing for being encrypted. In the end, the play, "lifeless" in rehearsal, has, like a quickening fetus, "suddenly assumed a life of its own" (90).

The closeted jouissance of the Whitsuntide play recurs more conspicuously when Stephen accompanies his father to Cork to sell off the family's remaining properties. Combining this introduction to insolvency with an initiation into patrilineal fellowship, both of which bear the lineaments of colonial abjection, Mr. Dedalus takes his son on a tour of his alma mater. In the "darkness and silence" of an anatomy theater, Stephen comes upon the word *Foetus* "cut several times in the dark stained wood" (95). The evocativeness of this word for Stephen is richly overdetermined. At Whitsuntide, the "mocking smile" of the covertly masturbating priest presented a sexualized "legend" for Stephen to read (89), the outward sign of the enigma of another's inner life, while, in Cork, the "sudden legend" that Stephen sees carved on a desk represents a shocking externalization of such sexualized spaces of body and mind (95). A gestating fetus is decisively internal, and information about fetuses and how they are created is also "internal," both secret and associated with forbidden imaginings that Stephen lacks the words and the will to express. The legend "expresses" those imaginings for him in an uncannily intimate yet alienated form: the Queen's College anatomy theater reveals "in the outer world a trace of what he had deemed till then a brutish and individual malady of his own mind" (95), grotesquely echoing Stephen's earlier desire "to meet in the real world the unsubstantial image which his soul so constantly beheld" (67). He finds this "trace" in an isolated and "startling" word of rich, obscure implication, a happenstance that serves to foreground, at a crucial point in Stephen's psychosexual growth, the enigmatic power of the signifier.

To appreciate the occult importance of this legend, one must take notice, first, that Stephen responds to the medical graffiti as though the word were not *foetus* but *masturbation*: the "mad and filthy orgies" that it brings "thronging into his memory" surely involve not unborn babies but rather self-titillating fantasies that might, if acted on, create them (95–97). It is, moreover, the self-administered orgasms to which these fantasies drive him that occupy, in his internal sexual economy, the prohibited position of the illegitimate fetus in the external social order (24). This equivalency is what makes the term *foetus* monstrous and sickening, a traumatic sign of shame and abnormality. Just as in "The Sisters," a contagion of taboo sexual energy involving a form of symbolic parent-child initiation unfolds here through the misrecognized substitution of ambiguously charged signifiers (simony, foetus) for unmistakably taboo sexual concepts (sodomy, masturbation).

But one must take notice, further, that the "legend" proves no less galvanizing than traumatic, or rather that it is galvanizing precisely owing to its traumatic force. Stephen's vertiginous spell of eroticized self-estrangement provokes the single most lucid, detailed and imaginative mental picture that he manages to beget over the course of the novel, a promising "fetal" development halfway between evanescent private fantasy and objectifiable creative vision. The word "startled his blood: he seemed to feel the absent students of the college about him and to shrink from their company. A vision of their life, which his father's words had been powerless to evoke, sprang up before him out of the word cut in the desk" (95). Since the question of Stephen's aesthetic potential is at the heart of this *kunstlerroman*, it is of surpassing importance that the strongest evidence of his having a literary vocation (far stronger than his stilted villanelle) should find its catalyst in another intrusively yet ambiguously sexual signifier. Moreover, the word Joyce selects to describe this signifier, *legend*, not only denotes its engraved status, which answers to its searing impact on Stephen's psyche, but also, in its other function as a narrative and symbolic intensifier, implicitly calls attention to the power of the signifier qua material signifier—to the power, that is, of its sensible properties on which its sense is raised. It is not simply a "legend" in the sense of inscription, but also a legend in the sense of hyperbolic semiological reality.

Joyce links the combined aesthetic and sexual inception and initiation in the Queen's College anatomy theater with Stephen's literal sexual initiation in Nighttown through a logic of superfetation, the wedging of one birth, one reproductive issue, within another—a logic that is normative and non-normative at the same time. Both the anatomy theater and the Nighttown scenes complexly interweave key moments in the reproductive cycle, from arousal and ejaculation through conception and childbirth, in a multilayered sequence in which teleology is both maintained and disrupted. In the Queen's College scene, insemination leads to conception, but the inseminating figure is the word *foetus*, so that while at the narrative level, insemination leads to conception, at the figurative level, an already-conceived fetus leads to insemination. The insemination in this scene leads, in *A Portrait of the Artist*'s subsequent Nighttown episode, to an initiatory act of sexual intercourse, with its attendant pleasure, figured forth as its reproductive terminus, a birth, with its attendant pangs. In the passage that precedes the sixteen-year-old Stephen's scene of completed sexual initiation in Nighttown, the novel's interwoven gestational and masturbatory images explode in welded tropes of violent sexual intercourse and childbirth.

Joyce further elaborates this sexualized/traumatized fetus imagery in *Ulysses*: in the imagined contents of the midwife's bag in "Proteus," in the ways the dead body of the eleven-day-old Rudy fragmentarily bobs to the surface in both Leopold's and Molly Bloom's streams of consciousness, in the simultaneously delectable and unthinkable contents of Plumtree's Potted Meat containers, and in the "staggering bob" that evokes their contents. Indeed, Joyce's enigmatic fetal imagery stands in a relationship of literary/cultural *nachträglichkeit* to the enigmatic/traumatic commodity sarcastically promoted in Jonathan Swift's "Modest Proposal," wherein the tender corpses of Irish children are effusively commended as a delectable and readily replenished cash crop with the potential to set to rights all of Ireland's imperially imposed misery. Viewed in light of Laplanche's schema, whereby the enigmatic message is always being relayed both backward and forward in time, as both "the belated effect of the traumatizing event," and a retroactive effect of "the second event" (Caruth 2016, 11–14), Joyce's enigmatic *foetus* reverberates with the horror that Swift's famous black comedy articulated but also occluded by way of knowing laughter. By the same recursive token, in its complex conjoining of sex/birth/life and violence/death/abjection, the scandal-charged fetal imagery of contemporary Irish literature activates Joyce's historically freighted but also prescient enigmatic signifier—from the drowned Charlie in *The Land of Spices*, to the dead calf in *The Country Girls*, to Mary's deceased sibling in *Down by the River*, to Grace's drowned toddler in *The Long Falling*, to Veronica and Liam's dead infant brother in *The Gathering*, to Ma's stillborn child of sexual enslavement in Emma Donoghue's *Room*.[14]

As Stephen prowls the streets of Dublin, "inarticulate cries and . . . unspoken brutal words rushed forth from his brain to force a passage" (106). Beginning with the phrase *force a passage*, the fusion of these image patterns continues in the description of "some dark presence" that Stephen feels moving "irresistibly upon him from the darkness, a presence subtle and murmurous as a flood filling him wholly with itself. Its murmur besieged his ears like the murmur of some multitude in sleep; its subtle streams penetrated his being. His hands clenched convulsively and his teeth set together as he suffered the agony of its penetration" (106). The tableau is one of being invaded and filled in an agonizing manner that figures Stephen both as rape victim and laboring mother. The curious simile, "like . . . some multitude in sleep," evokes a more collective plight and subtly allows Stephen's metaphorical condition to incorporate the iconography of Mother Ireland, poised between the rape of colonial occupation and the delivery of a new national being. The chain of symbolic associations linking Stephen's sexual and ethno-national subjectivity at this point of crisis indexes how the desires and frustrations generated in the former register might be discharged or sublimated in the latter.

Having completed a laborious journey through a dark, filthy passageway that is, symbolically, both anus and vagina, Stephen abruptly emerges to find himself among "women and girls dressed in long vivid gowns" (107). Stephen's sense of wonder gilds the scene with a mythic or fairy-tale exoticism. His initial guess that he had "strayed into the quarter of the Jews" suggests that Judaism is the greatest cultural alterity of which Stephen is aware, and locates the world of prostitutes on the periphery of the Symbolic Order of Victorian Dublin, at once within and beyond its purview. This world is the site of shameful transgression (Stephen's labyrinthine progress through a "maze of narrow and dirty streets" evokes a descent into hell à la Stead's "Modern Babylon" as well as Dante's *Inferno*), and for that very reason, it is also a site of potential rebirth, creativity, and transcendence. Hence, upon arriving, Stephen feels "he had awakened from a slumber of centuries" (107).

The moment of Stephen's ultimate initiation, of the "first intercourse" type, strongly reasserts the fusion of embodiment and immateriality that is Stephen's quintessential mode of processing the enigmatic power of the erotic ("darker than the swoon of sin, softer than sound or odour"; 108). Indeed, the free indirect description of his sexual contact with the prostitute might stand as an exemplary characterization of the enigmatic signifier as such: "the dark pressure of her softly parting lips" penetrating to "his brain" act as "the vehicle of a vague speech" (108). Perhaps nowhere in literature do erotic sensation and the signifying function meld so completely or find their rapport staked on such a powerful sense of the equivocal, the cryptic, the estranged—a simultaneous intensification and disruption of the social communion that each might respectively be imagined to entail.

This climactic juncture in Stephen's *bildung* not only crystallizes the operation of the enigmatic signifier but also interlinks the two signifying chains that we have seen proceed from that operation: the image pattern conflating bodily lust and spiritual transcendence, and the image pattern identifying sexual transgression and poetic expression. As we have noted, both of these chains unfold "in darkness," taking the shadows as their proper or imposed milieu, and this scene, in which Stephen loses his virginity, brings together all the various symbolic resonances of this obscurity: the shroud of mystery or uncertainty, the fear of exposure, the hope of fertilization, the shame of ostracism, and the unconscious as the locus of both repression and untapped creativity. By this arrangement, Joyce frames sexual consummation as an enabling trauma in manifold registers simultaneously.

In phraseology that recalls both the Monte Cristo fantasies and the tram ride, Stephen achieves a sense of transcendence in and through the experience of bodily weakness, exposure, and vulnerability: "His lips would not bend to kiss her. He wanted to be held firmly in her arms. . . . In her arms he felt that he had suddenly become strong and fearless and sure of himself. But his lips would not bend to kiss her" (107). Stephen's characteristic stance of proud, aloof insecurity collapses into a paralysis of inexperience that can be resolved only through the assertiveness of a sexually masterful woman who, in labially penetrating him, fulfills the logic of both chains of signification, her tongue a word made flesh and flesh made word. Stephen is thus confirmed as a subject by surrendering "belief in himself" to the "incertitude," and specifically sexual incertitude, that will figure so centrally in his crowning aesthetic achievement, his Shakespeare theory in *Ulysses* (Joyce 1986, 9.463–64, 9.842).

JOYCE'S POESIS: THE SEDUCTION EFFECT

Once we consider the prominence of sexual initiation in Joyce's fiction and come to understand the decisive operation of the enigmatic signifier in those narratives, important new light is shed on Joyce's signature narrative style. In articulating his famous "Uncle Charles Principle," Hugh Kenner observed that Joyce plied the indirect free style to develop a slippery relationship between the narrative voice and those of the characters. In Kenner's words, "[Joyce's] fictions tend not to have a detached narrator, though they seem to have. His words are in such delicate equilibrium, like the components of a sensitive piece of apparatus, that they detect the gravitational field of the nearest person. One reason the quiet little stories in *Dubliners* continue to fascinate is that the narrative point of view unobtrusively fluctuates. The illusion of dispassionate portrayal seems attended by an iridescence difficult to account for until we notice one person's sense of things inconspicuously giving place to another's" (Kenner 1978, 16). Whereas Kenner's calibrated analysis emphasizes the representational agility of Joyce's prose method, its innovation on existing modes of verisimilitude, we would like to call attention to the pragmatic implications of that "iridescence difficult to account for." As we have seen, the instances of sexual initiation in Joyce's early fiction hinge on a certain inscrutability of the exact valence, sexual and otherwise, of the seductive transaction.

The strategic withholding of information in these stories constrains the reader to share in the protagonist's incertitude and in the state of anxious desire aroused thereby. What offense or misfortune, for example, has "crossed" Father Flynn's life, and does it mark him out as reprobate, crucified, or both? Whose sister is being caressed by Davin's, and not Cranly's, hand in Stephen's obscure incest fantasy, and in what form of sexuality does this imagined scene implicate Stephen himself? It is, however, that additional play with narrative detachment, the periodic shifts into and out of the protagonists' own idioms, the variable participation in and distance from their points of view, that serve to reproduce, by sexual-textual analogy, the jouissance of seductive incalculability in the reader.

The eroticized indefiniteness of a seduction resides, for either party, in the imperfect but evolving legibility of the other's intentions and their import, conscious and unconscious, in their mutually informing relation to the likewise imperfectly legible signals furnished by the context. That is to say, in Joyce and elsewhere, the seduction effect depends on the eroticizing absence of an erotic metalanguage. Joyce puts the reader in intimate yet "unobtrusively fluctuat[ing]" and so unreliable contact with the protagonist's mental and emotional response to the unfolding seduction drama. He thus strives to relay the "enjoy-meant" of the highly charged interpretive suspension—the vivacity without transparency of apprehension—that characterizes his scenes of sexual initiation. Joyce inescapably impresses on the reader, through this "iridescence difficult to account for," the eroticizing impossibility of a fixed sexual code. In other words, this "iridescence" both effects and marks a kind of erotic seduction of the reader that is the purport, in a pragmatic sense, of his invention of *jouis-sens/joyceance*, and may be a reason we so enjoy (in the properly psychoanalytic sense) Joyce's writing. Certainly, the same enigmatic signifiers that mediate the seduction of the boys *in* these texts mediate the seduction of the reader *by* these texts. As such, they may be said to rivet the analogical or transferential link between the delineated and the interpretive experience, or, to be more precise, these signifiers constitute the textual joints at which the analogical aspires to the mimetic or the self-same. The acoustic properties of individual signifiers, like "the word *paralysis*" or "the word *simony*" (Joyce 1992a, 1), form an interface between the boys' sexual and the reader's textual initiations. The acoustic and visual properties of the oddly capitalized and italicized *Foetus* in *A Portrait of the Artist* do as well. As a result, the words that "sounded strangely" in the boy's ears in the opening frame of *Dubliners* sound a little strangely in our own, the "legend" that leaps off the anatomy theater desk leaps off the page, and these uncanny sensory vibrations are the materially inscribed reserve of signifying jouissance, an effect/affect the words harbor in excess of their semantic determinations. The enigmatic signifiers focalizing the interpretive undecidability that the boys experience in their sexual encounters not only ground our own sense of interpretive undecidability as well, they do so on the same material, acoustic basis, producing a sort of (dis)harmonious convergence of traumatic enjoyment.

It has often been said that Joyce displays an acute sensitivity to the word as object, to its thingness. In recognizing that the erotic potential of language lay in the exorbitancy of its thingness to its meaning, its sensuality to its sensibility, Joyce contrived to strike not only an extraordinary connection between the psychosexual mysteries represented in the text and the textual surface of their representation, but also a correspondingly direct, even tactile connection between that textual surface and the hidden springs of interpretive erotics.

To summarize properly Joyce's achievement in this regard, it is necessary to take into account the occulted relationship between sexual initiation generally and sexual abuse scandal in particular. Bathed in the light of public exhibition, the enigmatic signifier is alchemically transfigured into a scandal signifier, which is collectively enacted, consumed, and reacted to without giving rise to assured collective understanding. In brief, the scandalous is scandalous in that it draws on reservoirs of pleasurably traumatic excess originally formed and sealed at the very point from which individual, libidinal, affective, and social identity emerge: the traumatic/ecstatic encounter with the enigmatic message of the parental Other. Because that message remains taboo and therefore stubbornly unconscious, it can be processed or metabolized only in the form of misrecognition. Enigmatic signifiers must undergo some psychic defense—denial, disavowal, projection, and so on— in order to create the illusion of radical discontinuity between the universal, implicitly incestuous grounds of subjectivity and the monstrous or aberrant practices that scandalize. That is to say,

A. We are all interested in sex scandals in the etymological sense of the word: *inter-est*, or "being between," or, in this case, being between the potentiating condition and the actuality of the sex scandal scenario; and

B. We are all equally concerned to dissimulate that state of inter-est, that being between, and to establish an absolute psychic, social, or moral cordon sanitaire structurally prohibiting any possibility of our being implicated in that scenario. In this respect, we are committed, as a part of our everyday ego-maintenance, to not understanding, or to misunderstanding, the general economy of child sexual scandal.

Joyce's work proposes to elucidate the psychosocial operations of such scandal by mobilizing his audience's inter-est in the act of reading itself. This is precisely a function of that analogical or transferential link, remarked above, between the delineated and the interpretive experience. The reader is situated between Joyce's poesis, with its seduction effect, and Joyce's diegesis, with its representation of child sexual seduction—between the enigmatic signifier, the sensory reverberations of which resonate with the reader's own sexual initiation, and the signifiers of scandal, which unfold, in oblique fashion, various types of socially reprehended sexual initiations. The reader thus observes depictions of untoward sexual induction conveyed in a language with sensuous, material properties that evoke the traumatic jouissance imbuing their own infantile sexualization. Joyce not only stages thereby the irreducible connection between the enigmatic and the scandal signifiers, so that his reader might discern its reality, but does so interactively, so that his reader might feel its reality at a visceral level.

In grasping this irreducible connection as both intellectual proposition and sensory intuition, Joyce's readers come to appreciate, or at least are given to appreciate, how the dynamics of child sexual abuse rehearse the dynamics of every passage into sexed subjectivity, including their own. Securely repressed, this structural implication of the primal roots of sexuality in its most reviled enactments fuels the pressure among observers of sex scandals to dissociate themselves and their "own" (their community, their church, their relatives) from the whole ugly business. They feign ignorance, avert their gaze, disavow their suspicions, discredit accusations, or impute the supposed atrocities to some unimaginable alien other. Once brought to consciousness, however, as Joyce's fictions aim to do, this same structural implication imposes on scandal observers generally—all of us in sum—an ethical mandate to overcome those very pressures and treat the scandal of child sexual abuse as our collective responsibility. That Joyce's attempt to represent this "censored chapter" in Irish history was itself subject to prolonged censorship as literature suggests just how difficult those pressures are to overcome, and the subsequent history of this Irish scandal, including its literary history, demonstrates how difficult is the ethical imperative to surmount them. But Irish history has also borne out Joyce's sense of the stakes involved and his confidence in the indispensable role that literature has to play in addressing them. Writing to Grant Richards in an effort to secure publication for *Dubliners* at last, he proclaimed, with prophetic grandiosity, "I seriously believe that you will retard the course of civilization in

Ireland by preventing the Irish people from having one good look at themselves in my nicely polished looking-glass" (Joyce 1965, 64).

NOTES

1. In the epiphanies, a series of short sketches written from 1898 to 1904, Joyce aimed to record verbatim interactions he had witnessed, capturing them immediately so as to maximize accuracy. In a detailed entry on the epiphanies, the James Joyce Centre website offers relevant insight into the particular effect Joyce was aiming to capture in these brief, immediate transcriptions, noting that "Joyce's brother Stanislaus saw the epiphanies as something more like records of Freudian slips. Writing after Joyce's death, Stanislaus claimed the epiphanies were ironical observations of slips, errors and gestures by which people betrayed the very things they were most careful to conceal. Further, Oliver St John Gogarty, a friend of Joyce's and one of the models for the character Buck Mulligan in *Ulysses*, noted that Fr Darlington of University College had told Joyce that epiphany meant 'showing forth,' and that an epiphany was a showing forth of the mind in which one gave oneself away" (accessed November 6, 2018, http://jamesjoyce.ie/epiphanies).

2. Stephen's unwillingness to speak to Isabel in a register that would, as seen from her perspective, signify moral and spiritual corruption is not due to pusillanimity. Rather, it stems from Stephen's understandable unwillingness to attempt a form of communication that would be legitimately experienced by Isabel and indeed by Stephen himself as incestuously intrusive, owing to the Irish Catholic moral episteme's hypersexualization of all discourses outside those of Catholic piety.

3. Simon Dedalus's condemnation in *A Portrait of the Artist* of William Walsh, or "Billy with the lip," for his part in Parnell's destruction offers a vivid sense of Walsh's central role in advancing virulently anhedonistic, post-Famine Catholicism. Walsh's role would fully blossom once he successfully declared Irish children of the 1913 Lockout to be better off dead than outside Catholic oversight (Joyce 1992b, 33). For a fuller account of this subject, see this book's introduction.

4. Yet Stanislaus Joyce was already noting this augmentation of language's inherent capacity to simultaneously hide and expose when Joyce was still collecting epiphanies with the enthusiasm of a lepidopterist pursuing unusual specimens. "'Jim,' Stanislaus wrote in his journal, 'is thought to be very frank about himself but his style is such that it might be contended that he confesses in a foreign language'" (Ellmann 1982, 148).

5. On the relationship of Joyce's work to the thought of Ellis and Albert, see Brown (1985, 28–35, 52).

6. The phrase *après la lettre* here alludes to the famous essay "The Agency of the Letter in the Unconscious," by Jacques Lacan, the foremost exponent of the linguistic turn that has come to define post-Freudian psychoanalysis.

7. For recent discussions of this seminar with reference to Joyce, see Thurston (2004, 94–97, 161–66), Harari (2002, 23–27, 171–77), and Rabaté (2001a, 154–82; 2001b, 1–23).

8. For discussions of the *sinthome*, see Harari (2002, 203–42), Rabaté (2001a, 157–62), and Žižek (1989, 71–79).

9. While Freud did famously shift his emphasis away from actual sexualized trauma to internal drives as the root of adult neurosis, this shift was never as absolute as many contemporary critics would have it. He argues, for instance, in his "General Theory of the Neuroses," that

"phantasies of being seduced are of particular interest, because so often they are not phantasies but real memories" (1917, 370).

10. In an unpublished essay, Roy Gottfried has discussed the influence on "The Sisters" of the story "The Priest and the Acolyte," widely credited to Oscar Wilde when it appeared.

11. See, for example, the shrewd reading in Mahaffey (1988, 29–32).

12. For sublimation as the unsolved mystery of psychoanalytic theory, see Dean (2000, 257–59).

13. For an early and classic reading to this effect, see Kenner (1987). See also Henke (1982, 82–107); Day (1998, 59).

14. As Kathryn Conrad points out, conservative Catholic rhetoric in Ireland's serial abortion debates aligns the Irish state and the fetus, each as "an autonomous entity threatened from without" (2004, 158). In addition to sharing a presumed external threat, as Irish nationalist scandal culture evolved, the always-imperiled Ireland and fetus also came to share and indeed mutually constitute each other's absolute innocence. Images of fetuses—photo-realist or stylized, whole or mutilated—would eventually remain as the movement's last, irrefutable trump card. Ostensibly appealing to the viewer's protectiveness with its extreme vulnerability, the decontextualized fetus's enigmatic charge inheres more powerfully in its subliminal, off-putting abjection. The anti-abortion fetus image works by arousing an immediate, visceral revulsion that in turn induces guilt, prompting, in a split second, the viewer to angrily project his or her initial, aversive reaction onto constituencies posing a known threat to children. This version of the scandal of imperiled innocence would remain potent in Ireland into the twenty-first century, long after other such scandal structures had given way. That even the scandalized fetus trope ultimately failed owes much to later authors' development of Joyce's enigmatic fetal trope, incorporating traumatic violation and desire in turn-of-the-twenty-first-century literature of scandal. In the spring of 2018, the graphic images of fetuses that have long been a staple of the anti-abortion movement in both Ireland and the United States burgeoned in all the cities and byways of Ireland, visibly representing what Ireland's declining nationalist Catholicism had viewed as its final, unanswerable assertion of the movement's scandalously assailed innocence. Yet even this last bastion of conservative Catholic ideology failed by a landslide in May 2018, at least partly owing to the alternative representations of the complexities of children's relationships to sexual awakening, seduction, sexual molestation and abuse, and involuntary pregnancy—as seen through the eyes of Irish children themselves.

2

BETWEEN (OPEN) SECRET AND ENIGMA

Kate O'Brien, *The Land of Spices,* and
the Stylistic Invention of Lesbian (In)visibility

> No honourable and sincere man, said Stephen, has given up to you his life
> and his youth and his affections from the days of Tone to those of Parnell
> but you sold him to the enemy or failed him in need or reviled him for
> another. And you invite me to be one of you. I'd see you damned first.
>
> JAMES JOYCE, *A Portrait of the Artist as a Young Man* (220)

STEPHEN DEDALUS'S UNCHARACTERISTIC ROW WITH the good-natured
Davin over Irish nationalism begins when Davin confesses himself deeply
troubled by the secrets Stephen has confided in him (Joyce 1992b, 219). In
terms that recall Mary Douglas's formulation that social pollutions reflect
"an image of the body, whose primary concern is the ordering of a social
hierarchy" (1966, 126), Davin describes how "those things about [Stephen's]
private life" had physically sickened him, so he could not even "eat [his] dinner" (Joyce 1992b, 219). He assures Stephen, "I was quite bad," and that he
had lain "awake a long time that night" (219). When Davin subsequently
pleads with Stephen to allay his distress by pledging himself to the nationalist cause Stephen reacts with a famous string of escalating charges, first
against Irish nationalism and ultimately against the nation itself, culminating in his famous charge that Ireland is not only a negligent but a filicidal
mother—an "old sow that eats her farrow" (220).

According to Douglas, when we reduce all transgressions relating to
pollution, contamination, and contagion to their fundamental components,
we arrive back at the old definition of impurity, or dirt, as "matter out of
place" (1966, 36). Feeling "a tide [beginning] to surge beneath the calm

surface of [his] friendliness" (Joyce 1992b, 219), Stephen vigorously contests the implication that his secrets are "out of place" inside Davin's body by insisting on his own legitimate place within Ireland.[1] By claiming his status as an Irish compatriot, Stephen is effectively asserting his right to implant within Davin as an open secret what Davin has (wrongly) internalized as a disruptively alien enigmatic message.[2] Davin, he claims, thinks he is a monster, presumably owing to Davin's sickened visceral reaction to Stephen's secrets. Stephen gives evidence to the contrary—that he is a kinsman, not a stranger or monster—by invoking the brute empirical fact of his Irishness: "This race and this country and this life produced me" (220).[3]

Although he denies thinking Stephen a monster, Davin cannot accept him as a compatriot; he earnestly pleads with Stephen to join the Irish community: "Try to be one of us" (220). Surprisingly, it is not the character of Stephen's secrets themselves but Stephen's liminal status relative to the Irish community that Davin finds unbearable. Davin, accordingly, wants Stephen to resolve the internal turmoil the secrets are causing not by changing the status of the secrets through, for instance, confession, repentance, or a pledge to reform, but rather by changing his social status, by trying "to be one of us": a proper Irishman among Irishmen. Here we can see clearly an instance in which "pollution rules" and "moral rules," though connected, are not congruent (Douglas 1966, 133). That is, in the course of this exchange, neither Davin nor Stephen is particularly interested in the moral status of Stephen's nauseating secrets. Instead, the young men have entered into a heated debate about the placement of social boundaries and whether Stephen is an outsider (a monster), a fully fledged community member (an Irishman), or whether he is, as Davin believes, liminal (or, as Douglas would have it, still an initiate; 105). Stephen, for his part, responds not by declining Davin's request but by contesting its founding assumptions, by categorically denying that joining the nationalist community can reliably ameliorate either his own or Davin's "bad" condition (220).

As Stephen parses the bargain that Davin urges on him, he is being asked to "pay in [his] own life and person" the debts his ancestors incurred when they "threw off their language" and "allowed a handful of foreigners to subject them" (220). Concerning the category of "dirt," where the anthropological and the psychoanalytic converge, Stephen is being asked to serve (along with all other correctly constituted Irishmen of his generation) as a scapegoat or sin eater, ritually consuming on behalf of his social order a historical residue that would be termed *dirt* or *impurity* by the anthropologist and *dirt* or *shame* by the psychoanalyst, and receiving, in return, a social certificate of good health. He caps this formulation with the contemptuous rhetorical question: "What for?" (220). Davin's ingenuous reply, "For our freedom," unwisely concedes Stephen's premise: that Davin wants Stephen to decontaminate the insalubrious secrets that are giving him social dyspepsia by trading his life and person for membership in the Irish nationalist community. While Davin unwittingly concedes Stephen's premise, Stephen strenuously refutes Davin's. In particular, he angrily rebuts his friend's conviction that Stephen will render his potentially disruptive secrets safely inert—as open secrets—by placing himself fully within the nationalist community, completing an initiation that Davin argues is already in progress ("In your heart you are an Irishman but your pride is too powerful"; 220). Irish nationalism, Stephen argues, far from protecting the private lives of its adherents, always treacherously betrays their secrets. Stephen points out that the institution of the Irish open secret has a well-established pattern ("from the days of Tone to those of Parnell") of breaking down in times of crisis, with catastrophic results for Ireland itself and, as Stephen finds especially offensive, for every "honorable and sincere man . . . [who gives up] his life and his youth and his affections" for the Irish cause (220). Both Davin and Stephen finally set aside moral questions in favor of group boundaries, which, Stephen argues, become predictably unsustainable for Irish nationalism at particular moments of political crisis (such as the 1798 Uprising and the fall of Parnell).

If we think of the open secret as a means by which a community's avowed moral priorities may be systematically superseded by "rules of pollution," then what goes wrong in these moments of crisis is that broader definitions of nationality are externally imposed, often in the prevailing media, thereby reframing the contents of an open secret that had been heretofore contained within regional, orally constituted communities. The open secret, abruptly exposed in the harsh light of competing national print cultures, thereupon collapses.

"The Well-Known, Old, but Still Unbeaten Track": *The Land of Spices* and the Enigmatic Signifier

Close attention to certain categories of secret that everyone knows about (sometimes consciously and sometimes subliminally) and that everyone denies helps account for a curious contradiction that is of particular importance in this chapter and the chapter to follow. In our reading of Kate O'Brien's *The Land of Spices*, and in a far different way of Edna O'Brien's *The Country Girls*, we are training our critical sights on the long-standing visibility of and tolerance for nonstandard sexual practices and subjectivities in many Irish communities. To do so, we explicitly disrupt the ongoing reticence in Irish literary criticism concerning what is, manifestly, a cornucopia of deviant desires, episodes, and identities in modern Irish literature. Residual rules of open secrecy have continued to stifle critical commentary on the queer, the nonnormative, and the perverse in Irish women's literature particularly, even when the literary open secret constitutes the means by which a text's most important effects are produced.

As Angela Bourke has strikingly documented in *The Burning of Bridget Cleary* (2001), rural communities in late nineteenth-century Ireland witnessed rapid and violently uneven social transformations. This ongoing process of change was punctuated by periodic, devastating clashes between two quite differently constituted social orders, both of which answered to the names "Irish nationalism," "the Irish people," and "Ireland." Two distinct Irish nationalisms had heretofore coexisted both peacefully and invisibly: one, the orally based folk communities that defined social inclusion and exclusion in terms of purity and pollution, and the other, the broader ecclesiastical-national system in charge of Irish morality and Ireland's reputation in the eyes of the world. For the greater part of the eighteenth and nineteenth centuries, these two Irish "civilizations" coexisted side by side,[4] with a comfortably tacit understanding of what areas of human life were the legitimate purviews of each.[5] As the expansion across much of the island of new media and communications technologies rendered the language and perspectives of the imperial metropole increasingly inescapable, however, these two Irelands came into increasingly open and heated conflict. We might, following Bourke, look at the violent confrontation between a middle-class, literate Irish nation, to which the Irish Catholic hierarchy and the British state both contributed, and a long-established Irish folk culture, as a newly destructive version of a well-established "toggle" between the rules of pollution and the rules of morality that emerged in the late nineteenth century and that would continue to invisibly organize both social stigma and violence in the modern Irish state thereafter.

Kate O'Brien's 1941 novel, *The Land of Spices*, depicts a culture of open secrecy in transition. In the novel's convent school setting, during the period from 1912 to 1916, sexual (or eroticized) open secrets continue to circulate as coded referents in a community that has not yet been staggered and reorganized by the inimical powers of the media sex scandal. Yet local systems of communal, conscious secret-keeping are already perceptibly inflected by the unconscious system of traumatic unknowing that would increasingly characterize modern, media-saturated, English-speaking Ireland. The rise of the British sex scandal in the late nineteenth century and the subsequent consolidation of Ireland's scandal of imperiled innocence never altogether neutralized the established operations of the open secret. The rise of a public scandal culture in Ireland did, however, consolidate socially forbidden or disavowed sexual desires, sensations, and practices traditionally shrouded in open secrecy into a taboo, collective reservoir that paralleled, in macrocosm, the intrapsychic, unconscious operations of the enigmatic signifier.

In order to pursue our reading of the enigmatic signifier's operation in *The Land of Spices*, which evokes a vast, silent sea change in an Irish Catholic convent school, we must start with the observably transitioning mode of open secrecy that prevails in the world of the novel's convent school. Over the course of the story, the easy schoolgirl traffic in eroticized open secrets, which the older nuns in O'Brien's novel both oversee and overlook, is giving way—in the second decade of the twentieth century—to the regime of pathologizing and punitively inciting surveillance that Michel Foucault famously ascribes to nineteenth-century educational and psychiatric institutions (1980, 46). In their totality, the novel's intricately limned striations of public, communal, and intrapsychic secrecy and unknowing both reflect and convey, in microcosm, painful transformations in the Irish Catholic moral episteme.

The Land of Spices registers the moment when a global community of specifically women's Catholicism, organized principally in terms of purity and pollution and maintained through well-defined curricula and age-old rituals of admission, initiation, and membership, was coming under intense pressure from a specifically Irish, male-dominated Catholic nationalism. This new, post-Parnellite Irish Catholicism was resituating itself in relation to the Irish community with which Davin identifies in exhorting Stephen to "be one of us." The inhabitants of the novel's Belgium-based *La Compagnie de la Saint Famille* are regarded by the new mode of statist Catholicism as outsiders, and thus, during this period, as the novel makes clear, certain long-established open secrets that had been accepted in convent life were becoming untenable. In the course of the novel, male representatives of the Irish Catholic Church, which had long accepted de facto limits on its right to meddle in private areas of Irish social life, repeatedly intrude into the world of the convent. Such intrusions are evidently unrelated to doctrinal matters. Rather, in multiple scenes, "mansplaining" Irish male clerics leave neither the Reverend Mother nor the reader with any doubt about the nature of the perceived infractions periodically in need of male correction. As a community of Catholic women, many of whom were born or trained abroad, the order of nuns clearly appears increasingly improperly Catholic because—as Irish Catholicism is becoming more synonymous with Irish nationalism—it is excessively female and insufficiently Irish.

The society-wide shifts in definitions of community that O'Brien represents in *The Land of Spices* inexorably disrupt certain long-held open secrets in a manner that O'Brien makes manifest by drawing on both her native fluency in Irish taboo culture and her queer modernist mastery of enigmatic transmissions made visible. She does so, moreover, without providing ammunition that could be used to facilitate attacks against either convents or nonheterosexual women. Indeed, to continue to disregard O'Brien's textual deployment of contemporary open secrets so as to vividly render a distinctive social world that could be seen and felt, but not scandalized or pathologized in its own time, would be to remain blinkered to the novel's greatest achievements.

As Eibhear Walshe observes in his biographical study, *Kate O'Brien: A Writing Life*, O'Brien came of age during a period when public conceptions of physical and emotional intimacy between women were in flux. Love between women was losing the sanctioning mantle of the Victorian "ideal of romantic friendship" and was coming under the pathologizing eye of the new sexological discourses (2006, 46–47). This transition, from a de facto to a cultivated lesbian invisibility, occurred not only over time but also unevenly across social space (Ferriter 2009, 208–9). The shift from the blinkering of the social gaze on female homoeroticism to the shuttering of female homoeroticism against a censorious social gaze occurred later and more gradually in Ireland than in many other parts of western Europe. Thus, as O'Brien herself came of age and moved eastward,[6] and particularly after her post–University College

Dublin relocation from Dublin to Manchester, the lineaments of a specifically lesbian closet—a dialectical site of en/disclosure and hence a structure of potentially open(ed) secrecy—were consolidating around her. Under these circumstances, as Walshe contends, "it is not surprising that [O'Brien] never defined herself publicly as a lesbian" (2006, 46). But as Walshe and other critics have shown, O'Brien did, in lieu of "coming out" publicly, telegraph her lesbian identification in other ways. Given her historical and geographical positioning with respect to an as-yet incomplete and ill-defined lesbian closet, however, she was unable to draw on an established reservoir of performative and discursive cues that other queer Irish men and women, from Micheal Mac Liammoir to Nell McCafferty, would draw on so as to speak unmistakably, but with plausible deniability, to a loosely woven but finite community, ensuring incomprehension beyond and, as needed, disavowal within its borders. Accordingly, O'Brien's public signals, while clearly inspired by Joyce's and other extant strategies of disclosure, including faint performative allusions to Radclyffe Hall's *The Well of Loneliness*, were more evocative or numinous.[7] That is to say, instead of relying on heavily coded indices legible to certain parts of the national community and illegible to others, O'Brien crafted a mode of self-presentation that opened itself to a reading of sexual dissidence without encouraging or importuning it.

The enigmatic signifier, as theorized by Jean Laplanche, can be thought of as the open secret's dialogical obverse, which both depicts and replicates the experience of sexual initiation as an always traumatic because always undecidable proposition. Instead of the openly secret, which is available and potentially legible but inappropriable except by the initiated insider (so that those who know don't tell and those who tell don't know), the enigmatic signifier, owing to its origins in infantile sexual development, remains irrevocably uncertain, ever "secret" and yet unconsciously accessible to all readers.

The distinction to be made here is between the following:

A. A symbolic ensemble that implies or looks to define a hermeneutical situation to which potential addressees either belong, however deniably, or do not belong, a notionally closed communicative circle or "closet"; and

B. A symbolic ensemble that puts the hermeneutical situation itself in question, that introduces an interpretably (or meta-) hermeneutical situation.

In the first case, one has the condition of the open secret; in the second, the operation of the enigmatic signifier. For Laplanche, the enigmatic signifier functions in the first instance as a vehicle of infantile sexualization in response to the implantation of "something coming from outside," an enigmatic message, that takes on meaning (that is, becomes both sexual and traumatic) only belatedly, when the original seduction is "reinvested in a second moment" (Caruth 2014, 7). The material conductor of messages whose seductive power resides in the confusion of sexual and nonsexual valences, the enigmatic signifier exceeds and yet depends on its capacity for determinate meaning and range of association.

It is in the penumbra of uncertainty created by this fissure of sensuality, sensibility, and sense that the seductive potential of the signifier, its reserve of jouissance, is lodged. Because this signifier, like any signifier, is inherently iterable, the erotic current with which it is vested at the moment of infantile sexualization remains available to be reactivated under other circumstances, especially those recalling or approximating this traumatic origin, such as subsequent instances of sexual initiation or introduction. Moreover, because the eroticized zone of undecidability, or "enigma," remains intimately bound up with, while exceeding, the signifier's determinate meanings or valences, it imparts a sexual energy not only to the specific contents but also to the so-called signifying chain of metonymic differences delimiting them. Understanding the enigma in this fashion, not as an exceptional case but rather as an exceptional function latent in all cases, helps explain how a limitless array of objects, scenarios, experiences, and identities might come to be libidinally infused and thus the focal point of unconscious fantasy.

If the context of O'Brien's coming of age created both the necessity and the opportunity for her to fashion her self-image out of indefinite, radically interpretable cues of taboo sexual identity, the process of doing so may well have enabled her to reflect in her coming-of-age, autobiographical fiction, *The Land of Spices*, on the role of such cues in catalyzing the often wayward desire that notions of sexual identity aimed to reify. At the same time, in following the path of her literary forerunner, James Joyce, whose iconic *bildungsroman* her own *Land of Spices* closely tracks, O'Brien would have recognized how the increased self-reflexivity of the modernist novel was geared to the narrative deployment of indefinite or enigmatic signifiers.[8] That is, literature of the sort Joyce pioneered was becoming a space *about* as well as *of* interpretation, a hermeneutical field that interrogates its own limits and possibilities. This, the condition of so-called modernist difficulty, is also the proximate condition, as noted above, of the enigmatic signifier.

Indeed, it would not be going too far to propose that the enigmatic signifier represents a specialized instance of modernist difficulty. While an enigmatic signifier does not positively balk interpretation, it does function both affectively and semiotically without insisting that the occult relationship it encodes between those two levels be apprehended. Therein resides its peculiar suggestiveness, a faint resonance of traumatic erotic potential toward which the reader is permitted to maintain an unconscious and thus quite plausible deniability. In *The History of Sexuality*, volume 1, Foucault (1980) famously uncloaks the disingenuousness of Victorian protestations of ignorance concerning sexual activities everywhere inscribed in Victorian discourse. We would argue that in Irish society, with its legacy of Jansenist Catholicism, a like structure of vigorously buttressed ignorance, undergirded by a strict knowledge of what and where to overlook, persisted through much of the twentieth century, making it easy to mis- or underinterpret the more subtle literary strategies, like the enigmatic signifier, of cryptic sexual representation.

As regards lesbian visibility, the critical reception of *The Land of Spices* affords a conspicuous, even originary, case in point. The novel's intimations of female homoeroticism have often gone completely ignored, as exegetes interested in O'Brien's depiction of sexuality (Boylan 2000; Dalsimer 1990; Tighe-Mooney 2008; Walshe 2006) have trained their attention on the single euphemistic reference to a male-male "embrace of love" that put the novel under ban for a time in Ireland. Far more telling, however, is the surprisingly large number of O'Brien scholars who, in a classic act of Freudian denegation, explicitly deny the existence of any lesbianism in *The Land of Spices*, even though no one asserted it in the first place. Indeed, the critics who have contributed most substantially to our critical understanding of lesbian overtones throughout O'Brien's oeuvre are among those who pause to argue specifically against any lesbian presence in *The Land of Spices*. For instance, Aintzane Legarreta Mentxaka holds that "Kate O'Brien made regular use of subtext to hide lesbian content," but she excludes *The Land of Spices* from even this shrouded expression of female homoeroticism (2011, 72). Emma Donoghue introduces her discussion of the novel with the assertion, "Another Kate O'Brien novel which is not about lesbians, by the way, is *The Land of Spices* . . . the lesbian school or college novel was already a cliché and one O'Brien was determined to avoid" (1993, 49). Elizabeth Cullingford opines that "although in several of her novels, O'Brien codes lesbians as nunnish she nevertheless avoids [in *The Land of Spices*] coding her nuns as lesbians: the relationships between them are empowering rather than erotic" (2006, 21). Mary Breen, in her reading of the protagonist Anna Murphy's valedictory moment of attraction to her classmate Pilar, actively dissociates Anna's artistic epiphany from any lesbian inference, asserting that Anna's "gaze is an appropriating one, certainly, but the appropriation is artistic, not sexual" (1993, 176). (At this moment, Breen seems to forget that this lakeside scene is O'Brien's homage to the famous seaside scene in *A Portrait of the Artist*, where Stephen's explicitly sexual gaze, trained on the "bird girl," serves as the portal to his artistic vocation [Joyce 1992b, 185–86]).

As if responding directly to Breen, and indirectly to the run of *Spices* criticism, Patricia Coughlan concurs that "there is no explicit indication . . . that either Anna's reception of Pilar's beauty, or her appreciation of its effect upon herself, is a sexualized one; nevertheless, it seems to me, to feel obliged entirely to edit out this aspect of O'Brien's usual construction of feminine beauty from the scene would be the reaction only of a reader determined at all cost to maintain silence on the issue of lesbian sexuality" (1993, 81). The tortuous syntax of Coughlan's formulation sends the message of O'Brien's critics back to them, as Lacan would say, "in reverse order." Whereas they might feel that O'Brien is "determined to avoid" any suggestion of a lesbian school novel, Coughlan intimates that it is these critics themselves who seem "determined" to "maintain silence," to keep secret "the issue of lesbian sexuality" (1993, 81). Yet by the same token, just as previous critics cannot keep entirely silent on a lesbianism the presence of which they dispute, so Coughlan cannot unreservedly affirm the lesbian presence she circuitously acknowledges.

In every case, we are witnessing the effect of the enigmatic signifier. This semiotic mode not only facilitates plausible deniability but encodes such deniability in the very object to be apprehended, confounding what is to be known and what left unknown. It places an affect that cannot be dispelled in exorbitant relation to a sense that may well be doubted, inducing denials excessive in their protest and avowals yielding in their conviction. As a literary device, in a text like *The Land of Spices*, the enigmatic signifier becomes still more complicated, in that it operates in two dimensions at once: for the characters within the narrative and for the readers of the narrative, thereby knitting together the eroticism represented with the erotics of reading. Rooted in the oedipal taboos surrounding childhood sexuality, the enigmatic signifier serves as a particularly effective vehicle for representing the experience of initiation in or introduction to the very socially forbidden or disavowed sexual desires, sensations, or practices traditionally shrouded in open secrecy. Just as the exorbitancy of jouissance to whatever signification seems to animate it enables that libidinal affect to be readily displaced along a chain of associated symbolic forms and behaviors, so the same continuing exorbitancy lends those forms and behaviors an effective margin of autonomy from whatever sexual energies infuse and enliven them. That is to say, the constitutive semidetachment of jouissance from its source entails a like semidetachment of its associated signifying destination from jouissance. As a result, the relation of libidinal affect to signifying cause does not necessarily tend toward a recognizably erotic manifestation. To be sure, any social practice must express in some form the associated jouissance that fuels it; but owing to its "external" character, the association itself, which is the emergence of a sexual investment, may go unremarked yet unrepressed, may operate unobtrusively without being actively inhibited or concealed. As a result, the shameful or illicit nature, even the sexual tenor itself, of the libidinal stirrings triggered by an enigmatic signifier may readily go unacknowledged or disavowed, sheltered not in a closet of secrecy but in a mist of uncertainty or inadvertence. The enigmatic signifier produces sexual desires dissimulated in their very emergence, giving the novel's characters the license of ignorance and the novel's readers a corresponding license to ignore.

"The Irony of . . . the Nun's Locked Secret"

The first ambiguous index in *The Land of Spices* is the convent setting itself. The genre of convent school fiction has a history that comprises not only tales of lesbian sexual initiation and love, as Donoghue observes, but also tales that feature pubescent innocence, naivete, immaturity, even asexuality and that harbor the ingrained assumption of principled celibacy for their adult cast. The narrative context for *The Land of Spices* thus serves to reinforce the undecidability of the individual enigmatic signifiers dispersed throughout the text.

The first such signifier occurs at the very outset of the novel, in its opening paragraph, in which the Reverend Mother hopes "no one would faint" in the unseasonably warm October chapel (K. O'Brien 1988, 3). The reader, of course, cannot know that fainting, which seems at first to allude to the chapel's warmth, has any sexual implications. However, the Reverend Mother's train of thought goes on to note a "hysterical fuss towards the back of the school benches" (3). Neither "warmth" nor "fainting" is automatically a sexual term, but each can carry such connotations, and with the "hysterical fuss towards the back of the school benches," the ambiguity deepens, as—in a post-Freudian era—*hysteria* bears its own connotations of occulted sexuality. The underlying cause of the fuss completes the demonstratively (if still undemonstrably) erotic picture while introducing the novel's exemplary enigmatic signifier: the commotion arises out of "*Schwärmerei* for Eileen O'Doherty, who was at that moment receiving the veil" (3). The term *Schwärmerei* translates as "excessive or unwholesome emotion," alternatives that may be read as straddling, in much the same way as does the term *hysteria*, the line between a pathologized psychic condition of a strictly affective or an implicitly sexualized type. Its introduction in the novel's first paragraphs as a distinctive, familiar collective affect in the convent school immediately and explicitly introduces the theme of female-female desire, reminding those readers who know the word of an open secret they share with the author and her characters, while simultaneously initiating neophyte readers who have not spent time in convent schools.

But it is as an uppercase, untranslated meme in an English-language text and world that *Schwärmerei* performs its most direct and ramified function as an enigmatic signifier. First of all, only in its untranslated form does *Schwärmerei* take the colloquial sense of intense, collective, pubescent female devotion. On the one hand, such attachment may be distinguished from proper lesbian desire, as Donoghue does, on the grounds of its being a "shallow" and juvenile emotional expression (1993, 49). On the other hand, however, given the infantile derivation of eroticism as such, to counterpose *Schwärmerei* and lesbian desire along these lines is to admit a developmental continuum of homosociality and sexuality along which no bright line between different modes of affection may be drawn. The cues surrounding the introduction of the term elaborate on this aporia.

Three years earlier, at the graduation of Eileen, a senior renowned for her beauty and her physical prowess ("she played hockey like a goddess"), "the school had been all but unmanageable with *Schwärmerei*" (K. O'Brien 1988, 3). On that occasion, Eileen was moving beyond the reach of their community into the world of heterosexual attainments for which she seemed destined: presentation to the English court, a collection of male hearts among the English clubs and Irish garrison, a round of dating, blissful mating, and inevitable child rearing. That outbreak of *Schwärmerei* responded both to the loss of a beloved icon of sexual attractiveness and to a mass identification with the romantic triumphs in Eileen's future: that is, with both the termination and the genesis of certain erotic possibilities. On the present occasion, the Reverend Mother envisions hysterical girls fainting at a graduate's change in sexual status, one that will put her off-limits for the kind of heterosexual romance with which the girls, through her intercession, had earlier identified. In the same motion, however, her change in status commits her forever to a community of women, returning her, by a different sort of symbolic proxy, back to the girls, for whom she remains a preeminent object of collective desire. The intense, now familiar wave of emotions marking the ritual confirmation of her choice yet again registers the vicarious experience of both an end and a beginning of eroticized possibility, both a loss and a recovery, self-denial and indulgence—in short, a profoundly ambivalent experience of jouissance. The shifting and conflicting terms of the schoolgirls' worship of Eileen issue in an affect undecidable in its erotic quality, and that is where the enigmatic signifier, *Schwärmerei*, figures so importantly. In its untranslated state, the term *Schwärmerei* can resonate— in its vowel sounds, its rhythms, its feeling in the mouth, its translingual eye-rhymes (swarm, *mère*, Marie, *mari*)—of the entire homosocial-sexual spectrum, without determining a single point or distinguishing among the various points thereon. An umbrella term in the fullest sense, *Schwärmerei* shields its subjects from knowledge of their own erotic investments by the very sweep or range of its implications. In the process, it not only evinces an undetermined form of erotic passion but also lends an eroticized resonance to the experience of indeterminacy itself. The signifier and the signified of the unspeakable (in the sense of both the ineffable and the taboo) prove utterly flush and coextensive with one another.

A further order of complexity emerges in this opening scene with the shift of Reverend Mother's gaze to Anna Murphy, the youngest and newest student in the school and the co-heroine of the unfolding narrative. Reverend Mother's thought at this moment, "At least there is no *Schwärmerei* in that face," reflects an amused approval corresponding with a disdain for the swoon of *Schwärmerei* in general (5). For her part, Anna appears fixated on yet unmoved by the ceremony, "as if," in Reverend Mother's phrase, "she is memorising the whole affair, for critical purposes" (5). Over time, and against this backdrop of barely contained schoolgirl eroticism, Reverend Mother conceives a singular affection for Anna that she understands to be grounded in a certain kind of intellectual like-mindedness: both are concerned that serious things be treated seriously. From Reverend Mother's perspective, of course, nothing could be more serious than young women receiving the veil, and so her objections to the present display of histrionics combined with Anna's compelling imperviousness to the surrounding emotional contagion might invite us, should we take this opening scene on its own as-yet independent terms, to read O'Brien as invoking the immature and potentially embarrassing homoeroticism of *Schwärmerei* only to repudiate it, in a characteristic defensive maneuver. In Reverend Mother's condemnation of, and Anna's freedom from, the practice, O'Brien might be seen to emulate other intellectual women of the period—Dorothy Sayers springs to mind—in raising the issue of lesbianism only to clear herself and those intellectual female characters of whom she approves of any such proclivities.[9]

But far from operating as a self-contained vignette, this opening scene turns out to be the launching pad for O'Brien's intensively interconnective narrative strategy of metalepsis: hints are progressively dropped in advance of and in preparation for what has *already* transpired as the Reverend Mother's (and the novel's) traumatic "primal scene," which will be revealed, in a piece of structural symbolism, at the novel's meridian. Tapping Reverend Mother's overlapping memories of the anticipation and the aftermath of that life-altering event, these continuous auguries (one might say openings) of a secret past function as enigmatic signifiers in themselves, building a sense of suspenseful foreboding, with an increasingly sinful yet indefinitely sexual tenor. In this respect, the novel's many illegible foretokens replicate for the reader Reverend Mother's own traumatic experience of sexual initiation. And this, as we have observed, is precisely the original province of the enigmatic signifier.

We learn that Reverend Mother was "chilled" by a "shock which drove her to the purest form of life . . . hardened in all her defences against herself" (20); we learn that her vows "sealed up girlhood and its pain" and that she regarded the architecture of her new convent home with the "too emotional word 'bitterness'" (19, 12); we learn that a "blow" of "agonising pain" would "always leave her limping," and as a result, "ordinary life had lost a young woman of gifts and rippling sensibilities" (22); we learn that she "had been horrified at eighteen . . . hurled by dynamic shock into the wildest regions of austerity ever out of reach of all that beauty of human life that she had inordinately believed in . . . trained most delicately and lovingly in that belief by . . . its unwitting destroyer [her father]" (23); and we learn of conversations with her father that were inflected by "the irony of . . . the nun's locked secret" (31). Ultimately, our riddling path to the central crisis of Reverend Mother's youth merges with her own groping path of discovery as a girl. Upon learning of her father's impending death, Reverend Mother remembers the family leaving Cambridge under a cloud, the simultaneous break with her grandparents and the loss of the family's annuity, the odd disproportion in her parents' love for one another, and the sense that their marriage was "undertaken in darkness," her father falling "into some offence against society," living "in exile," and enduring other "small punishments" on that score (161).

Even as these anticipations gesture, however enigmatically, to the novel's deferred primal scene, they are interspersed with reflections and, more importantly, judgments on the young Helen Archer's reaction to that still unnamed, seemingly unspeakable event—adverse reflections and judgments, which, taken seriously, alter the dimensions of the traumatic event itself. We find that because of the incident her nunly vow of chastity was less a virtuous commitment than a "perverse seduction . . . needed at a moment of flight from life" (19); that her flight to the convent, driven by a need to "hate in blindness" and a desire for "vengeance in an unexplained cutting-off . . . was stupidity masquerading offensively before the good God" (23); that her initial, "stupid" if "understandable" response to the still unspoken offense left her regretting her own "cold, wild judgments, the silly self-defence and self-dramatisation of an ignorant girl" (21); and that, with a "belated mercy towards humanity in general," she is left respecting, however uncomfortably, "the courage required by the vulgar . . . to live" and "even . . . the courage of the outright sinner" (21).

"Father Would Like This Child"

The Reverend Mother's mentor, Mère-Générale, the head of the order, worries at her lieutenant's inability to realize her true spiritual potential— "saintliness"—owing to a fear "of love, even the love of God," a fear born of her traumatized response to that primal scene (26). Mère-Générale proceeds to instruct Helen, amid a discussion of her errant father, that "God is love, my daughter . . . and He is served by love. Don't take it on yourself to quarrel with that complicated fact" (29). In keeping with the enigmatic tack of the narrative, Mère-Générale's counsel can be read as a conventional directive to follow the mosaic commandment to honor one's parents, an equally conventional Christian precept to forgive those who trespass against us, or a more unauthorized exhortation to tolerance of a sexual episode about which, the text makes clear, she has no knowledge whatsoever. As Reverend Mother's internal response indicates, however, so far as her own case is concerned, honoring any one of those tenets implies embracing the other two anyway: "Yes, there was the rub. She had decided that He was equity, detachment, justice, purity—anything good that was not love. Anything good that was cold and had definition—of which love, it seemed, had none" (29).

Love, for Reverend Mother, is *the* enigmatic signifier, her indefinite "love" at once incorporating a sexual component in the name of the human and casting it out in the name of the divine, and, most crucially, never accommodating a final decision as to whether human love is primarily a pattern of divine love to be pursued or a rival of divine love to be eschewed. The undecidability of the latter question, underscored in the exchange with Mère-Generále and indeed throughout the novel, renders Helen's repudiation of her father in favor of her Father not just "stupid" and "hysterical" but self-contesting. (It is no accident that as she composes her final reconciliatory prayer—"Father, forgive me—I know not what I did"—"she did not know whether she addressed it to Heaven or to her earthly father"; 168.)

Thanks to the novel's dual track of ominous foreshadowing and recriminatory afterthoughts, the primal scene at which they converge expands to encompass not only the moment when Helen witnesses her father and his musician-protégé, Etienne, in the "embrace of love"—the phrase for which the book was banned in Ireland—but also the intense jealousy she felt almost immediately thereafter (165). If the tableau itself, filtered through Helen's internalized religious and social repugnance, explains the attitude she evinces toward homoerotics generally, as signaled in the metaleptic signs of her trauma, her overwhelming jealousy helps explain the inimical judgments she comes to render on those same homophobic attitudes.

Here we arrive at the innermost knot of the enigma of love that binds Reverend Mother in a state of affective paralysis. At first blush, it seems as if her sexual initiation supervenes in a brutal flash, in her vision of her father committing a most reprehended sexual act. But, in fact, she has long been implicated, unconsciously, in a likewise illicit if heteronormative sexual crush on her father: "She thought her father very beautiful. It always delighted her to come on the sight of him suddenly and realise, always with new pleasure, that he was different from other men, stronger and bigger, with curly, silky hair and eyes that shone like stars" (149). The phrase *delighted her to come on the sight of him suddenly* is clearly designed to chime with the primal scene, where she comes suddenly on the sight of her beautiful father, only to find he has another lover, of another gender, and her paternal cathexis surges forth in the more openly, if negatively, sexual form of jealousy. Young Helen so energetically recoils from homosexuality not because the "sight" of it has stained her innocence (as she imagines) but because that sight at once shatters and threatens to expose her unconscious oedipal fantasy. The spectacle breaches her psychic defenses concerning her relations with her father, giving her a glimpse, however fugitive, of the primal erotic charge that the enigmatic signifier at once holds and hides, in accordance with the dictates of the patriarchal family cell.

In demystifying the enigma of Helen's rapport with her father, the homosexual episode and her jealous reaction precipitate a new, more permanent enigma that molds her mature years, an enigma that goes to the paradoxically defining character of love itself, its lack of sure "definition" (31). The love to which she flies upon forsaking her father, her experience of divine love as purity, confesses itself to be allied with the parental-filial bond (in its commandment to honor one's father and mother, in its figuration as a Father, in its summons to its children) and even, in a developmental sense, to be modeled on that bond. The reason Helen continues, despite her great piety, to shrink from the very love she seeks, the reason she remains "afraid . . . even of the love of God," is that it has been, from the moment she conceives it, always already alloyed, not to say corrupted, by her sexually inflected love for her earthly father (26). In a profound affective paradox, she can flee to her heavenly Father only by way of a love imbued with or at least tinctured by a libidinous charge that is the illicit, "jealous" counterpart of the love from which she is fleeing: her earthly father's homosexual ardor. Considered in this light, Helen's violent flight to the convent looks somewhat familiar. Described by Helen herself as "the silly self-defense and self-dramatization of an ignorant girl" (21), defending against sexual awareness by way of histrionics, hovering somewhere between excessive and unwhole-some emotion, her self-exile from the "beauty of human life" begins to look a lot like an extended bout of *Schwärmerei*.

Returning to the opening scene, where *Schwärmerei* reigns supreme, we can now clearly see that Reverend Mother's distaste for the practice in no way reflects either the author's take thereon or her attitude toward the female homoeroticism that *Schwärmerei* might betoken. On the contrary, the dim view Helen takes is retroactively exposed and undercut as a species of unconscious reaction formation to her own hysterical displacement of a disreputable form of erotic attachment. Her jaundiced view of *Schwärmerei* may grow, as we shall see, from its perceived connection to homoeroticism, but its roots are elsewhere, in other forms of sexual transgression in which she would rather not feel incriminated. Her identification with Anna Mur-phy, in turn, goes beyond a like-minded seriousness; rather, she sees in this youngest of the schoolgirls her own prelapsarian past, when she believed that her bond with her father was one of almost intellectual purity, grounded in his tireless cultivation of her earnest aptitude for learning.

The next *Schwärmerei*-driven ritual, which occurs on the very evening when Eileen O'Doherty "had broken uncounted hearts," ratifies our profile of Reverend Mother's disposition toward these institutionalized bouts of sentimental effusion. If anything, the "Sunday marks" sessions, where each girl receives a weekly grade, are still more libidinally freighted than the veil ceremony: "some girls felt a delicious danger" in the event (69), "pretty girls became excitingly pretty in the brightened atmosphere," and some "might flaunt a flower . . . or jingle a forbidden bracelet. . . . Others had been worked upon by more restricted pleasures" (70). To heighten the mood of barely controlled exuberance on this occasion, Rosita Malone and Madeleine Anderson openly breach convent decorum by arriving late to the ceremony, partly dishabille, having spent their afternoon blissfully united in the shared scopic gratification of spying on Eileen O'Doherty, an erotic adventure they know will make them heroines: "She saw us once, and she only laughed . . . Oh my heart is breaking! I'm mad about her. I won't sleep a wink to-night . . . there never were such eyes in all the world" (74). In so doing, the girls unwittingly bring to crisis a rift between two strains of Irish Catholicism represented in the school: an earlier, earthier, yet more aristocratic variety represented by the lenient Mother Eugenia and a newer, nationalist, middle-class variant represented by the rigid Mother Mary Andrew. Whereas Mary

Andrew seeks to crush this public outbreak of schoolgirl passion as "foolish and disgusting" (74), Mother Eugenia pleads for the offenders because "within . . . 'civilised' limits [she] enjoyed the follies of *Schwärmerei*" (82). Reverend Mother is effectively called in as the ultimate, late-inning arbiter of the girls' cases, and in this role, the overriding of her present inclinations by her past troubles is, to say the least, instructive.

Despite Reverend Mother feeling so out of sympathy with modern nationalist Irish Catholicism that she has that very day written a request for transfer out of country, despite her considerable personal as well as ideological partiality for Mother Eugenia, and despite her private conviction that Eugenia's laissez-faire posture toward schoolgirl passion might, in the end, be the most practical, her own personal experience prevents her from endorsing the latter's jocular "indulgence" of *Schwärmerei*. The third-person narrator emphasizes Reverend Mother's resistance to any estimation of *Schwärmerei* as essentially harmless, let alone beneficial, in the following terse observation: "Reverend Mother did not like such jokes. . . . Moreover, she told herself as she shrank from the situation, that it was this easy stride with human nature, this random willingness to take psychological risks—indeed this happy blindness to them, which perhaps best commanded the dark places of segregated life. Nevertheless she could not endorse such naturalness—for she was afraid—for the young—of many natural things" (82–83). The most salient aspect of this passage for our purposes is Reverend Mother's new construction of *Schwärmerei* as something very much along the lines of the enigmatic signifier. She sees it as a phenomenon of psychic uncertainty ("psychological risks") running cover and giving license ("a happy blindness") to dimly apprehended homoerotic possibility, or, in Catholic parlance, occasions of sin ("the dark places of [gender-] segregated life"). That is to say, she recognizes Mother Eugenia's "civilized limits" as a kind of *cordon in-sanitaire*, where what we have seen as the secretly irreducible mixture of carnal and spiritual love receives open confirmation and affirmation: "After all," says Mother Eugenia, exculpating Rosita, "the beautiful beloved has only this morning renounced the world" (82).

Nevertheless, Reverend Mother's judgment on *Schwärmerei* does not go directly to its lesbian implications but percolates through her own traumatic sexual history. The phrase *happy blindness* bears patent if unconscious reference to her own ingenuous state before she had "come on the sight" of her father *in flagrante delicto*, and the parenthetical phrase qualifying her fears—*for the young*—just as palpably adverts to Anna Murphy, the young girl, whom Helen identifies with the intellectual cocoon of her own childhood. Most strikingly, Reverend Mother fears for Anna not unnatural things, the accepted social designation for homoeroticism—whether her father's overt acts or her charges' coded passions—but rather "many natural things." The single germane example of the "natural things" Reverend Mother fears is, of course, her own "natural" but incestuously tinged and therefore illicit father-love, once likewise sheltered in a "happy blindness," the loss of which led to a catastrophic "unexplained cutting-off" corresponding both to her entering the convent and celibacy and, symbolically, to Freud's classic account of the oedipal crisis that the primal scene precipitates.

In certain respects, this juxtaposition of infantile, juvenile, and adult perversity—male-male and female-female eroticism and homo- and heterosexuality—in Reverend Mother's unconscious thought processes typifies O'Brien's approach to representing sexual deviancy in general and her own presumed lesbianism in particular. Several critics have noted that novels such as *Mary Lavelle* and *As Splendor and Music* treat lesbianism as one of various forms of human love, all of which exist in an abrasive or competitive relationship with divine love and all of which are thus to be had only at an inescapable cost.[10] As we have endeavored to show, however, the difference here—what may be the distinctive quality of *The Land of Spices* in O'Brien's corpus—is that human passion subsists in a simulacral, supplementary, and even symbiotic relation to divine love as well as an abrasive and competitive one. Reverend Mother must, in consequence, reckon not just with "the price of passion," as Donoghue asserts, but also with sexual passion's positive virtue and necessity (1995, 182–83).

Reverend Mother learns this lesson in full from the very girl, Anna Murphy, whom she had mistakenly sought to safeguard from it. In order to steer her young ward more firmly away from the suggestive blandishments of *Schwärmerei* to the more respectable pleasure that Anna evidently takes in poetry, Reverend Mother concludes the evening's festivities by asking her to recite a verse. The poem Anna selects, "Peace," just happens to be one taught to young Helen herself by her father, thus bringing to Helen's consciousness Anna's developing role as her juvenile surrogate. In Anna's voice, Reverend Mother "heard her own nights of uncomforted sobbing, and now felt once more . . . the dark convulsions and intersections of the path that lead innocence to knowledge and desire and dream to reality. She saw this baby in herself, herself in those tear-wet eyes" (K. O'Brien 1988, 86). But it is in the words through which the voice reverberates that "she heard a storm break in her hollow heart . . . from past and future," to swell "the strong, irrational assault of sorrow, demanding to be faced" (85–86). These words are "full of echoes and prefiguring . . . hints and symbolisings" (86), just like the metaleptic narrative of her life, and like that narrative, they insist on the stubborn imbrications of the bodily and the sacral, the sexual and the spiritual. They are the words of Henry Vaughn, whose metaphysical verse, with that of Richard Crashaw and of course George Herbert (from whose poem the novel's title derives), aims at yoking in single images or tropes the human and divine manifestations of love, agape and eros, the passion of the Christ and the less elevated passions of humankind, without in any way eliding the discordance between them.

Helen's father devoted his life to the metaphysical poets, motivated by a cognate aspiration "to reward his own pleasure and indulge it" with "the gleam of the spirit, the hint of grace" (86).[11] He emerges, accordingly, not just as the figure or memory with whom Helen is to make amends but a figure or persona of the sort of (necessarily imperfect) reconciliation to be achieved—that is, a partial, still dissonant composition of her tainted human love for him and the rarefied divine love she sought in forsaking him. Such a reconciliation, then, entails a similarly conflicted or ambivalent iden- tification, requiring a new tolerance for her own frailties no less than his: "I am after all at once his daughter . . . and a victim of his—his personality. Therefore, from two angles, coward though I am, I know of sensitiveness, of what it can do and what it can suffer" (88). At this, the climax of her emo- tional epiphany, the ills of the sentimentality Mother Eugenia approves are no match for the insensitivity of "Mother Mary Andrew's voice" (88). Rever- end Mother abruptly decides to stay at her post in order to protect Anna— not from the likes of her father, from the code of *Schwärmerei*, or from the dangers they incarnate, but from the new, puritanical Irish Catholicism that would be the scourge of all such *sensitive* things.

Given the role that metaphysical poetry plays in orchestrating the cli- mactic resolution, personal and conceptual, of Helen's story, the decision by O'Brien to name the novel after a phrase in Herbert's poem "Prayer" would seem to herald an aesthetic agenda on her part. This seems all the more true since this poem, which Helen intones over the news of her father's death, so pointedly conjoins earthly delights and heavenly promises in a series of figural substitutions. The "land of spices" itself is both a metaphor of the titular "Prayer" and a metonym of sensual intoxication, tropes riven together along a chain of iterative association. O'Brien may thus be seen to celebrate and to emulate an art that not only traffics in but sublimates the enigmatic signifier, promoting the undecidability of an erotic implication to the undecidable proximity that implication might bear to spiritual transcendence.

For this reason, it is suggestive that before Anna Murphy delivers her inspiring recitation, she registers her first visible susceptibility to indefinitely eroticized attraction, a tiny crack in the unreceptivity she previously showed to *Schwärmerei*: "She was glad to see Letitia Doyle arrayed in the broad blue sash of the Seniors. They were lovely stiff sashes. Anna longed to run her hand up and down Letitia's" (83). Are we to read this linkage of the aesthetically pleasing and the erotically stirring as lending to Anna's voice the power it shortly exhibits to effect in Revered Mother an emotionally transformative satori? Is this convergence of aesthetic and erotic desire in Anna's perception of Letitia Doyle's sash an analogue of the feeling Helen's father bore for the violin maestro Etienne? And is it this unification of sex and sensibility that enables Anna to be father not to the man but to the nun, as the cherished, distinctly homoerotic Oxonian aestheticism Helen and her father once shared revives in Helen's sudden, harkening awareness that "Father would like this child" (86)?[12] With all of the contingencies at work, these questions remain too difficult to answer; they leave us by design in a state of brightening uncertainty.

However, two things are clear. First, art constitutes a privileged arena for mediating between the different planes of existential desire in the novel, for dignifying the sexual and materializing the supernal. Second, in limning Anna as her fictive alter ego, her "portrait of the artist," O'Brien repeatedly marks her as an extraordinarily cerebral creature, more interested in books than people; yet she is careful to build faint but discernible moments of same-sex eroticism into Anna's time at *Saint-Famille*. What is more, by way of underscoring the importance of these lesbian impulses to her specifically aesthetic development, O'Brien places the moments of their appearance in illustrative parallelism with incidents from Joyce's *A Portrait of the Artist*, the model text for Anna's *kunstlerroman* narrative. In one such example, Anna is unjustly denied an academic honor by the cruel Mother Mary Andrew, and when she complains of this malignant treatment, the Mother Scholastic physically abuses her for doing so. The episode unquestionably invokes the famous pandying scene in *A Portrait of the Artist*, wherein Stephen is unjustly and painfully chastised by Father Dolan despite an academic performance that has elevated him to class leader. Stephen's punishment is part of a terrorizing disciplinary sweep of Clongowes in the wake of a homosexual scandal, precipitated by what is perhaps literature's most famous enigmatic signifier, *smugging*, among the upper lines. Anna's punishment, conversely, leads to her being comforted in her bed by a girl, Molly Redmond, whom she has long admired and in a fashion that Mother Mary Andrew, upon discovering the girls together, deems "immodesty" (113). While by no means an overtly lesbian encounter, this is the only scene in the novel pushing a still indefinite homoeroticism to the point of physical contact, the sort of indefinite but forbidden contact that might be considered the female equivalent of the "smugging" activity at Clongowes Wood. In a dramatic irony pertinent to Reverend Mother's crowning reconciliation, her decision to stay at *Saint-Famille* in order to shelter Anna from Mother Mary Andrew (a pledge she carries out forcefully after this incident) runs counter to her earlier hopes of screening Anna from the kind of pathological sexuality that her own father, in her eyes, personified.

What Reverend Mother winds up nurturing in Anna is something along the lines of the aesthetic consciousness that her father had once implanted in her. The correlation of that consciousness with sexual desire finds further confirmation in our penultimate view of Anna, touched on earlier, in her lakeside tête-à-tête with the beautiful Pilar, Anna's version of Stephen Dedalus's seaside muse. In the "birdgirl," Stephen stumbles on a figure who appears to him a synthesis of bathing beauty and Madonna, hence an emblem of an aesthetic vocation dedicated to "transmuting the daily bread of experience into the radiant body of everliving life" (Joyce 1992b, 240). Under Anna's searching eyes, Pilar likewise transforms into an eroto-spiritual "motive in art" (K. O'Brien 1988, 286). It is, for O'Brien, the motive *of* art to address and transfigure the sexual dimension of life, and she accomplishes the feat so effectively in this interlude that her readers have, as we have noted, either read past the lesbian "gravity" of the scene altogether or reduced it to "subtext" (a literary closet of the reader's own making, wherein he or she deposits imperfectly legible effects of the text itself). Through free indirect discourse, O'Brien positions her alter ego as growing into the principle on which her own literary method is based: enigmatic signifiers mobilize the alembic power of art, enabling it to rarefy without concealing the erotic energies on which it draws. If this is not a strictly lesbian homoerotic principle, it must be accounted a queer one. As Anna "stared at [Pilar] in wonder," as she realizes "her lustrous potentiality" and feels it to be "a long-awaited, blessed gift," as she follows these sentiments by acknowledging her "secret need [for a] passage of beauty," the erotic intent is by no means nugatory, nor is it hidden somewhere beneath the surface (287). Rather, it gathers in the accumulated feeling that the signifiers convey and produce in only loose association with their semiotic values. This is precisely how the "prayer" in Herbert's poem passes through a series of evocative but counterintuitive juxtapositions, including "the land of spices," to become in the end "something understood." O'Brien would have *The Land of Spices* understood in related fashion, not as a loving elaboration of the enigma of prayer but as a kind of prayer on the enigma of love.

Envoi

Anna Murphy renews within Reverend Mother numinous words and meanings that she has long known but that had lain dormant for decades, becoming Reverend Mother's symbolic parent by rejuvenating erotic potentialities long disavowed. By the end of the novel, Reverend Mother returns the favor, becoming symbolic parent to the child who begot her. One key aspect of her spiritual integrity that remains consistent throughout the novel inheres in her extreme discretion: the good she does, she does altogether invisibly, accepting and also quietly exploiting the nearly universal misconstructions that are placed on her motives owing to her English accent and seemingly distant persona.

Like the novel she defines, and like the author who created her, Reverend Mother is content to be presently misunderstood in the name of a more equitable future. A transformed future, however, cannot be brought about altogether in silence. Just as *The Land of Spices*'s textual web of signification concerning homoerotic love must hinge on one unmistakable instance, in Helen's father's explicitly sexual coupling with Etienne, so just once in the course of the novel must the Reverend Mother visibly act on Anna's behalf, using her clout openly to ensure that Anna can accept the university scholarship to which her abilities entitle her.

Reverend Mother is thus both the beneficiary and the begetter of her unknowing protégé, Anna Murphy, a queer, female intellectual traveler into a futurity the Reverend Mother will never know, coming of age at a most inauspicious moment in the history of Irish Catholicism. And with her, into this future she carries an enigmatic message initially transmitted to and subsequently received from Reverend Mother, herself the bearer of an originary seduction bearing the passionate energies of an English, Protestant, male homophilic lineage.

Kate O'Brien, like her Reverend Mother, elected to work, in a sense, invisibly, so as to nurture the next generation. In *The Land of Spices*, she crafted a beautifully wrought, shimmering account of one educator's unspoken self-appointment as a queer ally who quietly ensures for the next generation that of which her own beloved father was bereft. Paradoxically, however, in the novel it is only by means of the voice of the queer child that the Reverend Mother is able to understand herself, to make sense of the words and affect that she has, unwittingly, hoarded away safely from her childhood, uninterrogated, unsullied. In *The Land of Spices* itself, O'Brien likewise hoarded her own erotic truths, which she encoded fulsomely, exhaustively, and emphatically, in terms that themselves invoked the time-honored and otherwise inexplicable misapprehension of the novel's import by the scholarly community. Due to the welcome, well-advanced dismantling of the Irish lesbian closet, for which O'Brien deserves some credit and gratitude, it is now possible to set aside this residual form of open secrecy.

NOTES

1. As Douglas (1966) has it, "where there is dirt, there is a system" (36). Through such systems, she contends, all societies systematically transform myriad sensory stimuli that would otherwise register as an endless onslaught of sensory white noise and static into a stable order of recognizable shapes; and "dirt" is the by-product of this ongoing, social conversion of "sound and fury" into a legible, predictable world. Dirt, Douglas argues, or "matter out of place," is thus the category that all social orders must have in order to account for and ritually manage anomalies that threaten to disrupt their social patterning (36). Crucial to the maintenance of every culture's epistemological system are clear lines of social hierarchization and demarcation that "provide a frame for experience" and make statements about the home (65). Pollution thus occurs when such boundaries are transgressed or rendered contradictory (126).

2. In Cathy Caruth's 2001 interview with Jean Laplanche (published in 2014), Laplanche places great emphasis on the strangeness of the other who implants the originary enigmatic message, and the strangeness of the enigmatic message itself. He explains the spatial dimension of the enigmatic signifier in relation to "a biological model," according to which "an organism has an envelope, and something happens inside, which is homeostatic, and something is outside," emphasizing that in the enigmatic encounter what is meant by strangeness or extraneity is "something very much more 'outside' than [that implied by something external to the

biological organism's homeostative envelope]" (Caruth 2014, 25). Laplanche argues that the "reality of the other" in the enigmatic encounter is "absolutely bound to his strangeness" and that, in fact, for "the human being, the baby," the messages of the other are enigmatic "because those messages are strange to themselves" (27).

3. Stephen's terms notably prefigure those that Leopold Bloom in Barney Kiernan's pub makes in self-defense following the similar charge of pollution laid by the Citizen, who accuses foreigners like Bloom of "filling the country with bugs" (Joyce 1986, 12.1141–42).

4. We allude here to D. P. Moran's famous essay "The Battle of Two Civilizations" (1901) to suggest that there were decisive fissures in late/postcolonial Ireland other than the Pale versus the Gael.

5. In *Poets and Dreamers*, Lady Gregory's insightful commentary on the Biddy Earley stories that she collected points to the competition these stories frequently engender between the priest and Biddy Earley (1974), betokening a long-standing traditional belief that private troubles the church cannot or will not treat may and should be handled by traditional practitioners, using traditional means. In *The Burning of Bridget Cleary*, Bourke (2001) describes this established movement between the church and folk practitioners as it occurred in an increasingly unstable and uneven modernity.

6. From Limerick to Dublin to London, to the Basque Country in the north of Spain, and then, in her one move west, back to Manchester.

7. For Joyce's strategies of homoerotic disclosure, see Joseph Valente (1997, 47–76) and (2006, 124–48).

8. For more on O'Brien's debt to Joyce, see Owen Weekes (1990, 122–23); Legarreta Mentxaka (2011, 105).

9. See, in particular, *Unnatural Death* (1938) and *Gaudy Night* (2016).

10. See Donoghue (1993, 50–53; 1995, 182–86); Coughlan (1993, 74–77); Dalsimer (1990, 112–15); Tighe-Mooney (2008, 125–37).

11. Anna asks Reverend Mother, in an instance of symbolic irony, "Did your father compose it?" (87).

12. We should note the subliminal echoes here of the homophonic phrase "father *is* like this child," because Reverend Mother discovers the phrase "Father would like this child" oddly floating on the "quiet surface of her mind" immediately after Anna's "little voice" unleashes "a storm [breaking] in her hollow heart, which was not her own storm, for that was over, but was rather an assault, a sentimental menacing appeal, from past and future and from nowhere, from the child's voice and from her father's." Thus, we have here a textbook reactivation of the enigmatic signifier, an internal "storm" experienced as an external "assault," as from the past, the future, and from nowhere, and as only from the child, and from her father, and in her stalwart insistence that whatever Anna's little voice has broken open within her, it was "not her own storm, for that was over" (86).

3

COUNTRY GIRL

Groomed, Seduced, and Abandoned

No NOVEL SINCE *ULYSSES*, IT seems fair to say, occasioned a greater or more sanctimonious paroxysm of Irish scandalmongering than Edna O'Brien's debut, *The Country Girls* (1960).

Written in a creative white heat over the course of her first three weeks of self-imposed, Joycean exile, *The Country Girls* incurred the wrath of church, state, and society in Ireland. Both the archbishop of Dublin and the minister of culture declared O'Brien a "smear on Irish womanhood" (Kernowski 2014, xviii). The pastor of O'Brien's local parish summoned his congregants to bring their copies of the book to the church grounds for a ceremonial burning (Lawson 2014, 75), O'Brien's own mother thought the book a "most terrible disgrace" (Guttridge 2014, 60), the local postmistress told O'Brien's father that she "should have been kicked naked through the town" (Guttridge 2014, 60), women were said to have fainted over the book's contents (Kernowski 2014, xviii), and all of this occurred immediately after its appearance, since in short order it was banned throughout O'Brien's native land.[1] In sum, it touched a nerve. That much is obvious. The question of why the novel incited such outrage is less evident, we would argue, than it might appear. Was the source of self-righteous agitation the frankness of O'Brien's language, which her mother took to "inking out" of her own copy (Lawson 2014, 75)? Was it the sexualized expression of rebelliousness, amounting at certain points to sacrilege, that the protagonist, Caithleen, and her fair-weather friend, Baba, periodically vented? Was it the disreputable portraits

Figure 3.1. "Ann Lovett: Death at the grotto." Granard grotto of the Virgin Mary. *Irish Times,* January 31, 2004, article commemorating the twentieth anniversary of Ann Lovett's death. Photo credit: Brenda Fitzsimons/courtesy of the *Irish Times.* © *Irish Times.*

of the families and townspeople involved in the girls' upbringing (those characters that Philip Roth denominated the "rural Dubliners"),[2] or the cruel, tyrannical picture of the nuns in charge of their convent education? Was it the vision of Irish Catholic patriarchy as a backward regime consumed with the subjugation of women? Or was it merely the sexual errancy, in thought and deed, exhibited by Caithleen and Baba as a signature feature of their personal *bildung*? Was it the accumulated effect of all these goads to the pietistic sensibility of post–de Valera Ireland? Or was such gross offense taken on still other grounds that have remained obscure?

Without discounting any of the listed rationales, we propose a more decisive if less conscious point of sensitivity (or perhaps more decisive *because* a less conscious point of sensitivity) animating the initial, disproportionately censorious response to O'Brien's maiden novel. In our view, *The Country Girls* hints subliminally but powerfully at the endemic operation of sexual or sexualized abuse in the youthful development of rural or small-town Irish girls—a traumatizing abuse sufficiently endemic, sufficiently interwoven in

the fabric of everyday social life, to pass more or less unremarked by participants and bystanders alike.

Published at the chronological midpoint of our survey, *The Country
Girls* constitutes a pivotal moment in the gathering canon of child-abuse
literature, when its sexual dimension was becoming available for recognition yet going largely unrecognized nevertheless. The novel does not,
accordingly, represent scandal so much as the scandalous, that which would
become scandal. In this sense, *The Country Girls gives* scandal and, in so
doing, became a scandal unto itself.

FATHER—THE CRUX OF HER DILEMMA

Taken from Samuel Beckett's *Molloy*, the epigraph to Edna O'Brien's memoir, *Mother Ireland*, begins, "Let us say, before I go any further, that I forgive nobody" (Roth 2014, 41). Addressing O'Brien's proud irreconcilability,
Philip Roth queried her in an interview, "Who is the most unforgiven creature in your imagination?" "Until the time of his death [1983]," O'Brien
replied, "it was my father," and she goes on to cite "his anger, his sexuality, his
rapaciousness" as the grounds for her reproach (Roth 2014, 41). The loosely
biographical tenor of *The Country Girls*, acknowledged by O'Brien herself,
leaves little doubt of her intention to pass the baton of unpardonability from
her own father to the father of her fictive alter ego, Caithleen Brady.[3] As the
critic Peggy O'Brien contends, Mr. Brady, "perceived as sexually rapacious
and perpetually absent" (1987, 485), is a projection of the original father
figure—in his savagery, his intemperance, and his calamitous fecklessness.

The various specimens of Mr. Brady's domestic violence are an ongoing source of childhood trauma, taken from O'Brien's prodigious memory
and rendered in fictional form.[4] But thus translated, they are not, as Elizabeth Weston holds, "a straightforward instance of trauma" (2010, 85). To the
contrary, the effects of Mr. Brady's manifold paternal malfeasance are profoundly traumatic insofar as they are not straightforward but compound,
pervasive, and mutually reinforcing. Full weight needs be given to Baba's
summary assessment of Caithleen's fate in the epilogue to the *Trilogy*, the
heading to this section: "Father—the crux of her dilemma" (E. O'Brien
1986, 531). Caithleen's father represents the crux of her dilemma in the sense
of being the essential traumatic core or hub of all of her subsequent travails,
but he does so because he is also the crux of her dilemma in the sense of

being the point at which it divides and redoubles, exists crosswise with itself. Father is "the crux of Caithleen's dilemma" in that her troubles, leading to her untimely death, arise primarily from the chiasmatic structure of the trauma he inflicts.

Evidence of the split and intersecting impetus of her traumatic relation to Mr. Brady presents itself from the very beginning of *The Country Girls*. The novel opens with Caithleen awakening abruptly, her heart "beating faster," in a panic that her delinquent father had once again "not come home" (1960, 5). Yet the anxiety gripping her in the hour before dawn is, if anything, exceeded later that day by her fear at the prospect, and then the reality, of his homecoming, which he validates with "a punch under the chin so that my two rows of teeth chattered together" (33). The establishing framework of the novel thus positions Caithleen in a terrorized double bind: she quakes in oscillating if unequal measure at her father's habitual truancy and his habitual violence, or what Peggy O'Brien calls his rapaciousness and his perpetual absence. Caithleen is rattled to sleeplessness by his disappearances and panicked to paralysis at his reappearances. By the same token, turning matters around, Caithleen is paradoxically invested in both his staying away and his coming home (being stricken at his visitation and afraid of his abandonment). She regrets her father's prolonged absence as well as his overbearing presence, even though vicious and to her mind lethal assaults on herself and her mother attend the latter. No model of "straightforward" trauma can readily explain Caithleen's psychomachia on this score, her conflicting desire for her father to be and not to be away from her altogether.

The extended dynamics of Laplanche's general theory of seduction can help us understand the thorny crux of Caithleen's paternal dilemma. As noted in our discussion of O'Brien's literary hero, James Joyce, the general theory of seduction holds that parental figures bring their unconscious stirrings—desires, cathexis, transferences—to bear on their children in enigmatic signifiers carrying ambiguous psychic messages. In their highly charged indeterminacy (and the indeterminacy of their charge), these enigmatic signifiers elicit the nascent libidinal fantasies of the child, inducing thereby a shock of traumatic jouissance.

Retroactively forbidden—the primal seduction always rings twice— this overload of enjoyment serves to institute the *spaltung*, or fissure, between conscious and unconscious mentation fundamental to subjectivity as such (Laplanche 1997, 661). This primal mode of seduction cannot be reduced to the fantasy of the child since, as Slavoj Žižek observes, it "does refer to a traumatic encounter with the Other's enigmatic message." But neither can it be located in some "actual interaction" between child and adult, since that very message depends entirely for its meaning and its effect, its existence qua message, on the fantasy frame determining the child's reception (Žižek 2009, 20). The primal seduction, then, emerges as a virtual phenomenon at the doubly inscribed interface between a real and an imagined encounter, where the encounter activates the phantasmatic staging that actualizes the encounter, where the encounter is vertiginously the effect of its own cause. Put another way, the primal seduction is simultaneously an intrusion of adult sexuality as if from within the psychic interiority of the child *and* a staging of an endogenous fantasy emanating paradoxically from without.

Pedophilic child abuse draws upon and exploits this primal seductive scenario, rehearsing its basic elements along more deliberate, predatory, and explicitly genitalized lines. In so doing, even as such abuse maintains a degree of dialogical uncertainty necessary to the effect of seduction, it shifts the epicenter of the encounter away from that interface where the real and the imagined, external event and interior fantasy, are mutually constitutive, and toward the former dimension, into the parameters of an "actual interaction." As such, it brings the now taboo elements of the original scenario of seduction and the child's own subliminal investment therein to the brink of their awareness. That is, it threatens to breach the conscious/unconscious barrier that the undecidable contours of the original seduction worked in part to establish. The libidinal energies that the child first experienced as a part of his or her subject formation are tapped and evoked only to be turned against that now formed subject, to his or her undoing. Traumatic jouissance, wherein shock and disturbance pervade an economy of surplus pleasure, turns into full-fledged sexual trauma, wherein erotic pulsions and attachments, retroactively tainted, are subsumed within an economy of violent psychic mortification. It is precisely owing to the metonymical displacement of primal seduction in child sexual abuse that the attempt to remedy the psychic wounds of the latter, to disentangle its traumatic violence from the formative traumatic jouissance, so often leads to a repetitive cycle of abuse, specifically the self-injurious pursuit of sexualized occasions of overwhelming distress.

But the sexual and the violent complements of child abuse can also unfold in reverse order, as they do in *The Country Girls*, to its distinction among Irish novels taking up this theme. Given that a sexual assault on a child, inflicted by a parental figure or surrogate, necessarily evokes the scenario of primal seduction and thereby induces a traumatized response in its victim, a physical assault on a child inflicted by a punitive parental figure structurally implicated in that primal seduction will inevitably evoke that scenario as well—that is, it will resonate erotically at the unconscious level and induce a sexualized response. As Freud's famous essay "A Child Is Being Beaten" (1963) leads one to infer, parentally administered corporeal discipline cannot entirely avoid sexual, potentially sadomasochistic implications. Child victims subject to extreme, overtly sadomasochistic encounters with parental violence are often pressed into a converse abusive cycle: the attempt to repair the psychic wound or damage suffered in childhood leads to its repetition, in a self-punishing pursuit of traumatic occasions of sexual attachment and excitement.[5]

Caithleen's psychosexual predicament or "dilemma" in *The Country Girls* follows just this latter itinerary, which helps explain her otherwise baffling sense of dread at what might seem the liberating incidence of her abusive father's perennial defections. Mr. Brady himself betrays a subliminal awareness of the eroticized thrust of his own brutality. On his initial return home, when he "chattered" his daughter's teeth with his fist, he proceeded to rebuke her as follows: "Always avoiding me. Always avoiding your father. You little s—. Where's your mother or I'll kick the pants off you" (33).[6] His verbal formulation oddly yet aptly combines a conscious disciplinary idiom—"I'll give you a swift kick in the pants"—with a less customary view to forcible denuding—"I'll take the pants off you." That is to say, Caithleen's father threatens a method of chastisement that will leave her uncovered and exposed, an eroticized spectacle, even, implicitly, an available and defenseless sex object. His introductory complaint, that she is always avoiding him, bespeaks a frustrated desire for proximity that, in context, carries a libidinal tinge. Caithleen's reaction to her father's ambiguous message is answerably bifold as well. She calls for her friend, Baba, but not upon being punched, only after her father threatens to kick her pants off. Yet she claims to have done so strictly to protect herself from her father's physical brutality, not from any attack on her modesty. In a similar manner, we can see in Caithleen's dread at her father's presence a conscious reaction to the onset of his savage, preemptory discipline, and in her anxiety at his absence an unconscious reaction to eroticized destitution.

After her mother's enigmatic disappearance—a source of sexualized trauma unto itself—and as Caithleen prepares to leave for convent school, she once again has occasion to be "avoiding [her] father." Only this time, the libidinal tincture in Mr. Brady's frustrated desire for his daughter's recognition or attachment runs a little deeper. His advances shift from the confrontational to the solicitous: "'Don't forget your poor father,' he said. He put out his arm and tried to draw me over onto his knee, but I *pretended not to know what he was doing* and ran off to the yard to call Hickey for his tea" (56; emphasis added). Mr. Brady's overture might be classified as undecidably amorous. Is it an invitation to an innocent embrace? An index of a murkier, even forbidden complex of feelings? A prelude to something approaching molestation, or even a conscription of Caithleen as a substitute, symbolic or otherwise, for her deceased mother? Caithleen's reading of her father's tender is correspondingly indefinite. She is sufficiently sensible of something untoward to be wary and uncomfortable, but what she knows and pretends not to know does not coalesce into a concrete, or concretely erotic, surmise. Her father's movement insinuates without signifying, admits without requiring, a sexual interpretation. This is to say, the encounter evokes for Caithleen the original scenario of enigmatic seduction, even partakes of that scenario retroactively, but does not crack the repressive lock that protects her from any conscious memory thereof.

The incident thus takes its place as the most prominent of the routinely equivocal inklings of an errant, furtive sexual energy percolating in the distressed Brady household—for example, Mrs. Brady's monitoring of the groundskeeper Hickey's filthy nighttime emissions; sounds from the parental bedroom, such as the cracking of Mr. Brady's knees, overheard from an out-of-order bathroom serving as an impromptu whispering gallery; the moans, coughs, rustles in bed, and screams of Caithleen's mother; and Hickey's sly wink and commentary, as when he disrupts the "very close" embrace of Caithleen and her mother with the words "Old mammypalaver" (8). Indeed, the casualness of Caithleen's report on her father's attempt to corral her betokens a likewise routine occurrence, the implicit erotic motives of which leave but a vague, uncertain impression on the surface of her mind, while depositing themselves deep in her unconscious.

Mr. Brady here initiates his solicitation of Caithleen with the same appeal to filial devotion with which he prefaces his teeth-rattling blow to her jaw. The rhetorical iteration not only signals a psychic connection between his physical brutality and his claim on her affection; it intimates that paternal violence might be his defense against what Lacan calls *"père-version"* (1997a, 167). In a bookended scene, his response to her expulsion from the same convent school betrays a cognate form of psychic projection. He calls her a "filthy little—,"and then, upon hearing her "vehemently" rancorous rebuff ("I hate you"), he "struck [her] a terrific blow," blaring, in an unwitting double entendre, "I'll do what I like to her" (117). Since Caithleen surely knows the sort of violent retribution her scornful back talk must incur—she has experienced this brand of corporeal punishment over and again—one must infer an unconscious masochism that also "likes" what he'll "do to her," even as Caithleen her-"self," Caithleen in her ego identity, "hates it" and him. Such is the wrench that child abuse throws into the desiring machinery of its victims.

In her landmark study, *Trauma: A Genealogy*, Ruth Leys (2000) contends that "from the moment of its invention, the concept of trauma [has] been balancing uneasily—indeed veering uncontrollably—between two ideas, theories, or paradigms":

1. A mimetic theory, which holds that "because the victim cannot recall the original traumatogenic event, she is fated to act it out or in other ways to imitate it." What is more, because the traumatic occurrence undergoes psychic dissociation, it never fully enters the victim's "ordinary memory"; she cannot cleanly distinguish the traumatic locus from the traumatic source, her own agency from that of the other, what has supervened from without and what has emerged from within. In the very state of suffering a trauma, on this paradigm, the victim identifies with and internalizes the cause. As a result, any attempt to repair the original insult issues in a displaced repetition thereof.

2. An anti-mimetic theory. Here the victim is "essentially aloof" from the traumatic experience and "remains a spectator of the traumatic scene, which she can therefore see and represent to herself and others." Under this model, the victim apprehends the violence suffered "as purely and simply an assault from without"; a "purely external event" thus befalls, without substantially compromising, "a fully constituted subject." Ordinary memory continues to function in the recovery of the event, and since, as Freud contends, we repeat instead of remembering, no imitative acting out need transpire (Freud 1966, 273–77; Leys 2000, 298–300).

As we have seen so far, however, the mimetic and anti-mimetic paradigms are not mutually exclusive in *The Country Girls*. To the contrary, in what may be the novel's signal contribution to Irish trauma narrative, they operate simultaneously at different levels of the same ordeal. Mr. Brady's physical aggression toward his daughter, the overt concussive attacks, plainly fall under the anti-mimetic reading. Caithleen bears witness to the violence she suffers; she processes it as "a purely external event." She can recall the particulars without dissociation, and she well understands these experiences as grounds for "always avoiding" him. The sexual valences of her father's attacks, by contrast, affect Caithleen along the lines of the mimetic paradigm. In this respect, the barrier to "ordinary memory" of the primal seduction on which they draw remains prohibitive. As indicated in that later groping scene, Caithleen cannot recall the traumatogenic event that lends her father's behavior toward her its sexual import.

Because it is the master enigmatic signifier of subject formation, the scene of primal seduction is always and necessarily occulted by a likewise primary, or foundational, repression. At the same time, the impulse to identify with and internalize the traumatic cause or agency is enjoined by the very structure of primal seduction, which confounds self and other, endogenous fantasy and intrusive libidinal communique. Caithleen is doubly fated, therefore, to imitate the toxic jouissance that her father catalyzes, doubly bound to pursue it self-reflexively—by repeating, in various guises, the scenario and the dynamics of its coming to be.

Because Caithleen can bring to conscious recognition neither the erotic dimension of her filial connection nor its lateral reemergence in her father's alternating bouts of belligerence and dereliction, the underlying connection between the two likewise remains under the ban of repression, whence it continues to fuel and shape the metaphoric repetition and metonymic displacements of her acting out. A cardinal instance of these psychic operations is manifest in her ongoing fear of her mother's death at her father's hand. To be sure, her worry is not unrealistic, given his volcanic temper, but it also speaks to her reflexive association of the traumatically habitual eruption of parental violence and the seminally traumatic intrusion of parental sexuality. The anxiety she feels for her mother's vulnerability dovetails with her own dread of paternal violence, and with the unerring reverse logic of unconscious thought, she projects the sexual element of that dread back onto her parents' relationship.

Consider the image of the mysteriously vanished Mrs. Brady that Caithleen invokes as a reason for "avoiding" her bedridden father and disregarding his likely wishes: "I didn't go up to see him, though I knew he would have liked a cup of tea. I hated going into his room when he was in bed. I could see Mama on the pillow beside him. Reluctant and frightened as if something terrible were being done to her. She used to sleep with me as often as she could and only went across to his room when he made her" (58–59). In this mental tableau, the intimations of battery alternately infect and override, on different planes of recall, the conjugal mysteries of the parental marriage bed. At the level of Caithleen's ordinary memory, the threat of bodily assault to her mother predominates, relegating the conjugal implications of the scene to the background. The image of Mama "frightened" models Caithleen's own fear of continued physical abuse, and Mama's ensuing retreat to Caithleen's bed ("to sleep with me") binds them in a partnership of terror and mutual protectiveness, which Caithleen's present refusal to visit her father recalls and, in a sense, honors. At the level of Caithleen's dissociated memory, however, founded as it is on the scene of primal seduction, violence may be seen as a concomitant of the conjugal mystery, as part and parcel of sexuality itself. Here, the image of Mama "reluctant" models Caithleen's reluctance to attend her father abed, while eliding the sexual grounds of such reluctance. As Caithleen remembers, her mother's retreat to her bed, and hence their partnership, did not extend to those evenings when "he made her [mother]" go to him, a euphemism for marital rape. In other words, the mother-daughter terror-bond did not extend from spousal or filial abuse, of which Caithleen bears a knowledge both conscious and intimate, to sexual abuse, of which Caithleen's knowledge is indirect and shrouded in deniability. (In this respect her apprehension of her mother's plight is nearly akin to her subliminal sense of the erotic inflection of her own abuse.) Thus, Mrs. Brady functions in Caithleen's memory as her double, not only in the metaphorical sense, as a mirror image of her own family-centered trauma, but also metonymically, as a vehicle or objective correlative of the scission to which that trauma was subject (mimetic/anti-mimetic, conscious/unconscious, physical/sexual).[7]

The split between the mimetic and anti-mimetic strains of Caithleen's filial trauma, between what she is able "to represent to herself and others" and what she cannot, translates into a second breach, this one within the anti-mimetic register itself: an epistemic divide opens between the traumatogenic event, her father's violence, reliably witnessed by Caithleen, and the longer-term effects thereof, which are honeycombed with traces, residual and abusively renewed, of a traumatic jouissance that she cannot access. While she never loses sight of the concussions, she cannot, as a structural matter, gain insight into the repercussions. Absorbed into the volatile brew of her unconscious promptings, the aversiveness of battery by a cruelly super-egoic father, however delegitimized, lends a comprehensive and stultifying ambivalence to the course of Caithleen's future sexual adherences, which are the main narrative focus of the novel.

Ticklish Desire

The critical consensus on Caithleen's pubescent/postpubescent amorous history has been that she longs for and fantasizes about romance, protection, and economic security in an effort to restore all that her father's deprivations and her mother's untimely death have cost her, both emotionally and materially. Peggy O'Brien holds that a "morbid" Caithleen "yearns for romantic fulfillment" (1987, 484). Lynette Carpenter finds this "need to fulfill her romantic ideals" to be combined with and complicated by a "competition for economic security" with Baba (1986, 265). Tasmin Hargreaves sees Caithleen "desperately attempting to find safety and wholeness" (1988, 291). According to Elizabeth Weston, finally, Caithleen follows an "imagined arc of romance narrative," which provides but "momentary escape" from her traumatic suffering before thoroughly exacerbating it by "inculcating submission to a problematic, socially constructed image of femininity" (2010, 85, 93).

On each of these readings, Caithleen exhibits what we might call white-knight syndrome: she seeks older men, father substitutes, better versions of her father, to rescue her from the dilemma he has created. Not surprisingly, this approach allies closely with the feminist critique of O'Brien for creating women "obsessed with and victimized by their relationships with men" (Cahalan 1995, 61). Caithleen has been understood to hazard, even invite, the exploitation that befalls her. But in the process, her misfortune appears a byproduct of gendered misrecognition, an attachment to a romance script fettering her to a certain image of femininity, as opposed to proceeding from the vicissitudes, however imposed or extorted, of her own sexual desire—and this despite O'Brien's statements concerning the inveterate masochism of her female protagonist.

In our view, the white-knight gloss on Caithleen's early adolescent adventures badly underestimates the extent to which her filial trauma engenders in her a subliminal, specifically erotic investment in its replication—that is, the extent to which her impulse to repair the damage her father so violently wrought converges with the countervailing impulse to repeat the sexualized trauma trailing in its wake. That is to say, the tribulations she encounters as a young adolescent are not only the lamentable offshoot of her quest for romance, protection, and economic security but also the outcroppings of a larger if deeply unconscious design: a design instilled in her from without as if it were her own.

In a very real sense, the oscillations of her father's sadistic attentions and desertions groomed Caithleen for her conflicted—at once zestful and oppressed—participation in what, given her tender years, must be deemed serial instances of pedophilic interference, if not outright violation. His grooming of her in this regard may be unintentional. But in effect he does groom Caithleen by or rather *for* proxy. He grooms her to seek out and enter into child sexual transactions or relationships that serve to confine her perdurably within the original calamitous terms of her family romance.

From the age of fourteen, Caithleen repeatedly engages in liaisons that rehearse in some fashion her dysfunctional and destructive relationship with her father, "the crux of her dilemma." But while most of these liaisons involve the white-knight type of older, tutelary men who can feed her appetite for well-upholstered domestic romance, she is not exclusively attached to this generational type, nor to this gender for that matter. She actually begins her course of sexual dalliance with her lifelong frenemy and doppelgänger, Baba, an incident to which we will shortly return. Much later, now allied with Baba on the dating scene in Dublin, she explicitly rejects her counterpart's plan to target the wealthy, middle-aged prowlers of the pub scene and argues for more youthful, one might say age-appropriate options. These exceptions to the avuncular rule indicate that the predominate spur to Caithleen's desire, the object cause that magnetizes her postpubescent psychosexual economy, resides not in the paternal imago (identity markers like age and gender) or in the paternalistic function (social roles like provider or safeguard), *except* insofar as these harbor associations with the domineering enactment of paternal authority generative of her filial trauma. Without exception, all of Caithleen's prospective intimates, irrespective of gender, generation, or class background, are in some way authoritative and aggressive figures. In this respect, and despite the settled reputation of *The Country Girls* as a heterocentric bildungsroman, Caithleen's sexual penchants tend to queer the heteronormative standards of her Irish Catholic community in the very act of adhering to them. That is, she cathects the middle-class, male-identified faculties of domination to such a degree that they accrue a value detached from the received gender, class, and generational subject-positions themselves.

To be sure, in certain cases, such as that of Mr. Gentleman, these same faculties can and do merge with the accoutrements of mature and successful manhood in appealing to Caithleen's sense of dependency and her corresponding wish for deliverance, both emotional and material. But precisely in putting herself at the disposal of such authoritative aggression, Caithleen not only courts enthrallment (in every sense), she thereby expresses in action the perverse, antithetical wish that marks every erotic pairing: to re-engage in some form, to "mimic" if you will, her traumatic upbringing. She exemplifies in this regard how, as intimated earlier, child abuse does its most lasting damage in setting the victim's mechanism of desire at cross purposes with itself.

The bipolar split in what Caithleen wants from her several schoolgirl crushes manifests as a profound ambivalence toward the crushes themselves. Just as she is not exclusively attached to any one type, so she is not entirely attached to anyone. Rather, she lurches between different kinds of positive and negative estimations of each of her erotic interests. Her often adoring attitudes, extensively remarked on in the criticism of the novel, syncopate with less frequently noted but no less pronounced strains of mockery, enmity, disdain, and disgust. It is not too much to say that with respect to Hickey, Baba, Jack Holland, and even Mr. Gentleman, Caithleen inclines toward what puts her off and is repelled by the very thing she fancies.

This, the perverse logic of Caithleen's desire, both results from and testifies to the childhood abuse that renews the traumatic jouissance of primal seduction. Owing to the evocation of that jouissance in her coming of age, Caithleen does not just repeat that trauma in order to repair its effects, the dynamic explored in Freud's *Beyond the Pleasure Principle* (1961); she also seeks to repair that trauma as a strategy for repeating it, in its connection to a debilitating enjoyment. Moreover, given her still juvenile status, her earliest relationships with paternal surrogates do more than draw on the cycle of childhood sexual abuse; they continue it. Caithleen's profound ambivalence toward her crushes, then, answers quite precisely to the dual return of the repressed, both bodily and psychic, that they induce: the intrusive retroactivation of a self-fissuring surplus enjoyment.

Caithleen's early relationship with her lifelong peer, Baba, provides a crucial and entirely overlooked instance of this psychosocial economy. To begin with, the parallelism of Baba to Mr. Brady is manifold and conspicuous, not in the externals of the Imaginary register, of course, but in the symbolic position that she assumes toward Caithleen. O'Brien inscribes this symbolic doubling directly onto the surface of the text, its "characters" serving as clues to the characters. Caithleen calls her terrible father "Dada" and her terrible friend "Baba." The names are both doublets; they have the same number of letters identically disposed; the consonants of each wherein their phonemic difference lies are the lowercase reversed images of one another, as in a mirror; and, of course, the names, the vehicles of the symbolic positions, rhyme, allowing for a certain confusion of the two.

Like Dada, Baba is at once commanding and contemptuous of Caithleen. In the latter's words, Baba is her "bully" (18), a classification that perfectly summarizes Mr. Brady's style of paternal rule. Like Mr. Brady, Baba denigrates Caithleen as a form of human waste: whereas Brady calls his daughter a "little—[shit]" (33), Baba repeatedly labels her "trash" (58, 68). However, Baba goes still further in slighting Caithleen, likening her to a "bloody sow," her hair to "old mattress stuffing," and her nose to a "petrol-pump" (60, 32, 26). Caithleen's terror of her father has its match in her fear of Baba: "I'm afraid of Baba; she makes so little of me" (59).

Like Mr. Brady, Baba asserts her authority parasitically, with Caithleen as her chief mark or target of exploitation. Baba steals flowers, demands food-stuffs, and inveigles jewelry from Caithleen, all the while displaying a cavalier attitude toward the gifts she extracts and absolutely no sense of indebtedness for her appropriations. She even calls out Mr. Brady for his cadging ways, a moment that invites the reader to draw the pot-kettle comparison. Finally, like Mr. Brady, Baba intersperses her dictatorial and manipulative efforts to bind Caithleen to her will with edicts of enforced separation. Whereas Mr. Brady periodically abandons his daughter, Baba periodically banishes her. Replicating, after her own lights, Mr. Brady's toggling gestures of cruelty, Baba elicits a similarly conflicted response from Caithleen: anguish in Baba's presence, overriding misery at prolonged division.

Emotionally abjected by, yet also dependent on, her sole if nominal friend, Caithleen comes to hold Baba in deeply ambivalent esteem, at once loathing and admiring her charisma, which is manifest in her ability to compel Caithleen herself to serve her every whim (Baba's own father tells Caithleen, "you've always been Baba's tool"; 118). At the same time, in reigniting the scenario of Caithleen's filial trauma, her ambivalence toward Baba passes smoothly into homoerotic attraction. Thus, Caithleen only vents her childhood animus toward Baba in the midst of complimenting her alluring physical appearance: "hysterical with temper" over Baba's bullying, Caithleen thinks, "I could smell her soap. The soap and the neat bands of sticking-plaster, and the cute, cute smile; and the face dimpled and soft and just the right plumpness—for these things I could have killed her. The sticking-plaster was an affectation. It drew attention to her round, soft knees" (22–23). Baba's sexual appeal thus takes root in the very insults that she adds to Caithleen's formative injury.

Caithleen's most tangible sexual encounter with Baba comprises the same blend of wound and want, resuscitating essential features of her primal seduction, the enigmatic signifier included. She reports how "Baba and I sat there and shared secrets, and once we took off our knickers in there and tickled one another. The greatest secret of all" (10–11). In more than one respect, the enigmatic signifier here, the vehicle of an ambiguously fetching psychic message, is the word *tickled,* which carries both sexual and nonsexual, naughty and innocent, inviting and threatening, pleasant and unpleasant connotations. The primary signification of *tickled* in this context would be "titillated, stimulated to excitement and delight," as in the metaphorical saying "to tickle one's fancy." In this instance, with the girls' knickers off, this signification would carry an erotic and specifically a homoerotic reference, severely reprehended in the post–de Valeran Republic. Hence, of all the secrets shared by the girls, their mutual caresses are, to Caithleen's mind, "the greatest secret of all." If the illicit nature of the sexual activity incites a certain jouissance or surplus enjoyment in Caithleen—and "greatest" can mean most wonderful as well as weightiest or most serious—this is in part because it brings a traumatic element to bear on the proceedings, infusing Caithleen with a complex of fear, shame, and self-doubt redolent of the abuse scenario. For her part, Baba reinforces and exploits this traumatic dimension as if her own desirability depends on it, which it very well may. She bullies and blackmails Caithleen by threatening to disclose their forbidden, clandestine tryst, "and every time she said that [she would tell], I gave her a silk hankie or a new tartan ribbon or something" (11). Caithleen's added phrase, *or something,* misleads in its offhand insouciance. Bestowed ritualistically, in a scripted exchange ("every time Baba said that"), the type of gifts specifically mentioned count as romantic tokens or favors, a way of perpetuating the romantic encounter along other, nongenital but masochistic lines, and thereby preserving a reminder of the traumatic jouissance it yields.

However, as addictive as the displaced reenactment of childhood (sexual) abuse may prove for its victims, like Caithleen, it is aversively, even repulsively so. And the ambivalence it arouses can only be exacerbated when this reenactment takes the form of likewise taboo sexual practices requiring concealment, like the erotic revelry of two young girls. It is therefore to be expected that Caithleen might seek to forswear without divulging (i.e., to disavow in the Freudian sense) her liaison with Baba, even as she prolongs their perverse romantic friendship. Immediately after reporting her sexual ties to Baba, she finds occasion to tell Hickey, "I'm going to be a nun when I grow up; that's what I was thinking" (11). Hickey's rather cryptic reply suggests that perhaps "the greatest secret of all" wasn't so secret after all, or was rather an open secret, an intuited if unadmitted understanding of the abrasive intimacy the two might share: "A nun you are in my eye. The Kerry Order—two heads on the one pillow" (11). Caithleen's visceral reaction to his words, "I felt a little disgusted," signals not just an unease with Hickey's suspicions or his snarky way of expressing them but an unease with herself, a momentary breach in her wall of disavowal.

The word *tickled* forms a brick in that wall, as a part of its enigmatic function. Indeed, in this context, the word *tickled* marks the point at which the enigmatic signifier and the open secret meet, tenor to vehicle. To use the word *tickled* to describe her closeted intercourse with Baba is to leave open an anerotic, or at least less transparently erotic, interpretation thereof, something along the lines of "just play," tickling pure and simple. With the ambiguous *tickled*, Caithleen introduces a patina of undecidability to her narration: does she or does she not have sexual relations with that girl, and does the answer to that question hang on what the meaning of *sex* is? How determinate or elastic is the range of its application? The effect on the reader is to render the event portrayed a little more equivocal, a little less categorical, and hence seductive rather than graphic. We know but cannot be entirely sure. We are in on the "greatest secret" but with its final gist suspended. Or, to put it another way, the enigmatic signifier, *tickled*, transforms a closed case into an open secret for us as well.

The secondary sense of *tickle* (paradoxically its primary denotation), to touch lightly causing laughter and bodily twitching, has its own distinct emblematic value as pertains to the reenactment of primal seduction. Whereas the metaphorical application of *tickle* places emphasis on sexual gratification, this literal sense also entails a significant measure of discomfort, sufficiently intense to induce queasiness, nausea, and dread. That is to say, whereas the figural tickle imparts enjoyment, the literal tickle incorporates a traumatic admixture.[8] Ironically, then, in deploying the euphemism of tickling to soft-pedal the sexual nature of her secret encounter with Baba, Caithleen winds up making allusion to the innermost nature of their secret liaison, its trauma-roticism, the distal reverberations of her filial abuse.

Predictably, in keeping with her vexatious role in Caithleen's embattled *bildung*, Baba brings to the fore the traumatic dimensions of the tickle by exploiting it for bullying purposes. When Caithleen first enters into a pedophilic relationship with the village toff, Mr. Gentleman, her display of bliss—"I want to sit here all night and dream" (68)—provokes Baba to jealous inquisition as to the name of her conquest: "'Tell me, or I'll tickle it out of you,' and she began to tickle me under the arms" (69).[9] In a neat reversal of her earlier strategy of extortion, Baba's gambit in this instance keeps in play the ambiguous sense and enigmatic force of the tickle.

Having previously threatened to divulge information about their pleasant erotic tickling in order to extract amorous tokens from Caithleen, she now threatens unpleasant, anerotic tickling in order to extract the name of Caithleen's new amour. Further reinforcing the layered affective duality of the tickle, Caithleen herself initially feels her erotic attraction to Mr. Gentleman as "an odd sensation, as if someone were tickling my stomach" (16), and she ultimately capitulates to Baba's demands on the grounds that "I'd do anything not to be tickled" (69). The tickle thus encapsulates in a single complex of sensations what Caithleen desperately wants, what Caithleen desperately wants to avoid, and what Caithleen cannot avoid repeating, thus affording Baba the perfect fulcrum of manipulation. By the same token, the tickle affords O'Brien a perfect fulcrum of representation. Compressing in its different modalities of sensation the warring affects associated with a loss of control—the ecstatic and the agonizing, the torturous and the titillating—it proves an apposite narrative metonymy for the effects of primal seduction, abusively renewed, on child victims like Caithleen.

According to Caithleen, this incident of Baba's bullying "had broken my heart, destroyed my life," and permanently severed the bond between them: "'We will never speak again, ever,' I kept repeating, under my breath" (68). The remainder of her narrative, however, not only belies this assertion, it shows the very opposite to be true. What Caithleen keeps "repeating" is, in fact, a reconciliation with (which is always a conciliation of) Baba herself. Indeed, far from severing the relationship between the two girls, this quarrel proves a decisive stage in its continuation. It represents the point at which the forbidden homoerotic intimacy explored earlier in the relationship is sublated into a more socially approved homosocial sodality and rivalry. Caithleen's surrender of the name or pseudonym in question sets off a current of triangulated desire between the two girls, with Mr. Gentleman at the mediating vertex.

As Eve Sedgwick (1985) has adduced in her landmark study, *Between Men*, English literature abounds in examples of male same-sex desire accommodating the mandates of compulsory heterosexuality and the corresponding stigma of homosexual dissidence by positioning a female figure as simultaneously a love interest and a channel of eroticized identification between her competing male admirers. The "between (country) girls" ménage bears the same structure as the erotic triangles that Sedgwick unpacks, only with the genders flipped. However, given the asymmetrical power relations between men and women in the comprehensively patriarchal society of modern Ireland, this gender transposition itself makes for a corresponding reversal in political agency and effect. The traffic in women central to male homosocial relations, Sedgwick remarks, serves to facilitate the promotion of men's individual and collective self-interest, the enhancement of men's privilege, and the consolidation of their authority (1985, 3–4). It is, if you like, the sexual-romantic cell of the modern patriarchal system. By contrast, the nascent competition of Caithleen and Baba over Mr. Gentleman conduces to *his* aggrandizement, both individually and as the allegorical representation of gentlemen tout court. The homosocial dynamic conducted by *The Country Girls*, accordingly, accedes to the heterosexual imperative as part of a more general submission to the system that its opposite number, male homosociality, sustains and reproduces.

The patriarchal Symbolic Order, of course, has effectively sponsored Caithleen's filial experience of abuse, if only by sanctioning her father's disciplinary authority, enabling his brutality, and conniving at its sexual overtones. Moreover, obligatory heterosexuality constitutes the cardinal mandate of the Symbolic Order; it is the predicate and guarantor of the traffic in women, and its specific embodiment in modern Irish society at once determines and mystifies the course of Caithleen's traumatic *bildung*. We might say, her submission to the heterosexual imperative obscures and mitigates what we have identified as her "queer" masochistic sexual affinity for figures of authoritative aggression, irrespective of gender. Although her same-sex flirtations continue in the gender-segregated space of the convent school, her expulsion from its corridors, based on a blasphemously hetero-sexual sketch of its officers, inaugurates a fully, resolutely heteroerotic orga-nization of her mid-to-late adolescence around the Gentleman/Gentlemen.

During this period, post-Famine economic anxieties and changes in the rules of inheritance had normalized exaggerated age differences in agrarian Ireland between prospective grooms (preferably established on the land) and prospective brides (preferably still fertile for years to come). Extending well into the twentieth century, these rural marriage arrange-ments camouflaged and capitalized on the sorts of daddy issues with which filial trauma encumbers Caithleen. Her social habitus encourages a sexual development, an itinerary of desire, that will in the future incline her toward older men, paternal surrogates in the Imaginary and Symbolic registers, in imago as well as function. But more significantly, and more scandalously, the social habitus encourages her to gravitate in the present moment, as a fourteen-year-old, toward paternal surrogates as potential mates, and to conceive of herself as available to them, at least notionally, for flirtatious foreplay pointing in that direction. Indeed, what we earlier adjudged Mr. Brady's grooming of Caithleen by/for proxy can be so readily actualized only in a context where sexual trifling with the local girls, by kith and kin, is a regular and seemingly normalized occurrence. Consequently, although unwitting on Brady's part, the effects of his grooming prove so consistent with the casually predatory ambience of the town as to seem collectively intentionalized.

The "Gentlemen"

The workman, Hickey, is the first of the socially sanctioned paternal substi-tutes to adopt an inappropriate attitude of seduction or solicitation toward young Caithleen. Hickey represents her first girlhood crush, toward which she bears a deeply conflicted attitude, as one might expect, considering its fraught transferential basis. She breathlessly informs her icon of the Blessed Mother, "I love Hickey" (6). But under the Virgin's icy stare, "from a gilt frame," she partially retracts her declaration: "'Yes, I love Hickey,' I thought, but what I really meant was that I was fond of him" (6). Lurking in the passage is the enigmatic signifier prompting the sudden qualification of her fervor: the single word, *gilt,* describing the frame from which the Virgin hears Caithleen's incessant prayers of "penance." The implicit pun on *guilt*—underscored by the fear of hell driving her nightly vigils—marks an unconscious sense of the untoward implications of her long-standing wish to marry Hickey and its likewise muted or repressed connection to her paternal "dilemma." Sure enough, Caithleen immediately proceeds to retract not only that wish but her assertion of romantic love as well, by reference to Hickey's unsavory physical features and unhygienic habits. Over a very short span, Caithleen espouses toward Hickey an attitude of unreflective ambivalence that aligns with his role as an avatar of the mimetic, which is to say amnesiac, sexual elements of her filial trauma.

As it happens, Hickey exhibits those attributes particularly attractive to Caithleen, authoritativeness and aggressiveness, in a markedly eroticized fashion. While Hickey tends to deflect Caithleen's pleas for him to protect her from her father's unhinged wrath, he does step in to perform the classically oedipal function of disrupting the intimate mother-child dyad that she and Mrs. Brady share until the end: "'Old mammypalaver,' Hickey said. I loosened my fingers that had been locked on the nape of her soft white neck, and I drew away from her, slyly" (8–9). On a related note, Hickey assumes the traditional paternal role of disciplinarian, threatening corporeal chastisement à la Mr. Brady: "Be off, you chit, or I'll give you a smack on your bottom" (12). The scandalized phrasing of Caithleen's answer, moreover, suggests that with her sexual maturation the proposed spanking has gathered a libidinal as well as a punitive aspect: "'How dare you, Hickey.' I was fourteen and I didn't think he should make so free with me" (13). Hickey proceeds to confirm as much by importuning Caithleen for a "birdie," his "private name for a kiss" (13), indicating an abashed desire to keep the kiss itself private.

Here again, the discomfort caused by Hickey's coded solicitation has more to do with the stage of Caithleen's sexual growth than with a lack of precedent; Caithleen points, somewhat indignantly, to the fact that she "hadn't kissed him for two years" (13). But the incident she invokes with these words is, if anything, far more unseemly than the present contretemps. On that occasion, Mrs. Brady bribes Caithleen with sweets to kiss Hickey ten times as a reward for his having purchased a heifer on the cheap. If we consider the following items—

A. Mrs. Brady has, in the vernacular, effectively pimped out her daughter, traded her favors of affection in compensation for material services rendered;
B. The transaction occurs under quasi-incestuous circumstances: Hickey clearly stands in as both provider and head of household for the convalescing Mr. Brady, whose absence is said to license the frivolity; and
C. Mrs. Brady is the very same woman who shares an intense bond of identification with Caithleen as joint survivors of eroticized domestic abuse.

—then we can begin to grasp just how systemic, how familiar, how normalized is the sexualization of young girls in the rural Ireland of O'Brien's experience and imagination. So endemic and accustomed is the practice that it does not seem to register in that moment as unacceptable. Even for Caithleen, Hickey's attentions register as inappropriate only in the mode of *nachträglikeit* or deferred action, what Laplanche calls "afterwardsness" (Laplanche 2016, xi). Paradoxically, it is only when Caithleen has traversed the gap between childhood and pubescence (precisely and not accidentally the two-year gap between Hickey's kisses) that the intimations of pedophilia in Hickey's fatherly affections come dimly to view, casting their shadows backward in time.

The second socially sanctioned paternal substitute to adopt an unseemly posture of seduction and solicitation toward Caithleen is the shopkeeper and family friend, Jack Holland. Caithleen bears him the same sort of traumatic ambivalence as she does Hickey, only in reverse. Whereas she repeatedly professes her devotion to Hickey only to withdraw from his blandishments, she repeatedly takes exception to Holland and his advances yet circles back to his shop over and again, unconstrained and sometimes unbidden. Caithleen first encounters Jack directly after the "birdie" incident with Hickey, and his own paternal surrogacy is immediately established: "Jack Holland was waiting for me. . . . At first I thought it was Dada. They were about the same height and they both wore hats instead of caps" (13). The backstory of Jack's connection to the Brady family further solidifies his place as a perverse father figure to Caithleen, a *père de jouir*. Mr. Brady has already caught Jack fondling his wife, and Caithleen suspects that his suit in this area is ongoing. Rather than invalidating his interest in Caithleen, however, his continuing ardor for Mrs. Brady serves to introduce a second, parallel line of transference to this extended family romance. Just as Jack stands in for Mr. Brady in Caithleen's abusively contoured unconscious fantasy, so

Caithleen stands in for Mrs. Brady in Jack's pedophilicly inflected unconscious fantasy.

In a subtle, highly literary, autoethnographic version of a Freudian slip, Jack discloses, to the alert ear, his romantic conflation of mother and daughter. By way of corroborating Caithleen's suspicions about her mother, Jack abruptly, and apropos of nothing in particular, pays Mrs. Brady a fulsome compliment drawn from the miraculous conclusion to W. B. Yeats's nationalist tour de force, *Cathleen ni Houlihan*: "There are kings and queens walking the roads of Ireland . . . ploughing the humble earth, totally unaware of their great heredity. Your mother, now, has the ways and the walk of a queen" (16–17). The subliminal import of Jack's paean—what is in his words more than what they mean to say—lies in the precise outlines of the traumatic tableau they invoke. The eponymous heroine of Yeats's sovereignty drama acquires "the walk of queen" only upon undergoing a generational metamorphosis from old woman to "young girl," from mother (Ireland) figure to daughter figure. Witness—

> PETER. Did you see an old woman going down the path?
> PATRICK. I did not, but I saw a young girl, and she had the walk of a queen.
>   (Yeats 1953, 57)

On the analogy mooted by Jack's allusion, the mother and older woman, Mrs. Brady, attains to the "walk of a queen" strictly by identification with and incorporation by the "young girl," the daughter figure, who by no coincidence whatever happens to share the name of Yeats's Mother Ireland. Caithleen thus emerges as the secret object or alloy of Holland's desire; she embodies unto herself the essential splendor he finds in the mother. Jack's subsequent, oxymoronic reference to Caithleen, "a juvenile lady friend" (17), underscores this generational fusion, while his allusion to Padraic Colum's poem "The Drover" highlights the supersession of the older figure by the younger that Yeats stages in his play. Those who set about "plowing the humble earth," in Holland's phrase, are concentrated into the single figure of the Drover, whose thoughts likewise focus on a single figure, "my thoughts on . . . the King of Spain's daughter" (17), her mother, and his queen, having been elided as surely as the old woman in the sovereignty myth and Yeats's revivalist adaptation. In aligning the unrequited Jack with the famously unrequited Yeats, who notoriously attempted to replace the recalcitrant Maud Gonne with her daughter, Iseult, O'Brien calls to mind the ongoing eroticized fungibility of mothers and daughters in the Irish Imaginary. Beyond Jack's ken, but well within O'Brien's, finally, the allusion brings the preeminent nationalist iconography of Yeats's rural drama into libidinal, even scandalous alignment with the pervasive sexual abuse anatomized in *The Country Girls*. The call to a noble martyrdom for Ireland, effected through the transformation of the sovereignty goddess (Cathleen) in Yeats's drama, plays on the same motive force that drives the ignoble behavior of a Jack Holland—the eroticized figure of the "young girl" (Caithleen).

O'Brien foregrounds the operation of this lust for youth along more quotidian lines in the very next encounter between Holland and Caithleen. Jack uses the necessity of informing an anxious Caithleen that "your mam is gone on a little journey" to solicit kisses from her and her companion, Baba (23). The latter side-steps Jack's overture "airily," but Caithleen, following her, "tripped over a mouse-trap" in a literal Freudian slip—that is, an active expression of an unconscious self-punitive desire sabotaging the conscious will (23–25). Caithleen effectively traps herself alone with the insistently amorous shopkeeper, and she is forced to confront the sort of harassment that she would, yet seemingly cannot, avoid. At this point, her only recourse is to plead the simple truth that rather gives the game away: "'I'm too young, Jack,' I said, helplessly" (25). She thereby calls attention to a sociosexual regime that is not just precipitate when it comes to young girls ("I'm too young") but pressurized, if not predatory ("I said, helplessly"). Indeed, the most significant narrative property of Jack's advances is the fidelity with which they mirror Hickey's a short time earlier; for taken together, their targeting of Caithleen for "favours" looms over the early stages of the novel and suggests *an everyday atmosphere of open season on pubescent females*. O'Brien thus establishes an uncanny synchrony between the individual configuration of Caithleen's paternal trauma, "the crux of her dilemma," and that of the Symbolic Order in which she struggles to survive and resolve it—not least in the way her own mimetic tendencies, her repetition in lieu of remembering, unfold under a social dispensation that reproduces as a matter of course certain sexual elements of the trauma.

Jack Holland turns out to be more serious and persistent in his suit than Hickey, with an upshot at once telling and ironic. Instead of comforting a stricken Caithleen upon the news of her dear mother's drowning, he pulls her aside and apologizes for being unable to indemnify the Brady

family estate against their creditors. His mea culpa, however, is but pro-
logue to machinations whereby he would not only take over the property
himself but also leverage it in an importunate bid to secure Caithleen's
consent to marriage. His gambit reveals how material dependency is a necessary, instrumental condition of child sexual harassment and abuse. The
insolvency of Mr. Brady proves a key supplementary factor in the dynamics of predation-by-proxy that we have outlined, and Caithleen's oft-noted
romancing of economic security proves a predictably double-edged plan of
campaign: seeking to escape the financial constraints that leave her prey to
the harassment of older men, she must put herself at the disposal of just such
older men.

At the symbolic level, Jack's gambit introduces a perverse twist on the
sovereignty drama he cited in extolling Mrs. Brady's virtue. A letter to Caithleen at convent school reiterates the imagined restoration of the mother/ni
Houlihan figure in the daughter Caithleen, only this time with the express
hope that the native Brady lands might be restored to her as well. The "full
implication" of the letter, as Jack subsequently makes clear, is that "in time
to come I hope to marry you" (103), her repossession of the Brady property
being contingent on his taking possession of her. In the "full implication"
of the Yeatsian intertext, Jack promises to play the role of Irish patriot, to
win back Caithleen's "beautiful green fields" by marriage (Yeats 1953, 53),
but only after having expropriated them in the first place, in the manner of
the "strangers in the house" whom Cathleen ni Houlihan rails against in
the play (Yeats 1953, 53). Thus, the "young girl," Caithleen, would come to
live again on her native land only after she has been incorporated in an Act
of (connubial) Union with the comprador, Jack Holland. In other words,
Holland attempts to engineer a localized, native version of the metropolitan
marriage.

For her part, Caithleen remains very much focused on the erotic "threat
that the chapped, colorless lips would endeavor to kiss mine" (103–4), and
as if to show just how thoroughly Holland has twisted the whole abuse scenario, Caithleen actually conjures up her "waiting" father as protection from
him. On the logic of traumatic repetition, however, her desperate flight on
this occasion still does not deter her from visiting Jack once more before she
leaves town, exposing herself, yet again and unnecessarily, to his unwanted
liberties.

Mr. Gentleman is the most significant, enduring, and overtly pedophilic of Caithleen's socially sanctioned paternal surrogates. Only Mr. Gentleman's presence and influence spans the entirety of *The Country Girls*. Only Mr. Gentleman's interest in Caithleen can be accounted truly scandalous by the social mores of their small town, and this owing to its adulterous rather than its pedophilic tenor. Only Mr. Gentleman plots a long-standing yet noncommittal and disposable affair with Caithleen, crossing the (always implicit) line from harassment to outright grooming, from seduction to violation, from morally reprehensible sexual "interference" to legally actionable child sexual abuse. (The relationship between Mr. Gentleman and Caithleen begins early in her fourteenth year and grows more serious during her fifteenth year. The age of consent in Ireland at the time was sixteen.) Only Mr. Gentleman possesses and aggressively exerts a personal authority recognized not just by the Brady circle but by the town as a whole, greatly increasing his stature in Caithleen's eyes. Only Mr. Gentleman, correlatively, is able to secure and hold Caithleen's enduring affection. Whereas the ambivalence attendant to traumatic mimesis manifests as a conflict between attraction and repulsion (or vice versa) with regard to Hickey and Holland, her ambivalence remains internal to her devotion to Mr. Gentleman, a conflict between its determinants, which leaves her an especially exploitable resource for his ego and sexual gratification.

As befits its central role in Caithleen's development, the narrative thread involving her liaison with Mr. Gentleman is among the most tightly structured in the novel. It unfolds in three distinct segments corresponding to three stages in Caithleen's infatuated submission to Mr. Gentleman's predatory designs. Each stage contains an explicit identification of Mr. Gentleman with Caithleen's father, thereby referencing the fatal origins of the affair; each stage identifies Mr. Gentleman's gaze, or mien, with sorrow or disappointment, thereby presaging the fatal end of the affair. Each is punctuated, finally, by Mr. Gentleman's removal. The stages are thus linked metonymically by the progressive narrative and metaphorically as microcosms of the whole. In this respect, the form of this narrative thread encodes the aporia of traumatic reenactment: progress toward redress ensnared in the toils of re-dress.

The first stage (54–64) is that of grooming. It commences by proxy, with just a hint of the traffic in women: Caithleen's father sends her to cajole a loan out of Mr. Gentleman, instead of pleading on his own behalf. Mr. Gentleman follows up in a classic predatory scenario; he hails his mark from his luxurious automobile as she waits for a bus, and he proceeds to arrange an assignation. Consenting, Caithleen observes, "There was something about him that made me want to be with him" (61). While she cannot say exactly what the attraction might be, her comment is sandwiched between two telling references to the remarkable sadness of his eyes. The first and most compelling in a persistent series of nonverbal harbingers of gloom and rue, his eyes signify from the start the doom that hangs over their romantic prospects and, more importantly, the doom that positively magnetizes Caithleen's traumatized desiring apparatus and impels her to pursue those futile prospects on account of their very futility.

At the ensuing luncheon appointment, Mr. Gentleman pulls out the full battery of conventional grooming devices. He seeks to impress Caithleen with his wealth and refined taste. He orders her the finest items on the menu, aggressively plies her with wine, despite her "Confirmation pledge," and inquires after her sexual innocence. More pointedly, he exerts his authority by instructing her on what men like in "young girls" ("Men prefer to kiss young girls without lipstick, you know"; 62–63). By adducing the taste of men en masse, he seeks to normalize his otherwise illicit pedophilic ardor, yet those collective proclivities just happen to match his own: "'The next time we have lunch, don't wear lipstick,' he said. 'I prefer you without it'" (64). Finally, he caresses her with his "wistful" gaze and "settle[s]" on her neck, which is just that physical attribute of which Caithleen seems most self-satisfied (64). Nothing galvanizes his grooming technique, however, like the leaving off. In proclaiming, "You're the sweetest thing that ever happened to me," before he "slipped away from [her]" as if nothing had happened, in giving her a look "which seemed to be saying 'Don't go,'" only to go himself, Mr. Gentleman establishes himself as her "new god" by reviving the terms of primal seduction: he frustrates the desire he arouses and compromises the enjoyment he induces (65).

What is more, Mr. Gentleman previews the longer-term rhythm of a seductive method that plays on Caithleen's personal traumatic history: intense emotional contact followed by extended periods of separation and radio silence. Indeed, after the first grooming encounter, Mr. Gentleman disappears without a word and does not correspond until they meet again the following Christmas. Riding to convent school with her father, Caithleen refuses "to acknowledge him" but rather envisions, almost hallucinates, Mr. Gentleman as a replacement (72–73). And indeed, Mr. Gentleman comes to embody the same traumatic contradiction as her father, the oscillation between Leys's mimetic and anti-mimetic modalities. On the one hand, her conjuring of Gentleman's powerful gaze represents the first time that Caithleen consciously and explicitly entertains a paternal transference onto one of her gentleman callers. On the other hand, in true mimetic fashion, she remains drawn to what she cannot apprehend, the reenactment of her father's traumatizing habit of dereliction and disappearance in Mr. Gentleman's like pattern of unannounced withdrawal and abandonment.

SEDUCED

The second stage of Caithleen's entanglement with Mr. Gentleman is that of the seduction proper (89–101). After a long, uncommunicative parting, the two reunite at Christmas to much kissing and many professions of love. At the heart of their holiday rendezvous is an impassioned automobile excursion, described at feverish length:

> Softly the flakes fell, softly and obliquely against the windscreen. It fell on the hedges and on the trees behind the hedges, and on the treeless fields in the distance, and slowly and quietly it changed the colour and the shape of things . . . and I knew that before the flakes began to show on the front bonnet Mr Gentleman was going to say that he loved me . . . and very solemnly and very sadly he said what I had expected him to say. And that moment was wholly and totally perfect for me; and everything I had suffered up to then was comforted in the softness of his soft, lisping voice; whispering, whispering like the snow-flakes. . . . He kissed me. (99)

In a brilliant exercise of dramatic and intertextual irony, O'Brien has Caithleen construct a quintessential Hallmark card moment—the heavily romantic atmosphere, the first and climactic proclamation of love, sealed with a kiss—and filters it through a stylistic pastiche of the famous peroration to James Joyce's "The Dead." That scene, also at Christmastime, centers on the breakdown, the routing, of Gabriel Conroy's romantic fantasies about his marriage to Gretta, and as such it provides a frame of reference that subverts

Caithleen's fantasy of true love. This subversion operates on multiple levels simultaneously. At the simplest level, the Joycean frame indicates that Caithleen has completely misrecognized the depth and nature of Mr. Gentleman's feelings, much as Gabriel has misjudged Gretta's feelings that holiday evening. The careful blending of Mr. Gentleman's whispers of love with the whispering of the snowflakes from "The Dead" reinforces this level of irony. More complexly, the Joycean frame indicates that Caithleen misapprehends the nature and the direction of her intimate relations with Mr. Gentleman. Her sense of a "wholly and totally perfect" moment, in which they have finally come together, is expressed in a vocabulary that raises, like a revenant, the already ghostly scene from "The Dead" in which Gabriel and Gretta are coming apart. The ghost in Caithleen's phantasmatic machinery, of course, is her traumatic relationship to Dada, which, like any revenant, and like the repressed, perpetually returns. Caithleen's sense of being "comforted" in that "wholly and totally perfect" moment for "everything that I had suffered" both sharpens and complicates this level of dramatic irony. If Caithleen does indeed find comfort in this moment for the pain of Gentleman's unexplained severance of all communication in the past, his alternating pattern of truancy itself, of which this moment is but a part, renews the more profound, unconscious suffering begotten by her father's abusive desertions.

At the same time, her evident masochistic attachment to that suffering supplies a final, most intricate layer of irony. It is crucial that Gentleman's profession of love, the key to that "wholly and totally perfect" moment, is delivered "very sadly," at once recalling and anticipating the sadness of his eyes on virtually every occasion of their intimacy. In this case, these embodied signifiers of misgiving and foreboding herald the foundering of their relationship at this, its very founding, which is precisely what, from the vantage of Caithleen's traumatic mimesis, gives the moment its warped perfection. The Joycean palimpsest infiltrating Caithleen's great love scene, then, not only undercuts the perceived fulfillment of her conscious romantic desires but also encodes the unconscious, traumasochistic desire that is already coming to fulfillment.

After their snowbound tryst, Gentleman holds to his seductive pas de deux of assertive advances and self-protective retreats. He bestows a "small gold watch" on Caithleen, "so small that [she] had expected it to be a toy," but then tells her she must "put it away" and hide it from everyone. He moves to finish his presentation with a kiss, but then "he drew back from [her], guiltily." He whispers, "I love you," but then tells her, "We'll have to be very careful," and "I can't see you too often, it's difficult" (106–7). When Caithleen inquires, "Can I write you?" he says no, "firmly" (107). Gentleman's temporizing and equivocation become so patent that Caithleen grows sensible that her "suffering," far from being comforted or compensated by endearment, as she believed, is actually being exacerbated. She even stages a muted rebellion. She admonishes him to "show more feeling" and wonders mopishly, to his noticeable irritation, "And will I ever see you?" Yet so answerable, so commensurate, so complementary is Gentleman's seductive method to Caithleen's insensible need to repeat as well as repair her traumatic history that she not only accepts but embraces a long-term dalliance shaped by Gentleman's perennial detachment and periodic disappearance (107).

The denouement of the seduction stage sees Caithleen settling for irregular assignations with Mr. Gentleman, one of which features the single most chilling transaction in their entire association:

> In the summer Mr Gentleman took me out in his boat. We rowed to an island far out from the shore. . . . It was a happy time and he often kissed my hand and said I was his freckle-faced daughter.
> "Are you my father?" I asked wistfully, because it was nice playing make-believe with Mr Gentleman.
> "Yes, I'm your father," he said . . . and he promised that when I went to Dublin later on he would be a very attentive father. (110)

Having won Gentleman's accession to his role as father figure, Caithleen immediately subjects that title to a Freudian disavowal: "because it was nice playing make-believe with Mr Gentleman." "Make-believe" here functions to invert the logic of transference that actually defines the place of Gentleman in Caithleen's psychic universe. Her notion of make-believe fatherhood is not just a knowing pretense but a wish-fulfilling fantasy that elevates Mr. Gentleman to the status of fairy-tale hero. Psychic transference, on the other hand, is a make-don't-believe—that is, a making, a psychic projection of reality, by way of a failure of recognition, the erection of a psychic reality without the awareness necessary to belief. Instead of a knowing play-act, Caithleen's transference issues in an unknowing reenactment of the reality of paternal abandonment in her "new god." In this context, Mr. Gentleman's pledge to be "a very attentive father" when she moves to Dublin can only remind her of his habits of detachment and defection in the past, while reminding the reader of his impersonation of Mr. Brady in this regard, hence of the unconscious source of Caithleen's attachment to him. It was also, of course, just such a pattern of delinquency that drove Caithleen's mother to seek a replacement for her husband in Tom O'Brien, with whom she embarked on a doomed nautical adventure, which, at another level of transference, Caithleen here rehearses with Gentleman.

And Abandoned

Caithleen's stay in Dublin with Baba contains the longest stretch of the story without an appearance by Mr. Gentleman, belying his promise of much attentiveness. He fails to even send Caithleen a "postcard" from his travels. When he does arrive, beginning the stage of abandonment (166–88), he offers to repay Caithleen's patience with a trip to Vienna, where, he promises, "We're going to be together. I am going to make love to you" (172). He strangely envisions the sexual consummation of their liaison, however, in terms of evacuation, saying, "We have to get this out of our systems," and its telos he envisions in terms of separation upon return (173). In other words, he imagines the apotheosis of their love as inseparable from the dissolution of their relationship. Abandonment is inscribed in the very proposal of seduction. For her part, Caithleen does not take his proffer at its romantic face value; she is well aware of his propensity for estrangement and of how it has always made her feel: "And already I was sad. No one would ever really belong to him. He was too detached" (178). She is by no means fooled or bamboozled by his gesture. That she goes along with his plan—from their mutual disrobing and fondling in her room to their orchestrated meeting at the quays—is a testament not to her naivete but to a compulsion to repeat born of a life history where wound and want, trauma and enjoyment, are inextricable, each secreting (hiding/exuding) its complementary other.

Her particular history with Mr. Gentleman gives her no reason to believe that he will act to break, as opposed to renew, this cycle of affective violence. Certainly, her history of being neglected by him gives her no reason to believe that he will show up for an expedition so equivocally projected in the first place, and the immediacy with which she grows anxious at the quays evinces as much. By the same token, without such heartfelt expectation, it would seem that deep down she is not really waiting for him at all, as evinced by her continuing to linger long after she has dismissed any possibility of his arrival: "I knew now that he wasn't coming; but still I sat there.

An hour or two later I got up" (186). What she does await is the inevitable, that which her grooming has taught her will come. She waits, precisely, to be abandoned, to see that mode of abuse through to the end. Or, as Caithleen tells a passer-by, with greater symbolic significance than she apprehends, "I'm waiting for my father. . . . We're going away somewhere" (185). Consciously, of course, she refers here to Mr. Gentleman as her make-believe father. But on an unconscious level, the reference to her father acknowledges his place as the foundational and summary figure, her epitome, of a patriarchal dynamic of authority and aggression, entitlement and predation, abuse and abandonment, inherited on both a local and national scale by men like Hickey, Holland, and, above all, Mr. Gentleman. The latter bears witness to this fact, metaphorically, in attributing his final act of desertion and betrayal primarily to the influence of Mr. Brady. His telegram explaining his default on the excursion begins, *"Everything gone wrong. Threats from your father"* (187). Giving them their most general range of application, these words— Everything. Wrong. Threats. Father—might well be taken to encapsulate the assault on Caithleen's adolescence that is virtually coterminous with her *bildung* in *The Country Girls*. The crux of her dilemma, indeed.

Envoi

Effectively the last word in *The Country Girls*, the telegram proleptically enfolds into the text a signifier of the cultural logic of scandal at work in its reception. In the father's outrage, expressed in threats, we have the source and morally responsible agency of the most reprehensibly traumatizing and scandalous conduct in the novel proclaiming himself scandalized by its subsequent manifestation in the romantic career of his daughter. In the outrage of the Irish Catholic Church at O'Brien, catalogued in detail at the outset of this chapter, we have the source and morally responsible agency of the most reprehensibly traumatizing scandal (the ongoing sexualized abuse of children) in the nation's history proclaiming itself scandalized by its manifestation in the *bildungsroman* of *The Country Girls*. The telegram itself then functions as an envoi, a message to the future, the ultimate import of which could only be appreciated in full once the child sex scandals of Ireland seeped into public view. In this respect, Caithleen's *bildung* in *The Country Girls* is written to completion not in the latter installments of the *Trilogy* but rather in O'Brien's later novel of the X case, *Down by the River* (1997).

1. O'Brien herself took to calling *The Country Girls* "my wicked book." Quinn (1986, 141).

2. Quoted in Kernowski (2014, ix). O'Brien remarks that readers from her home county, Clare, find her works not caricatures at all but "too revealing" (McCrum 2014, 64).

3. In her 2013 memoir, *Country Girl*, O'Brien makes it altogether clear that her own father and Caithleen's are one and the same. In the chapter "The Doll's House," O'Brien recalls her mindset as she wrote *The Country Girls*, enumerating a series of images and feelings that came to her in dreams and memories of a "former world" that was returning "before [her] eyes . . . infinitely clear" (139). Following her graphic account of a sexual dalliance with a local girl with whom she recalls committing acts of painful mutual penetration with stalks of wild iris, O'Brien shifts abruptly to "the novel's opening paragraph," which "centered on the fear of my father" (140), an affective state of decisive relevance to our reading of the novel.

4. O'Brien amazes no less a mnemonic novelist than Phillip Roth: "I was struck . . . by the vastness and precision of your powers of recall" (Roth 2014, 43).

5. For a compatible view of the social and psychoanalytic operations of sadomasochism, see Hinton (1999).

6. Caithleen's father's threat conjoins violence and sex to an unusual, even a grotesque degree—particularly when we remember that he is not threatening to "debag" her, as Buck Mulligan playfully offers to do to Haines in "Telemachus," but rather to kick her knickers off. The idea of violently pulling or even kicking someone's trousers off foregrounds violence and humiliation while its erotic implications remain latent, as with "a kick in the pants." In this case, however, sex is explicitly conjoined to violence, with each merging seamlessly into the other. That Edna O'Brien was by no means exaggerating the conjuncture of mutually inciting sex and violence that simmered close to the surface in her hometown is confirmed with a vengeance by the postmistress who remarked to O'Brien's father that she regretted his daughter had not been "kicked naked through the town." Since O'Brien knew this story, her father must have enhanced the atmosphere of eroticized violence by recounting this sadistic fantasy to his own daughter.

7. It should be noted that Caithleen's mother's disappearance is announced in the midst of a performance of *East Lynne*, when Caithleen is first informed that her mother has gone off on a boat with Tom O'Brien (41). As with *East Lynne*, sex and death are notably contiguous in the story that is told to explain Caithleen's mother's disappearance, and, moreover, there is a real possibility that the immediate and insistent promoting of death as the more definite import of Mrs. Brady's absence serves primarily to obscure the far more scandalous and also far more definite evidence that exists for her having gone off on a tryst and failed to return.

8. The tickling episode derives from a real-life event reported in *Country Girl*: "One summer Sunday, a girl with ringlets lured me in for an 'op,' short for operation. It was quite dark, and we were hidden by the low-lying branches as we took off our knickers, then pulled up the stalks of the wild iris that grew in a swamp and stuffed the wet smeared roots into one another, begging for mercy. Our cries flowed together and were muffled by the drones of bees and wasps that swarmed in and out as we swore eternal secrecy." This incident quite remarkably interfused the erotic and the anerotic, trauma and enjoyment, agony and ecstasy, in a single bundle of sensation (E. O'Brien 2013, 140).

9. Baba's blackmail likewise has its roots in that real-life incident of mutual penetration (n8). Having "lured" O'Brien, her ringletted friend said that she would "tell unless I gave her my most prized possession, which was a georgette handkerchief with a pink powder puff stitched into it. And so I did" (E. O'Brien 2013, 140).

4

"FROM THE PITS AND DITCHES WHERE PEOPLE HAVE FALLEN"

Sex Scandal and the Reinvention of the Irish Public Sphere in Keith Ridgway's *The Long Falling*

THROUGHOUT THIS STUDY, WE ARE concerned to mobilize Jean Laplanche's elegantly textured psychoanalytic conceit, the enigmatic signifier, as an instrument for illuminating, simultaneously, the cultural dynamic of child sex scandal in modern Ireland and the specific role of modern and contemporary Irish novels in responding to and participating in this dynamic—first, by exhuming its ethico-political bases, and second, by delineating its social and intrapsychic ramifications. In Laplanche's theory, the enigmatic signifier functions as a vanishing mediator of infantile sexualization, the coded material whereby each developing subject receives from the adult world ambiguously beckoning psychic messages laden with repressed desire and unconscious libidinal energy.

As Laplanche (re)reads Freud's seduction theory in an interview with Cathy Caruth:

> There are always at least two scenes that constitute a traumatic "event," and . . . trauma is never locatable in either scene alone but in "the play of 'deceit' producing a kind of seesaw effect between the two events." . . . [Freud's] theory explained that trauma, in order to be psychic trauma, never comes simply from outside. That is, even in the first moment it must be internalized, and then afterwards relived, revivified, in order to become an internal trauma. . . . First, there is the implantation of something coming from the outside. And this experience, or the memory of it, must be reinvested in a second moment, and *then* it becomes traumatic. (Caruth 2014, 25–26)

More than a vehicle of (unconscious) seduction, the enigmatic signifier is a seductive vehicle whose power resides in the eroticized indefiniteness of its suggestion: a confusion of the sexual and the nonsexual, of knowing and not knowing, and of innocence and incrimination, which carries a traumatic charge of jouissance. If the sexual tenor of the signifier renders it enigmatic, the enigmatic force of the signifier sexualizes it in turn.

Because like any signifier, the enigmatic signifier is iterable, the erotic current with which it is invested at the first moment of implantation remains available to be "reinvested" in a series of later moments recalling or approximating the original enigmatic encounter. Moreover, because like any signifier the enigmatic signifier bears its semiotic values as a part of a chain of metonymic differences, the traumatically fraught valences infusing any such activation of the enigma can extend to a wide array of scenarios, experiences, objects, and identity forms. That is to say, the enigmatic signifier makes new sense of Freud's *nachträglichkeit*, which Laplanche translates as "afterwardsness" and redefines as both instigated by and accounting for the uncanny disappearance and subsequent traumatic recurrences of an enigmatic message deposited in infancy by the adult other.[1] Scandals of endangered innocence constitute especially explicit and powerful sites for the collective reactivation of the enigmatic signifier and its ambivalent effects, both because they center on the coercive sexual initiation of a minor, thereby recalling the peremptory force of the infantile exposure to adult sexuality, and because they rehearse for the public at large the traumatic play of knowing/unknowing endemic to sexual initiation as such. A scandal of any variety comprises not only the precipitating exposure of a transgression but also a second stage of cover-up, dissembling, and gradual, uneven disclosure, and then a third stage of seemingly abrupt but always imperfect revelation, which transforms the concealments of the second stage into an outrage in their own right.[2] In a child sex scandal, the intermediate passage from disavowal and undecidable awareness to incomplete transparency and residual doubt or deniability takes shape in and through the workings of the enigmatic signifier, which revivifies for the scandal's participant-observers (and in scandal, all observers are participants) the traumatic jouissance of their own primal scenes.

Even as they represent fictional versions of the scandals of imperiled innocence that have bedeviled and defined modern Ireland, the novels under study here also reproduce the sexualized phenomenology of scandal itself—that is, by staging the eroticized dynamics whereby individuals are interpellated not just as consumers of scandal but as subjects of scandal culture, agents whose consumption of child sex scandals goes, recursively, to the roots of their own subject formation. To this end, as we have shown, such literary texts as *Dubliners*, *The Land of Spices*, and *The Country Girls* deploy enigmatic signifiers in two dimensions simultaneously: for the characters in the narrative and for the consumers of the narrative. In the lived experience of reading, these dimensions can neither be fully conflated with, nor dissevered from, one another. The shimmering overlap between the two issues, for the reader, is a higher or sublimated form of sexualized psychomachia. On the one hand, the traumatically charged erotic scenarios represented in the text, whether explicitly or implicitly, are bound up, knitted together, with the eroticism of reading about them; such scenarios pull the act of reading about them into their libidinal force field, so to speak, however aversive or repudiated the libidinal expressions on offer might be. On the other hand, precisely this enigmatic, ambivalently charged connection between the narrative and the interpretive event allows the sort of critical reflection encouraged in serious literary practice to be extended from the scandal dynamics unfolding on the page to the reader's vicarious involvement in those dynamics (though when it comes to scandal, the line between immediate and vicarious can prove unexpectedly faint).

It is a major goal of our project, enacted with particular force in this chapter, to delineate the distinguishing structure of a specifically literary or aesthetic (as opposed to religious, journalistic, partisan, or tabloid) response to Ireland's child sexual scandal. As we show, the literary response engages a dialectic that (a) interpellates the audience as already implicated in the process of collective judgment not only entailed in but constitutive of scandal itself and (b) does so precisely to lend that audience greater perspective on the stakes—ethical, political, and otherwise—of that implication. Or, to put the matter in the terms of our titular quote from *The Long Falling* (Ridgway, 1999), the literary response to scandal casts its readers into "the pits and ditches where people have fallen" so as to render palpable the overlap or proximity between scandal observation and participation, to overcome the surface effect, endemic to scandal culture, that a bright line exists between the two modalities of engagement. As our chapter title further suggests, the novel performs this literary-aesthetic function vis-à-vis its readers by folding the observer/participant dialectic back into the contours of the narrative. That is to say, it foregrounds in the design of the story the irreducible linkage between scandal observer and participant, "readers" and "protagonists," and then teases out the two overriding effects of their correspondence:

1. However disempowered and abused, the victims of an atrocity in one sociopolitical register are not immune to finding themselves incriminated in the burden of scandal enacted in another register.
2. As a result, the enigmatic elaboration of the original scene of outrage opens up multiple lines of libidinal affective identification with perpetrators and victims alike, all the more so as each party stands in a different relationship to the normative ideologies of modern Ireland, the institutional mechanisms of regulation, and thus to any given "imagined community" of moral or legal judgment. The opportunities for projection and misrecognition on the part of any given scandal subject thus prove abundant, as *The Long Falling* dramatizes.

The narrative focus of the novel is the Quinn family, all of whom find themselves embroiled in at least one major scandal as an agent or participant and connected to another as a victim or observer. Moreover, each of these seemingly discrepant or opposed roles meld together, affording a kind of diegetic metonym for the simultaneously conflicted and collaborative nature of scandal culture. A series of traumatic convulsions in the Quinn family erupt along three axes of authority and disempowerment. The first is generational and involves what we are calling *the disposable child*, instanced in Michael Quinn's vehicular manslaughter of an adolescent girl and, less graphically but as saliently, in the criminal negligence of the main protagonist, Grace, in the drowning death of her toddler, Sean. The second is gender, involving the category of *the abused woman*, instanced in Michael's routinely brutal (and drunken) battery of Grace after her truancy in Sean's death, and in her correspondingly plausible defense for her later vehicular murder of Michael himself. The third axis is sexuality, in response to *the abased queer*, and instanced in the domestic and neighborhood furor occasioned by the coming out of Grace's second son, Martin, an event that prompts his father to assault him, verbally and physically, and actuates Grace herself to fund his flight from rural Monaghan to cosmopolitan Dublin.

Behind this interlacing network of family contretemps looms one of the most notable scandal figures in recent Irish memory: Girl X. In 1992, having been, over a three-year period, repeatedly raped and finally impregnated by a friend of her family, the 14-year-old X was in London awaiting a scheduled abortion when her parents contacted the Irish authorities to consult with them about the use of DNA samples in obtaining a conviction of her rapist. Her parents were ordered to return her to Ireland immediately, and she was thereafter restrained from travel and subsequently placed on twenty-four-hour suicide watch to ensure against harm to the developing fetus. Although X won the right to travel on appeal, her traumatic and highly public scandal trajectory ended abruptly and inconclusively in a (literal) miscarriage, and the constitutional wording that not only allowed for but mandated the assemblage of an extraordinary theater of cruelty as the requisite state response to a protracted sequence of assaults on a minor remained unchanged until 2018. It might also be noted that although the Irish Constitution certainly did not in any way mandate the reduction of her rapist's sentence from fourteen years to two, this was to be yet another pain-inducing sequel to X's horrifying scandal trajectory.

As these events unfolded, the so-called X case became a rallying point for mass resistance to the intrusive sovereignty asserted by a theocratic, patriarchal state over women's bodies and reproductive decisions. Although the "long falling" into disgrace of Ridgway's Quinn family culminates with Grace Quinn's arrest for murder while participating in the giant Dublin march on X's behalf, the figure of X herself does not appear or perform any discernible narrative function. Nevertheless, as the few critics who have written on *The Long Falling* would agree, Girl X is the symbolic hub on which the entire structure of the novel pivots. We would add, moreover, that Girl X is not just the novel's premier figure *of* scandal but also its premier figure *for* scandal, the public enigmatic signifier of scandal's cultural and sociopolitical economy.

It is vital to X's central if enigmatic place in the symbolic pattern of the novel that her plight comprises each of the categories of traumatic violence on offer. On these grounds, she emerges as a potential analogue for each of the main narrative actors, whose scandalous transgressions, suffering or dishonor likewise derive from their place within and subjection to the patriarchal regime. In keeping with her algebraic designation, the novel seems to pose X both as a vanishing nexus interlinking the other characters along lines of indignity and as a common denominator, soliciting the reader to evaluate the other scandal scenarios by comparison with her own.

However, this role of X and the invitation it presents, while no mere illusion, does turn out to be self-negating, a false lead paradoxically necessary to arrive at the truth. Her status as an exemplar, rather than a mere example, of the scandal figure serves in the end to interdict the very sort of universal transference that her pervasive haunting of the events of Ridgway's narrative would seem to solicit. Unlike the other main characters, X embodies all of the target registers of systemic violence: generational, gendered, and sexual. And thus, unlike any of the novel's central characters, X is never situated so as to participate in the victimization of others. She retains a radical, symbolic innocence not unlike that of Sean Quinn, son of Grace and Michael and brother of Martin, who drowned in infancy. As a result, any equation of X's subject position with the novel's protagonists winds up exposing: how they possess a measure of social agency denied her, while forfeiting a measure of moral authority in turn; how each partakes of an empowered collective identity from which she is excluded; how each is fractionally complicit with the social hierarchy weighing on her; and how neither an express solidarity with nor a structural affinity for a particular mode of victimization stands proof against some level of incrimination in the web of social relations engendering it. As the narrative's all-purpose double or doppelgänger, then, X proves to be undouble, even unheimlich, bearing toward each of the main characters (Michael, Martin, and Grace) a mode of resemblance, kinship, or identification whose underlying rationale or impetus will not hold.

For this reason, the letter X in *The Long Falling* always bears its notational import as a chiasmus, a trope that combines repetition with reversal. The plenary victim, X, doubles the other scandal characters and, in the same motion, reverses that likeness, revealing a muted but decisive contrariety in their respective moral and political postures or profiles. The clearest and richest case of this chiasmatic swerve is the relationship of X to Grace Quinn. The vicissitudes of this relationship encapsulate the moral journey on which the novel takes both Grace and the reader, its scandal protagonist and observer.

The narrative's ultimately insupportable parallel between Grace and X follows a dialectical pattern of doubling over the course of the novel. In the first stage, or what scandal theorists Chris Greer and Eugene McLaughlin (2013) term *activation*, there obtains a purely external bond between them, a structural counterpoint in which emphatic parallels in their social position and experience are shaded with less conspicuous but ultimately definitive differences.

Both Grace and X have endured iconic forms of misogynistic violence—domestic abuse and rape, respectively—and both face periods of state-imposed incarceration as a direct or indirect consequence. The suffering of both accordingly spotlights the imbrication of male dominance and state power (Grace's spurious confusion of Detective Brady with her deceased husband dramatizes this point) in an Irish state whose theo-cratic origins continue to structure an uneven distribution of protections and liabilities across the body politic. In addition, both are disposed at the periphery of the Irish community, with England serving in either case as the marker of their marginal status, their faulty claim to full inclusion. Grace is an immigrant *from* England, resented by her neighbors on this score. X has traveled *to* England, openly seeking, in contravention of native law, the alleviation of one of the many forms of harm her rapist has inflicted on her, and she is herself criminalized on these grounds.

Grace thus represents the novel's most thoroughgoing counterpart to X in the register of gender, signifying, at first, as her sister-victim of the patri-archal church/state complex. At the same time, however, Grace also repre-sents an antitype to X in the generational register, as the delinquent parent of her own disposable child. Less compelling at first than their gender align-ment, this generational antinomy becomes the dominant factor in Grace's ethico-political education, as child abuse slowly emerges as the novel's cen-tral problematic.

The generational disparities between Grace and X come to the fore in the novel's second stage, *amplification*. Once Grace is on the run, she herself internalizes their structural affinities as a full-blown identification with the girl. She configures X as a projective version of her own best, most ethic-ally viable self, an unfairly accused scandal victim. By implicitly equating her own (justified) killing of Michael with X's (entirely justified) proposed abortion, Grace simultaneously endeavors to occult her own sense of culpa-bility in the death of her firstborn son.

In a symmetrical turn, her second son, Martin, initiates the third stage of the dialectic—*justice*—by convincing Grace that she is indeed blamewor-thy, not for the death of Sean but for the killing of Michael. The effect, though not the intent, of Martin's *j'accuse* is to drive Grace to cognize and accept an extraordinarily thorny ethical proposition endemic to the child abuse scan-dals in Ireland: although she is in no way responsible for the abuse she has suffered, never to blame for her victimization, that abuse, that victimization, remains undecidedly tethered to other harm for which she is accountable. In a novel staked on the concept of falling and fallenness, the original sin of the modern Irish nation takes the form of this aporia: whatever its citi-zens suffered, however the patriarchal system constrained, coerced, or even terrorized them, they continued to be answerable to the children, who, like Sean, went unheard or overlooked.[3] Coming to this insight greatly complicates and ultimately balks Grace's identification with X. She becomes aware that she is not only X's semblable but also her antithesis and, on this basis, must imagine another form of community or solidarity with her.

Grace's moral journey entails a process of gradual anagnorisis, not the final resolution of obscurity into transparency, but rather the gradual consolidation within obscurity of a painful truth—to wit, her own compromised status. As a survivor of vicious domestic abuse, Grace earns the reader's sympathy and retains it through the various misprisions that mark her unflaggingly earnest struggle to come to grips with the moral complexity of her circumstances and her self-fashioning therein. At the same time, the sensitive reader's affective and interpretive experience of the enigmatic signifier that informs the three scandal registers on offer should prompt them to share, at a remove, Grace's growing awareness of her implication in each register. The virtually universal critical failure, up to this point, to do so, betokens a collective denial that the novel, like the other fictional accounts we are examining, endeavors systematically to contest.[4]

STAGE ONE

Beyond the striking correspondences in Grace's and X's social predicaments, Ridgway employs an array of literary devices to establish a compelling counterpart relationship through their manifold associations with crime and abuse, scandal and notoriety. At the novel's outset, an intertextual strategy unfolds, featuring a brace of extended allusions to Gabriel Conroy's iconic closing vision in "The Dead": "It rains on Cavan, Monaghan; rains on the hills and the lakes and the roads; rains on the houses and the farms and the fences between them; on the ditches and the fields, on the breathing land" (Ridgway 1999, 3). Mimicking with uncanny exactitude the rhythms of Joyce's famed denouement, the passage transforms the cleansing fall and the anesthetizing coverlet of snow over Michael Furey's graveyard into the raw, soaking rain more typical of rural Ireland. With this meteorological inflection, the metaphorical focus of the passage shifts from the desired burial of the past to the ineluctable exposure of the present— that is, to the afflictions of scandal rather than their elision. Moreover, the change of weather shifts the elusive focus from Conroy, snow aficionado, to his wife Gretta's ex-suitor, Furey, who perished in an untimely drenching (like many such uncanny scandal doubles, from Anna's brother Charlie in *Land of Spices* to Veronica's brother Liam in *The Gathering*).

The long-departed Furey holds a place in Gretta's memory primarily through the song he would sing while courting her, "The Lass of Aughrim," whose title character, a folkloric double of Furey himself, is still more germane to the twinning of Grace and X. The Lass is callously abused by Lord Gregory, much as Grace is abused by her "Lord and Master," Michael Quinn, in a series of events that leaves her, likewise, locked out and exposed. The Lass is also sexually exploited, impregnated, and abandoned by Lord Gregory, as X is exploited, impregnated, and left to her own devices by a friend of her family. What is more, the Lass's infant, like Michael Furey but also, more pointedly, like Grace's own little child, Sean, dies of something like a drowning.

The initial installment of the novel's dialogue with "The Dead" triangulates the figures of Grace and X through the folkloric "Lass of Aughrim" as paired victims of cognate patriarchal violence and malefaction. Everything the reader learns in the immediate aftermath of this opening gambit seems to justify Grace's standing among Ireland's brutalized and exploited innocents. In response to her son's death, as it is first innocuously described, Grace suffers merciless vituperation from Michael—for example, "she was a stupid woman, more stupid than an animal" (9). Her husband disseminates his opinions ("all that he had to say"; 11) to their neighbors, who begin conspicuously to avoid her and to stigmatize her by look and word. At the same time, Michael commences beating her, apparently in reprisal for their boy's death. Because the narrative voice, a variable frequency of free indirect discourse, channels Grace's initial sense of guiltlessness without setting forth Michael's perspective, his verbal and physical abuse of her registers as not only cruel and barbaric but gratuitous. Michael appears to exact vengeance for a tragedy suffered rather than a wrong committed. In this respect, Grace's status as faultless scapegoat unmistakably corresponds to that of X, who was confined for the crime of being raped. The patriarchal subjugation connecting Grace and X in their metaphorical lineage to the seduced and abandoned Lass of Aughrim thus involves not just a blaming but a disciplining of the victim.

This perverse logic continues to mark, and mar, Grace's marriage once her husband has "killed a girl," another analogue of X, in a drunk driving accident (5). Whereas Michael receives an unconscionably light prison term for his crime, Grace pays a correspondingly disproportionate price in community ostracism and obloquy. In other words, Grace takes significant blame for a homicide fueled by the same alcoholic excess at work in her husband's assaults on her. The previously noted link between her "accident" with Sean and her husband's auto accident (both victims are stowed in that same car) suggests that the latter weighs as a symbolic extension of the former, with Grace unjustly bearing the recriminatory weight for both. As we shall see, such melding of different offenses is a note sounded repeatedly in the novel, even as the offenses and offenders themselves keep changing. Thus, in a variation on this theme, Michael escalates his beating of Grace after his release from prison, seeking to expiate his negligent homicide by violently calling Grace to book for hers.

Up to this point, the parallelism of Grace and X remains circumscribed within the category of abused womanhood. Accordingly, when the time comes, the sympathy that the beaten and socially ostracized Grace has attracted from the reader qua scandal-observer can be enlisted in a moral, if not legal, defense of her spousal homicide. Gradually, however, suppressed memories that contravene Grace's conscious account of Sean's death begin to surface, and her sense of blamelessness begins to waver. As this change is channeled through the novel's prismatic indirect discourse, the reader's allowances for Grace may grow more equivocal as well. This dual shift in attitude unfolds not in response to Grace's vehicular assault alone, but rather to the double articulation of the two deaths to which Grace has been party—specifically, to their simultaneous connection with and partition from one another in Grace's Imaginary.

On the one hand, Grace tends to confound the two incidents along a public-private axis: the guilt imputed to her by others (the police detectives, the journalist, her son Martin) with respect to Michael's killing is internalized by Grace with respect, instead, to her son Sean's misadventure. The official investigation into Grace's role in her husband's violent end winds up tapping her long-dormant, still largely repressed springs of compunction over her son's drowning. In one particularly telling instance of psychic transference, Grace realizes that "it had not occurred to her to worry" about being arrested at her husband's funeral "until that moment . . . in the grounds of the strange church," when she suddenly sees herself as "a mother ignorant of the whereabouts of her child's grave" (50).

On the other hand, Grace's self-absolving ruminations on Michael's brutality and on her last fatal rejoinder allow his slaying to stand, however perversely, as evidence of the innocence she has always maintained concerning her son's death. As she abruptly flees a church adjacent to Michael's final resting place in Cootehill, she explains her reaction: "It was not guilt. . . . It was panic. . . . But this time it came to her . . . as a thought that was as hard as it was irrational. She had sent her husband to the place where her son was kept. . . . Thrown one over the other like a cover, like a sheet. Why had she done that?" (49). The answer to Grace's query turns on the metonymy secreted within her lurid posthumous metaphor. At an unconscious level, she broaches the notion that her killing of Michael, here figured as Michael's corpse, acts as "cover" for her truancy in Sean's demise, likewise figured as his remains. That is to say, her manifest responsibility for a crime deliberately executed, openly acknowledged, but substantially mitigated if not excused by her husband's prior abuse serves to occult or camouflage psychically her irresponsibility in the tragedy that, on her own account, precipitated the abuse in the first place. As Grace's memories have it, Michael's wife-beating originated with virulent objurgations for her negligence in Sean's death, a delinquency she denied at the time. So by a reverse twist of logic, her ability to rationalize Michael's killing on these grounds only goes to support her original claim of innocence.

In keeping with the psycho-forensic relation that Michael's murder bears to the "letting die" of Sean, Grace shows no conscious awareness of her responsibility for the earlier tragedy, but in its stead, she carries in her memory an implicitly inculpating reconstruction of the scene of Sean's death:

> She had held Sean in her arms and pointed at the stars and named the shapes she knew. . . . And then she had put him down so that she could take the clothes from the line. She threw them over her arm. She took each of them down and threw them over her arm. Then she had turned and looked into the darkness, and she had known almost immediately that he was in the ditch. It was easy. She looked at the clean clothes and turned again and draped them carefully over the line, knowing that some of them would fall and be dirtied, but knowing that some of them would stay where they were and that she wouldn't have to do them again. Then she went and took her drowned son's body from the shallow water and carried it into the house and sat with it in her arms until her husband came in. He hit her. He hit her and tore her clothes and dragged her out and threw her in the ditch and left her there. She had tried to drown. She had tried to lose consciousness,

with her head under the water. But she could not. She could not stop herself from breathing, from gasping and sucking in the air in cold dark mouthfuls. When she climbed up out of the ditch she saw all the clean clothes lying on the ground.... It stayed with her more than anything else. Those clean clothes lying in the mud. (128)

In this passage we arrive at the primal scene of *The Long Falling*, the misrecognized origin from which the narrative's scandal axes extend. Yet this memory has gone almost entirely overlooked in the criticism to date. The reason for this glaring blind spot in some otherwise fine exegeses of the novel can be traced, in our view, to the operation of the enigmatic signifier. Focusing as it does on emblematic, suspicious, yet still peripheral and morally ambiguous details of the scandal tableau—such as the trope of falling, and dirty versus clean laundry—the passage implies without explicitly indicating that Grace's first (non-) response to Sean's dangerous fall was purposive, whether consciously or unconsciously, rather than merely inadvertent, as she contends. The gnomically matter-of-fact report, with its fastidious tonal neutrality, allows for a less chilling interpretation of Grace's part in Sean's fate (which surely was sealed at some point during those precious minutes Grace devoted to rehanging laundry she had just taken off the line) than the details reported tend to invite, if not demand.

This discrepancy between poesis and diegesis, in turn, appeals to what we have termed the moral episteme of the audience, which is inscribed directly in the text in order to expose its limitations. Proceeding along binary lines, scandal narratives rely on Manichean scenarios for their cultural comprehensibility; to function at all, they must produce the kind of black-and-white judgment that eschews seeing the grossly sinned against as capable of grossly sinning, the injured innocent as, at another level, a likely transgressor. Grace's son Martin speaks precisely to the sentimentalizing dichotomies of this moral episteme in response to the inclination of his partner, Henry, to condone his father's murder: "Everybody loves a battered wife.... That's all you have to tell them. He hit me. So I murdered him. Oh, that's all right, missus, on your way now, there's a good woman" (227). Having been shown from the start of the novel that Grace is indeed a "good woman," and a long-suffering woman to boot, readers have found it difficult to reckon—midway through the narrative—with her liability in the death of a toddler.

Nonetheless, a close inspection of the above quoted passage makes it difficult *not* to issue some sort of indictment—of Grace herself and of the scandal morality that would exonerate her. At the heart of this difficulty lurks the novel's shortest and most elliptical sentence, "It was easy" (128). Although the referent, *It*, remains willfully ambiguous, its positioning limits the statement's conceivable import to the following:

A. It was easy to know that Sean had fallen into the ditch.
B. It was easy, in the dark, to have lost the child in the ditch, to have let him fall.
C. It was easy to leave the child in the ditch, easy to let him die.
D. It was easy, or easier, to leave the child in the ditch while she rehung the laundry, so that she "wouldn't have to do [the clothes] again."

In context, the sentence's referential indeterminacy pointedly preserves a measure of psychic denial or deniability on Grace's part, thereby making one of the final two meanings most likely. Grace's subsequent, astonishingly disengaged reactions, which could be summarized as "taking it easy," supply evidence that one of the two latter interpretations must be the correct one. She registers no anxiety in response to her child's peril and exhibits no urgency to retrieve him from the ditch into which he has fallen; she does not attempt to resuscitate him once she has recovered him; nor does she recall either feeling or exhibiting violent grief over his sudden extinction. To the contrary, she averts her eyes from her drowning child in order to contemplate and rearrange her laundry with a deliberation that, intentionally or no, creates an interval of inattention sufficient for Sean to succumb.

It is impossible to know what possessed Grace at this point. Her excuse for the miscarriage—that she "had turned her back only for a moment" (9)—reasonably accounts for Sean's original fall but does not even touch on, let alone explain, her astonishing inaction after she was aware of the fall having occurred. Her attempt to drown herself in the same ditch, at her husband's furious instigation, demonstrates the depth and intensity of her subsequent emotional trauma but not its precise nature. Is she simply devastated, belatedly, by Sean's sudden death? Is she contrite for her part in the calamity? Is she ashamed at her lack of devastation, her failure to evince any conventional maternal feeling or expression? Is she each of these indeterminably? Does her gesture unconsciously enact an identification with Sean in his final moments, or is it an attempted administration of self-retributive justice, to exchange a life for a life?

Grace's muted response in this revised and summary account of Sean's last moments on earth opens a second, tacitly antagonistic version of Grace's symbolic kinship to X, centered on the category of the disposable child. If the allusive role of the Lass of Aughrim is to connect Grace with X, the Lass of Aughrim also marks a crucial division between them. Impregnated and abandoned by an older man, like the Lass, X is also, like the Lass, nameless in her own tale, a condition that bespeaks a lack of socially sanctioned authority extending well beyond the partly disenfranchised position of Grace, whose allies include members of the police force.

Importantly, as both an abused woman and a devalued minor, X aligns with both the Lass and her dead baby, whereas Grace's uncertain culpabil ity in little Sean's death aligns her, conversely, with both the Lass and Lord Gregory. Ridgway thus triangulates the spiritual kinship of X and Grace Quinn through a mythic nexus that serves to emphasize the difference between an *object* and a *representative* of Irish scandal culture. Whereas X exemplifies how the material effects of a scandal culture turn on the fervent and unquestioning protection (typically through institutional regulation and confinement) of a notional, absolute innocence, Grace embodies the lived moral contradictions that scandal culture systematically obscures.

As Grace strolls in Dublin the morning after her recollection, she senses "snow in the air," which in turn prompts the second in a series of textual allusions to the final passages of "The Dead." Her inward vision of a Monaghan reliquary in winter weaves together a chiaroscuro of similarity-in-opposition between Grace's mental picture of the snow-covered roadside memorial where both Michael Quinn and his young female victim breathed their last, and the scene it unmistakably evokes: Gabriel Conroy's culminating vision of the graveyard at Oughterard where his spectral rival, Michael Furey, lies buried. In Gabriel's vision, the pure, thickly drifted snow graces a series of items metonymic and iconographic of Christ's crucifixion—crosses, thorns, spears—all of which betoken a promise of redemption attaching to the figure of Michael Furey himself.

In Gabriel's vision, which occurs in the very depths of winter—a seasonal correlative for his desolate state of being—Gabriel is already, metaphorically, knocking at Easter's door. Grace's inner landscape has likewise already begun transitioning to an early spring tide, reflecting her hope of impending renewal and liberation in her adopted Dublin home. However, the seasonal interregnum in her mind's eye dismally intermingles atmospheric elements: a melting, half-liquified snow creates a muddled, muddy mélange emblematic of a moral infirmity and adulteration attaching not to that other Michael (Quinn) but rather to Grace herself: "She thought of

Monaghan, covered by snow. She thought of the narrow part of the road where the flowers were propped up against the hedge. She pictured them, the snow resting on the bright petals and the green stems, melting into the colour, confusing the brightness and the dark, making a mixture of them, a damaged halfway shade that fell pure, and rested in stained patches on the grey ground" (134). Whereas the snowfall in "The Dead" figures in its all-effacing purity a *felix culpa*, a "fall" out of which a higher innocence may come, the "stained patches" of Grace's imagined snowscape figure an implicit *mea culpa*, a "falling" from a pristine to a confounded and compromised state. Drawing back to the broader intertextual perspective, the gap introduced between Michael Furey as victim/savior and Grace Quinn as victim/unsaving bystander extends to the latter's relation to X, by way of their shared mythic antitype, the Lass of Aughrim, of whom Michael Furey is the modern exponent and "voice."

No less strikingly, for our purposes, this funerary passage simultaneously recalls an earlier sepulchral dream of Grace's, which posts her (like Gabriel in his reverie) at a still unvisited (and in her case neglected) grave site: "He is kept there, beneath the wet ground, hidden. She sees the flowers, sees the petals knocked loose by the rain, scattered on the grass. . . . Sees herself by his grave. . . . She sees her mouth in the uttering of words, sees her knees pressing petals into the mud, sees her hands scoop the earth from around him, until she holds him in her arms" (18). Not only the physical features of the scene, particularly the disarray of the petals, but her own kneeling posture and her uttering of silent, secret, prayerful words closely replicate the tableau of Michael Quinn at the roadside shrine just before Grace runs him over. At the same time, her vision stages a compensatory fantasy wherein she supplants the figure of her husband, and, with him gone from the scene of memorial, she acts to protect and rescue her son, to retrieve him from the "pit" she had originally allowed to swallow him. Via a complex logic of substitution and displacement, the dreamwork subtending this image reveals (a) how, in Grace's psyche, the murder of Michael equates to the earlier crime of letting Sean die and (b) how, by punishing Michael for slaughtering an innocent youth, the same murder pays off her own debt, reinstates her innocence, and restores her to the good-mother roles of safeguard and succor.

Her attempt to maintain that fantasy position in real time, however, specifically to adapt it with regard to her imago of X, is haunted, if not vitiated, by the reversibility of that same dream logic. Grace can stand as an ethical counterweight to her husband, as his victim and destroyer, only insofar as her legacy and his remain entangled concerning the two juvenile deaths at the heart of the novel, scandals closely related not just to one another, but to the evolving fate of X.

The sequence of allusions to the graveyard in Joyce's "The Dead," whence the buried Michael Furey returns to memory and imagination, performs a dual function in *The Long Falling*. As we have seen, these allusions resonate with Grace's connections to the three homicidal events that structure the entire narrative. At a deeper level, however, this sepulchral pattern objectifies in symbolic terms the embattled psychic defense that Grace rears against the guiltiest and most painful aspect of this entanglement, what Nicolas Abraham and Maria Torok (2005) would term her inner "crypt."

At one point, Grace imagines her son's grave "building itself inside her" (Ridgway 1999, 173), a cryptic metaphor, as Ed Madden has properly diagnosed, for "a psychic response of melancholia" (2010, 24). In its extreme form, melancholia impels an incorporation (or encrypting) of the deceased within the precincts of the bereaved's bodily unconscious (Abraham and Torok 2004, 131). This extreme condition arises from an inability to reckon with a loss owing to the continued involvement of the bereaved's very identity in some aspect of that loss. Melancholia represents a strategy for holding on to the dead not in memory or in symbolic terms but as an embodied and always ambivalent part of the self, without having to consciously acknowledge or even unconsciously sense the fact or mode of so doing. It should be evident at this point that Grace holds on to Sean in this exorbitant, not to say pathic fashion, as a kind of psychic reversal or remediation for her having physically "let him go" in the ditch. To incorporate the lost object, however, necessarily entails incorporating the self-corroding torment associated with the loss itself—hence the ambivalence that is endemic to melancholia. For Grace, that pain, that distress, comprises a traumatizing encrypted guilt at her own negligence in Sean's death, for which her own abuse at Michael's hands, and subsequently her retributive murder of Michael, serve as a psychically coherent earthwork.

There is, however, an overdetermined quality to Grace's crypt, one that gives it a distinctively scandalous as opposed to simply taboo structure. It functions as both a psychic safehold for the mourned object (Sean) and a psychic repository for the inadmissible secret of his passing, and it depends for this compound effect not, as one might expect, on some outward facade of virtue but on the supplementary reinforcement of a second, less fully occulted transgression: to whit, the murder of Michael.

In Grace's scandal crypt, one primordial secret lies buried within another more public or open secret—its outer wall, if you will—and remains concealed there even as the unconscious pressure it brings to bear forces the second secret, its protective barrier, into view. Retrospectively sanctioned by her identification with X as an abused woman, Grace's public disavowal of responsibility for Michael's murder keeps barred from sight, most importantly her own, her fault in letting Sean die. Conversely, without fully revealing itself to her conscious mind, the subliminal insistence of that primal scene winds up outing Grace as her husband's killer.

Stage Two

This cryptological dynamic unfolds most emphatically in and around Grace's big public reveal: the confessional scene located at the exact center of the novel. While Grace watches a television report on X with her son Martin, it occurs to her that "everyone might know" of her killing of Michael and simply "not mind" (136)—that is, everyone might have implicitly accepted the justification by abuse defense that she shares, in her own mind, with X herself. She resolves to test her hypothesis on the one person, Martin's journalist friend Sean, who seems most obstinate in his suspicions and, given his profession, the most likely to pursue them.

Her last thought before sleeping on her plan is of Sean: "The name of her dead son. She wondered for the first time what that meant" (138). On the face of it, Grace ponders an unremarkable and essentially meaningless coincidence, especially considering how common a name Sean is. The very fact of her wondering, however—her confidence that the coincidence must have a meaning—points in itself to the undercurrent of significance she senses. Her bid to ensure the presumption of her innocence among Martin's friends, her new social circle, stumbles upon the signifier in which her stirring but still repressed guilt over her son's death may be encoded, a signifier whose dual reference in this context taps her conflicting unconscious impulses mandating and prohibiting (self-)disclosure.

These conflicting impulses not only bear on the tête-à-tête with the adult Sean that Grace arranges for the following evening but also define its contours, and their respective points of psychic attachment mark its coordinates. Having initiated the interview as a kind of preemptive strike, a reconnaissance mission designed to forestall potential nemeses, Grace goes on the defensive from the start, sliding all too easily from agent of inquiry to subject of interrogation. Having been conceived in the televisual mirror of her identification with X as "abused woman in the news," the interview terminates with Grace answering to another innocent victim—her deceased son—adventitiously resurrected in the symbolic mirror of his journalistic namesake. Within Grace's testimony her two secrets—the two death scenarios—are internested to the point of confounding them altogether.

Her terse denial of her husband's murder ("Oh no"; 150) serves only to trigger an extraneous account of a matter not even at issue: her son's fatal mishap. Grace is impelled, perhaps, by the presence of *a* Sean—who by his current age and closeness to Martin has come to stand in for *the* Sean—to rehearse and refute the charge of negligence lodged by that other spectral elephant in the room: Michael Quinn. Answerable neither to her own reasons for this confabulation nor to any pointed questions or conceivable foreknowledge on Sean's part, her decision to recapitulate the particulars of her son's drowning, however favorably rendered, can only be in obedience to some inner compulsion, an unconscious will or need to unburden herself.

Grace may, in her own words, have been "talking about the wrong thing" (150), but she does so for a psychically compelling reason. Her exact motivation can only be gleaned from its destination, or from the ends or effects she actually achieves. As it happens, her unsolicited excursus ends with an origin. That is, the point of the story she tells Sean is how and why Michael first began to beat her, and Grace's ensuing delineation of Michael's progression from occasional to habitual violence carries her unerringly to the precipice at which the accumulating factors mitigating the murder crest and set off an avalanche of confession. Just after finishing the story of the death of her son, Grace suddenly "knew that she would tell him now" (151) of Michael's murder. In this respect, Grace's admission represents an unerring return of the encrypted. She is driven, beyond all sense, to plead to a murder for which she does not feel guilty to a figure whose name recalls an unprosecutable calamity for which she does.

The crux of this forensic odyssey appears just as Grace's narrative of Sean's drowning merges into the preamble to Michael's killing. As Grace details how the former event corrupted her husband's character, Sean inquires, "Did he beat you?" to which she replies, "Yes, but that's not an excuse" (151). Poised at the nexus conjoining the two accounts, the word "excuse" bears a Janus-faced, prospective and retrospective valence. The beatings, Grace concedes, were no excuse—that is, no explanation earning forgiveness or exculpation (for the killing of Michael)—and the beatings do not serve to excuse the past negligence by which she is still unconsciously haunted—that is, they do not confer expiation or absolution (for the death of Sean). In its double inscription, the signifier *excuse* marks Grace's earlier secret as providing the psychic impetus for her disclosure of her later "open secret"; conversely, it also marks the disclosure of that later, public secret as a psychic displacement of the earlier one, prompted by her ambivalent gravitation toward and fearful aversion to her own sense of responsibility. Either way, in displaying the elements of her psychic crypt to Sean, Grace has begun to imperil it. On this score, her predicament epitomizes the broader social dynamics of scandal, where the disavowal of an entire affair, the collective knowing without knowing, depends on the continued "unsaying" of each part, each item of evidence.

In keeping with the architecture of Grace's crypt, with its strange logic of skeletons guarding skeletons, once Grace has confessed to Sean her guilt for Michael's murder, her submerged remorse over her son heaves to the surface. Thus, she is infuriated on discovering that Sean has secretly taped their conversation. But owing to the unconscious force of the shared name, Sean, she rapidly becomes disoriented concerning who should receive censure and for what. She alternately "felt as if she had been robbed, or had stolen and been caught" (157). Allowing her fresh sense of betrayal to rebound on her own past, she confounds this Sean, to whom she responds with anger, and that Sean, for whom she was and remains guiltily responsible; she confounds the wrong done to her, for which she deserves an apology from this Sean, with the wrong done by her, for which she needs to apologize to that Sean. The word *Sean* thus possesses the diacritical property of the enigmatic signifier. It vehiculates a confusion between acting and being acted on, between willing and abiding, between inward drive and external force: "She looked up and it was Sean that she saw looking back at her. She had told him *what she had done*. She had wanted to say sorry to him for turning her back just for a moment. But this was a different Sean, who was interested in something else, who stared at her with a look that was not right" (156–57; emphasis added). The terms of Grace's psychic crypt concentrate themselves in the ambiguous phrase *what she had done.* On the one hand, the unambiguous referent of the phrase, *Michael's murder,* does not admit the same sort of mitigation as does the lapse that truly haunts Grace. Concerning her son, she can still cling to the casuistic qualifier, "just for a moment," signaling the slightest inadvertence and hence a margin of innocence. The name *Sean* recalls something that she regrets having happened but does not think of herself as having categorically "done." On the other hand, the more profound and authentic regret she feels for her passivity at the moment of Sean's demise, compounded by the unimpeachable innocence of the victim, renders the killing of her abusive spouse (which she has unquestionably "done") the wrong "something" to be "interested in," a misjudgment compounded by the shady tactics of her interrogator.

The breach in the wall of Grace's psychic crypt gives shape to the monumental symbol she tries and fails to adopt as her own upon fleeing Sean's apartment. Alone in the Dublin night, she encounters a gigantic eighty-foot cross mounted, for no evident purpose, over a "blank expanse," an emblem of the patriarchal theocracy that presides over the widespread social dysfunction dramatized in the novel. Grace immediately affiliates the cross with the one that marks her son's grave, and going a step further, she envisages the latter badge of salvation as a metaphor for Sean himself: "a small cross, a child's shape . . . in a throng of adult tombstones" (173). Now, as Grace can only surmise the size and shape of her son's grave marker, having never visited his grave site, her imaginary identification with the diminutive insignia closely parallels Gabriel Conroy's similarly visionary identification with the presumed iconography surrounding Michael Furey's grave in the oft-cited conclusion to "The Dead." By extension, this allusive web serves to tighten the textual web connecting Grace's deceased son with Furey himself and his band of likewise distressed youths, including the Lass of Aughrim, her deceased infant, and X.

Like Gabriel, however, Grace doubts her fitness for the figure with whom she would be met. No sooner does she take up the cross as a vehicle in solidarity with Sean than she feels herself coming unstuck, losing her grip on that Christian standard of abused righteousness. She thinks to herself, "If somebody comes and finds me and asks me who I am, I will tell them that my name is Grace and I have fallen off the cross" (174). Her self-styled fall, in turn, replicates Sean's stumble into the drowning pool; Grace even turns herself open-mouthed to the sky and inhales the rainwater, in an unconsciously enacted, topsy-turvy variation on Sean's last bodily reflex. There is a reversal in the physical trajectory of Grace and Sean here that corresponds to the reversal in what we might term their moral orientation. Sean's slip into a ditch carries him *up to* the cross in Grace's imagination, absolved of all responsibility and embalmed in the brute innocence of infancy. Grace slips *from* the cross and finds herself exposed in her fleeting dereliction of responsibility. The dyadic mirroring of mother and son is accordingly skewed. As her crucified attitude attests, Grace remains, no less than her son, a victim of the intersecting pinions of Irish Catholic patriarchy: generational, sexual, and class inequity. At the same time, she remains implicated in the operation of that leviathan, even as it bears down on her. Unlike her son, she models what it is to be a subject of scandal in full, to find oneself suspended on both sides of the moral ledger in an insupportable complex of circumstances that society itself connives at while condemning.

The crisis following Grace's confession delineates a subtle but decisive shift in the psycho-symbolic workings of her self-adjudication. It marks the moment when X ceases to be merely the most public of Grace's alter egos and comes to eclipse the departed Sean as her primary transferential object, the fantasy figure in whom she can see a plausible but still preferred image of her own moral estate. Grace's first act of psychic transference onto X occurs by way of the signifier at its most material, the bare shape of the letter. Perusing the morning newspaper, her eye gravitates toward the repeated inscription, X, and she is mesmerized by the figure itself:

> It was everywhere. It looked strange . . . not like a letter at all . . . a new symbol.
> The words were cautious and slow, and Grace had soon lost the thread of them. It was not just her exhaustion. They were small and inadequate next to the enigmatic figure, the cross fallen sideways . . . this hieroglyph. It was something discovered, revealed. Oddly familiar. (175)

At the center of this mediation, we can discern the grounds of the X's unconscious appeal for Grace, its heimlich/unheimlich quality. It is the vehicle of unconscious signification, internalized by yet still inaccessible to her. The X represents an "enigmatic figure" for Grace because it answers to her own self-styled insignia of the night before—the cross—and as a cross fallen sideways it answers to her position of having "fallen off the cross." The met-onymic connection here rings with especially audible overtones owing to the asymmetry it highlights. Grace's fall *from* the cross skewed her identifi-cation with her son, denoting her unworthiness to claim his brand of incul-pability. Concomitantly, the sideways falling *of* the cross, the sign of socially approved, religiously imbued persecution and redemption, suggests there is something skewed about the theocratic order of Ireland that it symbolizes.

It is precisely this systemic warping or deformation that fixes Grace's identification with the embattled X girl as wrongly condemned: "The X stared out at her from the folded newspaper. She closed her eyes and saw it still" (176).[5] At this point, she notes, "It was everywhere. . . . this hiero-glyph" (175). From this point on, we would note, Grace's lost son is basically nowhere; he does not return to her conscious mind for the rest of the novel. His only reappearance comes in one of her dreams, in which he is subsumed into the figure of X, thus rehearsing in little the terms of his original disap-pearance. Grace's shift in transferential identification has as its unconscious aim a remortaring of the psychic crypt so recently breached. Reviewing the headline of the evening papers, she thinks, "All they said was X. What was she now? A murderer?" (232). This incredulous question might easily refer to herself as well as X, especially given the technique of free indirect style at play. But this is also to say that Grace's growing sense of sorority with the girl derives from and gives precedence to the crime for which she feels hunted, the spousal homicide, rather than the authentic source of her com-punction, her son's death; or rather, it derives from and gives precedence to that spousal homicide so that her son's death may remain safely interred behind its psychic walls. Here, if you will, lies the reason for the abrupt and thoroughgoing disappearance of Sean from her waking thoughts. Denial, the ability to forget knowing what one knows, is a subject's last defense against scandal's defining malaise, the inability to avoid or dismiss by force of will some degree of incrimination in its workings.[6]

But as the cryptologists Abraham and Torok have noted, these edifices of profound denial and repression, these crypts, are not individual keeps but transpersonal, mainly familial compounds (2004, 157–61), and this mode of structuration compromises the solidity of Grace's defenses. As we have noted, Grace's remaining son, Martin, rejects the abuse justification for her murder of his father and scolds all who would license her action on that basis. His harsh judgment of Grace and his willingness to turn her over to the authorities nonplusses everyone who knows that Martin too suffered his own abuse and brutality at his father's hands upon revealing his homosexuality, and that Grace bankrolled his escape from the menace of Monaghan, a conservative Irish Catholic habitus, to the more liberal, hence far safer, remit of middle-class Dublin. Accordingly, Martin's vengeful attitude toward Grace positively demands closer analysis. While his mindset may not be the central narrative conundrum to be solved in *The Long Falling*, it is perhaps the most challenging of the narrative's major tributaries.

In a shrewd treatment of the novel's gender politics, Madden proposes that for Martin, a gay man in a deeply patriarchal if liberalizing society, "the assertion of political subjectivity . . . requires the erasure or silencing of his mother" (2010, 28), whose intrusive presence in his new urban life space leaves him almost desperately afraid. On Madden's reading, Grace represents the "corporeal, ancestral and non-national past" that threatens his commodiously modern "self-definition," a hereditary avatar "surrounding him, encircling him like a border" (28). To assume the place that the Irish nation has now made relatively secure for him, Martin not only enters into an "alliance with the State and the police" (29) but also becomes, in the words of his boyfriend, Henry, "[his] father's son" (Ridgway 1999, 293), subjecting his mother to emotional betrayal, a peculiarly heartrending form of abuse.

In his "final analysis," Madden finds Martin's identification with his gender and the civic privilege it enjoys, "over any sense of empathy for or connection with his mother, troubling and ironic given the violence he also suffered at his father's hand" (2010, 30). As astute as this analysis is, Martin's "troubling and ironic" enmity toward his fellow victim must rest on something more fundamental, more primordial, than gender solidarity or political instinct, and this primal psychic and emotional ground, the very heart of the family crypt, is revealed in aptly transpersonal fashion by Grace herself. As Madden observes, Grace discerns her son's emotional distance from her, which she attributes to their spatiotemporal separation. But the language with which she reports this perception taps another layer, a deeper vein, in this tortuous family romance. Recumbent in her bath, she muses, "There was a new air around him. He had learned a way of being in the world, learned how to manage his progress, his breathing, his life. Learned all of it without her. She breathed across the water. . . . He had dug himself a dry pit, cleared a space amongst the shadows of his growing up. He had set himself against his past" (Ridgway 1999, 108). The odd focus on Martin's "air" and his "breathing," followed by Grace's own breath "across the water," followed in turn by the metaphor of a "dry pit," a specifically *dry* pit, cleared against the "shadows of his growing up"—the whole tissue of Grace's reverie unfolds an unconscious contrast between Martin's "way of being" and his brother's mode of dying, between Martin's transcendence of his Monaghan wellhead and his brother's literal submersion therein, between Martin's achieved independence from Grace ("learned it all without her") and Sean's fatal dependence on her. In both her verbal and bodily figuration, Grace has Martin "set himself against a past" charged with, if not defined by, the dreadful legend of avoidable filial death.

Is Martin's own sense of this past similarly haunted by unconscious intimations of his brother's mortality? The "shadows of his growing up" from which he has "cleared a space for himself" clearly include Grace herself. Are those shadows darkened, is this separation from her tinctured, with a degree of subliminal misgiving or disquiet concerning her part in Sean's demise? On the occasion of Martin's coming out to his family, his father expresses the depth of his homophobic loathing with a series of murderous wish-fantasies, pronouncing, "Your mother killed the wrong fucking one, that's for sure," and, "You'd be better off if it'd been you that she killed," and again, "You drowned the wrong one. It's your fault." Martin stands up for his mother, insisting, "She killed no one." But Grace breaks with her usual custom and makes no protestations of innocence whatever (188–89). So at the very moment that Grace is to perform her most decisive act of maternal protection, delivering Martin from his father's rage, the opposed notion of Grace as a lethal force is being inculcated in Martin, surely not for the first time. More importantly, if this is a long-standing formulation on Michael's part, then Michael has made Sean's demise an implicit death threat issuing from Grace and delivered to Martin, symbolically turning her nurture to vitriol.

Stage Three

The unconscious impression left on Martin by his father's accusations proves durable. Upon his reunion with Grace in Dublin, after the still unsolved homicide, Martin grows suddenly mindful of a secret "strength" that he had found in his mother as a child, and by a seemingly reflexive mnemonic process he associates that inexplicable quality with "the smell of his father," the "lap of the water," and the "whole life" he had hidden from his father and placed in Grace's trust (95). In combination, these become enigmatic signifiers, redolent—undecidedly but therefore suggestively—of another story, his brother's story. Shortly thereafter, Martin reveals in thought and word how far his juvenile awareness of an enigmatic secret strength in Grace masked and continues to mask a lingering infantile fear of the power she rather carelessly held over his life and death. Calling to mind their rambles over the wintry Monaghan landscape, he remarks, "Do you remember going out walking at home, in the snow? You used to trip me up on slopes and go diving after me. It's a wonder we weren't killed on a covered rock" (140). Grace's rejoinder, "I only did it when I knew it was safe," cannot but belie itself in recalling her walk with Sean, when she thought "it was safe," and he wound up "diving-in" to the watery pit (140). In the transpersonal unconscious of the psychic crypt, Grace's assurance carries implications, has effects, unnervingly contrary to her consciously nurturing intent. In response, Martin phantasmatically conflates the symbolic threat Grace poses to his "self-definition" and civic belonging with a maternal threat to his bodily existence: "He galloped through words . . . all the time convincing himself more and more that his mother could expose him with a story . . . reduce his life to the few square miles of his childhood. He thought that if she wanted to, she could kill him. Tell him where he'd come from. . . . Kill him dead" (140–41).

Owing to the tragic enactment of the Quinn family romance, Grace's role as the avatar of Martin's "corporeal, ancestral and non-national history," as Madden has it (2010, 29), blends seamlessly into his *méconnaissance* of her as a prehistorical, mythological imago, the devouring mother, of whom Ireland boasts a wide range, from the Sheela-na-gig to the Caillac Beare to Joyce's Old Gummy Granny and the "old sow that eats her farrow" (Joyce 1992a, 220). The manner of Sean's death, drowning in a sinkhole, evinces a link between the collective phantasmagoria of the devouring mother and the Earth Mother, both anatomical (watery pit as birth canal/vagina dentata) and functional (the confusion of enwombing and entombing, bearing and burying).

In all of this, there is no disagreement with Madden's assertion that Martin has "identified with his gender over any sense of empathy for or connection with his mother" (2010, 30). There is, rather, a demonstration that the "shadows of his growing up" (Ridgway 1999, 108) make this particular instance of identification nothing less, at the level of infantile fantasy, than a matter of survival. Unconsciously, he experiences the threat she poses to his social "self-definition" (Madden 2010, 29) as a threat to his embodied self, the threat to his national belonging as threat to his very existence. The specter of her "surrounding him, encircling like a border" (Ridgway 1999, 160) shrinks from "the few square miles of his childhood" (141) to the dimensions of a watery hole in the ground. Martin's adherence to the patriarchal sex-gender system could not, accordingly, run any deeper, referring as it does to the symbolic threshold where subjectivity emerges on an already politicized gradient.

In expressing his consternation with Martin's sullen animosity toward Grace on behalf of an acknowledged scoundrel, Henry exclaims, "You hated him. You loved her. You knew stuff." Martin's reply, "What stuff?" signals not an absent but a double meaning to be attached to his boyfriend's words (239). By "stuff," of course, Henry intends the most legible Quinn family scandal, the history of spousal and familial abuse perpetrated by Martin's unexpectedly lamented father. But during that cardinal incident of such abuse, cited earlier, the spousal and filial violence unfolded simultaneously by way of that other, more confidential family scandal, whose disputed tenor—that Grace was, quite literally, a femme fatale—has received fresh credence from the addition of her accuser-husband to the roster of her alleged victims.

This retroactive validation of Martin's unconscious terrible mother fantasy, in turn, forges a transferential link in Martin's psyche between the figures of Sean and Michael, the dead brother and the dead father, both left by Grace to die (in this regard, it merits notice that Martin feels most aggrieved over Grace's decision to "just leave [Michael] there and head off home" [238], a move isomorphic with her decision to leave Sean in the pit while she finished hanging the laundry). Here we have arrived at the burden preventing Martin from "taking [his mother's] side" (239), as Henry and all of his other similarly classed and gendered friends do so readily. His outrage at his father's killing remains every bit as inexplicable as Henry claims, unless and until we understand it to be a displacement of

A. The subterranean anxiety that killing activated over whether Grace knowingly left Sean to drown (or really withheld aid while Sean was still alive); and

B. The infantile panic that Michael's death rekindled over what Grace might have let happen to Martin on those "covered rocks."

The metonymic slippage animating Martin's fantasy in this regard stems directly from his place in the Quinn family structure. In the aftermath of Sean's death, Martin was slotted as his replacement not only in Michael's patrilineage but also in Grace's affections and in those dangerous walks across the farm. Now, with Michael dead and Grace taking refuge in Martin's abode and in his social family, he is being slotted as a replacement not for an elder brother but for the father. Under these circumstances, Martin's prosecutorial reaction to the murder should be construed as proceeding not solely from some tribal "identification with his gender" but from an identification, largely imposed, with the fate of his two gendered counterparts, in a family romance freighted with mythic imagos. Henry is substantially correct, as most readers would concur, to call Martin out for displaying properties of toxic masculinity associated with his progenitor— obstinacy, obtuseness, mercilessness, and even cruelty. However, Martin is also his "father's son" in inheriting from the man a symbolic position for which the unconscious fantasy of the terrible mother, bolstered by real-life events, carries visceral, motivational power. Triangulated as it is by the manner of Sean's death, Grace's violent disposal of her husband weighs in the precarious balance of Martin's psyche as an assault—emotional, material, and potentially lethal—against himself.

Strikingly, Grace reaches much the same conclusion. Following a confrontation with Martin, she comes to judge her slaying of Michael as less (than) justified, precisely for the damage it has inflicted on her son. It is as if Martin alone can communicate to Grace the gravity of her action: "Martin had told her what she had done. Killed her husband. His father. As if she had needed telling. She had" (229–30). For this reason, the murder ceases, fully and finally, to function as the bulwark of her psychic crypt, the acknowledged but effectively rationalized crime that safeguards her denial of responsibility for Sean's demise. Instead, the murder of Michael seems to have replaced, in another key, the moral tenor of the prior bad act: Grace has once again inadvertently but culpably brought violent harm to a son. Indeed, Grace goes so far as to figure the effect of her misdeed as the sudden, startling loss of her second son, and it triggers the same type of grief as the death of her first, with which it is associated in Grace's topographical imagination: "A day begun here, unfolding in front of her like a Monaghan road ... a construction that had crumbled as it was built, that had come apart in front of her.... Her eyes in shock. She had lost her son. As quick as saying it, as sharp as that" (241).

Further on, Grace even tropes the motives and consequences of her homicide as a form of oral ingestion, an engorging. That is, as if to confirm the transpersonal nature of her psychic crypt, its status as, in every sense, a family plot, Grace frames the violence affecting her loss of Martin in terms uncannily congruent with his own fantasy of her as a carelessly but compulsively devouring mother: "I wanted to be free of [Michael], and so I did it, but I'm tied to him now like I never was.... I wanted to spit him out and I swallowed him instead. I shouldn't have done it" (300).

As the "construction" of Grace's psychic crypt "crumbles" under the pressure of Martin's virulent reprehension, her identification with X, the last layer of reinforcement, begins to fracture and give way as well. On the night before the Dublin X march, Grace indulges in a woozy, whiskey-soaked reverie in which she sustains a deep moral affiliation with the girl, a sisterhood of the wronged and wrongly indicted: "she might end up meeting the girl in prison. Murderers, the two of them. Grace would look after her, become her friend. Together they would move on.... They would have each other" (274–75). But feeling that her violence against her husband wound up damaging Martin, much as she had allowed harm to come to Sean, Grace can no longer pretend to that moral parity with X on which her sororal fantasy was reared.

The generational breach in Grace's doubling of X reasserts itself; what is missing from her desired at-oneness with X is the element of being a minor at the disposal of surrounding adults, as opposed to being, however disavowedly, herself a disposer. Grace identifies with X's scandal in the first place in order to obscure precisely this generational schism, as it played itself out with Sean. In predicating her identification with X on her self-justified murder of Michael Quinn, himself a notorious destroyer of children, Grace undertakes to forget or efface her own embroilment in this pattern of destruction. Her identification with X thus seeks, albeit unconsciously, to capitalize on the deniability structured into any enigmatic signifier (including a public scandal figure), that "occult zone of undecidability" that makes the enigmatic signifier such an effective encryption device.

But her identification finds its limit in this very motive; it cannot move toward completion, approach full determinacy, without exposing the fault lines sutured or shrouded by the enigmatic signifier. That limit imposes itself a short way into Grace's reverie. Her new friend, Mrs. Talbot, points out that X is "too young for an adult prison," implicitly reinstating the generational divide between the would-be cellmates (275). In Grace's universe, children do not kill; they die, and at the hands of adults: "[Grace] had murdered. She had done that. . . . The X girl had not murdered. She had not done anything" (276). Even though Grace continues to fixate on her bond of gendered oppression and resistance with X, as victims of the same "machinery" of the patriarchal state, her own image of how the "machinery" is "grinding" on X ultimately convinces her that "she was not the same as the girl" (276). Grace now envisions X as a fourteen-year-old, from which vantage she appears not as Grace's doppelgänger or counterpart but as a stand-in, a living emblem, of her dead son's occulted memory.

As Grace falls asleep and reverie morphs into dream, X stands forth in the unmistakable guise of Grace's own child. She not only "looked to Grace like her dead son" but like the son "who had held her hand on the way to the lake," which immediately mutates into "the shallow pool" in which Sean drowned (279). The dream concludes with X meeting a like fate, except that her body is symbolically ruptured and lacerated in the process: "From her hands fell drops of water, breaking on the ground with a splash of red and a flower of white bone" (279).

The dream image conflates the drowning pool with the "grinding" social "machinery," Sean's loss with the girl's abuse. The scene unfolds in the shadow of a "narrow church" with a "tall spire," an emblem of the theocratic authority underwriting that machinery. Turning to "[X's] face again," Grace "recognised" a "mix of Sean and Martin," a composite dream image that encapsulates the realignment of the dramatis personae that has taken place in Grace's mind (279). Whereas at first Grace internalized the parallels between herself and X as an identification with the girl, she ends by internalizing their salient difference. Grace's dream positions her as an agent as well as a victim of the Irish social machinery and X as an abstract, a summary type, of all the children devoured by it.

The moral recalibration staged in Grace's dream supplies a crucial guide to understanding the full significance of Grace's attitude upon her arrest during the great march. At one point, the crowd sings, "Let her go, let her go," in reference to X's desire to quit Ireland to receive abortion services

(302). In giving herself up, Grace plays on this coincidence in her parlay with Detective Brady:

> "Are you ready to come in with us, then?"
> "I am. You'll let the girl go."
> "... What girl?"
> "The X girl." (304)

Framing her request almost as a plea bargain, Grace proposes a certain fungibility of herself and X in keeping with her past identification. But this is fungibility with a difference. Plea bargains necessarily entail the freeing of the less culpable, or innocent, "in exchange for the [more] guilty" (304). Grace's proposed bargain aligns perfectly with her realization that however like, "she was not the same as the girl." More than that, Grace bids to trade in her greater fault in exchange for the greater good—in the terms we used earlier, to transform *mea culpa* into *felix culpa*. Having "fallen off the cross," she proposes, in effect, to climb back on it to redeem X, to barter for or buy back (re-deem) X as a way of saving her. Inasmuch as Grace had, the night before, enshrined X as the dream surrogate or double of her deceased son, her gesture also represents another unconscious attempt to reverse the outcome of that fateful night, which at this point we can safely designate the origin of Grace's "long falling."

But Grace's final démarche carries still more sweeping implications. Having internalized her own unwitting complicity in the social machinery grinding on both X and herself, Grace simultaneously offers herself as a savior for X, restoring her from scandal object to innocent victim, and as scapegoat for the nation-state that victimized X in the first place. That is to say, she acts to dissolve the scandal embroiling X and to take upon herself not just her own scandal but also the scandal of theocratic social power grossly abused, what we might call the systemic scandal underlying the narrative with its three categories of violence: the abused woman, disposable child, and abased queer. Grace does not just give herself up to "let her go," she gives herself up as someone who admits to wrong, and whose admitted wrong, following as it does on the sanctioned gender and generational violence of the Irish nation, is inextricably enmeshed with that social order. That is to say, the warrant that Grace presents to "let her go," her own wrong, is effectively commutable with the wrong that society itself has inflicted on X, including the wrong of incarcerating her. It is a "commutation" of X's sentence, warranted by the crime of having imposed it in the first place. By this psycho-symbolic gambit, Grace constructively, if paradoxically, transforms her final relationship to X. By relinquishing her spiritual kinship with the girl, she enacts a new mode of solidarity with her, one that circumvents the Manichean logic of public scandal itself.

NOTES

1. In "An Interview with Jean Laplanche," Caruth (2014) engages Laplanche in a focused and detailed account of the genesis and meaning of the enigmatic signifier, beginning with Laplanche's account of how latter-day psychoanalytic theorists and exponents of Freud became fixated on seduction itself, mistaking the event of early childhood seduction for a theory of seduction. Laplanche ruefully describes the reduction of Freud's theory of seduction to the mere statement that "seduction is important in the child," which, as he points out, "is not a theory, just an assertion" (26). Laplanche describes how, in *The Language of Psycho-analysis* (1973), he and J.-B. Pontalis unearthed Freud's original seduction theory qua theory, with its "very complicated . . . temporal aspects, economic aspects, and topographical aspects" (26). In Freud's "Project for a Scientific Psychology," Laplanche finds Freud's founding theory of seduction "very carefully elaborated . . . in the famous case of Emma." This theory accounts for "the complex interplay between the external and the internal" that occurs at the originary moment of seduction—a "wounding or 'piercing'" that occurs when "the small human being [who] has no unconscious . . . is confronted with messages invaded by the unconscious of the other" (30). It is in response to this infantile encounter with the other, which Laplanche describes as an implantation of "the strangeness of the other," that the child copes by building an ego. Thus, Laplanche argues, it is "in relation to the seduction theory that the subject builds himself as an individual." It is to internalize "the other's message" that the child first "builds an inside." And it is because, as Caruth notes, the ego "is so very closely linked to this temporal structure of originary seduction" that "the ego is, after that, always open to the possibility of being traumatized again" (30).

2. Chris Greer and Eugene McLaughlin, in their article "The Return of the Repressed: Secrets, Lies, Denial and 'Historical' Institutional Child Sex Abuse Scandals" (2015), posit four phases of scandal, the first of which, latency (which corresponds to the open secret), may or may not proceed to the second phase, activation, at which point the scandal process is inevitable. Henry Fielding, in *Tom Jones*, serves as an early scandal theorist when he notes scandal's propensity either to stay latent or, irreversibly, to cross the threshold into public visibility, when he observes that for "gentlemen who have the misfortune to have any of their rogueries detected . . . discovery seldom stops till the whole is come out" (2007, 99). After the "detection" phase, Greer and McLaughlin's remaining three stages, which ensue only (but then invariably) once a latent scandal has been "detected," correspond roughly to the three stages we describe—activation is defined as the point when a news organization has committed to publishing the scandal and naming the abuser, and it is driven by institutional responses that may entail denial of abuse, denial of knowledge of abuse, and/or denial of responsibility for abuse. Greer and McLaughlin argue that there is no such thing as a "deactivated" scandal. Once a transgression has become activated, the amplification phase shifts the focus of the scandal from the crime itself to institutional efforts to cover it up. The justice phase involves a reinstatement of the primary transgressions, new disclosures of incriminating evidence and supplementary evidence, and intensifying denunciation of the individuals and institutions involved. Sometimes the "trial by media" is prolonged, and sometimes individuals or institutions try to put an end to it through a public admission and apology (Whyte 2015, 113–23).

3. See especially Moira Maguire's *Precarious Childhood in Post-Independence Ireland* (2009), which breaks ground in several crucial ways. It presents a new "history of childhood" in Ireland and is a new account of the relationship of the Catholic Church to the Irish state. Most importantly for our purposes, it breaks ground as a sustained, disciplined examination of "the child" as a discrete, autonomous category, an examination that is not folded into (and thus distorted within) a broader account of, for instance, women, the poor, workers, Catholics, Protestants, and so on.

4. Virtually all prior critics have accepted the Grace = X equation that our reading here demonstrates Grace herself gradually and painfully discarding.

The long falling that Ridgway describes in his opening paragraph is relentless and inescapable, and it establishes a pattern. Then, abruptly, it stops, and the sunlight, like the snow in "The Dead," seems to transform and unify the whole of Irish society, ostensibly repairing harm that was heretofore ubiquitous; the whole country "looks new." Thus, the metaphoric Irish nation that the novel presents has recently undergone an apparent collective transformation from the society-wide condition of irremediable abjection to the shared enjoyment of equally universal protections. However, through the contrasting life trajectories of Grace Quinn and her son, Martin, Ridgway makes plain that for most Irish girls and women the pattern the rain put down remains in place. In this new Ireland, after the flood, the Catholic Church may look bigger than it is only owing to its ongoing "power of suggestion," but even now it "never moves." The prevailing atmosphere, "the sky," "moves behind it and changes it," but such changes are variable; bathed in the vacillating light of the Bishop Casey, Kerry Babies, and Ann Lovett scandals, the Irish Catholic Church, in response to the earliest of what will become an unimaginably protracted series of scandals, appears, by turns, "solid . . . and soft, depending" (Ridgway 1999, 4).

5. This scene, with its uncanny inculpating or condemnatory gaze, recalls the earlier scene when Sean, the journalist, looks at Grace with a look that was "not right."

6. Clearly, the subject's drive to avoid feeling or being shamed is fundamental to the operations of scandal. The following two studies look at scandal or public exposure through the lens of shame rather than noting shame only in passing as one of scandal's structuring effects: Koestenbaum (2011) and Munt (2007). The role of shame and denial in the pattern of forgetting that could be considered the final stage of scandal stems from scandal's constitutive relationship to trauma, via the enigmatic signifier. The propensity of the social order to treat scandal both as license to speak of the unspeakable but also as subsequently reinstating that unspeakability through a kind of reforgetting is apparent, for instance, in the repeated discovery and amnesia, the surfacings and submersions of facts, relating to Ireland's most iconic child abuse scandal, that of the Tuam Mother and Baby Home.

5

RETROFITTING IRELAND'S ARCHITECTURE OF CONTAINMENT IN TANA FRENCH'S *IN THE WOODS*

IN ELIZABETH BOWEN'S *THE HOUSE in Paris* (1959), the character Karen, on a ferry traveling from Queenstown to Holyhead, encounters a young Irish woman of approximately her own age who barrages her with free-wheeling reflections primarily expressing her interest in attractive males and the hope that she might meet one while in England. Everything about this young woman is strange to Karen, from her bright yellow outfit (Karen thinks of her as "Yellow Hat"), to her open excitement concerning the early and most entertaining stage of the dating-and-mating process, to her general and apparently unfeigned *joie de vivre*. Observing her at a distance, Karen thinks that she and Yellow Hat seem hardly to belong even to the same species. She reflects that there really ought to be more than two gender categories, given the degree of difference that can exist between what are both nominally young women (89).[1]

Bowen's Karen and Yellow Hat are so different, of course, owing to the very different spaces they occupy in the post–World War I world. Karen is awkwardly negotiating the mismatch between the domestic space of her liberal, well-educated, aristocratic family, which has remained largely unchanged for generations, and the cosmopolitan, gender-integrated postwar public sphere represented by her art school friends. And she is tacitly, shamefacedly wishing she could remain within the comfort, predictability, and privilege of the old order without having to forswear the challenges and opportunities, as well as the uncertainty and the risks, of the new one. Yellow Hat, on the other hand, though we know much less about her, clearly embodies an Irish "new woman," eager to enjoy all that the interwar period has to offer: travel, fashion, fun, and the chance to be admired and sought after. Whatever domestic sphere this young woman was raised in, she is eager to leave it behind.[2] We might think of gender in Tana French's *In the Woods* (2007) in a similar framework, as a detailed literary rendering of some of the many genders proper to Ireland's evolving public and private spaces in the later twentieth century, and to the role of childhood trauma, specifically sexualized childhood trauma, in constituting them.

Over the course of modern Irish history, certain spaces took on supercharged significance in the national imaginary, due to the various ways in which they mediated cultural, biological, and economic processes of social reproduction. In some cases, such as Kilmainham Prison or Dublin Castle, the reason for a place's privileged position in Ireland's socio-symbolic order invites little fine-grained analysis. These places are to Irish history what the Bastille is to French history: to learn about the culture and its history is to learn what these places mean, in learning what they are. In other cases, however, the role of particular places in conjoining economic distribution and biological reproduction with cultural significance and normative regulation has benefited from scholarly scrutiny. For instance, many who grow up in Ireland continue to read the Anglo-Irish Big House as an emblem of colonial and class oppression, yet work such as that of Declan Kiberd (1995) and Vera Kreilkamp (1998) on the role of the Big House in reproducing settler-colonial relations has helped us better understand its distinctive place in the Irish imaginary. In *Transformation in Irish Culture*, Luke Gibbons has cast light on the oddly paired, hypersymbolic position of the Catholic Church and the Irish pub after the Great Famine had razed all the other components of the native Irish infrastructure whereby a shattered social network might be recreated (1996, 85–86). Through the work of scholars and cultural commentators such as Kathryn Conrad, Mary Raftery, Frances Finnegan, Claire Bracken, James Smith, and most recently Catherine Corless, we can map how, in the post-Famine landscape, spaces of gendered incarceration and punishment like the Magdalene laundries emerged as both constitutive and paradigmatic of the broader, post-Treaty system of control and appropriation that Smith (2007) terms Ireland's "architecture of containment."

This work on the socio-symbolic meaning of particular spaces has great relevance for an understanding of French's Dublin-based crime novels, which merit serious critical attention in part owing to her attentiveness to the complex ways in which specific Irish places—especially those peripheral to Ireland's national self-definition—may hold multiple, contradictory historical and cultural meanings. In a nod to Kiberd's observation concerning Elizabeth Bowen's depictions of houses, we would add that for French, every place is like an operating manual that tells those in it how to conduct themselves (1995, 369). A recurrent theme of *In the Woods* is that how we read the instructions depends on how we define the space itself—that is, which elements in the space and its history are accorded significance and which elements are overlooked (see Lloyd 1993, 6–7; Pine 2011, 13–16).

In the hands of Tana French, the mystery/thriller genre affords rich opportunities to explore questions of how we make sense of finite social spaces and the incalculably myriad lives and histories each contains. Focalizing *In the Woods* to one specific and nationally liminal place, French deploys elements of unconscious fantasy, at once erotic and violent, that are never definitively corroborated or dispelled, and she thereby extends the inherent capacity of the mystery/thriller genre to complicate, problematize, and even thwart the very epistemophilic drive that it exists to elicit. Although the crime that sets the narrative in motion is ultimately solved, the elasticity of its sociohistorical context and psychosocial impetus forms a bewildering stay on the reader's understanding of its setting, Knocknaree, with all of its "self-contained worlds," inner and outer, "layered onto the same space" (French 2007, 222). In thus staging the difficulties and dangers of attempting to know even a single housing estate and the proliferating series of traumatic events at that single location, the novel unfolds what we might call a revisionist allegory: a framework that compels the reader to recognize that the initial temptation to treat various subject positions (gender, ethnic, spatiotemporal, etc.) as stable and binary rather than multiple and contingent can only serve to balk our comprehension of Ireland's topological imaginary—that is, how a specific locus knots together diverse histories with their respective mythopoetic alloys.

"Empty Your Heart of Its Mortal Dream": Traumatic *Bildung*

The Dublin murder detective of *In the Woods*, Rob Ryan, a narrator both sympathetic and in every sense unreliable, prepares us to receive his account of a harrowing murder investigation gone horribly wrong with the terse caution, "I crave truth. And I lie" (4). His paradoxical confession illustrates French's deft use of the police procedural to twist and intensify the dilemma posed to the reader by a narrator whose acute, introspective untrustworthiness intimates some ethically unsettling parallels between the work of the detective and the work of the fabulist or fiction writer. However, our primary interest in Ryan's opening caveat is more literal minded. We are concerned with Ryan's trumpeting of his systematic mendacity in enforcing the law as the first in a series of pointed comparisons between the work of detectives and other officials whose respectable status, income, and attitudes operate in the service and defense of the Irish state, and the mentality and conduct characteristically identified in the novel with psychopathologies of a broadly criminal type.[3]

It is perversely appropriate that the nexus connecting these respectively licit and illicit psychopathological performances in the novel should also be the primary vehicle of normative (and normatively traumatic) psychosexual development—that is, the signifier in its inherently enigmatic aspect. As noted in earlier chapters, as desiring subjects, parental figures inevitably impart to their children ambiguously eroticized psychic messages, encoded material to which Jean Laplanche has given the name the "enigmatic signifier." Such symbolic rudiments serve to enable and even enjoin, without positively enforcing, sexual constructions and responses at the unconscious level. For Laplanche, the introduction of (adult) sexuality into the child's life horizon elicits a traumatic enjoyment that binds the child to its symbolic occasions and thus furnishes the very condition of their subjectivity. The conduit of this traumatic enjoyment, or jouissance, is precisely the signifier in its extrasymbolic (as opposed to presymbolic) dimension, its infusion of the meaning it bears with a sensory and affective force that exceeds it. Jouissance nests in the material lining or penumbra of the signifier (the grace of a gesture, the kink in an expression) as an interval of undecidability, wherein what is imposed and what is invited grow indistinguishable. The act of seduction merges with the experience of being seduced; the subject and object of libidinal cathexis are confounded. That is to say, the enigmatic signifier is the site, the support, of a truly constitutive transference, the coming together of the (sexed) subject in the field of the other.

Because the signifying form is inherently iterable, the jouissance that is vested in moments of infantile sexual initiation remains available to be reactivated across a wide array of circumstances. The profound impact of primal libidinal excitation thus proves a contingently renewable resource that fuels various manifestations of sexual, sexualized, and sexually tinctured behavior. Moreover, because it functions as a penumbra of undecidability, wherein a certain confusion obtains between the impulses or affective stirrings of the parties involved, the enigmatic signifier is also the primary mechanism of psychosexual misrecognition and manipulation, which can likewise extend along an eroticized chain of association to all other matters of import for the subject in question.

What we are calling the psychopathological performances, of both the law enforcers and the lawbreakers, represent an extreme subspecies of such beguilement. The profound relationality of desire is drawn on and exploited, but in the mood of absolute refusal. That is to say, the radical transferential entanglement that results in the child's traumatic jouissance is reenacted along severed, dichotomous lines, with the psychopathological agent rising to the imaginary jouissance of a plenary subjectivity by submitting the other party to the trauma of violent objectification or instrumentality.

The psychopathology of everyday detection is so vital to the narrative structure of *In the Woods* that Ryan offers an illustration thereof even "before you begin my story," as a framing device for the whole (4). He details the stock interrogation tricks whereby the Murder squad detectives mount deceptive shows of vulnerability, empathy, and confidentiality to inveigle their marks, while inducing them to mistrust and ultimately betray their own friends and confederates. In the case at hand, Ryan begins by flirting with a girl named Jackie, the paramour of a robbery-murder suspect. Such flirtation is an exercise in eroticized indefiniteness, or undecidable eroticism, which pivots on a chain of enigmatic signifiers—vocal tone, suggestive gesture, ocular intensity, and so on—whose imperfect legibility allows them to function as indeterminable expressions of and lures for desire. Ryan proceeds to engage Jackie in a dialectic of transference, casting himself as an especially avid, committed version of her boyfriend ("telling her I can see why he would want to stay home when he's got her") and, by implication, casting her attractiveness as the gravitational force in their colloquy (3). He gives her this taste of sugared erotic agency precisely, and psychopathologically, as a means of brutally reducing her to a useful object: first within the fictional scheme her boyfriend had supposedly hatched ("He's claiming that she . . . gave [the unmarked bills] to him"; 3) and second within Ryan's law enforcement fiction that her boyfriend had thus implicated her. What

Ryan calls his "delicate crosshatching of discomfort and compassion at her man's betrayal" encapsulates the performative contradiction at the heart of psychopathology, the proffer of intimacy as a self-interested strategy of dissociation (3). And it is precisely the enigmatic signifier that facilitates this strategy by veiling its central contradiction, that fools a woman like Jackie into believing she figures in the scene as a desiring and desirable subject long after she has been relegated to the status of a disposable tool.

Ryan's effective deployment of the enigmatic signifier to seduce persons of interest into betraying hidden truths depends on his already-assumed or established credibility as an official and a man. Conversely, in a sort of double bootstrap, his credibility as an official and a man happens to derive in large measure from a classic repository of the enigmatic signifier, the lilt and grain of the voice, in which meaningful verbal counters register, and by which they are inevitably, if ambiguously, inflected. Ryan's credibility specifically inheres in his "good" English public school accent, a particularly valuable social and professional asset in Ireland, as he observes. The residual influence of what Valente has termed "the myth of manliness" lends Ryan's anglicized tonality an aura of intelligence and competence unmatched among the other Irish-accented officials around him. Of special import, accordingly, is the derivation of his "perfect BBC accent" (9), and hence his manly cachet, from a boarding school that he attended only as a refuge from the continuing childhood trauma incurred "in the woods" at Knocknaree. The vanishing of then-Adam Ryan's friends, by choice or by force, at the prompting or the hands of another, also marks the disappearance of Ryan's childhood into his adult condition, a departure likewise indeterminably sought and suffered.

If French's allusions to W. B. Yeats's poem "The Hosting of the Sidhe," by way of the novel's mythic locale, Knocknaree, serve to affiliate Ryan's lost friends, Jamie and Peter, with the stolen children of faery lore, they simultaneously link the psychosexual growth of Ryan, punctuated as it is with this inconceivable rite of passage, to the related Irish myth of the changeling.[4] On the one hand, the eerie crisis that befalls Ryan on the cusp of sexual maturity banishes him to the woods permanently, in a sense. Allegorically speaking, he remains lodged within the substructures of the national imaginary. Having vanished from public view almost as surely as his friends, he has, like them, run "into legend, into sleepover stories and nightmares parents never hear" (2), while in the public sphere, reports of their uncanny mishap are still periodically circulated by that modern organ of mythology, the tabloid. On the other hand, Ryan has been substantially deracinated, losing not only his country of residence, at least temporarily, and the friends who have been his social ground of being, but also his name and his ethnic idioms. While his own embedded history is definitively Knocknareean, he cannot claim it, tell it, or expect it to be recognized as his own. In this respect, Ryan's childhood has indeed been stolen and traumatically replaced by a dissociated adulthood that retains only a haunting, profoundly alienated (and alienating) trace of his child self. The present Ryan feels continuous not with that prior being but only with the experience of his disappearance and all that surrounded it. There no longer exists the aboriginal Irish Adam(ite) Ryan; there remains only an anglicized replicant whose name, Rob, punningly testifies to the enigmatic theft that his manly BBC voice obscures.

To say that Ryan undergoes a changeling course *au bildung* is to say that he straddles the traumatic *séjour*: he remains in the woods of his childhood dispossession, and he has, concurrently, come out on the other side; he lives the ambivalence of a being doubly inscribed in time, and he has been driven to surmount that ambivalence, more or less effectively, in his daily rounds. Ryan's psychopathological performances as an investigator recapitulate this self-agon. On the one hand, Ryan's nagging if shadowy consciousness of a catastrophically lost childhood sustains his self-deprecating awareness of the inauthenticity of his accent and the arbitrary mystique it confers. On the other, he finds himself unable to overcome his prejudices concerning the credibility and even the basic worth of various regional gender and class variants more suited to the modest social milieu of his Knocknaree childhood than to the tony English boarding school of his adolescence. Painfully uneasy about his own past—as his compulsory, awkward Sundays with his parents attest—Ryan repeatedly musters (even while self-consciously deprecating) his own contempt toward the déclassé subjects he encounters at work. Under the circumstances, this pattern of self-refuting snobbery seems to represent a projective attempt to override the discomposure of his traumatically staggered subject position. His ruthlessly manipulative interrogation techniques, in turn, are not just about ferreting out the truth in others but also refashioning the truth of himself. In entering into, only to repudiate, an affective connection with his lower-caste suspects, Ryan forcibly asserts a hierarchical distance from them and, in the process, from the associations they trigger of his own interdicted boyhood. His psychopathological forensic performances are thus designed to ratify his status as a "made man" in every sense: a vested member of the elite Murder squad, yes, but also a fully actualized, unassailable male persona.

As a new member of Dublin's elite investigations unit, Ryan suffers a certain amount of pro forma hazing, but the general unquestioning acceptance that he receives stands in stark contrast to the unit's collective response to their next addition, Cassie Maddox. Whereas the veteran detectives take the competence of fellow newbie Ryan at face value, they presume Maddox to be both unqualified and sexually manipulative, her demonstrated acumen as an investigator notwithstanding. Her gender, coupled with her youth, serves, in their minds, as prima facie evidence that she cannot have merited her position. Her youthful female embodiment stands, like Ryan's good accent, as an infallible index of her overall worth. Clearly, she has made some kind of illicit use of her attractiveness, through seduction, blackmail, or both.

It is, in fact, fair to say that Maddox, who becomes Ryan's partner, matches or surpasses his skill in executing the psychopathological performances endemic to their investigative métier, including the deployment of enigmatic signifiers of relationality. She is, however, considerably less comfortable than he with these institutionally prized stratagems. Whereas Ryan views the ruses of police interrogation with self-reflexive irony, as an extension of the primary imposture that upholds his entire professional standing, Maddox feels her bad-faith debriefing of subjects to be of a piece with the other performative feints and subterfuges required by the ongoing, gender-based precariousness of her professional position: a strenuously nuanced campaign of (de)sexual(ized) self-presentation to her coworkers; silence about the legitimate, even admirable grounds for her promotion to the Murder squad; confirmation of her heterosexuality without palpable emphasis on her femininity or sexual appeal; and so on. Unlike Ryan, whose manipulative interview style aims to draw a bright, because assured, line between the suspect classes (in every sense) and his own community of detectives, Maddox cannot draw on a similar sense of tribal solidarity with her peers, and the affective lines inscribed by her manipulative practices accordingly come with a blurred or double edge.

Maddox's superb mastery of the psychopathological performance, no less than Ryan's, derives from a traumatic episode that has had a formative impact on her mature personality and course of life. On the cusp of adulthood, while at University College Dublin, Maddox fell victim to a full-blooded, clinical psychopath, with a supremely insidious talent for playing on the affections of his companions. Seizing on the complexities that imbue youthful cross-gender friendships among heterosexually identified subjects—a felicitous scenario for enigmatic signifiers—Maddox's college friend successfully exploits the lurking erotic possibilities in their relationship so as to conduct a protracted slanderous campaign against her: he contrives to exile her from their social circle on the grounds that she has sexually victimized him. Having driven her out of the university and, by a circuitous route, into law enforcement, this ordeal prepares her, serendipitously, both to navigate the suspicions of her new circle of associates, the Murder squad, and to cultivate the self-doubts of the alleged offenders she interviews.

On the strength of this experience, Maddox becomes the squad's resident expert on psychopathy, its unofficial profiler. Thus, it is no coincidence that it is she who most pointedly summarizes the detective-psychopath correspondence and figures psychopathological manipulation in terms of sexual aggression. "After all," she says of the drug dealer who stabbed her (thereby qualifying her for the Murder squad), "he had a point: I *was* only pretending to be his friend to screw him over" (15). The novel extends her analogy to state officials generally, who routinely simulate care, solicitude, protectiveness, and outrage for complete strangers (voters) who are of merely instrumental concern to them. Ryan speculates that half of all government positions are occupied by psychopaths, and in the novel's climactic scene, the head of the Murder squad, O'Kelly, observes that one psychopathic suspect's bent for destructive manipulation is ideally suited to government work. For its highest authorities and its lowliest delinquents alike, success in the Celtic Tiger social order seems to rely on the assumption of an empathy one does not feel in order to sell plausible lies one does not believe to people one secretly loathes in the pursuit of ends diametrically antithetical to their interests and expectations.

As the novel unfurls, Knocknaree looms as a narrative emblem and national microcosm of this modus operandi. Built just prior to Dublin's belated transformation from a Victorian cityscape catering to a small metrocolonial elite and a teeming underclass, the remote Knocknaree was touted as a groundbreaking, modernizing initiative that would make middle-class housing, replete with shops and movie theaters, available to Dublin's burgeoning caste of low-grade bureaucrats and office workers. If we are to judge by results, however, Knocknaree was, in fact, a highly effective bait-and-switch scheme whereby politicians conspired with developers to build cheap houses on inexpensive outlying land, then to sell them at inflated prices using flashy brochures that promised to support an infrastructure that was never to materialize. This essentially predatory collaboration between the state and Irish venture capitalists is recapitulated in the novel's present, in which a coalition of anonymous real estate investors and corrupt city councilors reenact the crime of Knocknaree's inception by forcing the construction of a motorway through the iconic woods adjoining the estate. The novel's motorway controversy is a fictitious counterpart to the real-life furor that surged around the Irish state's decision to extend the M3 motorway directly through the Hill of Tara in the first decade of the twenty-first century. Writing during the years when the M3–Hill of Tara uproar was raging, French represents her culturally, historically, socially, and environmentally destructive motorway as a government/investor boondoggle that Knocknaree's residents are powerless to reject or even, thanks to threats from the powerful, to cash in on. As becomes clear over the course of the novel's central murder investigation, the corrupt machinations propelling the unwanted motorway's construction follow the same pattern of self-interested motives and malevolent intentions hidden behind reassuring expressions of care that are ascribed in the novel to both the skillful detective and the psychopath.

The woods of the novel's title, the site on which all the housing estate amenities were to be built, contain thousands of years' worth of Ireland's lived historical legacy, which a coalition of Knocknaree residents, archaeologists, historians, and concerned citizens have been fighting a losing battle to protect. These woods are also, for Ryan, a lost childhood paradise and the scene of that bizarre and still unexplained catastrophe that determined the course of his adulthood. Having been marked in the Irish media and social imaginary as the redemptively found child, the survivor of an incomprehensible sylvan tragedy that left him tainted, guilt-ridden, and vaguely suspect, the adult Ryan reenters these mythic woods after workers at the archaeology dig—desperate to salvage artifacts before the construction starts—find the body of a murdered twelve-year-old girl.

These woods are also home to ancient, occult, dangerous entities: a winged-voiced creature, a disembodied laughter, the pooka that is sometimes blamed for spiriting away Peter and Jamie, and so on. Their collective

Figure 5.1. "The Battle of Soldiers Hill." Woodcut commemorating the first concerted attempt of developers and police to drive away or remove activists encamped at the Tara Solidarity Vigil. Artist, Pixie.

presence is associated not only with the vanishing of Ryan's friends but also with its precursor episode, witnessed by these same children: the rape of the Knocknaree girl named Sandra by a trio of adolescent boys, one of whom, Jonathan Devlin, grows up to be the father of both the murder victim, Katy, and the murder's architect, Rosalind. These baffling entities would be most properly designated cryptids, monstrous creatures like the Thunderbird, Sasquatch, the Black Dog, or the pooka itself, whose collective existence has been widely attested but cannot be reliably verified or scientifically proven. In a sense, the cryptid is an existential version of the enigmatic signifier, in that it occupies a zone of indeterminability between a traumatic visitation of the other and an uncanny fantasy of the self, a positive or negative projection of desire. Entangling the appearances and reports of such cryptids with the criminal episodes to be investigated, *In the Woods* lends a phatic dimension to their enigmatic function: the cryptids embody the capacity of the horror/mystery genre, in its more sophisticated forms, to solicit and to thwart allegorical readings in one motion. The cryptid figures of *In the Woods* might be taken to signify the spectral power of the state, the pervasive influence of capital, the furtive predations of child sexual abuse, or the ineluctable corruption of human relationality by psychopathic energies. But they cannot be definitively affixed to or even affiliated with any of these points of reference. In its undecidability as a symbolic counter—built upon its ontological uncertainty—the cryptid proves an especially apt objective correlative of the novel's signature mode of moral-political obliquity. Evil and corruption, the text announces, originate just here, at the site of enigma—at the crux of the X—where interpretation is necessary in proportion to irresolubility.

"The Crux of the X": Dangers of Unsanctioned Memory

If, as Ernest Renan contends, the formation of a national identity requires selective forgetting (1990, 11), then any significant transformation of that identity and its attendant ethos, such as the unaccustomed and unforeseen prospects of the Celtic Tiger era, must enjoin similarly strategic species of amnesia on individual subjects formed during, by, and within these tectonic shifts. It stands to reason, for example, that the sudden influx of capital and the mutation in the social compact resulting from this altered terrain of economic power and dependency could not but generate intense if largely unconscious pressures and anxieties among those vertiginously in the ascendant, thanks to Ireland's giddy emergence on the world stage. For this neoliberal elite, revived memories and inklings, disruptive to the precarious social and moral coherence of the new national dispensation, would constitute a particularly sinister threat. No such revived memories could more grievously shock the Irish conscience than did the stream of nonstop turn-of-the-century scandals documenting systemic violence, sexual and otherwise, against Irish children. And no such revelation could more thoroughly shred the Irish social fabric than that this systemic violence against children had long been covered up by the same authorities, the same institutions, that were building and benefiting from the new order of affluence. No brute reality, accordingly, was more liable to the distracting mummery of the fairy-tale construct, the legendary explanation, or the paranormal excuse.

Composed along this historical fracture, where the excavation of these memories imperils the phantasmatic social architecture reared upon their entrenched repression, *In the Woods* stages in small this looming crisis at work within its narrator-protagonist, Rob Ryan, as a terrifying and obtrusive sort of *nachträglichkeit* or "afterwardsness."[5] Ryan finds himself bereft of crucial and terrifying memories, the recovery of which threatens to undo his mature persona. And as these memories continually shift and morph in an oneiric zone, just beyond the pale of conscious apprehension, they engender in Ryan a habit of anxious self-scrutiny that mirrors the anxious, hyper-vigilant moral atmosphere of Celtic Tiger Ireland. Ryan likens himself to someone living "on a fault line" (212). Because his approved but consciously fabricated version of manliness is predicated on the traumatic disappearance of his friends and the obliteration of his own juvenile identity, his every intimation of the past cannot but prove at once boon and bane, a promise of lost childhood recovered at the cost of manhood compromised. Ryan's superlatively, impossibly successful Celtic Tiger masculinity teeters on the brink of implosion; he is perpetually unsure whether some resurgent, long-suppressed memory will be "trivia or . . . The Big One that blows your life and your mind wide open" (212). Still more disturbingly, he cannot in his psychomachia distinguish his dread of such a quake from his desire for its mnemonic trigger. Of necessity, Ryan continually practices a secret forensics, an internal probe into his own personal and pathological history that resonates both with his detective work and with the archaeological enterprise that hosts his latest crime scene. French constructs her narrative precisely to articulate together these various types and scales of "digging."

The twelve-year-old Knocknaree resident Katharine (Katy) Devlin, whose death Ryan and Maddox are called on to investigate, is found laid out on a prehistoric sacrificial altar in what initially looks to be an easy invocation of Ireland's purportedly deep-rooted atavism. The dead girl on the prehistoric altar would seem to constitute a clear sign that in Ireland what Seamus Heaney terms "the old man-killing parishes" are still at it (1972, 47). However, the mythic series of violent, paranormal, possibly supernatural, upwellings affirmed in Ryan's narrative proves disastrously misleading. By the novel's end, it is clear that attempts on the part of both the detective and the reader to make sense of a contemporary child abduction and murder by construing it as a link in an inexorable chain of unmotivated human sacrifice have both impeded the investigation and abetted the ongoing misappropriations of which the murder, correctly understood, is an egregious symptom. The most flagrant vehicle for "recurring violence so exceptional as to be inexplicable" is folklore, on which the novel draws for its creepy ambience. French's never-abandoned realism, however, simultaneously proposes sensational media coverage as the modern-day counterpart to oral accounts of monstrous visitations and faery abduction. For instance, the modern newspaper scandal and the Irish oral tradition that informed Bram Stoker's famous vampire dovetail when Maddox draws a picture of a property developer with blood-dripping fangs in a corner of the visual map of Knocknaree that she and her partners are using to investigate the crime. Ryan recalls that he flinched every time he caught sight of it, a detail that makes clear that the property developers are no less frightening than the pooka, the folkloric evil that haunts Ryan's most terrible visions.

Maddox's account of her near molestation by a school custodian likewise blurs the line between the stuff of newspaper scandal and the stuff of fairy tale. She tells Ryan how she abruptly grasped the significance of this disturbing encounter thanks to the flood of revelations about child sexual abuse in the Irish media of the 1990s. In this regard, her epiphany recalls and could even allude to that of Veronica Hegarty in Anne Enright's slightly earlier and similarly preoccupied Celtic Tiger postmortem, *The Gathering* (2007). Like Maddox in this moment of recollection, Veronica in *The Gathering* has suppressed traumatic memories brought to mind owing to the Irish public sphere's constant infusions of child sex scandal: "Over the next twenty years the world around us changed and I remembered Mr. Nugent. But I never would have made that shift on my own—if I hadn't been listening to the radio and reading the paper, and hearing about what went on in schools and churches and people's homes. It went on slap-bang in front of me and still I did not realize it" (Enright 2007, 172–73). Understandably, for both novels, the burgeoning exposé culture of Celtic Tiger Ireland serves to disambiguate the enigmatic signifiers of childhood seduction for the adult women involved, whether as subject or witness. For Maddox, this *éclairissement* comes in the form of disenchantment, the custodian's original proposition having made an appeal, albeit unwittingly, to her juvenile capacity for magical thinking, a sensibility nurtured on fairy tale and the fantastic. She recalls that she had thought her would-be rapist might have been offering her marvels instead of marbles, that to enter his woodshed was potentially to become one of those children who pass through the wardrobe. Maddox's memories of the incident swerve from folkloric accounts of supernatural childhood abduction, the fairy tale in grown-up dress, to the gothic empiricism of media scandals and back again, with their point of intersection acting as a magnetizing hub. As Ryan notes, Maddox "has a mind like a clo-verleaf flyover" that can "spin off in wildly divergent directions and then," unexpectedly, "swoop dizzily back to the crux" (French 2007, 196).

In the Woods thus suggests that modern media scandals both mimic and complement ancient faery lore in their double-sided treatment of childhood ab/se-duction. At one level, the narratives circulating in either mode of discourse carry a certain frisson that rehearses, at a safe distance, the traumatic jouissance imbuing all such solicitations—whether they be to sexual contact, venal intrigue, or flight and disappearance—a blend of danger and blandishment, wonder and wounding. Both narrative genres, that is to say, translate the primal enigmatic signifier of infantile seduc-tion into a more emotionally digestible form. At a second level, and in the very process of doing so, folktale and scandal copy seek to blunt the menac-ing aspect of these solicitations by locating their source or context outside the bounds of accustomed experience or credible expectation. Newspaper scandals update faery lore in this respect by replacing, as the characteristic site of child enticement, supernatural visitation with unnatural deviancy, the paranormal event with the abnormal impulse. Both genres, that is to say, also function as social palliatives, anesthetizing the fear of child endan-germent by turning such instances into unfathomable anomalies, unlikely exceptions to the beneficent rule of nurture. In modern Ireland, as we shall see, public accounts that emphasize childhood predation as peripheral and inexplicable, through the idiom of folklore or scandal, create opportunities to reinforce the Irish nation's self-definition as a good mother, whose chil-dren are never exposed to jeopardy or, as Ryan proclaims, virtually never disappear without a trace.

The reassurances provided by the fairy tale and the scandal report turn on their systematic omission, mystification, or disavowal of the sort of low-grade psychopathic performances we have noted, which might be termed the psychopathia of everyday life: that is, displays of interest or intimacy for the purpose of instrumentalizing the other. The manipulation and exploita-tion of the affectively charged enigmatic signifier in child seduction or pre-dation is, after all, but an especially odious manifestation of that practice. Psychopathic conduct is not simply unethical; it stands outside, withdraws itself from, the ethical order, insofar as it lacks or suspends the recognition of socially accepted interpersonal norms. At the same time, it remains a fairly representative vein of human relationship itself. In this sense, psychopathic performance enacts the paranormal or uncanny motive so beloved of Irish folklore and scandal copy: it is literally *para*, outside or alongside the norm, as a departure *from* that is also a subset *of* the normal.

This is all the more true, or perhaps only becomes observable, in a social regime informed by a principle of universal commodification, including and most decisively the commodification of subjectivity. In the late capitalist order exemplified by the Celtic Tiger, psychopathic conduct as defined above exemplifies what Lacan calls the logic of the exception. It is an exceptional instance, specifically an exception to ethics as such, that discloses, even crystallizes, the truth of the system at large.

In the Woods attests as much in several key respects: symbolically, diegetically, and thematically. Symbolically, the methods of police interrogation detailed above tend to identify psychopathology with the Law itself in Celtic Tiger Ireland. Diegetically, the murder mystery centers on the intergenerational ties among three cohorts: the 1980s adolescents (Jonathan Devlin, Sandra Scully, Cathal Mills, and Shane Waters), the present-day adolescents (Rosalind Devlin, Katy Devlin, and Damien), and the investigative unit (Maddox, Ryan, and Sam), and each cohort is informed in both its internal dynamics and its relation to the other cohorts by the members' own experience, enactment, and/or (mis)apprehension of psychopathic performance. The homosocial psychopathia that issues in the rape of Sandra profoundly affects Jonathan's paternal bearing toward his psychopathic daughter, Rosalind, and her victim, Katy; Maddox's collegiate tangle with psychopathy leads her to doubt Ryan's capacity to distrust Rosalind; Rosalind bamboozles not only her co-conspirator, Damien, but also Ryan, resulting in an amorous bond between Maddox and Sam; and so on. Psychopathology operates everywhere, every day in the novel as the chief determinant of its multilayered plot. Thematically, psychopathia cements the plotlines of *In the Woods* to its sociohistorical context. The murder of Katy Devlin occurs, of course, on a tract of land to be developed in a naked profit grab and in spite of the adverse ramifications for nearby residents and the despoliation of precious archaeological resources. Of greater structural moment, however, is the psychopathic resonance of the two events: the objectification and instrumentalization of the other, instanced most shockingly in child victimization, finds its collective mirror image in the wholesale commodification of heritage that was endemic to the Celtic Tiger regime, whose dizzyingly abrupt onset was also shocking, in its own way, to the traditional *phronesis* of Ireland. Rather than treating child sexual assault as a deviant outlier set against the backdrop of a more respectable economic and financial corruption, French intertwines the exposure of these private and public outrages so as to peg them as cognate outcroppings of a morally unsound political economy. And it is precisely this narrative strategy that raises *In the Woods* from the rolls of genre fiction to the dignity of the novel of manners.

Violent Group Dynamics

Ryan's surprise upon finding that the murder victim's identity has been established discloses his predisposition to view the case as a replication of his own childhood trauma, an inexplicable and sui generis visitation somehow connected with the disappearance of his friends. As he reflects on the identification of the deceased child, Ryan seems to bear out his opening caution, "And I lie." For it is just here that he first informs us, all evidence to the contrary, and with the solemn credibility of a trained criminologist, that "a little girl—especially a healthy well-groomed little girl, in a place as small as Ireland—can't turn up dead without someone coming forward to claim her" (33). Doubling down at a later point in the novel, Ryan assumes that an ongoing sense of guilt haunts the detectives who could not determine what had befallen his childhood friends, because "in all Ireland's brief disorganized history as a nation, fewer than half a dozen children have gone missing and stayed that way" (156). It is this very assumption that makes the novel's individual disappearances so sensational, so seemingly mythic, and so plausibly linked; while in turn the sensationalization of the disappearances, both in Ryan's narrative and in the press, ratifies the common wisdom that Irish children never, in fact, disappear.

French invokes such popular wisdom to create added buzz within the story for its lurid central events. But she simultaneously and insistently exposes Ryan's repeated assurances that Irish children are altogether safe as a comforting but egregious lie, a self-serving instance of collective amnesia, outstripping thereby the generic conventions she so deftly employs. Scattered across the whole of the novel are numerous other near and quasi-child disappearances that recall the materially, socially, and culturally specific realities that underlie the novel's fantastic, gothic surface. Indeed, French systematically references virtually every category of juvenile disappearance that has been pervasive in modern Ireland.

Among these allusions is Maddox's account of her near molestation by a public school custodian, a plausible case of a near disappearance. Forcible incarceration and suicide are alluded to in Ryan's recollection of a Knocknaree resident named Mad Mick, who was said by Ryan's friend Peter to have made a girl pregnant. Peter told his friends, Adam and Jamie, that the desperate young woman hanged herself in the woods and that her face turned black, a detail that suggests that Peter was giving a firsthand account. After the young woman's suicide, as Ryan recalls, as though from his own firsthand knowledge, "one day Mick started screaming, outside Lowry's shop," and "the cops took him away" (174).

The incarceration of girls and women in the Magdalene laundries and the involuntary removal of infants from their unwed mothers both haunt the birth story of Ryan's other best friend, Jamie. In the early 1970s, Jamie's mother had an affair with a married friend of her parents, got pregnant, and insisted on keeping the baby. When Maddox and Ryan praise her courage, noting the ruin such a decision could have brought upon her, she tells them, "I think: [it was] a rebellion against the patriarchy" (182). As Ryan observes in response, "She had been lucky. In Ireland in 1972, women were given life sentences in asylums or convents for far less" (182). Finally, French calls attention to the large numbers of Irish children and young people over the course of modern history who suffered a kind of economic erasure through forced emigration or descent into the internal exile of extreme poverty. Of one Knocknaree youth whom Ryan remembers from his own childhood, the murdered girl's father, Jonathan, explains, "He was a casualty of the eighties. There's a whole generation out there that fell through the cracks" (234).

Only once does Ryan specifically reflect on the paradox central to his extravagantly contradictory accounts concerning children's status in modern Ireland: in a passage that attempts to reconcile his frequent claims that Irish children are always safe with the novel's relentless accounts of children disappearing en masse. In a meditation on why, before 1990, Irish adults had earnestly believed that Ireland's children were safe, even as it became evident they were not, Ryan struggles to find these adults at worst naive and misinformed, and therefore truly innocent: "It seems ingenuous to say that the 1980s were a more innocent time, given all that we now know about industrial schools and revered priests and fathers in rocky, lonely corners of the country. But then these were only unthinkable rumors happening somewhere else, people held on to their innocence with a simple and passionate tenacity, and it was perhaps no less real for being chosen and for carrying its own culpability" (75). The quality of innocence that Rob Ryan so desperately wishes to salvage and to valorize as the defining element of 1980s (pre–Bishop Casey) Ireland does not, however, protect even those children who ultimately were not casualties of 1980s Ireland, when "a *whole generation*" disappeared (234; emphasis added).

Crucially, in all the most significant tales of disappearance or abduction narrowly averted, the traumatic severance of communal bonds appears, in retrospect, to have been not averted at all, but merely forestalled. Maddox, for instance, is not raped, abducted, or murdered by the school custodian, and yet over the course of the novel the cruel severance of her singularly cherished bond with Ryan, her partner and friend, at last delivers the long-deferred blow that she has seen coming but cannot evade. Jamie's mother, too, evades being sent away to a Magdalene laundry only to wind up overwhelmed by the relentless demands of single motherhood in 1980s Ireland, and she ultimately resolves to relinquish (and then catastrophically loses forever) the daughter she had risked everything to keep. Conversely, when Adam, Peter, and Jamie put up a strong and unified resistance in order to keep Jamie in Knocknaree, they believe they have succeeded, only to find toward the end of the summer that Jamie's mother has been secretly proceeding with her plans to send Jamie away, a staggering blow that both precedes and seems to precipitate the mysterious disaster in which Jamie and Peter are lost.

Central to the trajectory of Maddox's inexorable loss of the community she had found with Ryan is her status as a sort of changeling (not unlike Ryan himself), a survivor of both a childhood calamity and the psychopathic cruelty of her classmate at Trinity College. The latter experience, far more than her parents' premature deaths in an automobile accident, her near molestation, or her stabbing by a deranged Trinity drug dealer, represents her defining trauma. The strong and verbally commanding Maddox is able to talk about these other occurrences and their psychic aftermath readily, yet she can only explain the devastating harm done to her by the psychopath's multiple outrages on her personhood—his claim that she had falsely accused him of rape, her resulting social expulsion, and his subsequent threats to rape her with impunity—as his having "[done] his thing" (246). When Ryan learns that Maddox's habitual nightmares rehearse her collegiate ordeal, he surmises that they involve her bodily violation, that "his thing" is rape. In retrospect, he realizes that positing physical assault as the deepest trauma one might suffer represents a fundamental error in judgment, perhaps his most disastrous misapprehension. He doesn't explain why he feels this way, however, leaving the reader to extend his insight and in the process to discern its pertinence to the larger narrative.

In strictly personal terms, Ryan's supposition that only trauma with a distinct bodily dimension, such as rape, can have severe and protracted psychic effects prevents him from fully cognizing the extent of the damage he endured in surviving the notorious vanishing, years before. Interpersonally, Ryan's confusion of psychosocial invulnerability with absolute invulnerability allows him to be manipulated by *his* psychopath, Rosalind Devlin, and causes his singular bond with Maddox to be broken. Finally, Ryan's failure to appreciate how Maddox's most painful ordeal could be caused by a purely symbolic as opposed to a material or somatic transaction badly misprizes the power of psychopathic performance in the very story he is given to narrate—a failure consistent with his beguilement by Rosalind Devlin. Although Ryan and all of us to a degree associate the psychopath with bodily violence, Maddox's ordeal reminds the reader that psychopathy primarily seeks to destroy the other as a subject—that is, as the bearer of a symbolic position, mandate, and value, of which the other's physical presence may or may not figure as the chief repository. To equate serious trauma with physical trauma, Ryan's self-confessed blunder, is to underestimate the prevalence of the psychopathic, both in the novel and in the cultural milieu it depicts. Accordingly, it is also to misunderstand in a fundamental way the novel itself, which is all about such underestimation.

Sparing the body yet leaving deeply eroticized scars, the changeling experiences of Maddox and Ryan are emblematic of the perils of growing up. After all, developmentally speaking, the disappearance of children happens as a matter of course, the approved course. It is constitutive of maturation.[6] For its part, sexuality is the component of the maturation process that furnishes its most definitive biopsychological impress. That is because it is the component that, having been already channeled and activated in infancy, perpetually harbors traces of the vanished child within its precincts and periodically stages the possibility of their recrudescence. This aspect of sexual being proves especially fraught in the property-based societies that French's Celtic Tiger Ireland epitomizes to the point of parody. Under broadly liberal regimes, where the ideal of individual sovereignty and private ownership are jointly enshrined, to pass from immaturity to maturity, from citizen apprenticeship to citizen subjectivity, is to become one's own person, to come into full possession of one's self, as opposed to remaining, legally and otherwise, at the disposal of another, indentured to another's will. In this context, sexuality constitutes an especially decisive stile in the growth process precisely because it is also, developmentally speaking, the most routinely contested. At sexuality's origin, as we have seen, lies a profound equivocation, vehiculated by the enigmatic signifier, between external solicitation and endogenous fantasy, the traumatic imposition of the other's unconscious designs and the enjoyable realization of the self's nascent desires, between a seductiveness that inheres in the actions taken and a seductiveness that inheres in the interpretation given, in the gestures made and the impressions left. The amphibolous nature of infantile sexuality persists even into the relatively secure identity formation of adulthood, wherein the subject might indeterminately be said to give oneself to and to take possession of the desire of the other.

Here we have the key to why psychopathological performances regularly involve forms of sexualized violence even when they do not, as in French's novel, necessarily entail bodily assault. By brutally objectifying, instrumentalizing, and depleting the other, these performances look to secure the (narcissistic) boundaries of the self against the unconscious traces of traumatic inmixing or embarrassment endemic to infantile eroticism. Psychopathological conduct, in short, sustains the impossible fantasy of plenary self-ownership through the effective, if localized, "owning" of another. Indeed, Rosalind may only come to be apprehended because she had been so hell-bent on directing Damien not only to kill her sister but also and in particular to rape Katy before doing so. She thereby evinces a self-aggrandizing will to instrumentalize her boyfriend and "own" her sister in the most gratuitously and sexually cruel manner imaginable.

Given the high existential stakes, psychologically speaking, for all parties to the psychopathological performance, it is perhaps unsurprising that those who undergo and/or rebel against such treatment in the novel often wind up behaving psychopathologically themselves. For instance, Jamie's single mother behaves manipulatively if not psychopathically in allowing Jamie and her friends, Peter and Adam, to think she has relented in her decision to send Jamie away, so as to stay their resistance until the moment of separation. It is shortly after the three friends have discovered that Jamie's mother had only pretended to abandon the boarding school plan—as Jamie protests, "all the time . . . she was just *lying!*"—that Jamie and Peter mysteriously disappear, leaving the young Adam Ryan in a state of complete dissociation. He recalls, "We had lived that whole summer trusting that we had forever. . . . I wanted to tell her I would go instead; I would take her place" (277–78), which, as it happens, he does, when he is sent away to boarding school in England in the aftermath of the vanishing. In a desperate, initial response to this perceived betrayal, and without regard to parental authority, the young Adam unexpectedly kisses Jamie, laying symbolic claim to a right of association and combination that was now being abrogated.

As attested by Ryan's osculatory assertion of prerogative, the conflict over Jamie's fate, immediately prior to the catastrophe in the woods, involves the ownership of a juvenile subject, a child citizen. Does Jamie's mother have the right to dispose of her at will, to impose on her an uprooting and displacement that is, after all, the moral equivalent of abduction or internment, if done against the child's wishes? Or is the child citizen already her own property and so collectively the property of, proper to, her own chosen "we"? As is simultaneously indicated by Ryan's kiss, this irresolvable generational conundrum remains deeply imbricated with, if not subsumed within, the sex/gender system against which Jamie's mother rebelled in the first place. For if Ryan can be read as sealing with a kiss the covenant of friendship joining Peter, Jamie, and himself as "proper" to one another, it must also be seen to mark Jamie as the outward sign, the totem, of that covenant, as symbolic property. With this new assertion of connection, Ryan enters the lists of heteronormative masculinity at the point of its central and most insidious contradiction: the enactment of intimate, interpersonal, and especially eroticized bonds harbors within itself the likelihood of psychopathological objectification.

To underscore this point, French links Ryan's eroticized assertion of solidarity, by both analogy and narrative coincidence, to the rape of Sandra in the previous Knocknaree generation of lost youths. For this purpose, she contours Ryan's narration so that he reflects on this episode not just as a possible antecedent to the crime at hand or as a counterpart episode to the disappearance of his friends, but also as an event to be mined in its own right for a triangulated sexual politics that he himself has lived and will live again—as Adam, with Jamie and Peter, and as Rob, with Cassie and Sam.

Of Jonathan's susceptibility to the manipulation of the novel's other onstage psychopath, Cathal, who orchestrates the gang rape of his girlfriend, Sandra, Ryan muses, "He had been lost somewhere in the wild borderlands of nineteen, half in love with his friends with a love passing the love of women. . . . I wondered what else he would have done for his cause" (233). In an epiphany recalling the diagnosis of a homosocial-homosexual continuum in Eve Sedgwick's classic work *Between Men* (1985), Ryan discovers in the motivations of the three boys who raped Sandra a desperate, because unadmitted, passion for one another, remarking that famous biblical aphorism of brotherly devotion, "surpassing the love of women." But if Ryan's cognate experience gives him insight into the group dynamics surrounding Sandra's violation, it also sets significant limits on his vision. He does not, cannot, recognize the profound ambivalence at work in the misrecognized and displaced homoerotic attachments that he discerns.

Sexual maturity in the novel tends to endanger the cohesion of cross-gender groups of children, because under the broadly patriarchal arrangements and assumptions still operating in Celtic Tiger Ireland, some group members, typically the girls, are shunted from being subjects to being (sexual) objects, and hence from partners to property. This shift transforms the remaining group members, typically the boys, into both partners and competitors with respect to the newly ordained property; they are ushered into a decisive homosocial attachment and antagonism, with the latter fueled by but also concealing the eroticized aspect of the former.

Surpassing the love of women yet acknowledging only the love or at least the desire for women, this homoerotic adherence (as Sedgwick famously established) threatens the very heteronormative masculinity it informs. It raises the specter of a certain gender instability at the heart of that masculinity and, as such, engenders an internal antagonism in the individual boys, experienced, however inchoately, as crisis. The erotic fellowship in question does not, as a result, merely surpass the love of women; it overtakes and poisons it. This is the psychopathological dimension of the homosocial dynamic with which Ryan fails to reckon. The group rape of Sandra is literally an effort to deposit the male antagonisms here described in the body of the other. But the rape does more than license the expression of this animosity as sexual violence. In combining Sandra's physical possession *by* the group with her violent moral expulsion *from* the group, the rape offloads and thus assuages that male antagonism in both its inner and outer forms, salvaging the homosocial affirmation of masculinity at the expense of its female vessel.

Or, it would be more accurate to say, attempting to salvage. For Ryan himself observes the irony that while the whole point of Sandra's rape was to bring the boys back together, it in fact set them irreparably at odds. The homosocial violence in question, and in general, is all about resolving that primal scene of traumatic enjoyment, the enigmatic signifier, which stages a profound con-fusion of subject and object, in the form of an internal prompting externally inflicted. Precisely because it is a scene of both wounding and enjoyment, abjection and the accession to subjectivity, this primal scene resists final resolution or, more precisely, takes its only possible resolution in the mode of repetition. No sooner, in this case, is the masculinity of the boys consolidated, their gender instability settled, and group cohesiveness resumed—through the violent reduction of Sandra from person to property—than the boys themselves are transformed into competitors over that property, menacing the group adhesion anew. Not only does the divisive question of sexual possession (who has the strongest, the original, the preferred, the most sustainable claim of possession on the phallus as the objectified female other) threaten to trump the bonds of shared male sovereign subjectivity, it casts doubt on those very bonds. Insofar as masculinity has been identified, in the very act of rape, with masterful possession, the admission of disputes and degrees of possessiveness reintroduces gender instability, reactivates the primal trauma of subjectivity, and releases homosocial antagonism on that basis.

Cathal's continuing claim on Sandra as his "real" girlfriend has the effect of dispossessing both Jonathan and Shane in their very (sexual) possession of her; indeed, the gang rape dispossesses them more assuredly than if they never took possession, if "taking her" had remained a future prospect. That Cathal himself proves one of the real, clinically diagnosable instances of psychopathy in the novel is surely no accident. As we have seen, psychopathological performance regularly unfolds here as the manipulation of intimacy to secure advantage and aggrandizement, and Cathal's stratagem works not only on his central victim, Sandra, but on his partners in crime as well.

The one indisputable thing to be said about the rape episode is that Cathal alone emerges with his fortunes unscathed and his life prospects intact, a successful socioeconomic agent in Ireland's new liberal order. If madness might be understood not as an extreme deviation from some absolute standard of rationality (which has never been established) but rather as a dysfunctional departure from the operational norms of a given society, from its forms of life, then Cathal, of all the participants in this squalid episode, is the least mad.[7] His psychopathy, psychopathy in general perhaps, looks like the very antithesis of madness in the commodified world of the Celtic Tiger.[8] To the contrary, a psychopathological course of personal *bildung*, from childhood to sexual maturity, would seem most closely aligned with and appropriate to the course of national development that incubated in that neoliberal, late-capitalist beast.

Psycho-State Formations

If we read the proprietary kiss that Adam Ryan bestows on Jamie as the most innocent point of a spectrum that includes, at its far end, the sexual outrage of a generation earlier, we might well deduce that the three musketeers would have come a cropper in the end, even had the great disappearance never transpired. In addition to the various metaphorical parallels between these incidences, they are metonymically linked to one another and to the larger narrative context by their locale: both occur in the purlieus of the heritage dig of Knocknaree, wherein the central homicide was committed and its victim's body displayed. Dedicated to the unearthing of Ireland's ancient origins, the site is also, for that very reason, expressive of Ireland's modern roots in the enterprise of revivalism, which from the fall of Parnell to the founding of the Republic served to conjoin the cultural nationalism of the Abbey Theatre with the revolutionary nationalism of the Fianna and the Volunteers. In this overlap of temporal registers, connecting the affect and the act of ethnological discovery, the venue coalesces and monumentalizes the evolution of Ireland from tribal territory confederated by blood and belief to liberal state held together by civic identification and property relations under law. Between the crimes and the scene of the crimes, then, there exists an analogy of growth and development—personal on one hand, national on the other. Is this analogy more than casual, more than a coincidence in narrative detail?

By digging deeper, so to speak, into the revivalist-cum-revolutionary heritage of modern Ireland, we can see that this is so. From the "98" through the Easter Rising to the Anglo-Irish War, Irish nationalists strove to overcome colonial, ethno-sectarian divisions and hostility through intensely homosocial paramilitary violence in the cause of reclaiming a country habitually figured as a woman (the Sean-Bhean bhocht, the SpeirBhan, Eire, Mother Ireland, the Blessed Virgin, etc.). In this regard, Sandra's rape (retrospectively) and Ryan's kiss (proleptically) reenact in personal terms the gendered dynamic of this insurgency, fought by youths loving each other with a love surpassing the love of women, youths whose rebellious assaults likewise ultimately pitted the participants against one another in a civil war, rather than consolidating the fraternity they sought. French's odd yet strategic phrase to describe how Sandra's assailants conceived their partnership—as "the cause"—serves to underscore the allegorical resonance of their seemingly unexampled rite of passage. In her depiction of a traumatic gendered ontogeny recapitulating Ireland's national phylogeny, French fashions the bodies of growing Irish children as ideologically sex/gendered time bombs, destined to burst into adulthood at their own expense.

In the decades after the Anglo-Irish Treaty (1922), residual division and animus—between capital and labor, landowner and tenant, Anglo and Celt, Protestant and Catholic—gave way to a new crisis of possession and dispossession of the sort miniaturized in the childhood cohorts of In the Woods. The Irish underclasses had come, following the era of revolutionary struggle, to occupy a position that was essentially analogous to their middle-class compatriots, or that could be made analogous in a nationalist rhetoric in which all committed patriots were the valued children of Mother Ireland, a condition explicitly invoked in the Easter 1916 Proclamation. But as a relatively small, insular elite laid effective claim to the cultural heritage of Ireland and, on its authority, captured the state apparatus—the instruments of governance, economic administration, and mass communication—other, more populous groups became or remained substantially if not formally disenfranchised. Their loyalty was in turn retained and national cohesion secured through the displacement of their class abjection—dispossession writ large, if you will—onto the women and the children metonymically affiliated with them. A new hegemonic narrative reorganized all of the existing histories of Ireland with reference to a teleology combining masculinist theodicy with middle-class triumphalism. The social order reflected in and served by this narrative exploited and instrumentalized women for the twinned purposes of biological and ideological reproduction, by mandating their conformity with an ultrarespectable, desexualized yet maternal ideal of femininity already identified symbolically with the nation itself (Mother Ireland as Blessed Virgin) and soon to be so identified legally in the Constitution of 1937.

Interlocking arms, the companionate, male-dominated institutions of Catholic Church and Gaelic state ruthlessly disposed of female and juvenile bodies within an "architecture of containment"—including orphanages, industrial schools, Magdalene laundries, and, yes, the surveilled family home—in order to enforce their moral authority as political fiat and their political power as morally unimpeachable. For most of the twentieth century, the Irish state not only routed vast numbers of women and children into the Irish Catholic Church for training and indoctrination but also institutionalized those, under the same aegis, who were understood to have refused such indoctrination or who behaved in any manner deemed contrary to its precepts of (sexual) morality. National cohesion was thus induced under a peculiarly gendered mode of duress, wherein women (and children) functioned as what Giorgio Agamben (1998) has theorized as the exception: they are included in the symbolic order but only as the excluded portion, vital agents of social belonging but only in being deprived of agency.

The lineaments of this distinctly gendered predicament reappear graphically in the case of Sandra and virtually in the case of Jamie. On this score, *In the Woods* mounts an organic species of historical allegory. The group dynamics of the novel's childhood cohort allegorize this rooted cultural psychopathology and mirror its homosocial contours, precisely insofar as they are its historical effect, its legacy. Hence Ryan's desperation to implicate Jonathan Devlin—one of Sandra's tormenters, who was peripherally present at the disappearance of Ryan's friends—in the death of his daughter Katy. It is the one finding that could weld Ryan's personal past and his professional mission into seamless unity, satisfying his imperious urge to impose cohesion on an irreparably ruptured life trajectory and make sense of his fractured experience.

In the hands of a lesser writer, this finding might also have served as a facile means for satisfying the reader's cognate urge for tidy narrative closure. But French is specifically concerned in her sampling of historical allegory to treat the discontinuities of the Irish boom with its own prehistory as a resource for complicating the itinerary of her crime plot. To this end, the vanishing of Ryan's cohort and the attendant voiding of his own place in the Irish social landscape of the time is made to stand for the voiding of the symbolic contract of middle-class theocratic masculinism that had defined his social terrain.

Now to say that this contract was voided is by no means to suggest that the effects of its long, robust implementation did not persist and persist robustly. As Raymond Williams (1973) has theorized, the residual aspect of any social dispensation remains fully in force in its amalgamation with that moment's emergent aspect. Accordingly, the cultural psychopathology indexed in the rape of Sandra or Rob's proprietary claim on Jamie does not simply dissolve as either a motivating factor or an explanatory gauge. Witness Maddox's nemesis at University College Dublin, who pointedly exploited obsolescent but deeply sedimented attitudes about sexual decorum and its manipulation not only to frame Maddox but also to rally all their peers, male and female, to ostracize her. Nevertheless, the emergent impact of the neoliberal winds blowing through the European Union and its member states did engender a new variation of that cultural psychopathology, which the novel's criminal mastermind, Rosalind Devlin, has been fashioned to represent.

Against Ryan's expectations, the reader's expectations, and the entire historico-ideological groundwork in which those expectations are embedded, the main psychopathic villain, like the victim of the featured atrocity of *In the Woods*, a rape-homicide, is both female and a minor. French flips the script, reverses both the gender and generational coordinates of the fictive and documentary annals of sexual outrage and violence that have magnetized the public imagination of Ireland over the past two decades, from the Murphy and Ferns reports to the Ann Lovett and Kerry Babies scandals to the Magdalene laundries and the recent Tuam Mother and Baby Home disclosures. This does not mean that French's choice of a homicidal psychopath is intended to allegorize a like reversal in the gendered and generational scheme of dominance that has obtained in the Irish republic since its inception. In casting so dramatically against type, however, she does prod her reader to apprehend a certain mutation in that scheme and in the particular brand of psychopathology it sponsors.

To be sure, the psychopathic tendencies of Rosalind Devlin germinated in the established postcolonial symbolic order, with its officially sanctioned and enforced sex/gender system. Her father, Jonathan, never outpaces the traumatic sense of guilt, isolation, and dispossession he incurred in raping

Fig. 5.2. "Names of 796 Tuam babies written on white sheets." From an art installation by nine Galway activists. TheJournal.ie, August 17, 2018. © Erin Darcy.

Sandra. His subsequent decision to marry the girlfriend he accidentally impregnated, a heroic attempt to turn himself into a proper citizen-subject, can only lock himself and his loved ones securely within what Kathryn Conrad (2004) has called the modern Irish "family cell," a carceral structure buttressed by a religiously saturated notion of respectability premised on compliance with normative gender hierarchies, sexual regulations, and reproductive imperatives. The angel of this (prison) house, Jonathan's wife, languishes in a state of chronic depression, which connects her to yet another female persona of Ireland, Mise-Eire, who is enshrined in an eponymous poem by Patrick Pearse as an emblem of Ireland's distress under colonial rule (French 2007, 323) but could easily be repurposed as an image of women's woe in the Irish republic. Given Cathal's assertion that she was insensible as "[yellow?] wallpaper" (240) and the fact that he has not seen Jonathan for many years, the evidence suggests that her depression preceded Rosalind's earliest experiments in manipulating her family members/inmates. Although her mother's incapacity cannot have caused Rosalind's psychopathy, her mother's affliction and resulting inadvertence in managing domestic affairs certainly supplied Rosalind with the opportunity to assume authority over, as well as responsibility for, her siblings and to learn young the psychopathic art of parlaying intimacy into power. Indeed, Rosalind ultimately contrives to reconfigure her family unit to her preference, eliminating the sister who was threateningly brilliant and self-motivated and bringing the other, weaker sister entirely under her control.

Rosalind is, in fact, gunning for the biggest game in her family ecosystem, her father, whom she has taken care to position so that he may, if she chooses, be incriminated in the rape-homicide she herself has orchestrated (370). Certainly, Jonathan has harbored (and been silenced by) his well-founded fear of Rosalind's formidable capacity to mount reprisals for any perceived infractions. And ultimately, Rosalind does "take down" her father, by the rumors she commanded Damien to circulate alleging that Jonathan had been sexually abusing Rosalind under Katy's instructions. After the novel's various final adjudications—Rosalind receives a three-year suspended sentence in exchange for testimony against her catspaw, Damien, who is sentenced to life imprisonment—we learn that Rosalind has ultimately succeeded in stigmatizing her father as a pedophile and forcing her family to leave Knocknaree. As Ryan recalls of his last conversation with him, Jonathan has met these injustices with stoical resignation: "Allegations of child abuse, no matter how baseless they may seem, have to be checked out. The investigation into Damien's accusations against Jonathan had found no evidence to substantiate them and a considerable amount to contradict them, and Sex Crime had been as discreet as was humanly possible; but the neighbors always know, by some mysterious system of jungle drums, and there are always plenty of people who believe there is no smoke without fire" (414). Rosalind's leverage over her father abides in the scandal context of Celtic Tiger Ireland, the revelations of rampant child sexual abuse and its cover-up, itself an outgrowth of Ireland's institutional deification of paternal authority, which put minors, especially female minors, at a discount. Owing to his involvement in the assault on Sandra, Jonathan is especially sensitive to even the tacit insinuation of this kind of blackmail, and his remorse over that incident gives warrant, in his estimation, to the threatened punishment. For her part, while Rosalind presumably does not know about her father's crime, she apprehends perfectly well the pall of suspicion cast by the ubiquitous child sex scandals of the time, and she is fully cognizant of her own profile as a potential victim. More importantly, her flirtatious overtures to Ryan, combined with the care she takes to conceal her status as a minor, indicate that she is both savvy and cynical enough to turn the recriminatory atmosphere to her advantage.

But even as the dimensions of Rosalind's criminal psychopathy depend on the broader framework of Ireland's modern cultural psychopathy—up to and including her insistence that Katy be not just killed but sexually violated, and by a man—her brand of turpitude neither aims nor conduces to carrying forward the ideological terms of that cultural psychopathy nor to reinforcing the gender hierarchies that it reflects in extremis. Indeed, what renders the disposal of Katy's body at the heritage site so ironic for the reader and so strategically misleading for the detectives is that the violent and vindictive perversity animating Rosalind's sororicide does not align itself, by design or by accident, with the sexual, generational, and institutional politics on which it is propped, like Katy's corpse on the ancient altar. So while Maddox and her crew eventually solve the murder, its underlying meaning, the social implications of Rosalind's scheme, remains illegible to the very end. Drawing on her prior experience, Maddox dismisses Rosalind's miscreancy as an interiorized and individualized psychic malady, an empathic default at once self-absorbed and self-delighting.

A further irony concerning the crime scene, however, extends the novel's historical allegory to situate Rosalind's psychopathy firmly in its cultural milieu: the heritage site on which Katy lies is to disappear imminently under the bulldozer of highway construction at the behest of real estate developers. So, in exerting a form of absolute possession and control (over her dupe, Damien, over the fate of her plucky sister, over her entire family), Rosalind's murderous sexual violence bears no communal impress or historically shared impetus, yet it chimes metaphorically with the will to possession of the Irish moguls and robber barons, determined to screw the Irish community out of any possession or control over the shared history lodged at Knocknaree. In the past crimes that frame the present ones—the gang rape of Sandra and the vanishing of Jamie and Peter—*In the Woods* reenacts the formation of community in violence, specifically the movement from a mythical state of universalized but unconstrained childhood or immaturity to the establishment of permanent bonds among citizen-subjects connected by guilt and sublimation. In the psychopathological performances of the police interrogation, of which Maddox and Ryan are past masters, *In the Woods* shows how the monopoly of violence exercised by the state serves to reenact the formation of the modern community or nation along its original exclusionary lines, abjecting and exploiting the "usual" gender, generational, and class suspects. By this means, infractions against the community are harnessed by the state to legitimate and harden the social hierarchies that form its very foundation. By contrast, while the present felonies at the heritage site tap into the same social hierarchies and feed on the sociopolitical environment delimited thereby, they do so for self-aggrandizing purposes at complete variance with the received agendas of the Irish people-nation at large, symbolized by the site itself, or of its legal and institutional manifestation, the state apparatus. At the same time, the malefactors pursue those antisocial ends with either the intentional cooperation or the inadvertent connivance of the state officials in charge. That is to say, here the transgressions harness state power to legitimate (in the case of the developers) or to exculpate (in Rosalind's case) their infractions. The script is flipped in both crime and punishment.

In the earlier scenarios we flagged, individual psychopathic performances metaphorize the insanity of state practices of self-preservation and aggrandizement; personal psychopathy stands as a microcosm of cultural psychopathy. Conversely, this climactic pairing of illicit activities, two different versions of rape-murder, features psychopathological performances that emblematize the hijacking of public institutions to private interests diametrically opposed to any communally approved good—whether it be the success of a local child celebrity like Katy or the conservation of prized heritage sites. This mutation in the Symbolic Order, which *In the Woods* looks to narrativize in all of its complex transactional relations to the original Gaelo-Catholic genome, is an Irish species of neoliberalism born in, but surviving beyond, the Celtic Tiger era.

NOTES

1. Karen thinks to herself, "She and I belong to the same sex, even, because there are only two: there should certainly be more" (Bowen 1959, 89).
2. See F. O'Toole (2009).
3. The novel's central paradox concerning the structural, not to say moral, equivalence of lawful and criminal or illicit psychological profiles is foregrounded when Ryan recalls Rosalind's enigmatic conclusion that he was perfectly suited to investigate her sister's murder: "*You're the perfect person for this case*, Rosalind had said to me, and the words were still ringing in my head as I watched her go. Even now, I wonder whether subsequent events proved her completely right or utterly and horribly wrong, and what criteria one could possibly use to tell the difference" (167). Jon Ronson's recent work of cultural journalism, *The Psychopath Test*

(2011), fascinatingly probes into the dizzyingly involuted definitional and ethical difficulties that attend any attempt to positively identify individual psychopaths. He ultimately concludes that the dangers and costs of maintaining psychopathology as a psychological diagnosis are unsustainably high. We are not in disagreement with Ronson's conclusion that the simultaneously medical and legal status of psychopathology as a DSM diagnosis constitutes an insidious gap in the (in any case sievelike) civil protections of modern democracies. However, taking our cues from the text itself, we are approaching the term from the angle pursued in the documentary *The Corporation* (Bakan 2005) and by the work of Philip Zimbardo in the Stanford prison study, documented in *The Lucifer Effect* (2007). Both media retain psychopathology as a legitimate, even crucial category for our understanding of individuals only when individual affect and behavior are understood within an institutional (that is, material and ideological) framework.

4. For the definitive work on changeling lore, see Bourke (2001).

5. This defining quality of the enigmatic signifier has been translated, from Freud's English-language translators, as "belatedness" but was retranslated into English by Laplanche as "afterwardness" to account for the enigmatic signifier's uncanny temporal bivalence. It serves as an originary message that can be apprehended (though by definition, never known) only in relation to a later, reactivating traumatic prompt that is itself apprehended only owing to the enigmatic first message. See Caruth (2014, 11–13).

6. For an especially insightful critical essay that reflects with great theoretical precision on a literary representation of "growing," see Norma Alarcón's classic article on Maria Helena Viramontes's short story "Growing" (Alarcón 1998).

7. In *The Secret Scripture*, Dr. Grene, Sebastian Barry's protagonist/commentator on the general state of Celtic Tiger Ireland's mental health, past and present, makes plain the pre-Treaty origins of Tana French's Celtic Tiger psychopathy when he observes of his mother's nemesis, Fr Gaunt—a figure for the Irish Catholic Church in its longstanding role as unanswerable arbiter of both sanity and morality—that he was "obviously sane to such a degree it makes sanity almost undesirable" (2008, 278). In writing about the post-bellum American South, a peripheral space merging into its metropolitan center, not unlike Knocknaree, William Faulkner designates the most rebarbative character in *The Sound and the Fury*, Jason Compson, the only "sane" character in the novel (1929, 420).

8. Perhaps the most satisfying of Maddox's and Ryan's many gendered, minutely coordinated psychopathological performances is the one that they ruthlessly launch against Cathal, interrupting him in the middle of a business meeting and placing Maddox in the dominant position, publicly barraging Cathal with sexually humiliating questions and suggestions that extract a certain childish pleasure (and the *childish* pleasure this scene provides is certainly part of its point) in subjecting Cathal, securely ensconced within and surrounded by his adult male cohort, to an act of malevolent humiliation that is satisfyingly akin in kind, if not in degree, to that to which Cathal subjected Sandra.

6

"ROARING INSIDE ME"

The Enigma of Sexual Violence in *The Gathering*

THE *GATHERING* OF LITERARY CRITICS

To reflect on Anne Enright's Booker Prize–winning novel, *The Gathering* (2007), is to reflect on trauma, the experience of trauma, the witnessing of trauma, the nature of trauma, and the consequences, individual and social, of trauma. From the time of its publication, literary critics and social commentators in and beyond Ireland have been deeply and rightly smitten with this novel's unparalleled capacity to speak about the unspeakable, about that which cannot speak in its own voice, be it in the novel itself or in the world the novel represents. Thus, in the years since the novel's publication, the focus of scholarly articles and book chapters dedicated to *The Gathering* understandably converges on the novel's myriad, complex representations of trauma. Moreover, because most of these essays draw their understanding and their accounts of trauma from the same canonical pool of trauma theory—such as Cathy Caruth's book *Unclaimed Experience* (2016), Judith Herman's *Trauma and Recovery* (1997), and Shoshona Felman and Dori Laub's *Testimony* (1992)—this shared thematic ground has resulted in an especially thoroughgoing interpretive consensus, issuing in a number of fine essays that remain relatively restricted in their scope.

The criticism on *The Gathering* has consistently brought similar elements of traumatic psychology and phenomenology to bear on the form and content of Veronica Hegarty's testimony of child sexual abuse—her brother's and, indirectly, her own. In this pursuit, each of the essays cited below begins its exegesis by quoting Veronica's prefatory statement of purpose, as an index of the traumatic cast of memory anchoring her narrative: "I would like to write down what happened in my grandmother's house the summer I was eight or nine, but I am not sure if it really did happen. I need to bear witness to an uncertain event. I feel it roaring inside me—this thing that may not have taken place. I don't even know what name to put on it. I think you might call it a crime of the flesh, but the flesh is long fallen away and I am not sure what hurt may linger in the bones" (Enright 2007, 1). Liam Harte (2010) speaks for the critical tradition in asserting, "This confessional beginning confirms many of the central insights of trauma theory: the radical disruption of memory and its reliability; the imperfectly known past; the body as the site of an unnamable wounding; and the belated overarching urge to testify to a dubious, haunting event that was not fully understood or integrated at the time . . . and which may or may not be susceptible to meaningful retrospective narrative formulation" (191). Following on the trauma theory that Harte invokes, the consensus holds the scenario of Liam's sexual abuse to be not only, in the context of Veronica's narrative, an object of doubt and obscurity (an "aura of uncertainty," "uncertain, almost, hallucinatory" [Oddenino 2011, 362], "fraught with distortions," "riddled with gaps" [Dell'Amico 2010, 60]) but also the originary (enigmatic) locus of doubt and obscurity, an overwhelming "event . . . not initially remembered or represented but . . . held at bay by dissociation," "cognitively unprocessed" (Harte 2010, 189, 192), "not available to the speaker" (Dell'Amico 2010, 65), "unprocessed and incomprehensible" (Downum 2015, 82). Until triggered anew by Liam's suicide, Veronica's memory of Liam's horrific ordeal is known in the body and felt in "the flesh" and "in the bones" rather than consciously apprehended (Enright 2007, 1). Veronica's body is understood to be "burdened, perhaps even possessed, by the story of the past" (Harper 2010, 77). As the vehicle of the trauma, Liam's sexual abuse, in turn, cannot "take the form of a remembered or narrative event" (Harper 2010, 76). Instead, it leaves a psychic wound to be expressed through the repetitive and displaced enactments of the suffering it occasions: the tale of Liam's and Veronica's trauma is disclosed only in its symptomatic effects—in Veronica's "alienated" relationship to her husband and her "emotionally distanced" posture toward the rest of her family (Downum 2015, 83), in her "association of sex with dirt, sickness and perversion" (Oddenino 2011, 371), and in her "inability to distinguish love from hatred" or intimacy from "annihilation" (Harper 2010, 81).

On this consensus, after the shock of Liam's suicide forces some inkling of the abuse into Veronica's mind, the traumatic import thereof positively disallows a lucid, temporally coherent narration of the "crime" to which she is driven to "bear witness" (Enright 2007, 1). Because "post-traumatic stress inherently creates partitions between experience and expression," a traumatized subject "must speak confusion . . . in order to tell the truth"— that is, must retell events in a fragmentary and jumbled fashion in order to capture the feel, as opposed to the bare facts, of the outrage (Harper 2010, 76). Denell Downum remarks, "*The Gathering*'s spiraling narrative structure reflects both the nonlinear nature of memory and the obstruction posed by an event so unbearable" (2015, 82). Her insights second Harte's earlier observation that Enright seeks "not merely to present trauma's effects [on her protagonist] but to encode them in the novel's form," thereby transferring them in some part to the reader (2010, 192). Other textual analyses proclaim what these glosses strongly imply: the acknowledged unreliability of Veronica's account of the summer at her grandmother Ada's house, which extends to the reality of the abuse itself, must be taken as a type of fidelity, a higher fidelity, to the anguished impossibility of traumatic witnessing. Two separate critics express this idea using virtually the same succinct formulation: Veronica's testimony "departs from the truth in the pursuit of an accurate expression of the state of being stricken" (Dell'Amico 2010, 63); or again, Veronica fabricates in order "to express the state of being stricken" (Downum 2015, 84). For Meg Harper, although Veronica "fills out her narratives with what she knows to be misinformation, infused with 'biases and blindnesses,'" she is "nevertheless utterly reliable in that she explores honestly emotional truths" (2010, 74). In the most extreme variant on this interpretive line, Carol Dell'Amico concedes that Veronica "makes up the past" outright, most flagrantly in the romance she invents between her grandmother Ada and Liam's rapist, Lamb Nugent, but insists nevertheless that Veronica "never lies" inasmuch as traumatic memory's truth is to be found in its imagined components. She argues that the traumatic exigency of speculation confers the "license of the fabulist" on Veronica (2010, 62). For all of these critics, the avenue of fantasy proves to be the shortest distance to the tormented reality.

For most of these critics, finally, both this path and this destination belong not just to Veronica Hegarty but to the Irish nation as a whole. The dissociation of her childhood memories, enjoined by their traumatic force, serves as the novel's double synecdoche for the larger cultural amnesia concerning child sexual abuse in Ireland, of which Veronica's specific state of PTSD is both a part and an effect. Seen through this optic, the narrative options she tries out to relieve the mnemonic void, the mythic components she rehearses to fabulate the irretrievable, do not spring from her mind unprompted but are formed in response to and in unconscious collaboration with the long-delayed revelation of child sex scandal across Ireland. From "listening to the radio, and reading the paper" (Enright 2007, 172–73), Veronica comes to discern that "individual memory is always at the same time collective memory and that repression is a social as well as personal response to traumatic injury" (Harte 2010, 178). For these critics, Veronica's body harbors the traumatic memory of Liam's abuse, unavailable to conscious recognition or narrative integration, by analogy to the way the Irish "body politic" has collectively secreted the traumatic grievances of its "members" in order to suppress the scandals that would ensue should they become a matter of public record. Taking the subplots surrounding Veronica's "mad," institutionalized uncle Brendan as evidence, prior critics construe the tort of Veronica and Liam to "refer to a host of national lapses," to "mediate a much larger grief and anger for the unacknowledged trauma endured by unknown Irish bodies made abject by postcolonial nationalism" (Harte 2010, 199). Such readings seek to trace out a "capillary network of tragic consequence" from orphanages to industrial schools to Magdalene laundries to the sort of "lunatic asylums" where Brendan lived, perished, and was anonymously interred in a mass grave (Meaney 2011, 158).

Shifting the Paradigm

The single-mindedness of the critical tradition on *The Gathering* goes to show how compelling and convincing the trauma theory paradigm has proven for any in-depth engagement with the novel's unsettling mode of narrative address. So indispensable, in fact, does trauma theory continue to be in this regard that we have found the project of shifting the paradigm to be coextensive with that paradigm's further development. We use the phrase *further development* advisedly. On the one hand, it is precisely the particularized deployment of the psychosocial elements and implications of psychic trauma theory, as our synoptic account details, that makes this criticism both a necessary and a sufficient foundation for an argument seeking to question, challenge, or qualify it. On the other hand, in aligning itself with the theories of trauma as such, whose most cited test case seems to be the Holocaust, this interpretive line on *The Gathering* has so far failed to reckon in a sustained, conceptually rigorous fashion with the particulars of the trauma delineated—to wit, the suffering and the witnessing of child sexual abuse, its peculiar character and effects, particularly as enacted in a middle-class domestic space rather than the institutions incarcerating Ireland's most disenfranchised and dispensable citizens. The psychoanalytic construct central to our study, the enigmatic signifier, can serve to facilitate and secure such a reckoning (Caruth 2014, 11–13).

In this context, the most telling function of the enigmatic signifier is as a conduit for the seductive transactions endemic to the parental-filial relationship, transactions at once dialogic (blurring the lines of unconscious agency) and traumatic (an unlooked-for impingement of adult sexuality into the child's psychic terrain). As we discussed in chapter 3, the enigmatic signifier mediates a sexual/sexualizing event or encounter that is reducible neither to infantile fantasy on one side nor to sexual assault or molestation on the other. In the ordinary course of things—from bodily care to physical affection to soothing vocalisms—parents will inevitably transmit ambiguously eroticized messages expressive of their own unconscious stirrings. The very transmission of this sub rosa material catalyzes without in any way coercing, stimulates without even necessarily summoning, answerable unconscious responses on the part of the child. The issue of this subliminal interchange is a traumatic jouissance, the vehicles of which are the associated or ambient signifiers, insofar as they possess a sensory or affective power that exceeds even as it vivifies the determinate meaning they convey. Permeated with such jouissance, the enigmatic signifier transmits an undecidable eroticism that is also a profoundly eroticized undecidability. According to Jean Laplanche's general theory of seduction, these sorts of unintended and uncontrollable erotic transactions serve to enlist the child into the Symbolic Order and hence subjectivity itself, which is predicated on the condition of desirousness and the metonymic substitutions it entails (Laplanche 1997, 661–62).

Whether perpetrated by a familiar or by a stranger, and whether inflicted through an abuse of consent or a brute attack, child sexual abuse taps into, draws on, and replicates in a pernicious and harrowing key the primal seduction mediated by the enigmatic signifier. That is to say, undertaken along these lines, child sexual abuse functions as what might be termed a "slow violence" (Nixon 2013, 2), which "interferes," as the Irish say, not just with the physical being or sexual organs of the child but with his psychic apparatus of desire as well. Such abuse is, one might say, the worst case or toxic version of the enigmatic message, implanting but also manipulating and exploiting the child's infantile store of jouissance, their phantasmatic wishes and appetites, aversions and ambivalences. This is by no means to suggest, let us be clear, that the child unconsciously "wants it" or that the sexual predator is merely taking advantage of an always already latent wish. Rather, the sexual predator implicates the child's circuitry of desire against their will and against their want, effectively turning juvenile desire against itself, psychically incriminating the child in an action that the predator alone commits and in a gratification that the predator alone seeks. By the same token, mobilizing the child's jouissance against the child, however effectively, not only does not in any way mitigate or moderate the violence of the sexual assault but rather exacerbates it: more than simply overriding or subjugating the will of the child, the assault works to repossess that faculty, to appropriate not just the child's desires but their command over them, hence to abrogate their still developing orchestration of their volitional powers.

In transactional terms, overt sexual assault forecloses the eroticized space of undecidability between the adult and child in the enigmatic encounter and forces it inward on the child as a traumatized space of doubt concerning their part in the action itself. In the primal, unconscious seduction constitutive of subjectivity, the implantation of adult sexuality into the infantile psyche carries a corollary traumatic charge or effect; in child sexual abuse, the violent, overwhelming erotic intrusion carries *nothing but* a traumatic charge or effect and thus works to negate the child's subjectivity outright.

The scenarios of child sexual abuse that Veronica envisions—remembers, imagines, or both—Liam's and her own, both fit the pattern of the latter assault-seduction. In both cases, the child is called on to manually stimulate and gratify the "member" of Lamb Nugent, who adopts a posture of jaded passivity: "like an old farmer getting his feet rubbed" in Liam's case (Enright 2007, 144) and as a "welcoming darkness" of sly intent in Veronica's more phantasmatic episode, where both parties submit to Ada's "livid" gaze (221). Obviously, Enright's purpose in portraying the children as physically active, or in portraying Veronica as conceiving them to be physically active, is not to cast them as initiating or even willing participants. What she has done, we would submit, is to provide a pragmatic allegory of the implication of their desire in its own brutal conscription. Liam's and Veronica's respective fondling of Lamb Nugent's penis amounts to a simulation of agency in an encounter over which they have no control. Thus, with the slightest nod to Freudian dream symbolism, Veronica punctuates the fable of her own sexual abuse and affirms the reality of her brother's by reference to Nugent's profoundly passive sexual aggression, his self-effacing appropriation of the children's *geist*: "I know he could be the explanation for all of our lives and I know something more frightening still—that we did not have to have been damaged by him in order to be damaged. It was the air he breathed that did for us. It was the way we were obliged to breathe his second-hand air" (224). Veronica's metaphor of moral contagion here, being obliged to breathe second-hand air, perfectly captures the predicament of spurious because constrained agency that the children suffer: they are "obliged" (forced or enjoined) to go through the motion of taking on (breathing) Lamb's toxic desires.

Unlike the bulk of the novel's professional critics, Veronica Hegarty neither omits nor shrinks from the implication of the children's sexual desire in the trauma they endured and its importance in understanding the nature and consequence of that trauma. To be more specific, Veronica's account consistently reveals—sometimes self-consciously, sometimes unknowingly—that the libidinal investments of the sexually traumatized child can coexist with and even reinforce the fear, disgust, and horror that they originally experienced. When the matter of her brother's death finally impels Veronica to "just say what happened [to him] in Ada's house" (142), she fights through a "terrible tangle of things" (144) (barricades against traumatic reactivation) to uncover a variant on the Freudian primal scene, an image of taboo sexual intelligence, here displaced from parental intercourse to a symbolically incestuous man-boy encounter: "And before the scene became clear to me, I remember thinking, *So that's what the secret is.* The thing in a man's trousers" (146; emphasis in original).

With this presentiment as a frame—the effect of the constitutive intrusion of adult sexuality into her psychic ambit—Veronica cannot but intuit the promise or specter of erotic enjoyment imbuing her brother's traumatic violation. Indeed, upon inadvertently interrupting the assault, she immediately "feel[s] that [she] ha[s] spoiled it for all concerned" (146). Veronica is by no means insensible to the distress her brother is undergoing. Amid her curious inspection of the mechanisms of the sex act ("the boy's bare forearm . . . made a bridge of flesh between himself and Mr. Nugent. His hand was buried in the cloth, his fist clutched around something hidden there"), she also observes that Liam is not only "shocked" but downright "terrified" at the proceedings (143–46).

But on narrative reflection, she refuses to reduce the affective content of the affair to a single valence, to disentangle the sexual from the traumatic components of the sexual trauma, unwanted gratification from undeserved torment, however morally satisfactory it may be to do so. In Nugent's face, she discerns a "struggle" that is "unbearable, between the man who does not approve of this pleasure, and the one who is weak to it" (144). Conversely, in her brother's plight, in the very depths of his terror, she divines the prospect of a likewise unbearable ambivalence: "There is also the pleasure of the boy to consider" (145).

In appraising the last comment, it is instructive "also to consider" what Veronica recalls as her own contemporaneous reaction upon witnessing the sexual violation of her brother. As Harte has argued, while Veronica may or may not have been a victim as well as a witness of Nugent's turpitude, "the distinction is in any case largely irrelevant, since witnessing has been clinically correlated with experiencing [an act of abuse] personally in real time" (2010, 192). All the more so when the witness and the victim are "Irish twins"—who "came out of her on each other's tails" (Enright 2007, 11)—and, as Harper remarks, "psychic doubles or doppelgangers" (2010, 78). Under such circumstances, correlation can and in this case clearly has passed into identification. Accordingly, it is of surpassing importance that Veronica remembers her immediate response to the spectacle of her brother's abuse along profoundly sexual lines: "I closed the door and ran to the toilet upstairs, with an urge to pee and look at the pee coming out; to poke or scratch or rub when I was finished, and smell my fingers afterwards. At least, I assume that this is what I did if I was eight years old" (146). As though to confirm that the witnessed tryst does in fact function as a primal scene, Veronica overlooks or represses the following:

A. That her response initiates a transition in her juvenile awareness of her own genitalia, from the exclusively excremental (pee and look) to the nascently but unmistakably erotic (poke or scratch or rub). The latter practice involves a genital stimulation corresponding to that which she has witnessed her brother give Nugent and which, importantly, she deliberately rehearses even as she records its self-solacing effect: "I pause as I write this, and . . . lick the thick skin of my palm with a girl's tongue. I inhale. The odd comforts of the flesh" (146).

B. That her response transmits mysterious and forbidden knowledge, which, being traumatic, lodges in her body, where it thereafter not only resides but presides as a knowing that can be unearthed only through the body but that perpetually stands between her body and its most visceral responses. Veronica's follow-up claim couches her childish ritual of genital scarification as the first step toward a self-lacerating release of information: "You know everything at eight, but it is hidden from you, sealed up, in a way you have to cut yourself open to find" (147). On this score as well, adulthood finds Veronica rehearsing her original reaction in barely displaced fashion. Abed with her college boyfriend, Michael Weiss, whose gentle intimacy she finds terrifying, she suddenly begins "hacking away at [her] inner leg, with a biro of all things" and then, to his horror, "running through the ineffectual blue lines with his kitchen knife" until she bleeds (130).

Later in her story, Veronica declares, "What is written for the future is written in the body, the rest is only spoor" (163). What was written in Veronica's body, what wounded her in the moment of witnessing, was written for a future in which she would have to write on/into her body once again (with a biro), wounding the same area (her inner leg) and thereby exposing, without yet fully understanding, what had remained "sealed up" in her eight-year-old self: not simply the hidden truth of sexual arousal, as she might have thought, but also the misrecognized consequences of child sexual abuse on both victim and witness. For Veronica, that consequence turns out to be an inextricable psychic imbrication of eros and trauma, or we could even say, eros and thanatos. Her libidinal attachments bear, even require, a traumatic component, which explains why her first love, "gentle, human Michael Weiss," was unable, as she remembers, to "talk me down" (130, 81).

Traumatic pain, conversely, triggers a sexual response for Veronica, if only as a defense, which is why her long-deferred attempt to "just say what happened" to her brother includes a "pause" to indulge the "odd comforts of the flesh." In simultaneously renewing and deforming the primal intro/seduction of (adult) sexuality, child sexual abuse can have the effect of both commingling and reproportioning the currents of desire and dread, wanting and wounding, at their wellhead. As a result, the line between the dissociated memory of trauma, as manifest in its inactive repetition, and the expression of libidinal investment, apparent in the selfsame conduct, can grow blurred to the point of indistinguishability.

Take, for example, Veronica's account of her sexual abuse by Nugent, which on her own testimony is more likely fantasy than memory, and for which reason, we submit, is all the more likely to be a symptom of the fraught experience of witnessing sexual trauma. Indeed, in her oneiric vision, she assumes the role of Liam, her hand clutching Nugent's "old penis," while her grandmother, Ada, takes Veronica's place in the perverse constellation as the interested bystander (221–22). As a young child, Veronica may well have assumed, however unconsciously, that the presiding adult of the household, Ada, must have known about and so connived at, if not condoned, Nugent's predations. As an adult, accordingly, Veronica erects her grandmother as the original, corrupt model of her own unavailing, erotically involved witness and hence a point of displacement for the guilt she has been carrying in consequence. At the conclusion of this interlude, Veronica proclaims, "This is the moment that we realise it was Ada's fault all along" (223). She thereby calls attention to the unconscious transference in the dreamscape itself, wherein Ada is positioned as a receptacle, not to say scapegoat, for the regrets that Veronica nurses concerning her own performance in the original event. What were her perceived failings?

The trauma literature, and in particular Felman and Laub's *Testimony* (1992), speaks eloquently of how witnesses like Veronica undergo survivor guilt along with remorse at having been unable to aid the primary victim. And to be sure, Veronica remains in the grip of this grievous emotional vise, exacerbated by her proximity to, her psychic twinning with, her brother. As the sibling witness to Liam's abuse and his self-appointed guardian in its aftermath, Veronica feels a profound sense of failure, amounting to truancy, at her traumatized dissociation from that primal scene: "Even your sister— your saviour in a way, the girl who stands in the light of the hall—even she does not hold or remember the thing she saw" (172). Not coincidentally, when the thing she saw comes back to Veronica in the shape of her own abuse scenario, it is triggered, directly and exclusively, by hallucinations that she has at Liam's wake of a series of victimized ghosts, culminating in the more vivid, entirely lifelike mirage of Ada, "as I might see an actual woman standing in the light of the hall" (217). That last phrase is especially significant. Its precise repetition of her self-description as "the girl who stood in the light of the hall" indicates that an unconscious metonymic association has been forged between this bodily placement and disposition, with its symbolic nimbus, and the role of "savior" or champion. For Veronica, to "stand in the light of the hall," which she remembers herself doing, is to be posted to defend and obliged to protect an endangered child. Charged with the care of Veronica, Liam, and their younger sister, Kitty, Ada was installed in the role of protector before Veronica's witnessing was thrust upon her. In keeping with this order of responsibility, Veronica's screen memory not only transfers to Ada her own perceived guilt at neither rescuing Liam nor remembering his plight, but also minimizes *her* guilt by comparison, putting it, one might say, in proper perspective. Whereas Veronica proved lamentably incapable of fulfilling her self-assigned role as savior, she portrays Ada as betraying that mission outright, as enabling, encouraging, even instigating Lamb Nugent's depredations. On Veronica's phantasmatic account, Ada looms as a monstrous version of Veronica's ineffectual bystander, allowing Veronica to forgive herself a little for her traumatically delinquent memory.

The specific nature of Ada's monstrosity, however, brings to bear, by mirroring forth, the implication of Veronica's desire in this primal scene, which is the key to its structure. More than a bystander to Veronica's servicing of Nugent, Ada exerts a gaze that controls the action. At the outset, Veronica feels "Ada's eyes are crawling down my shoulder and my back. Her gaze is livid down one side of me; it is like a light: my skin hardens under it and crinkles like a burn" (221). At the close of the scene, punctuated by Nugent's monomial appeal to that gaze ("the single word: 'Ada'"), Veronica wonders, "Is she pleased with what she sees?" (222). Here again, by the transferential logic of screen memory, Ada models a maleficent version of Veronica's witness, but in its voyeuristic rather than its helpless aspect. Veronica's ocular curiosity as to the function of the hidden penis in Liam's hand ("so that's what the secret is") takes on, when fused with Ada's grotesque authority, its own twisted, destructive agency.

At the same time, Enright takes care not to allow all traces of Veronica's scopophilic desire to be expunged from the "memory or dream" (222), lest the impressment of that desire to the predator's ends be omitted, along with the lifetime consequences of that impressment. Thus, Veronica frames the entire screen memory as an explicitly scopic mise-en-scène, using the term *picture* three times just to introduce the action: "I remembered a picture"; "it is a picture in my head"; "it is a very strange picture" (221). Within the frame, Veronica remembers the setting of her abuse as exuding the traumatic feeling it induces: "The walls are oozing [Nugent's] sly intent," "the pattern on the wallpaper repeats to nausea" (222). But her actual description of Nugent's sexual organ is unexpectedly, quite self-consciously, gobsmackingly appreciative: "Hot in my grasp, and straight and, even at this remove of years, lovely, Nugent's wordless thing bucks, proud and weeping in my hand" (222). Lovely? Yes, *lovely* is the word that shocks in this passage, marking a libidinal, visually inflected appeal, unravaged for Veronica by distance and time, a strange kernel of jouissance—unsought jouissance, unwelcome jouissance, toxic jouissance, but jouissance nonetheless. Her renewed access to this jouissance, another legacy of her brother's death, actualizes the insight that Liam likewise had his desire implicated against his will, that her psychic twin was similarly conscripted in the working of Lamb's desire: "I could also say that Liam must have wanted [Lamb] too. Or wanted *something*"—an all-important qualification (223). The homophonic bond between the two names, Liam and Lamb, under the inflection of an Irish brogue, further underscores the reciprocity of desire that child sexual predation orchestrates in order to compel.

With Veronica's account of her brother's ordeal and her own, the novel challenges, even confutes, the moral episteme that has dominated its reception to date. A *moral episteme*, as we are using the term, comprises a set of evaluative assumptions that precludes certain kinds of ethical analyses and judgments while prescribing others. In this case, the framework in question rules out the category of participant-victimage. That is to say, it takes those victimized by sexual abuse to be entirely passive and uninvolved psychically as well as physically in the event. This construction rests, in turn, on a largely unexamined premise that desire and will exist in perfect alignment with one another, such that one's libidinal energies cannot be mobilized, one's erotic stirrings cannot be elicited, one's fantasies cannot be tapped, against one's intent or volition. To put it another way, on this model, sexual violence reaches its limit in the brutal imposition of bodily force; it cannot turn the victim's psyche against itself, coercing its complicity in its own subjection. At a theoretical level, however, the formation of the unconscious itself constitutes the ever-present structural possibility of just such an unwilled participation in one's own eroticized violation. At an empirical level, primal seduction, the intrusion of adult sexuality into the infant's life and horizon, inevitably enacts that structural possibility, but child sexual abuse serves to weaponize it. As *The Gathering* illustrates, graphically and persistently, the prevailing moral episteme, blind as it is to the capture of unconscious desire in its own exploitation, not only fails to account for the forced implication of the Hegarty victims in their childhood abuse, but in so doing, fails to account for the specific reverberations of that abuse throughout their adult lives. This episteme thus fails as well to fully account for what *The Gathering* has to contribute to a broader understanding of how child sexual abuse has shaped the Irish social order.

Long before Liam Hegarty's suicide recalls some version of his sexual abuse forcibly, if indeterminably, to his sister's mind, Veronica has not only fallen into the standard pattern of repetitively enacting her traumatic experience, but also of doing so in terms of the desires forcibly if indeterminably implicated therein. Her mature sexual preferences gravitate toward the properties that she associates with the remembered, imagined, and/or speculative memories of Nugent's violations. Indeed, as she finishes her reconstruction of Nugent and Liam *in flagrante delicto*, she confesses to sleeping with men, meaning her husband, who resemble Nugent, in being torn between "disapproval" of their sexual appetites and "weakness" to them. That deep ambivalence is a source of torment to these men, and Veronica states, "I am attracted to people who suffer, or men who suffer, my suffering husband, my suffering brother, the suffering figure of Mr Nugent. It is unfortunately true that happiness, in a man, does not do it, for me" (129). The "unfortunate truth" of this declaration would still hold in the absence of the parenthetical "in a man." That is, Veronica's allergy to happiness in the other is strictly correlative to her aversion to any prospect of an unwounded or unscarred state of contentment for herself. In comparing her "suffering husband" to the suffering Nugent, she contends that "what he wants, what my husband has always wanted . . . is my annihilation. This is the way his desire runs. It runs close to hatred. It is sometimes the same thing" (145). It seems likely that she understands her husband along these lines, rightly or wrongly, because that is the way *her* desire runs as well, not toward mediated self-annihilation per se but toward the traumatic atmosphere created by such psychosexual aggression. As she herself concedes, "there is a part of me that wants to be hated, too" (180).

Nor is this traumatic magnetism that binds Veronica to Tom entirely the effect, as it has usually been read, of the emotional malaise that descended with Liam's death and Veronica's ensuing traumatic remembrance.

After all, Veronica's great love for Michael Weiss, which she continues to rehearse in her present testimony, could not hold her precisely because "he refused to own me" (82), which is to say he refused to reprise the violent implication of her desire in its own appropriation. Veronica finds that traumatic frisson—that displaced resonance of the primal scene—with her future husband from the very start of their relationship. It begins with "a little ruthlessness," "a spill of blood," over another woman (70), a brutality immediately incorporated into their own sexual practice: "in the early-early days, when it wasn't like sex so much as like killing someone or being killed" (73). In other words, the threat of marital annihilation after Liam's death does not differ altogether from the thrill of annihilation that fueled their initial conjugation. In either case, the libidinal and the lethal, the wanting and the wounding, not only internest but seem to interdepend in Veronica's consciousness.

From the common root of Veronica's childhood witnessing proceeds a double articulation of the erotic and the traumatic. On one side, because Veronica's sexual impulses were constitutively implicated in an unspeakable spectacle, her efforts to master its traumatic import through active repetition of various sorts remain saturated with enjoyment or jouissance, a cathexis shattering in its ambivalent intensity. In the case of childhood sexual abuse, the homeopathic response to trauma that took Freud "beyond the pleasure principle" continues to adhere in some measure to that principle. Such thanatotic enjoyment is, if you will, a diacritical marker of this type of trauma, one of the elements necessitating the targeted critical approach we have aimed to provide. On the other side, because a powerful associative link is forged between Veronica's early sexual stirrings and her helpless witness of an unspeakable offense against a loved one, her mature erotic arousal, attachments, and satisfaction come freighted with an unconscious alloy of remorse and the need for expiation. The signifier's triggering sexual attraction pulsates not only with the traumatic witnessing but also with the trauma witnessed, the desecration of the other. This consequence in turn reinforces, on a renewable basis, Veronica's subliminal guilt in not being able to save Liam.

Veronica firmly believes, for example, that Liam blames her for something, some hurt or problem not fully specified by him, faults her for "selling out" some unspoken, underlying compact between them. Yet she recalls no actual conversations to this effect, no carping or express accusations on Liam's part, thereby licensing if not encouraging the reader to impute to her some sort of traumatic projection. Veronica's ensuing denial of any credible moral basis for her own feelings of remorse only strengthens this impression while simultaneously knitting her individual case to a larger social dynamic:

> And you feel to blame, of course. You feel it is all your fault. (144)
> He managed to blame me. And I managed to feel guilty. Now why is that? (168)
> This is what shame does. This is the anatomy and the mechanism of a family—a whole fucking country—drowning in shame. (168)

The splicing of the register of guilt, inculpation, and wrongdoing with the register of shame, the sense of disgust in being oneself, is crucial in these passages. For it not only speaks to the dilemma of traumatic witnessing, in which the incapacity to do something redemptive inflicts feelings of self-worthlessness; it also speaks to the ambient power of sexuality to entangle one's being in an action or event in which one has not participated directly. Here, Veronica's sexual being itself and the libidinal dynamics of her whole family have been profoundly implicated in the miasma—personal, familial, and national—of child sexual abuse. Elsewhere, Veronica remarks that "[Liam] just had a contagious mind" (125). But what she responds to in her brother is the contagion of "shame" emanating from scandal.

This is a hard truth, an exceptionally hard truth, but one that Enright refuses to duck or dissemble. However censorious the emotions aroused by the contemplation of child sexual abuse—whether in person, in testimony, in gossip and rumor, or in media reports—they are themselves sexually inflected or tinctured. Disgust, contempt, abhorrence, repulsion—none escape the transfer of an affect imbued with erotic valences, which can themselves be acutely aversive, even traumatic, as well as enjoyable. Part of the motivation behind the amnesia surrounding child sexual abuse in Ireland was the avoidance or resistance to personal incrimination, and hence disgrace, and shame, through the bare fact of knowing, perceiving, or witnessing at whatever remove. Because of Veronica's proximity to her brother and to the primal seduction of the enigmatic signifier, the implication of her desire and her resulting shame is especially profound, impeding the standard mechanisms of avoidance and amnesia from operating efficiently. We have seen how, in keeping with current trauma theory, Veronica dissociates her memories of witnessing Liam's violation, forgetting cognitively while remembering somatically. The same holds true for the recruitment of her erotic cathexis in witnessing: she retains the vicarious, abusive seductiveness of the primal scene outside of consciousness through bodily reenactment. Veronica thus proves to be Liam's psychic doppelgänger in suffering not only traumatic *infliction* but also traumatic *conscription*.

On the night of Liam's wake, an event Veronica (reasonably) traces back to the sexual assault, she has what she calls "terminal sex" with Tom, and her brief sketch of the encounter recalls the childhood sex that has indeed proved terminal for her brother (218). She "did all the moves" as Liam did; she "made way for him" as Liam did; she "did not tell him to stop," again like Liam; and, most tellingly, she summarizes the state of her desire on this occasion in phrases eerily similar to those she uses in describing Liam's attitude toward Nugent's abuse: "So I must have wanted it too, or something like it" (219). The chiming of these two scenes speaks to the signature psychosexual harm of child sexual abuse generally, as it pertains to both Liam and Veronica. This most insidious damage is best represented not as a wound but as a short circuit. Both Liam, as a child, and Veronica, as an adult, seem to engage in a sex act voluntarily yet somehow athwart their own will. To put it another way, neither appears to own the desire that is nevertheless their own desire. Neither is a puppet, simply acting on the desires of others, of Nugent or Tom respectively. But that original appropriative intrusion of the desire of the other has left them abnormally estranged from the operations of their own desire, unable to recognize its limits or to reckon with its implications. As a participant-victim of Nugent's brand of passive sexual aggression, Veronica not only epitomizes this psychopathology but also discerns its operation as a family inheritance, one that creates traumatic parallels among the different generations of her people: from the orphaned Ada, perpetually on her compliant "back foot," to her mother, embracing the mandated violence of endless reproduction, down to Veronica's own generation and beyond. Taken on its own terms, her summary of this history is the single most incisive and important analysis in the entire novel of the legacy of Veronica and Liam: "It is not that the Hegartys don't know what they want, it is that they don't know *how* to want. Something about their wanting went catastrophically astray" (187). And Veronica's account can ultimately supply an attentive reader with an empirically cross-checkable understanding of when, why, and how.

As we have previously asserted, Enright encodes Veronica's traumatic amnesia and uncertainty not only in the narrative design at large, but also in the contouring of Veronica's libidinal cathexis by and within the traumatic frame. Taking account of what we might call the traumatic structure of her desire proves particularly useful, we would suggest, for an interrogation of the origins and the endpoint of Veronica's auto/biographical testimony, her self-reflective memoir of her brother. At the midpoint of *The Gathering*, Veronica introduces a pause in her narrative, a dramatic flourish that serves to heighten narrative tension, before proceeding to reveal the decisive, taboo secret driving Liam's abbreviated life and unexpectedly squalid demise: "I know, as I write about these three things: the jacket, the stones, and my brother's nakedness underneath his clothes, that they require me to deal in facts. It is time to put an end to the shifting stories and the waking dreams. It is time to call an end to romance and just say what happened in Ada's house, the year that I was eight and Liam was barely nine" (142).

The criticism has generally taken Veronica's "shifting stories" and "waking dreams" to be symptomatic of the traumatic amnesia and uncertainty wrought by the very event they have served to camouflage, if not conceal. In the unavoidable absence of assured recall, it has been argued, Veronica tries out different parabolic options, different fictive approaches to the same underlying truth. From this perspective, Veronica's willingness to foreground the apparent arbitrariness of the "romance" that she concocts between Ada and Nugent works to cement her paradoxical credibility as a fabulist. She necessarily fabricates, but she positively refuses to lie. In overlooking the role of Veronica's conscripted desire in her trauma testimony, however, this consensus fails to discern that even her disavowal of any truth claims and her admission of a certain narrative caprice might itself involve a significant degree of misprision.

Veronica acknowledges the fictive status of her story's central romance in the most magisterial way possible, by asserting absolute creative sovereignty over the temporal genesis of her plot: "Lambert Nugent first saw my grandmother Ada Merriman in a hotel foyer in 1925. This is the moment I choose." Yet her very claim to plenary authorial control of a given present is immediately divided against itself by the structure of its enunciation. Veronica in fact "chooses" at least two "moment[s]," and they coexist in a meaningful if subterranean relationship. In its conative function, *the moment* in the sentence refers to 1925 and more specifically to the moment "when Lamb Nugent first saw . . . Ada Merriman . . . [at] seven o'clock in the evening" (13). In its metalingual function, however, the "moment I choose" also marks the moment of enunciation or inscription, the point at which Veronica chooses her narrative opening.

Vexingly, though, the occasion and subject of Veronica's discourse, the traumatic implication of her formative desires in Liam's plight, involves unconscious processes, unassimilable to being "in the moment" or its pragmatic corollary, punctual decision-making, the self-coincident exertion of the will in time. The moment that Veronica chooses a Dublin hotel foyer in 1925 for her story's originary moment ("and the rest, as they say, is history"; 85) is itself a part and a precipitant of a causal chain—no—a causal "tangle" of physical and mental events shaping, following from, and recasting Liam's abuse, a congeries of overlapping perceptions and memories framed and filtered by one another, both in their emergence and then retroactively. It is this complex, metaleptic unfolding, time thrown out of joint by traumatic desire, that Veronica elaborates in the streamlined guise of a "romance." Her ostensibly germinal moment of choice springs already, if ambiguously, formed from the very prehistory barring access to the determining conditions of that moment and the import they confer on her decision.

Thus, what Veronica would have her audience believe is a purely discretionary and arbitrary choice of where to begin, and in what mode, must be seen, from a psychoanalytic viewpoint, as an unconsciously motivated effect of Veronica's place in the social dynamic she would rehearse (recapitulate/replay). We should not, accordingly, stop at the question of why Veronica fictionalizes the surround of Liam's sexual abuse (or her own)—to which the known effects of trauma supply a ready answer. We need to consider why she opts for this particular genre fiction, this particular romance, and this particular point of departure. Why is this, and no other, "the tale that [she] would love to write" (13)?

Seen from the perspective of the author's craft, Enright has set up her narrative to explore these questions, and hence to address the psychic rationale behind not just the fictiveness of Veronica's testimony but also the particular kind and course of that fictiveness. Insofar as this rationale is necessarily to some degree unconscious, Enright must supply evidence beyond the statements given by the protagonist herself. That is to say,

Veronica's skepticism as to the accuracy of her account and even her avowal of creative propriety over the romance she embroiders do not and, in a psychic sense, cannot supply or even admit the possibility of any meaningful interrogation into the whys and wherefores of her fabrication. To this end, Enright must open up some other form of internal distance within Veronica's narrative. At the same time, and herein lies the markedly complicating factor, Enright is equally concerned, as Harte indicates, to encode in the structure of the novel the difficulties of traumatic recall, including what we would call its repressed libidinal complement (Harte 2010, 192). In short, the itinerary of the novel must give prompts to a hermeneutics of suspicion that it will simultaneously act to balk, if not thwart.

To execute this ambidextrous strategy, Enright has recourse to a complex, chronological internesting, especially apt for the representation of mnemonic struggle and selectivity. She interweaves five separate divisions of time: the ancient romance of Ada and Lamb; the dimly remembered, vividly constructed childhood era when Liam was sexually abused; the desultory young adulthood of Liam and Veronica; the tightly focused period of Liam's suicide, wake, and funeral; and, following from the funeral, the volatile, dysfunctional present of Veronica's insomnia and alcoholic excess, during which she composes the story left us to read. By including this last segment, Enright is able to play off the chronology of the tale against the chronology of the telling, the *durée* of the plot against the moment of its enunciation. If there is a key to the novel as an experiential structure, a mechanism for orchestrating the dynamics of readerly engagement, it resides in this manipulation of temporal registers. What Enright accomplishes thereby is to feed her readers' expectations of narrative progress toward the sublation of adversity and the achievement of closure, only to counter this movement with the shock of recursivity, of the plotline turning back on itself and seeming to return to an earlier, torturous point in the story. Signally, as the novel nears its conclusion, it seems to gather a developing momentum, or momentum of development, toward full resolution, both psychic and narrative, thanks in large part to Veronica's discovery of elements new to the narration. As readers must continually remind themselves, however, these elements, which look to either clinch Veronica's speculative version of past events or to put her on a more positive footing for the future, have in fact occurred earlier in the plot sequence—that is, before the catastrophic period of Veronica's sleepless, inebriate inditing of this traumatic memoir. In narratological terms, Enright induces a confusion between the *fabula* and the *sujet*, such that the reader, anticipating the climactic resolution of the novel (the story as a whole), will mistake the earlier for the later development, will mistake a recursive movement *in* the plot for a linear progression *of* the plot. The published criticism has consistently turned on such misconstruals.

At the symbolic level, this involuted chronology works to simulate not just the effects of trauma per se but also the traumatic recruitment of libidinal energy: the forward movement of erotic cathexes or attractions captured and subsumed by their repetitive enactment of the traumatic event. Across the whole of Enright's text, a palimpsestic relationship obtains between different events and temporalities—past and present, childhood and adulthood, conscious and unconscious. Enright hereby stages how the damage specific to sexual trauma—the disruption of the psychotemporal coordinates of those involved, their chronotopes of sexual identity—makes the inciting episode, fugitive as it is to cognition, ubiquitous in effect and impossible to leave behind.

At the pragmatic level, however, Enright's involuted chronology does more than reflect the traumatic disturbances wrought on her narrator. It illustrates how these disturbances inform—in the sense of giving form to—her narrative, and in this respect, the novel's contrapuntal chronology serves Enright's ambidextrous strategy of ratifying the sincerity of Veronica's testimony while opening its unconscious motives to critical scrutiny. The introduction of new textual elements within disparate temporal frames simultaneously incites in careful readers a cognitive dissonance that compromises their alignment with the narratorial consciousness, compelling them to entertain different possible meanings or functions for these elements than those Veronica has assigned them, those she apprehends, or those she can admit—subliminal meanings or functions that convey the truth of Veronica's being rather than the truth of her discourse.

From Veronica's opening, establishing reflections on her intentions in telling her tale, found objects serve to anchor her overlapping, chronologically scrambled meditations, some explicitly fabricated and others scrupulously, photographically rendered, in a manner that allows Enright to broadly explore the multidirectionality of trauma. Starting with the "clean, white bones" that Liam once loved, and that Veronica herself surreptitiously collects, found objects serve as objective correlatives for Veronica's writing and, more importantly, as key elements in Enright's narrative strategy (1–2).

Dating back to Yorick's skull and further, to the Anglo Saxon "ubi sunt" thematic, found objects have been employed throughout literary history as focal points for narrative flexibility. A found object can be integrated in a storyline in order to advance, layer, or reinforce the dominant viewpoint. But it is also positioned, through its sheer givenness, to retain a discrete field of interpretive gravity in order to admit an alternative gloss that can test or controvert that viewpoint. In this sense, the *objet trouvé* bears something of the iridescent quality of the enigmatic signifier, at once compelling yet labile, forceful yet not definitive. This device is especially handy for Enright's purposes in that its bivalence can be so readily mapped onto the split-level chronology of *The Gathering*, its equivocal division between the time of the telling and the time of the tale.

One such found object is the cache of letters from Nugent to Ada, which Veronica believes decisively verify her speculative vision of the past, specifically the pivotal role played by Ada and Nugent's notional romance in the violation of Liam and, perhaps, Veronica herself. Not that these letters breathe any hint of romantic passion or erotic longing. Each specimen is nondescript, businesslike, and banal; in aggregate, they strongly support Mammy Hegarty's impression of Nugent as "the landlord" and nothing more. Veronica manages to read into these missives "a relationship of sudden pique and petty cruelty," though she has to concede, "I may be wrong—this may just be the way that landlords speak to their tenants" (235). With greater confidence, she detects "a sense of thrall," a suggestive yet underdeveloped notion of financial sway that Nugent exercised over Ada, leading ultimately to her connivance at Liam's abuse, even if she did not consciously collude therein. In Veronica's urgent drive to ferret out an explanation for the harrowing events of her childhood that is both documentable and bearable, she somewhat improbably tropes the landlord-tenant relation of Ada and Nugent as a relation of serf to liege, in which Nugent held some sort of *droit de seigneur* over the children. But does this feudal exaggeration of Nugent's petulantly exerted power really serve Veronica's stated purpose—that is, to locate the origins of Liam's violation in an aborted romance, where the protagonist-villain won neither the girl nor the affection he sought? Well, yes, it does, if the stalled yet smoldering romance is already established, as it has been over the previous thirty-five installments of Veronica's witness narrative. For under these circumstances, Nugent's lurid attitude resonates, as Veronica suggests, with a certain resentment at being slighted, feelings of frustration and entitled vindictiveness that result in his targeting of Ada's most vulnerable trusts: "When Nugent saw a child he saw revenge—I have no doubt about that" (236).

It is rare for Veronica to have "no doubt about" something, and it is one of the ironies of the posttraumatic condition that her unwonted assurance in this instance warrants serious critical suspicion indeed. The preexistence of the lurking attraction between Ada and Nugent to any further information about their interaction forms the predicate of Veronica's careful arrangement of events, the *sujet* of her narrative. For this reason it is all the more important to keep in mind how far the actual timing of events, the *fabula*, belies this arrangement. Veronica first comes into possession of the rent books and letters on the night of Liam's wake (217, 232), weeks before the period when she begins "to write down what happened in my grandmother's house the summer I was eight or nine" (1). That is also to say it is weeks before the fateful "moment I choose," the moment she chooses the moment in the hotel foyer as the point when "my romance" begins with thoughts of love on both sides. Before that decisive moment—the moment of Veronica's speculation and the scene that her speculation lights on as the ancient ground where "the seeds of [Liam's] death were sown"—there arrived those letters that would metaleptically extend and complete this imagined account (13).

But coming before the moment of invention as they did—and this is crucial—the letters do more to obviate than corroborate a romantic connection between Lamb and Ada as having given rise to the assault on young Liam. Nugent's status as the landlord at Broadstone gave him both means and opportunity for his predations, and his status as a landlord, at least along the feudal lines that Veronica envisages, also gives him plenary authority over the property's inhabitants, the license that accompanies ownership: "He had the house, and he had the woman, more or less, and he did what he liked with the children passing through" (235). The final element in any criminal prosecution is motive, and Veronica has already provided as much in her witness to the actual assault. "What he liked" was the sexual enjoyment taken from pedophilia, the pleasure, let us remember, to which he was "weak." The revenge motive that Veronica imputes to Nugent is not just forensically gratuitous in itself but it also depends entirely on a likewise superfluous tale of thwarted passion.

The significance of rebutting Veronica's romantic account lies not in the conclusion negated but in the questions raised. Since Veronica's history of her grandmother performs no indispensable function of explication, does it have some other function, equally vital to Veronica's avowed task of witnessing, and if so, what is it? The most compelling answer begins with the observation that what she calls "my romance" represents not any old version of romance—pulp fiction, medieval, teenage, or otherwise—but specifically a *family* romance in the proper Freudian sense. While Veronica credits "listening to the radio, and reading the paper, and hearing about what went on in schools and churches and in people's homes" with shifting her reflections on Mr. Nugent, her romance narrative in fact distances what went on at Broadstone from the mainly institutional forms of child abuse for which Ireland was becoming infamous (172–73). This model would be better exemplified by treating Nugent as exclusively a landlord-predator rather than a family member. By casting Nugent as Ada's jilted yet lifelong, ever-present spectral lover, Veronica modulates the child-predator scenario she witnessed into a symbolic version of an incest narrative in which her mode of witness, the stories she relates, plays a formative role. Ada, of course, is installed by the Hegartys themselves as a mother figure to Veronica, Liam, and Kitty, a surrogate for their Mammy, who was "not herself" that Broadstone summer (46, 86). But it is Veronica's elective romance that lends a distinctly paternal air both to Nugent's presence in the home and to the various grooming practices he deploys, be they the regular allowances of sweets that Veronica still remembers fondly, the display of curiosities, or the automotive mentoring. Introduced by Veronica in connection with "Ada's wedding picture" (21) and culminating in a graphically imagined sexual encounter, the enduring connection between Nugent and Ada delineates the scandal of Liam's abuse in familial terms. This fabricated romance constitutes Liam's abuse not as an open secret that everyone knows and yet disavows (though as Veronica concedes, Liam's status as an abuse victim was an open secret "all his life" [2007, 167]) but as what Nicolas Abraham and Maria Torok designate an *encrypted secret* (2005, 159–60), one that is collectively forgotten only to be preserved in the bodily containers of the associated individuals. It is not family life in general but this romance, this scandalous romance in particular, that Veronica references in her comment, "I do not think we remember our family in any real sense. We live in them, instead" (66).

The decision to trace Liam's sexual abuse to the imagined history of Ada and Nugent answers to Veronica's conscious desire ("this is the tale that I would love to write"; 13) because it answers to the implication of her unconscious desire in the dynamics of that abuse. To put it another way, in elaborating a family romance manqué as the expository structure within which her witness takes place, she in effect turns Liam's violation into a version of the primal seduction, the originary, enigmatic intrusion of adult sexuality, that the act of child sexual abuse evokes, replicates, and perverts. Thus, if the incrementally emerging focus of Veronica's saga testifies to the trauma of her brother's abuse, the saga's form testifies to the jouissance that Veronica cannot but find reenacted there.

As it turns out, Veronica's profoundly, confoundingly transferential relation to her brother's abuse is already encoded in that oft-quoted statement of purpose with which her chronicle begins: "I need to bear witness to an uncertain event. I feel it roaring inside me—this thing that may not have taken place" (1). As a witness, Veronica stands outside the event; yet she feels it "roaring inside" her. And while her phraseology certainly signifies her internalization of her brother's plight, a common effect of traumatic witnessing, it also indexes how the event taps into and amplifies stirrings interior to Veronica's affective and libidinal constitution. Indeed, her initial paragraph is entirely self-reflective; no mention is made of Liam, only of the continued life of the event within Veronica's body. The inference to be drawn, both from this prelude and from the ensuing family romance, is that the spectacle of Liam's seduction by Nugent reignited, powerfully if unconsciously, the tumult surrounding Veronica's own enigmatic sexual initiation. The result is an identification, amounting almost to a conflation, of inside and outside, of her brother's shattering and her own, and, most acutely, of his and her coerced desire. At the same time, such an unconscious identification on Veronica's part, while obviously painful, also serves as a defense mechanism against her sense of having betrayed her brother. Here again, Veronica's experience of her brother's "contagious mind," which zeroed in on people's "weaknesses" (125), their portals of shame, seems a legible enough displacement of the layered and conflicting sources of contagious shame inscribed in the traumatic yet libidinally charged ordeal they shared.

The extent of the transferential sibling identification occasioned by the signal events at Broadstone helps elucidate the delicate, asymptotic correlation that Veronica draws between the apparent reality of Liam's violation and the likelihood of her own. She does not envision her own abuse independently of Liam's, but neither does she equate the two. Hers consistently emerges as the less substantiated, less credible, less objective version.

Having said that, the two incidences do not break down, in her mind, along simple binary lines of observed versus hallucinated, or remembered versus imagined. She knows that "Liam was sexually abused," but with the caveat, "or was probably sexually abused" (224). She wonders, "Did it happen to me," and opines, "I don't think so." But she cannot rule out the possibility, which she continues to treat as a memory rather than a figment (222). To be sure, in recollecting Liam's violation, she must fight her way through a "tangle of things," while mnemonic access to her own is obstructed by thoughts in which "words and actions are mangled" (144, 221). The inner/outer, subject/object distinction here asserts itself in the language of her testimony. The rhyming and synonymy of "tangle" and "mangled," however, sets up a mirror relation between the two events, suggesting a joint and jointly obscured psychic origin that Veronica repeatedly calls the "missing thing," which in psychoanalytic parlance would be the primal seduction conjured in either instance of abuse. Finally, while Veronica presents her brother's violation as the more materially tangible, she elaborates her own as its symbolic supplement. By envisioning Ada and Nugent presiding together over her "interference," Veronica condenses her background family romance into an iconographic image of the primal scene as archetypal (family) ménage.

A New Epistemology of Child Sexual Abuse

In folding the problem of implicated desire into that of inflicted trauma, *The Gathering* powerfully destabilizes the classic roles of the abuse scenario— victim, witness, bystander, predator, enabler, deliverer, betrayer—and thereby brings forth a new epistemology of child sexual abuse, one in which the line between different modes of agency and responsibility, participation and observation, is irretrievably blurred without being entirely erased. Both the perspective of witness and the interpretation of the ensuing testimony are even further complicated in turn. While under this dispensation the roles in the abuse scenario are shown to be more permeable than previously assumed (including in current trauma theory), these roles are nonetheless liable to vastly different moral and social judgment and so incur shame and judgment in vastly unequal measure. As such, the sort of transferential identification among the involved parties that a participant-witness like Veronica Hegarty might unconsciously register not only molds her narrative but also compounds it with psychic defense mechanisms like repression, denial, displacement, and projection so as to alter substantially its testimonial impetus and value.

We have already treated instances involving the several figures and roles in the abuse scenario where the transferential identification incubated within Veronica's elective romance structure may or may not function as a mode of psychic defense. For example, is Veronica's belief that Liam "wanted him [Nugent] too . . . or wanted *something*" (223) a displacement of her own libidinal agitation at the startling spectacle of pedophilic activity, or her own inchoate wanting, or is it a disavowal of the full extent of Liam's jeopardy so as to rationalize her discomfort at failing to rescue him? That is, does her claim testify to her subliminal self-image as participant, co-victim, or complicit bystander? Correlatively, does Veronica's exclamation that "it was Ada's fault all along" (223) displace blame from the landlord to her grandmother in order to domesticate the harm done within family bonds, or does it displace responsibility for enabling Nugent from Veronica's passive moment of failed intervention to Ada's more aggressive if hypothetical orchestration of the episode, or does it simply vent a lingering resentment at the apparent inadvertence of the traumatized children's designated guardian? It is impossible to determine, finally, whether Veronica's vision of having fellated Nugent under duress represents the fundamental traumatic reality from which she has distanced herself by projecting that reality onto her brother, or whether it is an interjection of her brother's distress in order to assuage her survivor's guilt, or whether it is a more straightforward identification arising out of their Irish twinship.

It should be noted that these and alternative interpretations of each party's role in the episode of abuse are:

A. First put in narrative play by Veronica's decision, before writing, to treat the landlord's letters as appendages to the romance she "wants to tell" rather than on their own terms; and
B. Themselves potential factors in Veronica's decision to frame the narrative and to treat Nugent's letters as she did.

The vertiginous complexity of Enright's new abuse epistemology finds its answerable form in a Möbius-strip inversion of the figure/ground of her novel, the inaccessible traumatic Real and the *traumawerk* in which it is (dis)figured.

The reversibility of one figure-ground nexus in particular—concerning that Irish twinship of Liam and Veronica—solicits a profound and profoundly disturbing recalibration of the potential impact, import, and even reality of the sexual transgression at the heart of the novel. As we have mentioned, Veronica portrays herself as being preternaturally close to her brother in age, in alliance, and in affect; and that proximity, universally acknowledged among Enright scholars, has been seen as raising the stakes of Veronica's witness in every respect: its poignancy, the sense of guilt and responsibility it induces, the psychic and practical demands it imposes, the experiential transitivity it enables, and the identification and confusion it occasions. But the tropes Veronica selects to aver this proximity indicate that the scripting question might well be flipped. Rather than an organic immixture of their identities that intensifies the various aspects of Veronica's witness, their intimacy can be seen to arise precisely from their shared traumatic experience of premature and predatory sexualization. Veronica's instinct to cast that intimacy backward in time stems precisely from the contagiousness of the pedophilic transaction. Being galvanized by a libidinally invasive and overwhelming encounter, the intimacy of Liam and Veronica cannot but assume a likewise powerfully sexual complexion.

Thus, Veronica's initial description of her Irish twinship with Liam is markedly sexualized: "There were eleven months between me and Liam. We came out of her on each other's tails; one after the other, as fast as a gang-bang, as fast as infidelity. Sometimes I think we overlapped in there" (11). The individual metaphors constituting this remarkable portrait of the protagonists as young fetuses radiate throughout Veronica's narrative, resonating with far-flung passages relating to the abuse scenario, its imagined backstory, and its overdetermined aftermath. The metaphor "gang-bang" migrates into the idiom "slap-bang" in Veronica's comment, "It [Liam's abuse] went on slap-bang in front of me and still I didn't realise it," and the chiming of the two terms points to the incestuous sexualization of the siblings' "unholy alliance" as a factor in Veronica's dissociated memory (171, 173). The unusual interest, both positive and negative, that Veronica insistently expresses in her brother's looks might not signify an incestuous attachment, but as one element of a larger composite, her continual assessment of Liam's sex appeal is suggestive: "I remember thinking how good he looked; how handsome he might seem" (53); "At sixteen he was beautiful" (163); "Think of . . . the beauty of the boy" (236); "This grey thing . . . this horrible old fucker" (28); "He is a small grey heap of a man" (169). The migration of a second metaphor reinforces this suggestion. The image "we came out of her on each other's tails" reappears when Veronica receives news of Liam's death: it appears as a phantom sensation felt on Veronica's tail, "a warmth at the base of my spine," which she takes to be contact from Liam's disappeared, dead, but essential self (29). Later, at the wake, when her Mammy exclaims about what "great pals" Liam and Veronica were, she feels the exact same touch on her tail, "warm on the base of [her] spine," only literally this time, as a tactile hallucination (198). Despite the presence of Liam's deceased self, Veronica does not interpret the feeling as a spiritual communication from him but rather turns to see who has placed a "loving touch" on her and, finding no one, worries the question throughout the evening, and even later at the funeral (244). Her surprising failure to connect the two phantasmal touches with one another, or even to remember her prior association of the tail warming with Liam, counterbalances her deliberate affirmation of their all but fused identity with a reflexive repression or denial of its sexual dimension.

But that dimension is not lost to inspection; it is merely displaced and inadvertently encoded in the romantic narrative that Veronica "wants to write," in part because it substitutes for or doubles narrative possibilities that she would rather avoid. Such an interpretation is pointedly solicited by one more prenatal metaphor, in what is arguably the most horrifying fantasy scene in Veronica's imaginary history of Ada and Nugent. Directly after Nugent first meets Ada (and before their one and only "date"; 13), Veronica envisions Nugent as indulging in an erotic fantasy or memory in which he violates the sexually nascent, disease-ravaged body of his now deceased sister Lizzie. The scene proposes a sinister analogy between the two pairs of siblings, Lamb and Lizzie on one hand and Liam and Veronica on the other. Like Liam, the homophonically related Lamb is slightly older than his sister, whose bed he enters uninvited, as Liam enters Veronica's after their visit to St. Ita's asylum. Most importantly, at the incestuous culmination of his fantasy, Nugent feels the skin of his penis to be exactly the same as, at one with, the skin of his dead sister: "always damp, never sweating" (35). The commentary Veronica offers seems as gratuitous as the scene itself: "Because, in those days, people used to be mixed up together in the most disgusting ways" (35). But in fact her words consolidate the analogy as if by some unconscious compulsion. Liam and Veronica began life, on her own account, "mixed up together" in the womb, with similarly sexual overtones.

The mirroring of the respective sibling relationships of the child victim and the predator runs disquietingly against the grain of the narrative

Veronica "wants to write," and that is perhaps why it has gone largely overlooked to this point. As we have already previewed, however, the deeper significance of this parallelism derives from its place in the complex temporal framework of the novel, in this case the twist it gives to the chronology of Veronica's family romance. The placement of the fantasy scene situates Ada not as Lamb Nugent's first love but rather as a derivative or rebound interest. This development, in turn, implies that the true seedbed of Liam's abuse and eventual suicide is not in that future meeting of Ada and Lamb in a Dublin hotel lobby but in Nugent's taboo passion for his lost sister, for whom Ada turns out to have been a substitute. Their meeting, of which Veronica says, "This is the moment I choose," accordingly, is not the origin of her tale but already a part of "the rest" that "they say is history" (13, 85). Viewed psychoanalytically, the fantasy that Veronica attributes to Lamb Nugent bares her own unconscious promptings. Overriding her assertively self-conscious emplotment of her testimony, Veronica has laid at the foundation of her tale an incestuous attachment that doubles her own sexual enmeshment with Liam. Or, to take up another angle, she has at once divulged and denied her incestuous feelings by projecting them onto the figure whose predatory actions may have helped cultivate them. That is to say, Veronica's invented romance poses Lamb as a kind of demonic correlative to her ineffable bond with Liam because in the annals of her dissociated memory Lamb figures as the demonic catalyst of that bond. Given the precedence that Nugent enjoys in both narratives—temporal in one, causative in the other—they unconsciously attest, in combination, to the coercive activation of psychosocially inadmissible desire being a primary traumatic component of such child abuse. The infliction of child sexual trauma—whether in victim, witness, or witness-victim—always involves the conscription of a traumatic sexuality.

It is arguably owing to this forced elicitation of desire rather than to any brute traumatic shock to the system that Veronica's mourning process, in the words of Harte, "remains unresolved" (2010, 202). To advance her new abuse epistemology, of which this insight is a crucial part, Enright deploys her signature manipulation of the novel's temporal registers, again playing the *sujet* against the *fabula*, the telling against the tale, to create a sense of progressive, restorative momentum that proves at once diegetically recursive and psychologically regressive. Centering once again on a found object of vital import for Veronica's story, the chronological fold in the text opens to reveal an isomorphic crease in Veronica's response to sexual trauma, a dissociation between what she cognizes and what she somaticizes, what she thinks and what she is defended against knowing, what she repurposes and what she merely reenacts.

THE ROMANCE OF REPRODUCTION

The most sensational of the novel's found objects appears at Liam's funeral. It is a person, unknown as yet to the Hegarty clan, a boy, the son of Liam, whose resemblance to his father is uncanny. As Veronica tells her husband, "Oh, there's no doubting the child. . . . It's Liam. To the life" (245). The symbolic weight of her words cannot be mistaken, particularly in the context of her brother's passing. For Veronica, and indeed for the rest of the assembled, young Rowan personifies renewal, a surprise legacy of Liam that is also a revival of his genetic stock, and this in a narrative that takes as its mantra, "History is only biological" (162). The sudden upturn in the arc of the Hegarty family history at the funeral lightens the tone of Veronica's account, of the repartee among the guests, and indeed of the entire affair: "It is like we had never seen a child before. . . . Everyone wants to touch him. They just have to" (246). Enright thus stages, or has Veronica stage, a climax that looks to double as a classic mode of closure.

Liam's funeral serves to site a marriage of dominant social ideologies, what Lee Edelman calls "reproductive futurism" on the one hand (2004, 29, 58) and what Leo Bersani calls "the culture of redemption" on the other (1992, 1–2). The former is perhaps the defining creed of heteronormativity operating on a collective scale. It enshrines the figure of the child as both the emblem and the agent of the reparative power of the future—that is, the capacity of the future to indemnify the social damages and demerits incurred in the past and the present. For this reason, the child (functioning as an epitome of that hope) and the bringing of children into the world (undertaken as a pragmatics of hope) must be protected and celebrated. Reproduction thus becomes an art and a technology of redemption. This ideology has had an especially strong purchase in Catholic Ireland. Splicing the image of the innocent child with the redemptive agency of the Christ child, the Roman Catholic Church had, throughout the twentieth century, staked the future of a properly "Irish" Ireland on the moral and theological protection of children.

Representing for Veronica and her fellow mourners a symbolic resurrection of young Liam, Rowan becomes just such a child-epitome, the very pattern of reproductive futurism, the bearer of tomorrow's compensations and guarantees. That he assumes this status as the novel draws to a conclusion gestures toward an embrace of the culture of redemption. The latter centers, for our purposes, on the aesthetico-normative principle that literature possesses and should be in the business of exercising the power to repair or at least alleviate the problems, the anguish, and the sheer disappointment of everyday life. While traumatic witness or testimony plays in a somewhat different sociopolitical register than the culture of redemption, there are salient points of affiliation and even convergence between the two, plainly exhibited in the Hegarty chronicle. Inasmuch as Veronica comes to recognize, decades after the fact, the probable abuse of Liam as part of the larger, notorious sex abuse scandals consuming late twentieth-century Ireland ("listening to the radio, and reading the paper, and hearing about what was going on"), her story must be seen as a document of this very particular ill of Irish everyday life that *The Gathering* as a whole means to address. Accordingly, to stake the resolution of the book's narrative on the remediation of family and social dysfunction through the magic of an unforeseen birth, to find the possibility of closure in the promise that heteronormative reproduction affords a future renovation, to craft an ending that allegorizes the exorcism of the specter of Irish sexual abuse in the figure of an innocent, undefiled child—all of this seems to punctuate the novel's trajectory of development with a massive and frankly uncritical subscription to the culture of redemption.

But it is all a feint, a glorious feint, one of the greatest and most pointedly instructive feints in all of modern literary history. First of all, Enright invokes reproductive futurism and the culture of redemption to expose their mythic status, that is, their inflated reputation for fashioning satisfactory prospective resolutions. Veronica's infatuated reaction to Rowan indicates that she believes, at some level, in this idealizing myth, and her climactic placement of Rowan's tonic debut among the Hegartys predisposes the reader to believe as well. But while Veronica ushers in Liam's son at the end of her composition as an agent of reconciliation and rejuvenation, he in fact enters the tale itself, the *fabula* or sequence of events, weeks *before* Veronica's full-on psychic crash prompts her to compose her witness-narrative in the first place, during those late-night bouts of wine and sleeplessness. Gazing through the filter of Rowan's presence, Veronica sees her family dynamics in a more positive light and in colors predictive of a return to a more typical mix of tension and affection, love and antagonism, a blend unravaged by traumatic aftershock. In the recursive spiral of the novel's temporality, however, this sanguine moment actually *precedes*, and clearly does nothing to ameliorate, Veronica's subsequent breakdown, which places on display the whole array of traumatic injury and anguish: the inflicted, the suffered, and the collateral. Enright, it would seem, remains committed to toting up the full damage of child sexual abuse, and to do so means reckoning with the iron recalcitrance of the past, including its immunity to redemptive icons and ideologies.

Indeed, Enright takes this anti-redemptive anatomy of child sexual abuse a crucial step further. She shows how in collaborating to effect the enthronement of the innocent child as a simultaneously social and aesthetic ideal, these redemptive ideologies necessarily frame the child as an object of desire and so prove continuous with the dominant scandal of everyday Irish life that they are called on to dispel. Enright reinforces her critique by positioning her narrative-protagonist as the novel's main exponent of both ideologies. Veronica enacts the creed of reproductive futurism in her response to Rowan at the funeral. Precisely because her "brother's son" is "terribly like [his father]" and thus seems to resurrect him in untainted form, redeeming the traumatic losses of the past, Veronica professes "absolute regard" for his mother, Sarah, for whom she elsewhere expresses the harshest contempt (242). Enright thereby underscores the implicitly anti-feminist bent of an ideology that values women not for their present being in the world but strictly as bearers of a purportedly better future. Veronica enacts the creed of cultural redemption in her representation of Rowan's impact on both her state of mind and the Hegarty family mood, as the positive consummation of her testimonial project. With the arrival of Rowan, Veronica attempts, in her own mind, to convert her harrowing witness to the past, to "the flesh . . . long fallen away" (1), into a triumphant witness to the future, to the filial flesh, like her daughter's, that is falling nicely into place, "moulded and compact" (152). Far from denoting a final resolution of her traumatic backstory, however, Veronica's unspoken fantasies concerning Rowan bespeak its repetitive enactment. Specifically, these fantasies betray the residual implication of her own libidinal impulses in the sexual assaults she has witnessed and suffered. In this respect, her fantasies can be seen to adumbrate the psychic breakdown to come, unraveling the narrational metalepsis that tricks us into thinking she has already weathered it. Veronica's affective investment in Rowan is stunningly, even creepily, sexual. Indeed, it takes on precisely the language of child seduction: "Then I say, 'Hello Rowan,' again, 'Hello sweetie-pie,' wondering how I can trick or induce this child into my arms and, after a while, kiss him, or inhale him. How will I steal or filch permission to rub my cheek along the skin of his back, and play the bones of his spine, and blow thick kisses into the softness of his arms?" (242). And then she continues in phrases redolent of the notorious grooming process: "Perhaps over time. Perhaps I will be able to do it over time" (242).

A later reverie couples her eroticization of Rowan with her incestuous attachment to Liam, forged in their shared experience of abuse. Struggling, as the funeral service starts, to determine "what I want," Veronica first determines that she wants to know who at the wake gave her tail the "loving touch" previously associated with Liam's ghost. She immediately follows this option with, "Also, I want Rowan. I yearn for him, not with lips or hands, but with my entire face. My skin wants him. I want to nuzzle him, and feel his light hair tickle my chin. I want to flutter my eyelashes against his cheek." As if to insist on the reality and intensity of her ardor, she continues, "This spooling fantasy runs through my head through all that follows" (244). More surprising, perhaps, than the transparently erotic nature of Veronica's "want" in these moments is her evident obliviousness to its erotic overtones, to the untoward, pedophilic flavor of her expressed desire, let alone its incestuous triangulation with her brother. One must wonder how this is possible, especially for a subject whose extended traumatic witness so clearly proceeds from extraordinarily acute powers of introspection. We would submit that the diffuse yet fortifying assumptions of reproductive futurism, fully internalized by Veronica, license her libidinous fetishism as if it were something else altogether, something spiritual, uncompromised, innocent, and idealistic. Inasmuch as this reproductionist turn celebrates the child as a revelation not of truth ("the only thing that the dead require"; 156) but of hope and possibility, it rivets her testimonial all the more firmly to the culture of redemption, further insulating her consciousness from the embodied residue of traumatic sexuality feeding her delight in Rowan.

We have to wonder if the pervasive influence of these paired normative ideologies, the biopolitical and the aesthetic, helps account for the minimal attention that these glaringly scandalous passages have received from

Enright's otherwise canny exegetes. Certainly these passages cannot be dismissed as merely occasional. Once noted, they fit a pattern that extends beyond family gatherings, like the funeral, to Veronica's quotidian family life. She consistently represents her interplay with her daughters in suggestively carnal terms, as if the somatic memory of her premature sexualization is reasserting itself in displaced form:

> So I get a daughter on the sofa and manhandle her into loving me a little. . . .
> We cuddle up and there is messing. (38)
>   I know that her smell is there as I lie down with the thought of her
> beside me. I want to run my hand down her exquisite back, and over
> her lovely little bum. I want to check that it is all still there, and nicely
> packed, and happy. . . . I want to squeeze every part of her tight, until she is
> moulded and compact. (152)

It almost goes without saying that these scenes confuse the roles of mother and lover, parent and paramour, a psychodynamic intrinsic, at an unconscious level, to the enigmatic signifier in primal seduction and not entirely alien to the enigmatic signifier's overt, genitalized replication in child sexual abuse.

If one were disposed to doubt the linkage of this sexualization of Emily to Veronica's traumatized witnessing of Nugent's "interference" with her brother, her description of a photo she took of Emily and Liam together, during one of his last visits, should resolve any lingering doubts: "Emily is two; naked, straight as a dye, and more beautiful than I have words to say. Liam's hands are big, stuffed hands, wrapped around her middle as he holds her on. Her bum is neat and sharp, sitting saddle on one of his thighs. Behind her, the cloth of his trousers wrinkles and sags around a crotch that is a mystery no one is interested in anymore" (169). Beyond the fulsome tribute to Emily's attractiveness, Veronica's reflection features a comment on Liam's crotch that is entirely gratuitous were it not for its allusion to Nugent's "interest" therein. That unmistakable allusion in turn directs readers' attention to how Veronica's description lingers, a beat too long, on Liam's hands, which were of course importantly active during the earlier abuse episode. Given the posture of the photo's subjects, Veronica's editorial rendition of the tableau is reminiscent of the novel's traumatic primal scene, with Veronica herself once again in the role of witness. Enright hereby demonstrates how the repetitive enactment endemic to traumatized subjectivity passes from one generation to another. More than that, her staging of Veronica's narratorial consciousness reveals how the implication of the traumatized subject's coerced and repressed desires can be translated intergenerationally, via the family "crypt" described by Abraham and Torok (2004). Thus, instead of children as emblematic of future renewal, saving the Irish from the baleful effects of their sex abuse scandals, the baleful effects of those scandals threaten in hidden ways, and on a case-by-case basis, this generation's children and the very future they symbolize.

Veronica herself possesses unusually sensitive antennae for sexual threats to children, the consequence, no doubt, of remembering by way of the contemporary media what happened to her brother thirty years on. She can even acknowledge her own incrimination in this massive *affaire du scandale*: "And for this, I am very sorry too" (173). What she cannot face, however, is the guilty horror that her desire, what she wants, has somehow been incriminated as well. She has adapted a substitute language of desire, an idiom of interior-design consumerism focused on motifs suggestive of immaculate cleanliness: "Oatmeal, cream, sandstone, slate" (130). Just for good measure, she appends the phrase, "There is no blood here" (130), dissociating her life space from the "spill of blood" that marked her early sexual passion with her husband (70). Thinking of herself as now "beyond sex" (97), she levels unwarranted, even unhinged accusations against her husband that reflect her own desperate need to disavow the libidinal affect that has been forced on her: "You'd fuck anything. . . . You'd fuck the nineteen-year-old waitress, or the fifteen-year-old who looks nineteen . . . I don't know where you draw the line. Puberty, is that a line? It happens to girls at nine now" (176). And this bitter vitriol, notably, spills out months after the funeral and months after the seemingly redemptive appearance of child Rowan. In one sense, Veronica's overflowing invective simply treats her husband as a revenant of Nugent; Liam was, after all, exactly nine at the time of the assault. But her rant is also an act of projection that serves to defend her from what, at an unconscious level, she already knows and feels. The underlying, self-referential thrust of her attack becomes clear, appropriately enough, when her husband asks, "What are you talking about?" She replies, "Or not to your actual fucking, of course. But just, you know, to your *desire*. To what you want. Is there a limit to what you want to fuck, out there?" Then, in a direct apostrophe to the reader, she adds, "I have gone mad" (176).

Veronica knows whereof she speaks, even as she misrecognizes of whom she is speaking. Because the unconscious, as Freud observed, admits of no contradictions, it is the condition of unconscious desire to operate without definite limits; its lines of exclusion, prohibition, or unacceptability are not clearly drawn. Because Veronica cannot own the agitation of libidinal stirrings that are, in any case, not her "own," that are repugnant to her moral sensibility, she cannot master their unconscious effects. She cannot, that is, in refusing these stirrings' conscious recognition, as she must, set final limits to their unconscious circulation or the symptomatic disturbances they produce.

This catch-22 represents, if not the gravest, then surely the most insidious burden of her traumatized experience, whether as witness or victim, of childhood sexual abuse. The cardinal symptoms of trauma in general—the unreliability of memory, the somatization of awareness, the uncertainty concerning the past, the haunting power of the unmetabolized event—combine to protect the subject, paradoxically, from a recognition of how the specific trauma of sexual abuse has captured her desire behind her back, as it were, and so protects her as well from the intolerable shame such a realization would elicit. In the case of child sexual abuse in particular, however, some such realization proves necessary if the traumatic fetters on memory—the basis for all those cardinal symptoms—are to be released, so that the past might be cognitively processed instead of obsessively embodied and repetitively enacted.

Nothing in Veronica's final gesture toward recovery as she returns from self-exile in Gatwick Airport credibly promises an escape from this psychodynamic vise—certainly not her explicitly parodic indulgence in reproductive futurism, which she pitches, hypothetically, to her husband (in the recognizably wheedling voice of the officiously tea- and cake-pushing Mrs. Doyle from the 1990s' *Father Ted*): "Hey, Tom, let's have this next baby. Just this one. The one whose name I already know. Oh, go on. It'll cheer you up, no end" (260). No end indeed. Dedicated as she is to treating the evils of child sexual abuse with all the seriousness it deserves, Enright is also too honest a novelist to mitigate the evils she portrays by allowing them to subtend a comedy in the end. Instead, she elects to leave her narrator-protagonist up in the air, literally, and falling with equal symbolic speed back into Ireland and back into "my own life" (261). In the last sentence, she "is about to hit it now," a formulation that undecidably holds out the possibility that she might be coming smoothly down to earth at last—or crashing.

EPILOGUE

What about Brendan?

IT IS TIME TO CALL an end to family romance and to say what happened in Ireland in the years before and after Veronica was eight and Liam was barely nine. If Veronica has been "listening [carefully] to the radio" and "reading the paper" in full, and hearing about what went on in various Irish institutions, including but not limited to "schools and churches and . . . people's homes," she is well aware that abuse and exploitation of the powerless and marginalized have been endemic in post-independence Ireland, with child sexual exploitation being the most lurid, the most sensational, the most scandalous instance, but not a *singularly* horrific instance (Enright 2007, 172–73). Yes, "the anatomy and mechanism of . . . a whole fucking country— drowning in shame" (168) centers on scandalous revelations of child sexual abuse, owing both to Ireland's hyperbolic commitment to reproductive futurism, with its sanctification of children, and to the unique power of sexuality to elicit and transmit shame, for reasons that Jean Laplanche's theory of the enigmatic signifier throws into sharp relief. But that does not mean that there do not exist an array of other national atrocities equally deserving of collective remorse. Anne Enright demonstrates not just an awareness of this reality but an exemplary, because dialectical, awareness.

On the reigning critical consensus, *The Gathering* pools Brendan's story of abuse and abandonment into Liam's, establishing a gamut of disenfranchisement, according to which each variety figures as a like object of traumatized mourning and moral judgement. Gerardine Meaney, for instance, remarks that Liam's "injunction to give truth to the dead conjures up Uncle

Brendan," and Veronica discovers that her brother and her uncle are part of a larger story when she encounters the graves of the inmates of St Ita's, Brendan's mental asylum (2011, 157). Carol Dell'Amico designates Liam as "a figure for all those missing and unacknowledged in Ireland's past," an "entire panoply of lapses . . . at issue in *The Gathering*, most spectacularly the belatedly acknowledged dead" of St Ita's (2010, 66). Finally, Liam Harte eloquently observes that Liam's "fate is linked to that of . . . mad Uncle Brendan" and, further, that Veronica's "mourning of the bodily remains of her traumatized brother mediates a much larger grief and anger for the unacknowledged trauma endured by generations of unknown Irish bodies made abject by post-colonial nationalism and discarded anonymously in literal and metaphorical unmarked graves," such as those Veronica encounters at St Ita's (2010, 199).

To be sure, material and symbolic connections between the fates of Liam and Brendan inform Veronica's melancholic reflections and even the basic narrative itinerary of the period immediately following Liam's death. Veronica's comings and goings on behalf of her brother's memory and in post-traumatic response to his death (her efforts to retrieve his remains, to collect mourners like her sister, Kitty, to flee and reassess her own domestic situation, etc.) impel her to remember Brendan, to revisit St Ita's, and to reimagine the horrors she associates with being him and living there. Nevertheless, the linkage between her brother and her uncle as victims of neglect or bearers of trauma does not establish, as the criticism propounds, an easy continuity between the two as objects of grief, rage, and regret. To the contrary, there is a disparity between the ways Veronica envisions them, contemplates them, and reacts to and invests in their memory, which betokens the very different places they occupy, as child sex victim and mentally disabled subject, in the collective Irish Imaginary.

Let us begin with Veronica's mode of recalling the scenes of embodied suffering each endured. As we have seen, her memory of everything surrounding Liam's abuse remains uncertain, undependable, compromised, invented, even hallucinatory. Her memory of St Ita's, by contrast, is extraordinarily sharp, detailed, even crystalline. Her narrated memory of a childhood visit to the institution unfolds "under a hard white sky," and everything from Ada's dress, to the "longest, straightest" country road, to the man with two sticks hobbling along, to the shape of the handball court emerges with such bright-edged·clarity that Veronica concludes that "another part of me is still, these years later, walking along the road" (Enright 2007, 113–14). On a subsequent trip to St Ita's, returning from the airport with Kitty, Veronica notices, "There is no shift between my mind's eye and my real eye"; her memory is fully corroborated by and continuous with her immediate perceptions. As she turns into the hospital drive, she states, "It is as though we are driving through a sudden brief mist, on the other side of which is the past," completely preserved, perfectly accessible (158–59).

The dramatic disparity between her remembrance of Liam's and Brendan's respective plights derives, of course, from the starkly different positions from which she experiences them, and accordingly from the different kind and degree of her implication in them. Toward Liam's abuse she was a victim-witness, either a co-victim of Nugent's rapine or a victim simply by virtue of witnessing her brother's molestation, with all the sexual turbulence and moral implications that entails. Toward Brendan's abjection, she bore a far more distant, indirect witness. But at least in retrospect she was also something of a participant therein, a witness-participant whose childhood awareness of Brendan shared in the culture of phobic disdain for and discrimination against the mentally or psychosocially disabled. As she clearly recollects from her first visit, "we did not think of what lunatics did when they saw children—eat them, I thought, suck at their ears and jibber . . . and we did not tell [Ada] about the one loony we saw walking up the path from the sea, slow and stupid and dirty and terrible" (116).

As befits her intimate involvement with Liam, Veronica bears a highly personal and self-conscious sense of guilt for her failed witness in his case: "And for this, I am very sorry too" (173). Conversely, her past attitudes toward the disabled spur no such avowals of contrition, perhaps because her derision, while applicable to her uncle, strictly speaking, was never directed at him in specific. She does, in any case, revise her views on his life of disability in connection with the death of her otherwise impaired brother. Upon returning with Kitty from England, where Liam perished, she feels "this fact" of Brendan "suddenly kick into [her]" (156), a phrase that suggests a bond of pain is being formed. Nevertheless, she holds her emergent sense of solicitude and regret for her uncle at arm's length, rhetorically speaking: "I realise, as we land, that life in St Ita's was not a romantic one, but more likely a long dirty business of watching the piss gather in your lap, and nearly knowing what you were thinking, from time to time" (157). The lifelong cleanliness of Liam, however, which Veronica is careful to emphasize, contrasts with the squalidness imposed on Brendan by his disability, high-lighting a sharp *caste* distinction between the two despite their shared *class* origins. Whereas the vocabulary marking Liam's errancy breathes a certain scapegrace familiarity, his permanent belonging to the tribe from which he strayed (*"Pup, gurrier, monkey, thug, hopeless, useless, mad, messer"*; 163), the parlance of Brendan's disability—"lost to Largactyl and squalor. . . . He probably died wondering who he actually was" (156)—serves to underscore his foreignness even to himself, his profound exclusion from the tribe to which he belonged. In the very act of sympathizing with Brendan, or per-haps it would be more accurate to say pitying him, Veronica continues, in a different vein, her earlier practice of othering him.

This amalgam of familial compassion and ableist distance, pity and oth-ering, fuels in Veronica a sense of Brendan's ordeal, a commiseration with his suffering, which is powerful without being intimate, overwhelming yet impersonal. She rates Brendan the most aggrieved member of Ada's dam-aged progeny, yet she casts the affliction he endured in an objectified regis-ter diametrically opposed to the frame of fellowship in which she processes Liam's ruin. Thus, although she stops at St Ita's to conjure, with Kitty's help, memories of their uncle, she soon folds his ghostly image, with its "falling jowls," "unpleasant" eyes, and superior "Maths" into a broader vision of the institutional ravages of twentieth-century psychiatric practice, of which he was but one obscure victim (156–57). As they approach the "boiler house" of St Ita's, the institution suddenly morphs into a brick-and-mortar allusion to the Holocaust: "There are curious round windows on the boiler house, with the Star of David dividing the panes . . . I am thinking for a second, that they are burning mental patients in there, just to keep the hospital radiators hot" (159). By temporarily displacing Brendan from his Irish habitus, by invoking the ovens of Auschwitz and Buchenwald, Veronica annexes her uncle to a horror whose sheer scale and historical saliency magnifies the import of his fate, while dissolving its particularity and immediacy.[1]

As they quit St Ita's, Veronica espies an instance of that other staple of unspeakable modern atrocity, the mass grave. As she reads the sign implor-ing prayers for those residents of St Ita's unceremoniously deposited there, she "wonder[s] how many people were slung into the dirt of this field," with "no markers, no separate graves" (160). Veronica feels the ground beneath her quake, "boiling with corpses" (160), a phrase linking the boneyard to those spectral ovens. For us, the scene proves the single most haunting and

Figure 7.1. "The crumbling St Ita's Hospital, Portrane, Co. Dublin." © Media Drum World/Obscuraprints.

chilling in the entire novel, more astringent, and deliberately so, than those portraying Liam's sexual abuse. But the power and the poignancy of the scene—and this is most important—are predicated mainly on the permanent anonymity of the residents buried in that still unquiet earth, on the abjection and abandonment implicit in the failure to recognize their individual identities. It is a failure replicated by Veronica at this moment with regard to her uncle, who is not differentiated in her consciousness from the mass of "tangled bones" knitting the ground and catching like a "vague wind" at her thighs (160–61).

Later, on the night of Liam's wake, Veronica's final act of hallucinatory witness actually transforms Brendan into a personification of the teeming cemetery ground itself: "Brendan's bones are mixed with other people's bones; so there is a turmoil of souls muttering and whining under his clothes, they would come out in a roar, were he to unbutton his fly; if he opened his mouth they would slop out over his teeth. Brendan has no rest from them, the souls of the forgotten who must always be crawling and bulging and whining in there. . . . The only places clear of them are his unlikeable blue eyes, so . . . his shirt heaves and his ears leak the mad and the inconvenient dead" (216). Brendan looms as the last of a series of revenants, "disturbed" ghosts that parade before Veronica's distraught mind after a cryptic interview with her Mammy concerning Nugent's role in the family (214). On this occasion she explicitly declares Brendan to be "the worst" of "my nightmares," making official the status implied in her visit to St Ita's (215). But whereas the previous specters—Ada, Charlie, Nugent, and his chimerical sister, Lizzie—all bear the individualized impress of their respective roles in Veronica's traumatic family romance, the visitation of Brendan is the vehicle less of his own personal revivification in Veronica's memory than for a mass return of the forgotten, unknown, and nameless dead, of whom he remains but one example. As at St Ita's, the gut-wrenching pathos of Brendan and his "gathering" of ghosts rests on their comparative anonymity and the symbolic destitution it evokes even in their commemoration.

In this regard, Harte has astutely observed that Brendan stands for the not "properly dead," whose existence signifies a rupture in the social covenant between the living and the departed, an unpaid social debt that the former owe the latter (2010, 199). Enright has undoubtedly deployed Uncle Brendan to signal (a) the ethico-political failings of Irish society toward its disabled and disempowered members and (b) its continued moral default in allowing their systematic erasure from the national story. At the same time, she is careful to note how this function of Brendan's, and indeed this gesture of hers, cannot but bespeak the comparatively abstracted, alienated, or estranged relationship these "inconvenient dead" bear to the bereaved community, a relationship of ritualized obligation rather than deep-seated, heartfelt sentiment, of formal mandate rather than emotional devastation.

On this basis, Veronica finds herself implicated in the ongoing condescension toward all the forsaken and forgotten abuse victims, but not in the same visceral, affectional vein that implicates her in the degradation of her dear, obsessively remembered sibling. Enright underlines the discrepancy between Veronica's (and Irish society's) acute personal guilt for the plight of the sexually abused Liam and the inchoate, impersonal revulsion at work in Veronica's (and Irish society's) response to Brendan's fate, by way of Veronica's more intractable imperviousness to the abuse that she and Liam inflicted on their younger sister, Kitty. Throughout Veronica's maze of memories and compensatory romancing, Kitty functions as a scapegoat, as the family member toward whom Veronica need feel no empathy. In various ways, Veronica frames the childhood abuse of Kitty as normal or comical. Thus, the dichotomy between Veronica's complete decompensation in response to Liam's death and her heightened awareness of Brendan's utter desertion is underlined by the fact that she never ceases to justify or minimize the past sibling abuse that has been propelling her younger sister along a traumatized, self-medicating life trajectory strongly reminiscent of Liam's.

This disparity in the kind as well as degree of personal implication entails an incommensurability in the kind of mourning and/or melancholia that the respective cases of Liam and Brendan elicit, from Veronica certainly but also, by allegorical extension, from the hegemonic national Imaginary that an affluent lifestyle journalist from Dublin 4 might represent. The disabled, the institutionalized, and the abandoned, like Brendan and his fellows, may arouse a "much larger grief and anger" than Liam alone could focalize (Harte 2010, 199), but they have not enkindled the same deep, passionate, and gnawing "grief and anger" as all the Liams of Ireland, the child sex victims of respectable and relatable middle-class families.

In short, child sexual abuse does not represent, as Dell'Amico contends, the "saddest instance of collective forgetting" in the novel (2010, 63). That unfortunate distinction is held, rather, by the disabled and institutionalized—personified in Brendan. But child sexual abuse does emerge as the "instance of collective forgetting" that Ireland is "saddest" about and takes most fully to heart (which is paradoxically why it is *not* the saddest in the larger sense). By the lights of Veronica's narrative, it is the most worried, most consuming, most sentimentalized object of cultural forgetting, so much so that in order to bring Uncle Brendan into its order of significance, she speculates that he, like Liam and herself, owes his dysfunction to Nugent's predations (Enright 2007, 224). Of course, it will and should be said that her differently weighted investment in this matter arises naturally from her greater familiarity, greater affective entanglement, and correspondingly greater identification with Liam. But that is, at an allegorical level, just the point. The society of Irish journalists (lifestyle and otherwise), media exponents (social and otherwise), opinion makers, authority figures, professionals, churchgoers, job holders, and similarly classed subjects (from the upper to the lower range of "middle") have had, on average, greater familiarity and engagement with those who are known, supposed, or imagined to be child sexual abuse victims than with the mentally or psychosocially disabled once thought to require commitment to asylums like St Ita's.

In the years since the Ferns and Murphy reports, child sexual abuse has become "our" scandal, a heimlich site of open and public retrospective sorrow and remorse, in a way that the forced institutionalization of the disabled never quite has. As such, the scandal has also become what Kai Erikson has theorized as a collective trauma, in ways that the confinement of the mentally disabled never quite did (Erikson 1995, 183–99). That is to say, the child sex scandal has constituted a "blow to the basic tissues of social life that changes the bonds and impacts the prevailing sense of community" (Erikson 1995, 187), as Veronica herself observes. Locking the Brendans of the world away, sequestering them from their native community, perversely serves to insulate the "tissues" of that community from the traumatic effects of the violence it has perpetrated, at least until the claims of those most immediately harrowed have been substantially weakened by their disappearance into nameless obscurity, materialized in the mass grave. For individuals like Brendan, the classic response to mass atrocity, "never forget," has already been violated in advance, not least by those, like Veronica, who assume that the victims themselves had been forgetting all along: "He probably died wondering who he actually was" (Enright 2007, 156). The mourning of identifiable victims whose plight initiated a collective trauma differs, markedly and necessarily, from the mourning of victims whose grievances were precluded from doing so.

Enright's novel respects, by acknowledging, the stubborn reality of inequitable mourning, while advancing the ethico-political principle that things could and should be otherwise. It does so by insisting on the irretrievable anonymity of the departed "rejects" and outcasts while staking the outrageous urgency to grieve for them on that very anonymity. It does so by showing that the connection it unquestionably poses between Liam and Brendan as objects of mourning contains a significant hiatus or element of disjunction. Hence, the retrieval into cultural memory of one type or instance of erasure (Liam's) points to and invokes but does not necessarily lead to or accomplish a retrieval of the other (Brendan's).

On this score, *The Gathering* quietly touches on a robust debate in the global study of collective traumatic memory, recently canvassed by Michael Rothberg in his book *Multidirectional Memory: Remembering the Holocaust in the Age of Decolonization* (2009). The field is presently divided between two paradigms of cultural memory. The older form, competitive memory, holds that the practice of making present the past is tied to discrete, firmly bounded identity formations. In order to achieve the specificity and saliency of the traumas they have overcome, these different identity groups seek to command the public sphere with their historical perspectives, narratives, and demonstrations, thereby blocking out or marginalizing the cultural memory of others. The second form, the multidirectional memory of Rothberg's title, similarly tethers cultural memory to identity but judges such formations to be jagged and porous, to overlap with one another, and to share, accordingly, the building blocks of cultural memory: experiential points of reference, ethical codes, heroic ideals, narrative genres, and so on. On this model, disparate groups' remembrances of trauma and victimization do not unfold in a zero-sum game, wherein a spotlight on one eclipses the others, but rather open a space of negotiation, wherein these commemorative efforts might reinforce and even enable one another (Rothberg 2009, 1–27). The critical consensus on the mutual resonance of Liam and Brendan, of sexual abuse victims and the incarcerated disabled, as objects of mourning presumes the operation of this sort of multidirectional memory.

As Rothberg himself concedes, however, his model does not exclude so much as contain (in every sense of the word) competitive memory. The negotiations undertaken under the multidirectional model harbor contests for recognition and authority among the distinct, albeit interlocking, identity formations, issuing in contingent hierarchies of cultural memory that further negotiations look to dismantle. It is just this sort of dialectic, in our view, that Enright broaches in *The Gathering*. Veronica's traumatized reaction to the death of her brother, with whom she shares an identity—as psychic double—triggers a cognate sense of the more distanced victimization of her uncle, which is "always the worst" (215). This cognate sense reaches across boundaries of cultural memory but does not produce the full-throated investment or identification that it is shown to ethically demand. Multidirectional yet also hierarchical, Veronica's mourning process comes, as the novel moves toward closure, to constitute a site of perennially open negotiation, in which Enright is summoning her readers, Irish society, all of us, finally, to participate. The goal is to adhere in the fullest measure possible to the essence of traumatic mourning itself as cultural memory: to do justice, without favor, to *all* the "inconvenient dead" (216).

Figure 7.2. "The hospital was divided." Photograph of a hallway in the abandoned St Ita's. © Media Drum World/Obscuraprints.

NOTE

1. It is important to recall that the first victims of Nazi eugenics were the disabled; the targeting of the Jews, homosexuals, and the Roma people came later.

NOTES ON THE ILLUSTRATIONS

Cover. Paper doll cutouts representing the 796 babies and children who died at the Mother and Baby Home in Tuam hang on the rails of the children's playground at Galway's Eyre Square at a June 11, 2014, public vigil organized by Galway Pro-Choice.

This image appeared in the *Connacht Tribune* on March 10, 2017, accompanying two articles by Declan Tierney, 26–27. Tierney's articles— "Residents are left to wonder what still lies undiscovered" and "Strange silence falls on scene of shame"—describe a spontaneous memorial made of flowers, toys, signs, and letters at the entrance to the site of the one-time Tuam Mother and Baby Home, and the fear of homeowners in Tuam that their houses may be built "on the remains of dead children." These 2017 articles, with the 2014 photograph, appeared one week after the "Commission of Inquiry into the treatment of babies in the Tuam home" confirmed "the . . . discovery of human remains at the Tuam Mother and Baby Home." © *Connacht Tribune.*

Figure 0.1. "The 'spider web' of Tuam could touch anywhere." Poster with the words "Bury Our Babies with Dignity," surrounded by stuffed animals, commemorating the remains of 796 "Tuam Babies." This photograph of a memorial at the gates of the Tuam Mother and Baby Home site ran in the *Irish Examiner* with Donal O'Keefe's article "The 'spider web' of Tuam could touch anywhere" on Friday, July 27, 2018. The photo's caption reads, "Sophia Dilleen, 18-month-old granddaughter of historian Catherine Corless plays in a display by local people of Tuam." Catherine Corless's research initially broke the story of the "lost" infants and children at the Tuam Mother and Baby Home and elsewhere in Ireland, whose often preventable deaths over several decades went unmourned and unmarked in twentieth-century Ireland. O'Keefe's article describes an apparent attempt by the Irish government to set up a "false equivalence between those who want justice for the Tuam Babies, and those who would rather see the past covered up" that "backfired spectacularly." © Eamon Ward.

Figure i.1. *Homeless*. Held by the Bendigo Art Gallery, Bendigo, Australia, Thomas Kennington's *Homeless* (1890) is representative of the social realist paintings for which the artist is best remembered. Kennington (1856–1916) conjoined realism and melodrama to depict urban children who are emphatically both impoverished and, with their delicate porcelain complexions, ideologically English. Kennington produced a series of such social realist paintings in the last fifteen years of the nineteenth century, a period that marked a new homogenization of the English into a single, "white" race (Makdisi 2014), thereby both contributing to and visually archiving this period's new and increasingly politically potent sentimentalization of children. © Bendigo Art Gallery.

Figure i.2. "A dream of green fields." *Punch, or the London Charivari*. August 10, 1904. The cartoon's caption reads "The Children's Country Holiday's Fund is in great need of assistance. The Honorable Treasurer is the Earl of Arran, 18 Buckingham Street, W.C.I." The records of the Children's Country Holiday's Fund, established in 1884, are held by the London Metropolitan Archives. The fund's purpose was to provide periods of more than two weeks away from London for "worthy" poor children. The cartoon's caption identifies Arthur Gore, 1868–1958, sixth earl of Arran and Anglo-Irish peer, as the fund's treasurer, while the figure of Punch—the famously amoral spokesperson for England's purported national ethos—kindly directs the attention of "Dame Charity" to two homeless London children who are dreaming of "green fields." In addition to using the children's painful destitution counterintuitively to emphasize the British nation's compassion and generosity toward its most vulnerable constituents, the cartoon inverts the comparative positions of British and Irish children. The fields of the children's dreams might, at a glance, be taken as a visual reference to Ireland's depopulated post-Famine countryside—an effect the cartoon's title underscores—and an area of the United Kingdom that had not, in fact, been in any sense health-sustaining for children over a matter of centuries. Moreover, as these two children are evidently homeless, they would not have been eligible for Dame Charity's largesse: the benefits distributed by the Children's Country Holiday's Fund took the form of discounts and vouchers, with some balance to be paid by the parents of all "worthy" recipients, presumably to encourage and reward self-sufficiency. © Punch Cartoon Library/Topfoto.

Figure i.3. "Women of Britain say—'Go!'." A propaganda poster exemplifying the definitive (if often subliminal) role played by children in the powerfully gendered polarization that typified British WWI propaganda. © The British Library Board (World War One propaganda collection).

Figure i.4. "Orpen's war exam." Illustration by William Orpen (1878–1931) contained in a letter from the artist to Mrs. St. George with a sketch of the artist undergoing his military medical examination upon induction into the British military (March 1916). Ink and pencil on paper. Unframed: 22.8 × 15.3 cm. In this drawing, Orpen satirically undermines the masculinity of its subject by envisioning the rite of passage that defined masculine normativity for his generation—entering the military—as an occasion for a military doctor's discovery of some outlandish genital abnormality, which is left to the viewer's imagination. Orpen further visually undermines the normative claim of masculinity by depicting the inductee's naked body, seen from behind, as the body of a child. Thus, the military doctor's explosive reaction is comically suggestive of a jouissance contingent on a subliminal erotoscopic investment in the sexuality of all male inductees, constituted as boys, on the part of not only the doctor but also the larger, purportedly heteronormative British patriarchy that the doctor represents. Graves Collection of William Orpen Letters, Prints and Drawings, National Gallery of Ireland. NGI.7830.302. Photo © National Gallery of Ireland.

Figure i.5. The *Daily Herald*, now "dimly remembered as a forerunner for the disgraceful *The Sun*," originally "began life as a daily strike bulletin when the London print unions struck for a forty-eight-hour working week" (Coates 2009). The image "True to tradition" responds to a Dublin workers' march on September 21, 1913, that was attacked by the RUC, and the drafting of troops on September 26 to protect property and deliver coal to government bodies. It also captures the increasing centrality of children in what was becoming a society-wide ideological-moral crisis concerning Dublin business owners' overt use of starvation to bust nascent unionizing efforts on the part of Jim Larkin's ITGWU. The October 7, 1913 cover of the *Daily Herald* is captioned, in full, "[Dissatisfied with the pace at which the theory of industrialization was progressing among the women and children of Dublin, the Capitalists have called up their Police Reserves to finish with their batons the work begun by Disease, Filth, Rotten Tenements, and the other educational forces of Fat. In fewer words, the police have bludgeoned women and children in Dublin.] Fat (calling up its Police Reserves in its attack in Dublin): 'Remember, Gentlemen, the flag we fight under—Women and Children first!'" © Mirrorpix/British Newspaper Archive.

Figure i.6. "Food kitchen in Liberty Hall." Illustration by William Orpen. In November 1913, the Irish Citizen Army took Liberty Hall as its headquarters. The question of starving children posed difficulties for both sides, as both the employers who had locked out their workers and workers who refused to sign a pledge not to join the ITGWU were, from a public relations standpoint, potentially blameworthy. On September 27, the first of a series of food shipments from England, with its attendant scenes of hungry children waiting on the quay, exacerbated public anxieties. The Irish Catholic Church visibly stepped up efforts to appear more benevolent, with a spate of newspaper photos and publicity pieces depicting nuns feeding children, and young volunteers gathered for that purpose. After the failure of Dora Montefiore's "Save the Dublin Kiddies" campaign in late October, Constance Markiewicz and Maud Gonne oversaw the Liberty Hall soup kitchen, where trade unionists and their supporters labored frenetically, as Orpen's drawing vividly illustrates, to feed locked-out workers and their families. This image was reproduced in Orpen's 1924 memoir, *Stories of Old Ireland and Myself* (London: Williams and Norgate). Photo duplication courtesy of the Harry Ransom Humanities Research Center.

Figure i.7. Priest saves "Irish Child" from the shark, "Socialism," by pulling the child aboard a currach-like boat christened *The Faith*. In this allegorical illustration, workers' children are transformed into a single sentimentalized "Irish Child," and that child's safety is reduced to one zero-sum issue: the Church's absolute control over the child. This absolute ecclesiastical control, in turn, is legitimated by the self-evident danger posed by the large, toothy socialist shark that lurks in the waters surrounding *The Faith*. This image reframes Irish society as a Manichean space, locked in a moral struggle between Catholicism and socialism, with Irish children's eternal souls as the stakes. This cartoon appeared in the *Sunday Independent* on October 26, 1913, the same day on which the *Independent* gleefully depicted the arrest of Dora Montefiore and the "rescue" of numerous Irish children by Dublin police, clergy, and lay Catholics. As Lucy McDiarmid recounts the chaotic event, "over a period of several days, beginning on October 22, outraged priests and angry mobs recruited by the Ancient Order of Hibernians grabbed many of the children from the hands of . . . social workers . . . pulled others off boats . . . or off trains . . . attacked anyone attempting to leave Dublin with a child, and marched triumphantly along the quays singing 'Faith of our Fathers' after each day's successful 'rescues'" (2005, 125). Photo credit: TheJournal.ie (with permission of the National Library of Ireland).

Figure i.8. "Saving Dublin children." Paired photos from the October 26 *Sunday Independent*, featuring Dora Montefiore's arrest, side by side with two priests escorting an emaciated boy, named in the caption as George Burke, "rescued" from Montefiore's efforts to prevent his imminent starvation. We have been unable to find a legible version of the captions under the original photographs, first reprinted in McDiarmid's *The Irish Art of Controversy* (2005). Certainly, we cannot possibly ascertain the fate of George Burke, the right-hand photograph's emblematic rescued child—one of nearly three hundred children prevented from taking advantage of the "holiday" with families in England that Montefiore had arranged. There is, however, one compelling bit of evidence suggestive of this child's fate. We know from McDiarmid's extensive research in Archbishop Walsh's papers (2005, xvi) that Walsh had received private assurances from Montefiore herself, and subsequently "from Catholics in Liverpool," that the children would not be proselytized (126). Walsh's ostensible fears for these children (to wit, that the children might be converted to Protestantism or led astray by nonbelievers) were thus documentably spurious, even in their own terms. What we do know is that at the end of October, these children and their families had at least three winter months of worsening conditions still ahead and that Archbishop of Dublin William Walsh, who had firmly established himself as the one person in Ireland with the moral clout to intercede on their behalf, cared only that they had been prevented from boarding the ship to Liverpool. © INM (Independent News and Media).

Figure i.9. A scene from the play *Rebel in the Soul*, staged April 12–May 21, 2017, at the NYC Irish Repertory Theatre. Playwright, Larry Kirwan. Director, Charlotte Moore. Actors shown are Patrick Fitzgerald as Dr. Noël Browne, and John Keating as Archbishop John Charles McQuaid. Kirwan's play uses the late 1940s–early 1950s "Mother and Child Scheme" controversy to focalize midcentury tensions over Ireland's defining values, staged as an evolving confrontation among three competing, iconic figures for Irish nationalist Catholic morality: the Catholic socialist, Noël Browne; onetime IRA volunteer and human rights advocate, Séan MacBride; and the archbishop of Dublin, John Charles McQuaid. On the grounds that state-funded health care for mothers and children might entail treatment or guidance that would violate Catholic social teaching, the Irish Catholic hierarchy was willing to accept Ireland's high child mortality rate rather than cede control over any aspect of women's and children's bodies or lives. © Carol Rosegg.

Figure i.10. "State of shame: Report on schools reveals litany of abuse over 70 years." This figure appears in two articles run in the *Irish Independent* in response to the Ryan Report. Released on May 20, 2009, the Ryan Report represented a compendious and thoroughly damning investigation into child abuse in all forms occurring in Irish institutions from 1936 on. In the May 21, 2009, Metro Edition, the *Independent* ran this image of unnamed boys in an unidentified midcentury industrial school under the apt headline, "State of Shame." On May 25, 2009, the newspaper reran the image on page 14 with a commentary piece by Mary Kenny entitled, "Our decent society was in total denial about child sex abuse." Kenny's piece takes the position its title would imply: physical punishment, including severe beating, was normal and accepted in Ireland and most other societies and should be carefully distinguished from sexual abuse, which went unaddressed because it was unthinkable. The image for which we were able to obtain permission ran with Kenny's piece, but we have used the headline from the newspaper's first response. © INM (Independent News and Media).

Figure i.11. "The introduction of internment . . . for fourteen-year-old girls." Martyn Turner's celebrated rejoinder to the "Girl X" case derisively compares the Irish state's flagrant indifference to the rights of a pregnant female juvenile to its erstwhile concern for the human rights of the Northern Irish teenagers and young men interned by the British in the early years of the

Troubles. Cartoon of fourteen-year-old Girl X, "interned" on the island of Ireland. The full caption reads, "17th February 1992: the introduction of internment in Ireland . . . for fourteen year old girls." This cartoon was reprinted in the *Irish Times* on December 1, 2018, accompanying Diarmaid Ferriter's retrospective piece entitled "The multilayered genius of Martyn Turner." © Martyn Turner.

Figure i.12. "Credo that protected a monster" is the title of an article by Eamon Dunphy that swims around Wendy Shea's illustration of an amoeboid Brendan Smyth preparing to incorporate his next victim. Appearing in the *Sunday Independent* on October 16, 1994, this piece is representative of the media furor that followed the October 6, 1994 airing of the UTV Counterpoint episode "Suffer the Children." On April 23, 1993, the RUC had issued an extradition order for Smyth, who had been tried and found guilty of sexually abusing four siblings in Belfast in 1991. Smyth was harbored in the Republic through the end of 1993; he was extradited to Northern Ireland in early 1994, and on January 21, 1994, he pled guilty to seventeen counts of child sexual abuse. In "Suffer the Children," UTV journalist Chris Moore interviewed on camera multiple victims of Smyth's extensive, decades-long career of abuse. On November 17, 1994, Irish Attorney General Harry Welehan, who had stonewalled Smyth's extradition, resigned from office, as did the Irish taoiseach, Albert Reynolds. © Wendy Shea.

Figure i.13. "Shadow of a trauma." David Rooney's drawing of a child in bed, cowering under a looming shadow, illustrates Tim Ryan's article "Shadow of a trauma over Dail's holidays." *Irish Press*, Saturday, July 2, 1994. Above the image is the headline "Another X Case." As the Irish Dail was adjourning for summer recess, a court case had just been heard *in camera* concerning "a ward of the court . . . now in the same position as the original child [Girl X]." Ryan concedes that the pregnant ward of the state had, perhaps unsurprisingly, had a "change of mind," staving off an immediate scandal. He uses this close call, however, to point out that the February 1992 X case, precipitated when gardai ordered the parents of an impregnated fourteen-year-old rape victim to cancel a scheduled abortion in England, could recur at any time. The taoiseach, Albert Reynolds, who "first heard of the original X case" on the day he was elected, and his attorney general, Harry Whelehan, who "subsequently got a High Court injunction preventing [X] from travelling outside the country for an abortion," Ryan suggests, have good reason to fear the next juvenile rape victim, whose terrifying shadow already looms over their summer vacation plans. © David Rooney.

Figure i.14. "Pretty twisted stuff. It's almost Kafkaesque." The subheading of this piece is taken from the full text of a speech by Fine Gael TD John Deasy, delivered as part of the March 7, 2017, Dail debate over the Grace foster abuse scandal. This illustration heads the text of Deasy's speech on a full page of coverage that also includes Daniel McConnell's commentary, "If we do nothing, then we become the abusers," and Fiachra Ó Cionnaith's "Inquiry terms of reference scrapped after charged debate." Rather than an instance of dramatic rhetoric, the page's headline quote was, in fact, a literal explanation to the Dail of the legal implications of its proposed "terms of reference," which would have excluded from the inquiry under debate forty-six people with disabilities from the same foster home where for two decades, from the age of twelve, "Grace" had been documentably, spectacularly abused. Deasy, working in tandem with Fianna Fáil TD John McGuinness, supplied detailed evidence of senior health officials' consistent efforts to hide rather than redress serial abuses over the course of a three-decade, ongoing "foster care sex scandal." The abuse itself had been documented in the 2012 Conal Devine Report and in the Resilience Ireland Report, but at the time of the 2017 Dail debate, the Health Service Executive had delayed the two reports' publication for five years, citing garda advice. © *Irish Examiner*/Getty Images stock photo.

Figure 3.1. "Ann Lovett: Death at the grotto." Granard grotto of the Virgin Mary where fifteen-year-old Ann Lovett and her newborn infant died, January 31, 1984. Lovett's appalling death in childbirth at the feet of the Blessed Virgin occurred only months prior to the beginning of the Kerry Babies scandal, on April 14, 1984, when a newborn baby found dead on the White Strand, near Cahersiveen, launched what would become an obsessive, sensational investigation into the private life of a woman who could not possibly have given birth to the White Strand infant. Together these two major child sex scandals created the first cracks in what Tom Inglis (1998) terms the Catholic Church's "moral monopoly" over Irish society, placing new pressure on hegemonic definitions of "innocence" and "child." This photograph of the Granard grotto first appeared in the *Irish Times* on January 31, 2004, accompanying an article by Rosita Boland marking the twentieth anniversary of Ann Lovett's death, and was reprinted on January 31, 2017.

The 2017 caption reads, "From the archive: Thirty three years ago, a fifteen-year-old girl in Granard, Co. Longford, died giving birth in secret." Photo credit: Brenda Fitzsimons/courtesy of the *Irish Times*. © *Irish Times*.

Figure 5.1. "The Battle of Soldiers Hill." The Meath County Council first proposed the M3 Motorway in 1999. By 2001, a route through the Tara-Skyrne Valley had been decided on. Resistance to the M3 Motorway built along with public awareness, with protesters establishing a long-term encampment at Tara by 2006, as more and more heretofore unknown archaeological finds were discovered directly in the path of the motorway. On July 18, 2007, garda and construction workers set out to drive away or actively to remove protesters encamped at the Tara Solidarity Vigil. In the course of an extended confrontation on Soldiers Hill between protesters and garda, construction workers, and machinery, seven activists were arrested, and many more were injured. The motorway was opened on June 4, 2010. Woodcut: "Hill of Tara 18 July AD 2007." Artist, Pixie.

Figure 5.2. "Names of 796 Tuam babies written on white sheets." This photograph appeared in *TheJournal.ie* on August 17, 2018, accompanying an article by Ronan Duffy entitled, "Names of 796 Tuam babies written on white sheets and brought to Galway church." Duffy's article publicizes a vigil to be held in Tuam on August 26, 2018, to include Catherine Corless and relatives and survivors of the Tuam Mother and Baby Home, commemorating the lost children of Tuam. The vigil was in support of the call by Corless, relatives, and survivors for a proper burial for the "Tuam babies," whose abandoned remains had been found in a disused sewage tank. As Catholic Ireland prepared for a visit from the pope, nine Galway women wrote onto white sheets the names and ages of the 796 infants and children and 10 adult women known to have died at the Tuam Mother and Baby Home, and sewed the sheets to a fence at the grave site. The caption reads, "The sheets used in the project were sourced from local hotels, as a symbol of the work the women kept in religious institutions were forced to do." © Erin Darcy.

Figure 7.1. Photograph of the field in the foreground of St Ita's Hospital, Portrane, Co. Dublin. This image appeared in a photo essay in the June 8, 2014, *Daily Mail UK* titled "Eerie photographs reveal abandoned bedrooms and living areas of Victorian-era asylum that was still being used until last year [2013]." The overview for the photo essay reads, in part, "In 1895 Portrane Lunatic Asylum was the most expensive building in Ireland paid for by the British government. The hospital had an initial budget of £200,000 but this rose to £300,000 by the time it was finally completed. The facility was seen as being at the forefront of mental health care when it was opened in 1903." © Media Drum World/Obscuraprints.

Figure 7.2. Photograph of a hallway in the abandoned St Ita's. This depiction of an abandoned hallway in St Ita's Hospital appeared in a photo essay in the June 8, 2014, *Daily Mail UK* titled "Eerie photographs reveal abandoned bedrooms and living areas of Victorian-era asylum that was still being used until last year [2013]." The caption for this photo reads, "The hospital was divided between men and women, and then it was further divided into four further sections depending on the severity of the mental illness involved." © Media Drum World/Obscuraprints.

REFERENCES

Abraham, Nicolas, and Maria Torok. 2004. *The Shell and the Kernel*. Translated by Nicholas Rand. Chicago: Chicago University Press.

———. 2005. *The Wolf Man's Magic Word: A Cryptonomy (Theory and History of Literature)*. Translated by Nicholas Rand. Minneapolis: University of Minnesota Press.

Agamben, Giorgio. 1998. *Homo Sacer: Sovereign Power and Bare Life*. Translated by Daniel Heller-Roazen. Stanford, CA: Stanford University Press.

Alarcón, Norma. 1998. "Making *Familia* from Scratch: Split Subjectivities in the Work of Elena Maria Viramotes and Cherríe Moraga." In *Contemporary American Women Writers: Gender, Class, Ethnicity*, edited by Lois Parkinson Zamora, 220–32. London: Routledge.

Armstrong, Nancy, and Leonard Tennenhouse. 1989. "Gender and the Work of Words." *Cultural Critique*, no. 13 (Fall): 229–78.

Attridge, Derek, and Anne Fogarty. 2012. "'Eveline' at Home: Reflections on Language and Context." In *Collaborative Dubliners: Joyce in Dialogue*, edited by Vicki Mahaffey, 89–107. Syracuse, NY: Syracuse University Press.

Backus, Margot. 2013. *Scandal Work: James Joyce, the New Journalism, and the Home Rule Newspaper Wars*. Notre Dame, IN: University of Notre Dame Press.

———. 2014. "'The Children of the Nation?': Representations of Poor Children in Mainstream Nationalist Journalism, 1882 and 1913." In *Children and Childhood in Ireland: 1700–2010*, edited by Maria Luddy and James Smith, 357–77. Dublin: Four Courts.

Backus, Margot, and Joseph Valente. 2012. "An Encounter: James Joyce's Humiliation Nation." In *Collaborative Dubliners: Joyce in Dialogue*, edited by Vicki Mahaffey, 48–68. Syracuse, NY: Syracuse University Press.

———. 2013. "Kate O'Brien, *The Land of Spices*, and the Stylistic Invention of Lesbian (In)visibility." *Irish University Review* 43 (1): 55–73.

Bakan, Joel. 2005. *The Corporation: The Pathological Pursuit of Profit and Power*. Detroit, MI: Free Press.

Barry, Sebastian. 2008. *The Secret Scripture*. New York: Penguin.

Battersby, Eileen. 2014. "Dame Edna." In *Conversations with Edna O'Brien*, edited by Alice Hughes Kernowski, 53–57. Jackson: University of Mississippi Press.

Beja, Morris, and Ellen Carol Jones. 1982. "The Joyce of Sex." In *The Seventh of Joyce*, edited by Bernard Benstock, 249–58. Bloomington: University of Indiana Press.

Benjamin, Walter. 1998. *The Origin of German Tragic Drama*. London: Verso.

Bersani, Leo. 1992. *The Culture of Redemption*. Cambridge, MA: Harvard University Press.

Blake, William. 1982. *The Collected Poetry and Prose of William Blake*. New York: Anchor Books.

Bobotis, Andrea. 2006. "Rival Maternities: Maud Gonne, Queen Victoria, and the Reign of the Political Mother." *Victorian Studies* 49, no. 1 (Autumn): 63–83.

Bourke, Angela. 2001. *The Burning of Bridget Cleary: A True Story*. New York: Viking Penguin.

Bowen, Elizabeth. 1959. *The House in Paris*. New York: Vintage Books.

Boylan, Clare. 2000. Introduction to *The Land of Spices*, by Kate O'Brien. London: Virago.

Brake, Laurel. 2005. "Government by Journalism and the Silence of the *Star*: Victorian Encounters, 1885–1890." In *Encounters in the Victorian Press: Editors, Authors, Readers*, edited by Laurel Brake and Julie F. Codell, 213–35. New York: Palgrave.

Breen, Mary. 1993. "Something Understood? Kate O'Brien and *The Land of Spices*." In *Ordinary People Dancing—Essays on Kate O'Brien*, edited by Eibhear Walshe, 167–79. Cork, Ireland: Cork University Press.

Brown, Richard. 1985. *James Joyce and Sexuality*. Oxford: Oxford University Press.

Byron, Kristine. 2002. "'In the Name of the Mother . . . : The Epilogue of Edna O'Brien's *Trilogy*." *Women's Studies* 31 (1): 447–65.

Cahalan, James. 1995. "Female and Male Perspectives on Growing Up Irish in Edna O'Brien, John McGahern and Brian Moore." *Colby Quarterly* 31 (1): 55–72.

Carpenter, Lynette. 1986. "Tragedies of Remembrance, Comedies of Endurance: The Novels of Edna O'Brien." In *Essays on the Contemporary British Novel*, edited by H. Bock and A. Wertheim, 263–81. Munich: Verlag.

Caruth, Cathy. 2014. "Traumatic Temporality: An Interview with Jean Laplanche." In *Listening to Trauma: Conversations with Leaders in the Theory and Treatment of Catastrophic Experience*, 25–44. Baltimore: Johns Hopkins University Press.

———. 2016. *Unclaimed Experience: Trauma, Narrative, and History*. Baltimore: Johns Hopkins University Press.

Coates, Ken. 2009. Foreword to *The Miracle of Fleet Street: The Story of the Daily Herald*, by George Lansbury. Nottingham, UK: Russell Press.

Coe, Richard. 1984. *When the Grass Was Taller: Autobiography and the Experience of Childhood*. New Haven, CT: Yale University Press.

Colletta, Lisa, and Maureen O'Connor, eds. 2006. *Wild Colonial Girl: Essays on Edna O'Brien*. Madison: University of Wisconsin Press.

Colley, Linda. 1992. *Britons: Forging the Nation, 1707–1837*. New Haven, CT: Yale University Press.

Conrad, Kathryn. 2004. *Locked in the Family Cell: Gender, Sexuality, and Political Agency in Irish National Discourse*. Madison: University of Wisconsin Press.

Costello-Sullivan, Kathleen. 2018. *Trauma and Recovery in the Twenty-First-Century Irish Novel*. Syracuse, NY: Syracuse University Press.

Coughlan, Patricia. 1993. "Kate O'Brien: Feminine Beauty, Feminist Writing on Sexual Role." In *Ordinary People Dancing—Essays on Kate O'Brien*, edited by Eibhear Walshe, 59–85. Cork, Ireland: Cork University Press.

Cullingford, Elizabeth. 2006. "'Our Nuns Are Not a Nation': Politicizing the Convent in Irish Literature and Film." *Éire-Ireland* 41 (1): 9–39.

Curtis, L. Perry. 1979. *Apes and Angels: The Irishman in Victorian Caricature*. Washington, DC: Smithsonian Books.

Curtis, Liz. 1984. *Nothing but the Same Old Story: Roots of Anti-Irish Racism*. London: Sasta.

Cvetkovich, Ann. 1992. *Mixed Feelings: Feminism, Mass Culture, and Victorian Sensationalism*. New Brunswick, NJ: Rutgers University Press.

Dalsimer, Adele. 1990. *Kate O'Brien: A Critical Study*. Dublin: Gill and Macmillan.

Day, Robert Adams. 1998. "The Villanelle Perplex." In *Critical Essays on James Joyce's A Portrait of the Artist*, edited by P. Brady and J. Carens, 52–67. New York: G. K. Hall.

Dean, Tim. 2000. *Beyond Sexuality*. Chicago: University of Chicago Press.

Deane, Seamus. 1995. *Strange Country: Modernity and Nationhood in Irish Writing since 1790*. Oxford: Clarendon University Press.

Dell'Amico, Carol. 2010. "Anne Enright's *The Gathering*: Trauma, Testimony, Memory." *New Hibernia Review* 14 (3): 59–73.

De Man, Paul. 1979. *Allegories of Reading*. New Haven, CT: Yale University Press.

Derbyshire, Jonathan. 2010. "The NS Books Interview: Emma Donoghue." *New Statesman*, October 4, 2010. www.newstatesman.com/books/2010/10/fritzl-case-novel-child-room.

Donoghue, Emma. 1993. "'Out of Order': Kate O'Brien's Lesbian Fictions." In *Ordinary People Dancing—Essays on Kate O'Brien*, edited by Eibhear Walshe, 36–59. Cork, Ireland: Cork University Press.

———. 1995. "Noises from Woodsheds: The Muffled Voices of Irish Lesbian Fiction." In *Volcanoes and Pearl Divers—Essays in Lesbian Feminist Studies*, edited by Suzanne Raitt, 169–201. London: Onlywomen Press.

———. 2009. "Embraces of Love." In *Faithful Companions: Collected Essays Celebrating the 25th Anniversary of the Kate O'Brien Weekend*, edited by Mary Coll, 16–31. Limerick, Ireland: Mellick.

Dougherty, Jane Elizabeth. 2007. "Nuala O'Faolain and the Unwritten Irish Girlhood." *New Hibernia Review* 11, no. 2 (Summer/Samhradh): 50–65.

Douglas, Mary. 1966. *Purity and Danger: An Analysis of Concepts of Pollution and Taboo*. New York: Praeger.

Downum, Denell. 2015. "Learning to Live: Memory and the Celtic Tiger in Novels by Roddy Doyle, Anne Enright, and Tana French." *New Hibernia Review* 19, no. 3 (Autumn): 76–92.

Eckley, Grace. 2007. *Maiden Tribute: A Life of W. T. Stead*. Philadelphia: Xlibris.

Edelman, Lee. 2004. *No Future: Queer Theory and the Death Drive*. Durham, NC: Duke University Press.

Ellmann, Maud. 2003. "The Name and the Scar." In *James Joyce's* A Portrait of the Artist as a Young Man, edited by M. Wollaeger, 143–82. Oxford: Oxford University Press.

Ellmann, Richard. 1982. *James Joyce*. New York: Oxford University Press.

———. 1983. *James Joyce: The First Revision of the 1959 Classic*. Oxford: Oxford University Press.

Enright, Anne. 2005. Introduction to *As Music and Splendour* (1958), by Kate O'Brien. Dublin: Penguin Ireland.

———. 2007. *The Gathering*. London: Jonathan Cape.

Erikson, Kai. 1995. "Notes on Trauma and Community." In *Trauma: Explorations in Memory*, edited by Cathy Caruth, 183–99. Baltimore: Johns Hopkins University Press.

Fanon, Frantz. 1968. *The Wretched of the Earth*. New York: Grove.

Faulkner, William. 1929. *The Sound and the Fury*. New York: Random House.

Felman, Soshona, and Dori Laub. 1992. *Testimony: Crises of Witnessing in Literature, Psychoanalysis, and History*. New York: Routledge.

Ferriter, Diarmaid. 2005. *The Transformation of Ireland*. Woodstock, NY: Overlook.

———. 2009. *Occasions of Sin: Sex and Society in Modern Ireland*. London: Profile Books.

Fielding, Henry. 2007. *The History of Tom Jones, a Foundling*. London: Vintage. First published 1749.

Fink, Bruce. 1995. *The Lacanian Subject: Between Language and Jouissance*. Princeton, NJ: Princeton University Press.

Finnegan, Frances. 2004. *Do Penance or Perish: Magdalen Asylums in Ireland*. New York: Oxford University Press.

Fogarty, Anne. 1993. "Desire in the Novels of Kate O'Brien." In *Ordinary People Dancing: Essays on Kate O'Brien*, edited by Eibhear Walshe, 101–20. Cork, Ireland: Cork University Press.

Foucault, Michael. 1980. *The History of Sexuality*. Vol. 1. Translated by Robert Hurley. New York: Vintage.

Frawley, Oona, ed. 2014. *Memory Ireland*. Vol. 3, *The Famine and the Troubles*. Syracuse: Syracuse University Press.

French, Tana. 2007. *In the Woods*. New York: Viking Penguin.

Freud, Sigmund. 1917. "General Theory of the Neuroses." In *Standard Edition of the Complete Psychological Works of Sigmund Freud*. Vol 16. Translated by James Strachey, 243–463. London: Hogarth.

———. 1950. *Totem and Taboo*. Translated by James Strachey. New York: Norton.

———. 1951. *The Psychopathology of Everyday Life*. Translated by A. A. Brill. New York: Macmillan.

———. 1961. *Beyond the Pleasure Principle*. Translated by James Strachey. New York: Norton.

———. 1963. "A Child Is Being Beaten." In *Sexuality and the Psychology of Love*, 97–122. Translated by A. Strachey and J. Strachey. New York: Macmillan.

———. 1966. *Introductory Lectures on Psychoanalysis*. Translated by James Strachey. New York: Norton.

Gibbons, Luke. 1996. *Transformation in Irish Culture*. Notre Dame, IN: Notre Dame University Press.

Gifford, Don. 1982. *Joyce Annotated*. Berkeley: University of California Press.

Gottfried, Roy. n.d. Working paper that discusses the influence on "The Sisters" of the story "The Priest and the Acolyte," widely credited to Oscar Wilde when it appeared. Photocopy, Department of English, University at Buffalo, Buffalo, NY.

Greer, Chris, and Eugene McLaughlin. 2013. "The Sir Jimmy Savile Scandal: Child Sexual Abuse and Institutional Denial at the BBC." *Crime, Media, Culture: An International Journal* 9, no. 3 (December): 243–63.

———. 2015. "The Return of the Repressed: Secrets, Lies, Denial and 'Historical' Institutional Child Sex Abuse Scandals." In *How Corrupt Is Britain?*, edited by D. Whyte, 113–23. London: Pluto.

Gregory, Augusta. 1974. *Poets and Dreamers*. Buckinghamshire, UK: Smyth.

Groden, Michael, and Vicki Mahaffey. 2012. "Silence and Fractals in 'The Sisters.'" In *Collaborative Dubliners: Joyce in Dialogue*, edited by Vicki Mahaffey, 23–47. Syracuse, NY: Syracuse University Press.

Grometstein, Randall. 2010. "Wrongful Conviction and Moral Panic: National and International Perspectives on Organized Child Abuse." In *Wrongful Conviction*, edited by C. Ronald Huff and Martin Kilias, 11–32. Philadelphia: Temple University Press.

Guttridge, Peter. 2014. "The Books Interview: A School for Scandal." In *Conversations with Edna O'Brien*, edited by Alice Hughes Kernowski, 58–61. Jackson: University of Mississippi Press.

Hall, Radclyffe. (1928) 2015. *The Well of Loneliness*. New York: Penguin.

Harari, Robert. 2002. *How James Joyce Made His Name: A Reading of the Final Lacan*. New York: Other Press.

Hargreaves, Tamsin. 1988. "Women's Consciousness and Identity in Four Irish Women Novelists." In *Cultural Contexts and Literary Idioms in Contemporary Irish Literature*, edited by M. Keneally, 290–305. London: Colin Smythe.

Harper, Margaret Mills. 2010. "Flesh and Bones: Anne Enright's *The Gathering*." *South Carolina Review* 43 (1): 74–87.

Harte, Liam. 2010. "Mourning Remains Unresolved: Trauma and Survival in Anne Enright's *The Gathering*." *Literature Interpretation Theory* 21: 187–204.

Haule, James. 1987. "Tough Luck: The Unfortunate Birth of Edna O'Brien." *Colby Quarterly* 23 (4): 216–24.

Heaney, Seamus. 1972. *Wintering Out*. London: Faber and Faber.

Hegel, G. W. F. 1977. *Phenomenology of Spirit*. Translated by A. V. Miller. Oxford: Oxford University Press. First published 1807.

Henke, Suzette. 1982. "Stephen Dedalus and Women." In *Women in Joyce*, edited by Suzette Henke and Elaine Unkeless, 82–107. Urbana: University of Illinois Press.

Herbert, George. 2004. *The Complete English Poems*. Edited by John Tobin. London: Penguin.

Herdt, Gilbert. 2009. Introduction to *Moral Panics, Sex Panics: Fear and the Fight over Sexual Rights*, edited by Gilbert Herdt, 1–46. New York: New York University Press.

Herman, Judith. 1997. *Trauma and Recovery: The Aftermath of Violence—from Domestic Abuse to Political Terror*. New York: Basic Books.

Hinton, Laura. 1999. *The Perverse Gaze of Sympathy: Sadomasochistic Sentiments from Clarissa to Rescue 911*. Albany: State University of New York Press.

Inglis, Tom. 1998. *Moral Monopoly: The Rise and Fall of the Catholic Church in Modern Ireland*. Dublin: Gill and MacMillan.

———. 2008. *Global Ireland: Same Difference*. London: Routledge.

Joyce, James. 1963. *Stephen Hero*. Edited by Theodore Spencer. New York: New Directions Books.

———. 1965. *Letters*. Vol. 1. Edited by Stuart Gilbert. New York: Viking Compass.

———. 1968. *Finnegans Wake*. New York: Viking.

———. 1986. *Ulysses*. New York: Vintage.

———. 1992a. *Dubliners*. New York: Penguin.

———. 1992b. *A Portrait of the Artist as a Young Man*. Edited by Seamus Deane. New York: Penguin.

———. 1992c. *Selected Letters of James Joyce*. Edited by Richard Ellmann. London: Faber. First published 1975.

Kenner, Hugh. 1978. *Joyce's Voices*. Berkeley: University of California Press.

———. 1987. "The *Portrait* in Perspective." In *Dublin's Joyce*, 109–33. New York: Columbia University Press. First published 1956.

Kernowski, Alice Hughes, ed. 2014. *Conversations with Edna O'Brien*. Jackson: University of Mississippi Press.

———. 2014. Introduction to *Conversations with Edna O'Brien*, xi–xxii. Jackson: University of Mississippi Press.

Kiberd, Declan. 1995. *Inventing Ireland: The Literature of the Modern Nation*. Cambridge, MA: Harvard University Press.

Koestenbaum, Wayne. 2011. *Humiliation*. New York: Picador.

Kreilkemp, Vera. 1998. *The Anglo-Irish Novel and the Big House*. Syracuse, NY: Syracuse University Press.

Kristeva, Julia. 1980. *Desire in Language: A Semiotic Approach to Literature and Art*. Oxford: Blackwell.

Lacan, Jacques. 1957. "The Agency (Insistence or Instance) of the Letter in the Unconscious, or Reason Since Freud." Lecture presented in the Descartes Amphitheatre of the Sorbonne, Paris, May 9, 1957. Translated by Jan Miel as "The Insistence of the Letter in the Unconscious." *Yale French Studies* 36/37 (1966): 112–47.

———. 1990. *Television/A Challenge to the Psychoanalytic Establishment*. Translated by Denis Hollier et al. New York: Norton.

———. 1997a. *Le Seminaire Jacques Lacan XXIII: Le Sinthome*. Paris: Texte de l'association freudienne international.

———. 1997b. "Seminar V: Les foundations de l'inconscient." Unpublished; summarized in Joel Dor, Introduction to *The Reading of Lacan*, 93–155. London: Aronson.

———. 1998. *Seminar XX: On Feminine Sexuality*. Translated by Bruce Fink. New York: Norton.

———. 1999. *Écrits*. Translated by Bruce Fink. New York: Norton.

Lancaster, Roger N. 2011. *Sex Panic and the Punitive State*. Berkeley: University of California Press.

Laplanche, Jean. 1997. "The Theory of Seduction and the Problem of the Other." *International Journal of Psycho-analysis* 78: 653–65.

———. 1999. *Essays on Otherness*. London: Routledge.

———. 2016. *New Foundations for Psychoanalysis*. Translated by Jonathan House. New York: The Unconscious in Translation.

Laplanche, Jean, and J.-B. Pontalis. 1973. *The Language of Psycho-analysis*. Translated by Donald Nicholson-Smith. London: Hogarth Press.

Lawson, Mark. 2014. "Edna O'Brien." In *Conversations with Edna O'Brien*, edited by Alice Hughes Kernowski, 72–76. Jackson: University of Mississippi Press.

Legarreta Mentxaka, Aintzane. 2011. *Kate O'Brien and the Fiction of Identity: Sex, Art and Politics in* Mary Lavelle *and Other Writings*. Jefferson, NC: McFarland.

Levine, Judith. 2002. *Harmful to Minors: The Perils of Protecting Children from Sex*. Minneapolis: University of Minnesota Press.

Leys, Ruth. 2000. *Trauma: A Genealogy*. Chicago: University of Chicago Press.

Lloyd, David. 1993. *Anomalous States: Irish Writing and the Post-Colonial Moment*. Durham, NC: Duke University Press.

———. 2017. *Irish Culture and Colonial Modernity, 1800–2000: The Transformation of Oral Space*. Cambridge: Cambridge University Press.

Long, Edward. 1950. "Irish Piety." *The Furrow* 1/2 (March): 12–15.

Luddy, Maria, and James Smith, eds. 2014. *Children and Childhood in Ireland: 1700–2010*. Dublin: Four Courts.

Madden, Ed. 2010. "'Here, of All Places': Geographies of Sexual and Gender Identity in Keith Ridgway's *The Long Falling*." *South Carolina Review* 43 (1): 20–32.

Maguire, Moira J. 2009. *Precarious Childhood in Post-Independence Ireland*. Manchester, UK: Manchester University Press.

Maguire, Moira J., and Seamus Ó Cinnéide. 2005. "A Good Beating Never Hurt Anyone." *Journal of Social History* 38, no. 3 (March): 635–52.

Mahaffey, Vicki. 1988. *Reauthorizing Joyce.* Cambridge: Cambridge University Press.

Maher, Eamon, and John Littleton, eds. 2010. *The Dublin/Murphy Report: A Watershed for Irish Catholicism?* Dublin: Columba Press.

Makdisi, Saree. 2014. *Making England Western: Occidentalism, Race, and Imperial Culture.* Chicago: University of Chicago Press.

Malone, Carolyn. 1999. "Sensational Stories, Endangered Bodies: Women's Work and the New Journalism in England in the 1890's." *Albion: A Quarterly Journal Concerned with British Studies* 31 (Spring): 49–71.

McCabe, Patrick. 1992. *The Butcher Boy.* London: Picador.

———. 1998. *Breakfast on Pluto.* London: Picador.

McCarthy, Rebecca Lea. 2010. *Origins of the Magdalene Laundries: An Analytical History.* London: McFarland.

McCrum, Robert. 2014. "Deep Down in the Woods." In *Conversations with Edna O'Brien,* edited by Alice Hughes Kernowski, 62–65. Jackson: University of Mississippi Press.

McDiarmid, Lucy. 2004. *The Irish Art of Controversy.* Ithaca, NY: Cornell University Press.

McGahern, John. 2005. *The Dark.* London: Faber and Faber.

McKibben, Sarah E. 2010. *Endangered Masculinities in Irish Poetry: 1540–1780.* Dublin: University College Press.

Meaney, Gerardine. 2011. "Waking the Dead: Antigone, Ismene and Anne Enright's Narrators in Mourning." In *Anne Enright (Visions and Revisions: Irish Writers in Their Time),* edited by Claire Bracken and Susan Cahill, 145–64. Dublin: Irish Academic Press.

Moloney, Caitriona, and Helen Thompson, eds. 2003. *Irish Women Writers Speak Out.* Syracuse, NY: Syracuse University Press.

Moran, D. P. 1901. "The Battle of Two Civilizations." In *Ideals in Ireland,* edited by Lady Gregory, 25–41. London: Unicorn.

Morash, Christopher. 2010. *A History of Media in Ireland.* Cambridge: Cambridge University Press.

Morrison, Jago, and Susan Watkins, eds. 2006. *Scandalous Fictions: The Twentieth-Century Novel in the Public Sphere.* New York: Palgrave Macmillan.

Mullin, Katherine. 2003. *James Joyce, Sexuality and Social Purity.* Cambridge: Cambridge University Press.

Munt, Sally. 2007. *Queer Attachments: The Cultural Politics of Shame.* Hampshire, UK: Ashgate.

Murphy, Annie. 2009. *Forbidden Fruit: The True Story of My Love Affair with Ireland's Most Powerful Bishop.* New York: Little Brown.

Nic Congáil, Ríona. 2009. "'Fiction, Amusement, Instruction: The Irish Fireside Club and the Educational Ideology of the Gaelic League." *Éire-Ireland* 44 (1): 91–117.

Nixon, Rob. 2013. *Slow Violence and the Environmentalism of the Poor.* Cambridge, MA: Harvard University Press.

Norris, Margot. 1998. *A Companion to James Joyce's Ulysses: Biographical and Historical Contexts, Critical History, and Essays from Five Contemporary Critical Perspectives*. Boston: Bedford Books.

O'Brien, Edna. 1960. *The Country Girls*. London: Hutchinson.

———. 1986. *The Country Girls Trilogy and Epilogue*. New York: Penguin.

———. 1997. *Down by the River*. New York: Penguin.

———. 2013. *Country Girl*. New York: Little Brown.

O'Brien, Kate. 1988. *The Land of Spices*. London: Virago.

O'Brien, Peggy. 1987. "The Silly and the Serious: An Assessment of Edna O'Brien." *Massachusetts Review* 28 (3): 474–88.

O'Toole, Fintan. 2009. Review of *Occasions of Sin*, by Diarmaid Ferriter. *Guardian*, October 11, 2009. https://www.theguardian.com/books/2009/oct/11/occasions-sin-diarmaid-ferriter-fintan.

———. 2014. *25 Years of Irish Life: The Columns of Fintan O'Toole*. Dublin: The Irish Times e-Books.

O'Toole, Tina. 2004. "Kate O'Brien." Unpublished paper, delivered at An Evening with Kate O'Brien, University College Dublin, Dublin, Ireland, January 15, 2004.

———. 2013. *The Irish New Woman*. London: Palgrave Macmillan.

Oddenino, Ilaria. 2011. "Personal Wounds, National Scars. Reflections on Individual and Cultural Trauma in Anne Enright's *The Gathering*." *Studi irelandais* 1: 361–74.

Owen Weekes, Ann. 1990. *Irish Women Writers: An Uncharted Tradition*. Lexington: University of Kentucky Press.

Perry, Ruth. 1992. "Colonizing the Breast: Sexuality and Maternity in Eighteenth-Century England." *Eighteenth-Century Life* 16 (February): 185–213.

Peterson, Shirley. 2016. "Voicing the Unspeakable: Tana French's Dublin Murder Squad." In *The Contemporary Irish Detective Novel*, edited by Elizabeth Mannion, 107–20. London: Palgrave Macmillan.

Pine, Emilie. 2011. *The Politics of Irish Memory: Performing Remembrance in Contemporary Irish Culture*. London: Palgrave Macmillan.

Potter, Simon. 2003. *News and the British World: The Emergence of an Imperial Press System, 1876–1922*. Oxford: Clarendon.

Quinn, John, ed. 1986. *A Portrait of the Artist as a Young Girl*. London: Methuen.

Quintelli-Neary, Marguerite. 2003. "Retelling the Sorrows in Edna O'Brien's *The Country Girls*." *Nua: Studies in Contemporary Irish Writing* 4 (1): 65–76.

Rabaté, Jean-Michel. 2001a. *Jacques Lacan*. New York: Palgrave.

———. 2001b. *James Joyce and the Politics of Egoism*. Cambridge: Cambridge University Press.

Raftery, Mary, and Eoin O'Sullivan. 1999. *Suffer the Little Children: The Inside Story of Ireland's Industrial Schools*. Dublin: New Island Books.

Rains, Stephanie. 2015. "Nauseous Tides of Seductive Debauchery: Irish Story Papers and the Anti-vice Campaigns of the Early Twentieth Century." *Irish University Review* 45, no. 2 (October): 263–80.

Renan, Ernest. 1990. "What Is a Nation?" In *Nation and Narration*, edited by Homi Bhabha, 8–22. New York: Routledge.

Ridgway, Keith. 1999. *The Long Falling*. New York: Houghton Mifflin.

Rigert, Joe. 2008. *An Irish Tragedy: How Sex Abuse by Catholic Priests Helped Cripple the Catholic Church*. Baltimore: Crossland.

Ronson, Jon. 2011. *The Psychopath Test: A Journey through the Madness Industry*. New York: Riverhead Books.

Roth, Philip. 2014. "A Conversation Edna O'Brien." In *Conversations with Edna O'Brien*, edited by Alice Hughes Kernowski, 40–48 Jackson. University of Mississippi Press.

Rothberg, Michael. 2009. *Multidirectional Memory: Remembering the Holocaust in the Age of Decolonization*. Stanford, CA: Stanford University Press.

Sayers, Dorothy. 1938. *Unnatural Death*. London: W. Collins Sons.

———. (1935) 2016. *Gaudy Night*. New York: Harper.

Sedgwick, Eve. 1985. *Between Men*. New York: Columbia University Press.

Smith, James M. 2007. *Ireland's Magdalen Laundries and the Nation's Architecture of Containment*. Notre Dame, IN: University of Notre Dame Press.

Soderlund, Gretchen. 2013. *Sex Trafficking, Scandal, and the Transformation of Journalism, 1885–1917*. Chicago: University of Chicago Press.

Spencer, Theodore. 1963. Introduction to *Stephen Hero*, by James Joyce. Edited by Theodore Spencer. New York: New Directions Books.

Steele, Karen, and Michael de Nie, eds. 2014. *Ireland and the New Journalism*. New York: Palgrave.

Thurston, Luke. 2004. *James Joyce and the Problem of Psychoanalysis*. Cambridge: Cambridge University Press.

Tighe-Mooney, Sharon. 2008. "Sexuality and Religion in Kate O'Brien's Novels." In *Essays in Irish Literary Criticism: Themes of Gender, Sexuality, and Corporeality*, edited by Deirdre Quinn and Sharon Tighe-Mooney, 124–40. Lewiston, NY: Mellen.

Valente, Joseph. 1997. "Thrilled by His Touch: The Aestheticizing of Homosexual Panic in *A Portrait of the Artist as a Young Man*." In *Quare Joyce*, edited by Joseph Valente, 47–76. Ann Arbor: University of Michigan Press.

———. 2006. "A History of Queer Theory in *Ulysses*." In *Ulysses in Critical Perspective*, edited by N. Fargnoli and M. Gillespie, 124–48. Gainesville: University of Florida Press.

———. 2011. *The Myth of Manliness in Irish National Culture: 1880–1922*. Champaign: University of Illinois Press.

Valente, Joseph, and Margot Backus. 2009. "'An Iridescence Difficult to Account For': Sexual Initiation in Joyce's Fiction of Development." *ELH* 76 (2): 523–45.

Walkowitz, Judith. 1992. *City of Dreadful Delight: Narratives of Sexual Danger in Late-Victorian London*. Chicago: University of Chicago Press.

Walshe, Eibhear. 2006. *Kate O'Brien: A Writing Life*. Dublin: Irish Academic Press.

———. 2011. *Oscar's Shadow: Wilde, Homosexuality and Modern Ireland*. Cork, Ireland: Cork University Press.

Warner, Michael. 1999. *The Trouble with Normal: Sex, Politics and the Ethics of Queer Life*. New York: Free Press.

Weston, Elizabeth. 2010. "Constitutive Trauma in Edna O'Brien's *The Country Girls Trilogy*: The Romance of Reenactment." *Tulsa Studies in Women's Literature* 29 (1): 83–105.

Whyte, David, ed. 2015. *How Corrupt Is Britain?* London: Pluto.

Williams, Raymond. 1973. *The Country and the City*. New York: Oxford University Press.

Yeates, Padraig. 2000. *Lockout Dublin 1913: The Most Famous Labour Dispute in Irish History*. Dublin: Gill Books.

———. 2001. "The Dublin 1913 Lockout." *History Ireland* 9 (2): 3–36. http://www.jstor.org /stable/27724881.

Yeats, W. B. 1953. *The Collected Plays of W.B. Yeats*. New York: Macmillan.

Zimbardo, Philip. 2007. *The Lucifer Effect: Understanding How Good People Turn Evil*. New York: Random House.

Žižek, Slavoj. 1989. *The Sublime Object of Ideology*. New York: Verso.

———. 1994. *The Metastases of Enjoyment*. New York: Verso.

———. 2009. *The Parallax View*. Cambridge, MA: MIT Press.

INDEX

Page numbers in *italics* refer to illustrations.

abortion, 72n14; referendum, May 26, 2018, xiii; and X case, 134, 137, 159, 249

Abraham, Nicolas, 146, 152, 218, 230. *See also* crypt

afterwardsness (Laplanche), 51, 132, 195n5; *nächtraglichkeit*, 119, 132

Agamben, Giorgio, 189

Archbishop Walsh. *See* Walsh, William (Archbishop of Dublin)

asylums, 199, 233, 234–35, 238, 251, 252; Magdalene (*see* Magdalene laundries)

Barry, Sebastian (*The Secret Scripture*), 28, 32–33, 195n7

Benjamin, Walter, 31

Bersani, Leo, 225

Big House (Anglo-Irish), 164–65

Blake, William, 5–6

Bon Secours Mother and Baby Home. *See* Tuam Mother and Baby Home

Bowen, Elizabeth (*The House in Paris*), 163–65

Breen, Mary, 82

Browne, Noël, 19–20, *20*, 248. *See also* Mother and Child Scheme

Bourke, Angela, 76, 98n5, 195n4

Campaign to Save the Kiddies. *See* Save the Kiddies campaign

Caruth, Cathy, 80, 97n2, 161n1

Casey, Bishop Eamonn, 18, 23

Catholic Church, 78; fall of, xi; habitus, 37, 39n31; hierarchy, 76; history in Ireland, 45; and Irish identity, xi, 56; moral authority, 39n21, 45, 60; moral control over children, 42, 71n2, 71n3; moral episteme, 77; as patriarchal 61; power of, 61, 246–47; scandals, 72n14; and state, xi, 47, 57, 72n14. *See also* Irish Catholic Church

celibacy, 25, 83, 92

Celtic Tiger, 171–78

censorship, 21, 25, 39n25, 70

changelings, 168, 169, 181

child abuse: compartmentalization of, xii; exposure of, xi, xii; global, xi; institutional, xi; institutionalization (coercive confinement) as, xi; psychological, xi, xiii; sexual, xiv, xix; state collusion in, xi

child sex scandal. *See* scandal (child sex)

child sexual abuse, 248–49, 250; addictive reenactment, 114; Ferns report, 30, 190, 239; implantation of jouissance, 106, 201; material dependency, 122; Murphy report, 190; predation and grooming, 123–24; prevalence in post-Famine Ireland, 100–1, 119; as slow violence, 201

children (British), 3, 5–6, 244–45

children (Irish), 243–50, 251; at risk, xv; as citizens, xii; disavowed, 2; disposable, 134; and enigmatic signifier, 177; homelessness, xii; poverty, xii; of immigrants, xvii, xxii;

children (Irish) (*cont.*)
  mental health services, xii; needs of, xii; outrages against, xviii; seduction of, 177; sensational literary representations, xvi; sensational media representations, xvi; sentimentalization of, xix; sexual initiation of, xvi, 1; welfare of, xiii
confession as sexual control, 55, 56
Conrad, Kathryn, 23, 72n14, 164, 191
Constitution of Ireland (1937): Eighth Amendment, 8, 23, 135, 189; as theocratic, 30
convents, 31, 39n1; *La Compagnie de la Saint Famille* (*The Land of Spices*), 77–78; life inside of, 78
convent schools (Irish Catholic), 77, 83–84, 100, 117
Corless, Catherine, xvii, 243–44
Coughlan, Patricia, 82
Country Girls, The. See O'Brien, Edna
cruelty, xiv
crypt, 146; psychic crypt, 15
cryptids, 173–74
cultural memory, 239–40

Daily Herald, 13, 245–46
"Dead, The." See Joyce, James
Dell'Amico, Carol, 233, 238
Democratic Programme, Centenary of, xii
de Valera, Eamon, 30
direct provision for asylum seekers, xii, xvii
disavowed, 28, 30, 77, 83, 96
Donoghue, Emma, 1, 81, 82, 83, 84, 92
Dougherty, Jane Elizabeth: Irish girlhood, 39n26; sensational childhood, 2, 26
Douglas, Mary, 73–74, 97n1
Dubliners. See Joyce, James
Dublin Lockout, 1913: Archbishop Walsh and, 12, 13, 14, 15, 16, 71n3, 245–47. See also Larkin, Jim; Montefiore, Dora; Murphy, Martin; Save the Kiddies campaign; Walsh, William (Archbishop of Dublin)

Edelman, Lee, 225
Education: in Ireland, 77; Church control, 21, 100; female participation, 78. See also convent schools
enigmatic signifiers, 25, 34, 50, 77–80, 169; affective/erotic trauma and hermeneutic lure, 34, 36, 50, 65; circuitry of desire, 201; coded, 50; conduit for parent/child seduction, 50, 102, 200; constitutive blind spot, 3; deniability, 69; encounter, 2, 97n2;

encryption device, 158; eroticized indefiniteness, 131; foreshadowing, 84; genitalized replication in child sexual abuse, 229; Girl X as, 135, 151; infantile sexualization, 79–80, 131; jouissance, 35; literary device, 3, 35, 80, 82; licensing (reader's) ignorance, 82, 83; oedipal, 82–83, 89, 107, 113, 200, 229; open secret, 79; 114; penumbra of, 166; plausible deniability, 82; psychosexual manipulation, 166; public exhibition, 69; reactivating (reader's) enigmatic encounter, xix, 68, 70; reversibility, 59; scandal referents, 41; scandal signifiers, 70; "second moment," 80; self-betrayal, 168; sexual initiation, 52, 56, 66–67; modernist difficulty, 81; speech acts, 45; sublimation, 56; subliminal intensity, 167; tickling, 113–14. See also afterwardsness; Laplanche, Jean
Enright, Anne (*The Gathering*), xv, xxi, 196–99, 212–16, 221, 232; disabled and institutions, 238; "inconvenient dead," 236–37; institutionalization of mentally disabled, 238, 239; Liam-Lamb (homophony), 207; national shame, 232; split-level chronology and enigmatic signifier, 216; stigmatization of the disabled, 235; transferential sibling identification, 219
epiphanies (Joycean), 41, 71n1, 71n4
Erickson, Kai, 239
eroticism, policing of, 27–28

family, xx, 87, 89, 108, 110, 119, 153, 192, 193, 210, 211, 230, 237. See also crypt; Conrad, Kathryn
Famine. See Great Famine
Fanon, Frantz, 50–51
feminists, 8, 23, 25, 109, 227
Fink, Bruce, 31
Finnegans Wake, 44
Fogarty, Anne, 38n12
folklore, 37n4
Foucault, Michel, 30, 77; *History of Sexuality* (Vol. 1), 81; Irish post-independence theocracy and, 30
French, Tana (*In the Woods*), xx–xxi, 65–66, 172, 175–77, 179–80, 188–90; changelings, in, 169; cryptids, 173–74; Hill of Tara-M3 Motorway, 172, 173; psychopathology in, 165–68, 177–87, 189–95
Freud, Sigmund: adult neurosis, 71n9; *après la lettre* and post-Freudian psychoanalysis, 71n6; "A Child Is Being Beaten (1963)," 104;

belatedness/afterwardsness (*nachträglich-keit*), 191n5; *Beyond the Pleasure Principle*, 111, 209; family romance, 218; Father of the law (*père de jouir*), 39n30, 119; disavowal, 54, 127; infantile sexual theory, 33; hysteria, 84; taboo sexual knowledge, 202; Laplanche interview on Freud, 161n1; *l'école Freudienne* and, 48; oedipal desire, 49; post-Freudian psychoanalysis, 46; primal seduction theory, 50, 202; primal seduction vs. primal fantasy, 48, 51; sublimation, 56; seduction theory as (re)read by Laplanche, 131

Gathering, The. See Enright, Anne
Gibbons, Luke, 164
Girl X. *See* X case
Great Famine, 38n15; social aftermath, 11–12, 117, 164–65
Greer, Chris, 136; four stages of scandal, 161n2

habitus: Irish Catholic, 19, 39n31, 153; social, 117. *See also* Inglis, Tom
Harte, Liam, 197, 199, 203, 214, 233, 237–38
Herdt, Gilbert, 37n4
Holocaust, 200, 235
homophobia, 153
homosexuality, 89, 95, 116, 153, 185
"Hosting of the Sidhe" (Yeats), 168

Imaginary (Irish), 140
imperiled innocence, xii, xix, *xviii*, 4, 7, 9, 10, 13, 16, 17, 26, 27, 29, 37n4, 243–47, 249–50; 1913 Dublin Lockout, 11; Fall of Parnell, 11; imperiled children and national propaganda, 132; *A Portrait of the Artist*, 8
incest, 57, 67, 92; enigmatic signifier and incestuous grounds of subjectivity, 69; fear of, 71n2; quasi-incestuous relationships, 119; sexualization of narrative, 218, 222–24, 228; symbolic incest, 202; transformation of Freud's theory of primal seduction/primal fantasy, 49
In the Woods. See French, Tana
industrial schools, xi; Ryan report, 22, 248
Inglis, Tom, xvi, 19, 39n31, 250–51
institutional abuse, xi, xii, xvii, 164–65; 232–41; *Suffer the Children*, 249. *See also* asylums
Ireland: British newspapers on, 8, 11, 244–45; Catholicism in, 45; Church-state dynamics, 189; effects on women and children, 188;

folk culture in, 37n4; Giorgio Agamben and, 189; national identity, 174; national imaginary, 164; newspapers and journalism in, 38n11, 38n13
Irish Catholic Church, 99–101, *xviii*, 16, 17, 20, 22, 24, 26, *100*, 243–44, 246–48, 249, 250, 251; and moral episteme, 77; as synonymous with Irish nationalism, 78
Irish Catholic nationalism and women in, 77
Irish Constitution of 1937, 30
Irish Daily Independent, 17, 247, 248
Irish Imaginary and the fungibility of mothers and daughters in, 121
Irish independence (1922), xi
Irish national identity, 174
Irish nationalism, 30; sex scandals and, 44
Irish post-independence Catholic theocracy, 30
Irish Times and the Democratic Programme Centenary (No Child 2020), xii

Jansenism, 81
jouissance, 35, 47, 166–67; abuse as short circuiting, 211; and the enigmatic signifier, 200; trauma and, 34
Joyce, James, 8, 102, 125–26, 138, 146, 155; censorship of, 39n25; "The Dead," 138–39, 144–45, 150 (Michael Furey's grave); *Dubliners*, 44, 50, 52, 54, 67–68; photo-realist writing style 41; "household hints" in *Irish Homestead*, 38n12; Lacanian Joyce scholars and, 48; *Portrait's* Christmas dinner-table scene, 45, 58; *Portrait's* "bird girl" scene, 82; scandal-saturated air (in Dublin childhood), 44; sexual initiation 45–46; signature narrative style, 67; "The Sisters," 52

Kenner, Hugh, and "Uncle Charles Principle," 67
Kirwan, Larry, *20, 248*

Lacan, Jacques, 47–49, 71n6, 82, 106, 178; "Joyce le sinthome," 48; Joyce seminar, 47; Lacanian Joyce scholars, 48; logic of the exception, 178; subject formation, 47; *père-version*, 106
Land of Spices, The. See O'Brien, Kate
Laplanche, Jean, 31, 33–34, 49–55, 54, 65, 131; "afterwardsness," 119; ambiguously eroticized psychic messages, 166; and Lacan, 49; expansion of concept of the other, 97n2; expansion on Freud's concept of infantile

Laplanche (*cont.*)
  sexual theory, 33; Freud's *nachträglichkeit* revisited, 132; fundamental theorization, 33–34; general theory of seduction, 200; interview with Cathy Caruth, 33–34, 97n2, 131, 161n1; riddle of sublimation, 56; Symbolic Order, 200; theory of the enigmatic signifier, 79–80; transmission of shame, 232. *See also* enigmatic signifier; Caruth, Cathy
Larkin, Jim, 12, 15, 246. *See also* Dublin Lockout, 1913
"Lass of Aughrim," 145
Legarreta Mentxaka, Aintzane, 81
lesbian visibility, 81
Leys, Ruth, 106
libidinal cathexis, 212
literary devices: stream of consciousness, 64
literature: capacity to form unconscious reserve of history, 31; *fabula* and *sujet*, 215; found objects, 215; "hidden Ireland" of childhood sexual abuse, 32; literary devices, 214; manipulation of temporal registers, 214; Möbius-strip inversion, 221; shame and denial, 162n6
literature of child sex scandal, xviii–xxii, 2, 31, 36, 37n3, 51–54, 131–32, 133
literature of trauma. *See* trauma literature
Long Falling, The. See Ridgway, Keith
love: as enigmatic signifier, 88; as paradox, 89
Lovett, Ann, 23, *100*, 250

M3 Motorway protest: Hill of Tara, 172, *173*, 186–89, 251
Madden, Ed, 146, 153, 155–56
Maiden Tribute of Modern Babylon, 6, 11, 15, 38; child abduction, 21; white slave trade, 21
Magdalene laundries (Magdalene asylums), 5, 24, 31, 37n7, 164, 180; 133 Magdalenes, 24; "archipelago of institutional abuse," xi; "architecture of containment," 189
Maguire, Moira J., xvi, 21, 30, 62n3
masturbation, 61–63
McDiarmid, Lucy, 12, 39n23, 247
McLaughlin, Eugene, 136; four stages of scandal, 161n2
McQuaid, Archbishop John Charles, 19–20, 248
mental hospitals. *See* asylums
mimetic/anti-mimetic paradigms, 106–7
memory: collective, 239; collective forgetting and, 238; competitive, 240–44; cultural, 239–40

modern moral panic, 37n4
modernist difficulty: and the enigmatic signifier, 80–81
"Modest Proposal, A" (Swift), 64–65
Montefiore, Dora: Save the Kiddies campaign, 12, 247. *See also* Dublin Lockout, 1913
Moore, Chris. *See* institutional abuse
moral episteme, 142, 207
moral panics, 2, 6, 37n4
Moran, D. P., 98n4
Morash, Christopher, 38n15
Morrison, Jago, 37n3
Mother and Baby Homes. *See* Tuam Mother and Baby Home
Mother and Child Scheme, 19–20, 248
Mothers, 42, 47, 49, 57, 65, 105, 107, 108; Kerry baby case, 23; mother-child dyad, 118, 120; Mother Ireland, 65, 73
Murphy, William Martin, 12, 15. *See also* Dublin Lockout, 1913
myth of manliness (Valente), 11, 38n14, 168

nachträglichkeit. See afterwardsness
New Journalism, 6, 38n17; in Britain, xix; "Maiden Tribute" articles, 6, 11; sensationalizing techniques of, 11; W. T. Stead, 6
newspapers (British): child sex scandals and, 38n17; influence on Ireland and the Irish, 8, 11, 38n11; treatment of British and Irish children, 38n11, 38n13
newspapers (Irish): child sex scandals and, 6; nationalist, 38n17; treatment of British and Irish children, 38n11, 38n13
Nic Congáil, Riona, 38n17
noble cause corruption (Grometstein), 37n8

O'Brien, Edna (*The Country Girls*), 99–102, 111, 112, 113, 125, 130n3, 130n6, 130nn8–9; autobiographical aspect of *The Country Girls*, 101; *Down by the River*, 36, 65, 129; mother-daughter terror-bond, 108; repetition compulsion, 109–10; scandalized reception in Ireland, 99; "tickling" scene, 113
O'Brien, Kate (*The Land of Spices*), xx, 78–79, 80, 81–82, 93–94; culture of open secrecy, 77; enigmatic signifier in the modernist novel, 80, 93; enigmatic signifier operating in, 83; lesbian "closet," 79; and open secrets, 78; parallels with Stephen Dedalus's "bird girl;" 95; as prayer on enigma of love, 96; smuggling (female equivalent), 95; metalepsis, 86

occult zone of undecidability, 57, 158; encrypted secret, 218

Oedipal complex, 47, 49, 51, 57, 89, 92, 118

open secrets and the enigmatic signifier, 53, 75, 78–79

Orpen, William, *10, 14*, 245, 246

Other, the, 34, 97n2, 103, 235, 239

O'Toole, Fintan, xi–xiv, 39n22

Pall Mall Gazette, 6

Parnell, Charles Stewart, 42; fall of, 11, 44, 45; Katherine O'Shea, 45; Irish independence and, 45

Pearse, Patrick, "Mise Eire," 191

Pontalis, J. B., 161n1. *See also* Laplanche, Jean; Caruth, Cathy

Portrait of the Artist as a Young Man, A, 8, 94; Christmas dinner scene, 45, 58; Clongowes' smugging scene, 95; homosexual scandal depiction, 95; Parnell, 8, 11, 44–45, 58; sexual initiation in, 46; speech acts, 45

"Prayer" (George Herbert): significance in title, *The Land of Spices*, 93–94, 96

primal seduction, 103; weaponization of, 207; and pedophilic child abuse, 103; and traumatic jouissance, 103. *See also* Freud, Sigmund; Laplanche, Jean

print capitalism: melodrama and New Journalist sex scandals 5; Irish position in, 38n11; *Stephen Hero*, 43; open secret, 75; *Daily Herald*, 245

psychoanalysis: first law of, 25; Joyce's post-Freudian, 46; psychopathology as a psychological diagnosis, 194n3; and sexual identity formation, 46

psychopathia, 178, 183

psychopathology, 165–68, 177–87, 189–94, 194–95, 195n3

psychotherapy, 33; Jean Laplanche, 33–34

psychic transference, 127

psychosocial economy, 111–12

public opinion, xviii; manipulation of, xvi

public sphere, 37n3

punishment as eroticism, 31, 58, 61, 95, 106 (unconscious masochism), 36n2

queer modernism, 78; and open secrecy, 76

Raftery, Mary (*Suffer the Children*). *See* institutional abuse

Rains, Stephanie, 38n1

Renan, Ernst, 174

Ridgway, Keith (*The Long Falling*), xx, 131, 144, 162n4; enigmatic signifier in, 142, 149; "excuse" as signifier, 149; "X" as signifier, 151–52

Ronson, Jon, 194n3

Rooney, David, 27, 249

Rothberg, Michael, 239–40

same-sex marriage referendum, xiii

Save the Kiddies campaign (Save the Dublin Kiddies), 12, *13, 14, 15, 16*, 245–47. *See also* Larkin, Jim; Montefiore, Dora; Murphy, Martin; Walsh, William (Archbishop of Dublin)

scandal, xii–xiv, xix, xx, xxi, 1–3, 6; activation of, 136, 161n2; amplification of, 137, 161n2; child-related, xvii; empowering the powerful, xvii; imperiled innocence, 6; literary depictions of, xvii; sensationalism of, xvii; Smyth, Father Brendan, 25; stages of, 136, 161n2

scandal (child sex), xiii–xxii, 199, 250; accusation and believability, 37n4; as seen through the eyes of children, xvii; codes of, 44; damage inflicted by, 211, 225; Irish nationalism and, 233; Joycean scandal fragments, 44–45; "Maiden Tribute," 6, 11, 15; as moral panic, 2, 6, 21, 37n4; secrecy, 73, 75, 77–78, 113, 148 ; signifiers, 45

scandals exposing church/state abuse: Ann Lovett, 23, 100; Father Brendan Smyth 25, 26; Bishop Eamonn Casey, 18, 23, 24; Ferns report, 100; Kerry Babies, 100; mass grave of 133 Magdalenes unearthed in Dublin, 1993; Mother and Child Scheme, 19–20; Murphy report, 100; Tuam Mother and Baby Home, xv, *xviii*, xxii; 162n6, *191*, 243–44; X case, xx, 24, 134, 137, 159, 249

Secret Scripture, The (Barry), 32–33

Sedgwick, Eve, 116

sex, the Irish Catholic Church's control of, 45

sexual repression, Church ordained, 40n32

sexualized violence, 183

shame, xix, 11, 162n6

Shea, Wendy, 26, 249

"Sisters, The." *See* Joyce, James

slow violence, 201

Smith, James M., 39n24; architecture of containment, 8, 164

Smyth, Father Brendan, 25, 249

spaltung (fissure), 102

Stead, W. T., 6, 8, 11. *See also* "Maiden Tribute of Modern Babylon"

St Ita's asylum, 233, 236, *240*
Symbolic Order, 39n25, 46–47, 66, 116, 121, 164, 189–90, 194, 200

taboo. *See* disavowed
tickle as enigmatic signifier, 115
Torok, Maria, 146, 152, 218, 230. *See also* crypt
trauma (generally), xiii, xix; collective forgetting and, 238; collective memory and, 239–41; cultural memory, 239–41; disruption of psychotemporal coordinates, 215; hermeneutics of suspicion, 214; involuted chronology, 215; multidirectional memory, 240–41; recall, difficulties of, 214
trauma (sexual): activation of psychosocially inadmissible desire, 224; intrusion of adult sexuality, 219
trauma literature, 205
Tuam Mother and Baby Home, xxii, *xviii*, 243–44, 251
Turner, Martyn, 24, 248–49

unspeakable, the appeal and vulnerability of children, xix

Valente, Joseph, 11, 38n14, 168

Walshe, Eibhear, 78–79
Walsh, William (Archbishop of Dublin), 12, 38n19, 45, 71n3, 247. *See also* Dublin Lockout, 1913
Watkins, Susan, 37n3
Weston, Elizabeth, 101, 109

X (symbol, hieroglyph, *The Long Falling*), 134–35, 151–52
X case, 134–35, 151, 248–49; abortion and, 134, 137, 159, 249; *Down by the River*, 129

Yeates, Padraig, 15, 39n20
Yeats, W. B., 120, 168

Žižek, Slavoj, 57, 103

Joseph Valente is UB Distinguished Professor in the Department of English at the University at Buffalo. He is author of *The Myth of Manliness in Irish Nationalist Culture, 1880-1922*, *Dracula's Crypt: Bram Stoker, Irishness, and the Question of Blood*, *James Joyce and the Problem of Justice: Negotiating Sexual and Colonial Difference*, and *Quare Joyce*. He is editor of the annotated edition of *Dracula* by Bram Stoker and has edited (with Marjorie Howes) *Yeats and Afterwords* and (with Amanda Anderson) *Disciplinarity at the Fin de Siècle*.

Margot Gayle Backus holds a John and Rebecca Moores Professorship in the Department of English at the University of Houston. She is author of *The Gothic Family Romance: Heterosexuality and Child Sacrifice in the Anglo-Irish Colonial Order* and *Scandal Work: James Joyce, the New Journalism, and the Home Rule Newspaper Wars*.